Learning Without Lessons

CHILD DEVELOPMENT IN CULTURAL CONTEXT

Series Editors
Cynthia Garcia Coll
Peggy Miller

Advisory Board
Jerome Kagan
Carol Worthman
Barrie Thorne

BOOKS IN THE SERIES

Perfectly Prep: Gender Extremes at a New England Prep School
Sarah A. Chase

Academic Motivation and the Culture of Schooling
Cynthia Hudley and Adele E. Gottfried

Immigrant Stories: Ethnicity and Academics in Middle Childhood
Cynthia Garcia Coll and Amy Kerivan Marks

In a Younger Voice: Doing Child-Centered Qualitative Research
Cindy Dell Clark

Developing Destinies: A Mayan Midwife and Town
Barbara Rogoff

Bridging Multiple Worlds: Cultures, Identities, and Pathways to College
Catherine R. Cooper

Literacy and Mothering: How Women's Schooling Changes the Lives of the World's Children
Robert A. LeVine, Sarah E. LeVine, Beatrice Schnell-Anzola, Meredith L. Rowe, and
Emily Dexter

The Culture of Child Care: Attachment, Peers, and Quality in Diverse Communities
Edited by Kay E. Sanders and Alison Wishard Guerra

*Self-Esteem in Time and Place: How American Families Imagine, Enact, and Personalize a
Cultural Ideal*
Peggy J. Miller and Grace E. Cho

*Disability, Stigma, and Children's Developing Selves: Insights from Educators in Japan, South
Korea, Taiwan, and the U.S.*
Wendy Haight, Misa Kayama, Mary May-Lee Ku, Minhae Cho, and Hee Yun Lee

*Roma Minority Youth Across Cultural Contexts: Taking a Positive Approach to Research, Policy,
and Practice*
Edited by Radosveta Dimitrova, David L. Sam, and Laura Ferrer Wreder

Learning Without Lessons: Pedagogy in Indigenous Communities
David F. Lancy

FORTHCOMING BOOKS IN THE SERIES

Family as a Context for Development: Continuity and Change in Latin America
Edited by Mariano Rosabal-Coto and Javier Tapia Balladares

Acquiring Culture: An Integrated Paradigm for Children's Development
Suzanne Gaskins

*Growing up Latino/a/x in the Land of Lib: Drawing on Community and Culture to Face
Contextual Challenges*
Edited by Rosario Ceballo and Deborah Rivas-Drake

Learning Without Lessons

Pedagogy in Indigenous Communities

DAVID F. LANCY

Oxford University Press is a department of the University of Oxford. It furthers
the University's objective of excellence in research, scholarship, and education
by publishing worldwide. Oxford is a registered trade mark of Oxford University
Press in the UK and certain other countries.

Published in the United States of America by Oxford University Press
198 Madison Avenue, New York, NY 10016, United States of America.

© Oxford University Press 2024

All rights reserved. No part of this publication may be reproduced, stored in
a retrieval system, or transmitted, in any form or by any means, without the
prior permission in writing of Oxford University Press, or as expressly permitted
by law, by license, or under terms agreed with the appropriate reproduction
rights organization. Inquiries concerning reproduction outside the scope of the
above should be sent to the Rights Department, Oxford University Press, at the
address above.

You must not circulate this work in any other form
and you must impose this same condition on any acquirer.

Library of Congress Cataloging-in-Publication Data
Names: Lancy, David F., author.
Title: Learning without lessons : pedagogy in indigenous
communities / David F. Lancy.
Description: New York, NY : Oxford University Press, 2024. |
Series: Child development in cultural context |
Includes bibliographical references and index.
Identifiers: LCCN 2023040399 (print) | LCCN 2023040400 (ebook) |
ISBN 9780197645598 (hardback) | ISBN 9780197645604 (epub) |
ISBN 9780197645628
Subjects: LCSH: Indigenous children—Education. | Non-formal education. |
Culturally relevant pedagogy. | Educational anthropology. | Child development.
Classification: LCC LC3719.L36 2024 (print) | LCC LC3719 (ebook) |
DDC 371.04—dc23/eng/20231027
LC record available at https://lccn.loc.gov/2023040399
LC ebook record available at https://lccn.loc.gov/2023040400

DOI: 10.1093/oso/9780197645598.001.0001

Printed by Integrated Books International, United States of America

This work is dedicated to the memory of my cousins Rozsi and Pista, whose childhoods were terminated at Auschwitz. Never forget.

Also by David F. Lancy

The Anthropological Study of Play: Problems and Prospects
Cross-Cultural Studies in Cognition and Mathematics
Qualitative Research in Education: An Introduction to the Major Traditions
Children's Emergent Literacy: From Research to Practice
Playing on the Mother Ground: Cultural Routines for Children's Development
Studying Children and Schools: Qualitative Research Traditions
The Anthropology of Learning in Childhood
Raising Children: Surprising Insights from Other Cultures
Anthropological Perspectives on Children as Helpers, Workers, Artisans and Laborers
Child Helpers: A Multidisciplinary Perspective
The Anthropology of Childhood: Cherubs, Chattel, Changelings (3rd ed.)

Contents

List of Boxes	xi
Preface	xiii
1. Pedagogy and Culture	1
2. Babies as Students?	25
3. The Self-Starting Learner	51
4. Everyday Classrooms	82
5. The Chore Curriculum	106
6. The Transition to Structured Learning	133
7. Global WEIRDing	179
References	219
Index	269

Boxes

2.1 The Untutored Baby	33
2.2 Lessons in Kinship	44
2.3 Lessons in Social Behavior	45
3.1 Avoiding Hierarchy	53
3.2 Children Learning as Spectators	58
3.3 Principles of Indigenous Pedagogy	59
3.4 Children as Autonomous Foragers	73
3.5 Children as Innovative Craftspersons	75
3.6 Children as Pioneers	76
3.7 Avoiding Teaching	78
4.1 Learning in the Forest	92
4.2 Learning as a Nonparticipant	96
4.3 Reenacting Ritual	97
5.1 The Play Stage	114
5.2 The Errand Stage	117
5.3 Playing Becomes Working	118
5.4 Peers as Role Models	121
5.5 Strategic Intervention	123
5.6 Noting Milestones in the Chore Curriculum	126
5.7 Children as Reliable Workers	129
5.8 Managing Young Workers	130
6.1 Conforming to Expectations	152
6.2 Welcoming Initiation	154
6.3 Nyae Nyae Resistance to Schooling	164
6.4 Historical Resistance to Schooling	165
6.5 Conflict Between School and Work	166
6.6 Sharing Knowledge	170
6.7 The Paucity of Verbal Interaction	171

xii BOXES

7.1 The Disappearance of Chores	193
7.2 Truants from the Natural Classroom	195
7.3 The Decline in Crafts Learning	196
7.4 Indigenes Make Poor "Subjects"	211
7.5 Summarizing the Differences	212

Preface

In the interest of full disclosure, I must admit a failing. In second grade I received "Ds" on my report card under "Deportment." In fourth grade I was paddled by the principal for mischief. I barely avoided being expelled from high school and, later, college. I was a very poor student, but, fortunately, I was a pretty good learner. In graduate school and as a post-doc, I had considerable autonomy to engineer my own education, and I became a respectable student. My schooling experience left me with a profound appreciation of self-initiated and self-guided learning—cornerstones of what I refer to in this volume as "Indigenous pedagogy."

One of those personal initiatives was to conduct ethnographic studies of childhood in a remote Kpelle village in the Liberian interior. Although my agenda was quite open, I gravitated to the study of learning in various contexts, including play, work, initiation rites, and primary school. My first refereed publication appeared in *Human Organization* in 1975 with the title "The Social Organization of Learning: Initiation Rituals and Public Schools." An interest that was kindled fifty years ago has driven much of my work since. The titles of subsequent works reinforce this claim. But *Learning Without Lessons* is my first and last attempt to weave all these shorter strands into a recognizable textile.

The greatest challenge, tantamount to "writer's block," was the lack of widely agreed-upon terminology to label and sort the various components of a comprehensive portrait of children learning in culture. Numerous terms were considered and rejected. Ultimately, it came down to the urgent need to make a selection in order to compose a title. I am grateful to the series coeditors Peggy J. Miller and Cynthia Garcia Call and, especially, to Hayley Singer, Senior Associate Editor, Social and Behavioral Sciences at Oxford University Press, for getting me over this hurdle.

My gratitude to colleagues is profound, and I'd like to acknowledge a tiny fraction of them for their willingness to share with me their ideas and offer me good council. Among these I include Alyssa Crittenden, Courtney Mehan, Suzanne Gaskins, John Bock, Gabriel Scheidecker, Heidi Keller, John M. Roberts, Bob LeVine, Aaron Denham, Doris Bonnet, Alice Schlegel, Barry

xiv PREFACE

Hewlett, Sheina Lew-Levy, Karen Kramer, Annette Bates (Grove), Camilla Morelli, Chantal Medaets, Hillary Fouts, David Bjorkland, Peter Gray, Francesca Mezzenzana, Sid Strauss, Barbara Polak, Daša Bombjaková, Akira Takada, Susan Blum, Tom Weisner, and Adam Boyette. These individuals are delegates from a much greater constituency. Of course, my most significant role model and muse for the last thirty-five years has been Joyce Kinkead.

The final shout-out recognizes all those who labored to make this volume coherent and readable, including anonymous reviewers, copyeditors, and, especially, my friend and long-term editor, J. J. Delliskave.

January 23, 2023

1

Pedagogy and Culture

In most human societies, children become competent adults without
the help of . . . teaching . . . learning is achieved as a by-product, in
the course of interactions that have other purposes.

—Atran and Sperber (1991), 39

Introduction

This work is designed to fill a rather large lacuna in the fields of child development and education. A growing scholarly consensus challenges the
generalizability of Western-dominated research in child psychology. All
or most markers of the child's growth and development are now subject to
reexamination through a cross-cultural lens. By the same token, the study
of education has been similarly restricted since norms and theory are
constructed almost exclusively from research in Euro-American schools.
This work aims to fill a substantial portion of this gap by documenting and
analyzing the myriad processes that come into play as Indigenous children
learn their culture—without schools or lessons. I will characterize the con-
glomeration of learning-rich events as instances of "pedagogy in culture."
The construct has several connotations, but paramount is the idea that
opportunities for learning occur naturally in the course of activities, such as
work, play, and nighttime campfire stories, that are not primarily intended to
educate.

Since the founding of the American Educational Research Association in
1916, the field of education—schooling, curricula, teaching, and learning—
has been supported by a well-funded and scientifically based effort to document and analyze practice and theory. These ideas were exported around
the globe via the replication of Western-style schools using pedagogy from
the same source: institutionalized public basic schooling (Serpell and
Hatano 1997). The success or failure of that effort to transform Indigenous
communities (LeVine et al. 2002) is not my prime concern. Rather, it is to

Learning Without Lessons. David F. Lancy, Oxford University Press. © Oxford University Press 2024.
DOI: 10.1093/oso/9780197645598.003.0001

2 LEARNING WITHOUT LESSONS

argue for the belated study and analysis of Indigenous pedagogy as practiced in communities before the Western model became the norm.

Multiple sources of data have been drawn on: focused, empirical studies in cultural psychology and qualitative accounts of childhood in the ethnographic, historical, and archaeological records. These latter sources have been underutilized in speculation on the nature of child development and learning. The overall conclusion from this research is that the pedagogy found in communities before the advent of schooling differs in very significant ways from that practiced in schools and in the homes of schooled parents. These differences help to account for the failure of newly introduced schools to educate their naive students successfully.

Two studies will introduce the dramatic divide that distinguishes pedagogy found in premodern, Indigenous communities and postindustrial or WEIRD (Western educated industrialized rich democracies[1]) (Henrich et al. 2010). In the first study—conducted in a rural, Indigenous community in Mexico—fifteen trained teachers and thirty relatively unschooled mothers were selected to participate in two challenges: (1) construct a shelter for a market stall (*puesto*)—commonplace in the community; and (2) use math to plot out the ground for constructing *puestos* of proportionally larger areas (de Haan 2001). Teachers and mothers were each charged with assisting a single child in the completion of these tasks. From systematic observation as the process unfolded, the two groups carried out this assignment differently. The mothers assumed the child would learn through collaboration in the actual construction—the focus was on the task, with no provision for instruction or even verbal direction. Teachers first established the respective roles of superordinate teacher and subordinate pupil. Next, they formulated "lessons" for the pupil to follow so that their progress could be noted and adjusted. The task itself faded in importance (de Haan 2001).

> It is clear that the parent-child pairs start from a completely different organization of the . . . learning situation than the teacher-pupil pairs . . . Parents did not introduce the activity to the child or explain about the role they were supposed to fulfill as if the child did not know anything about this.

---

[1] The WEIRD acronym is nothing short of brilliant but needs to be tweaked to fit reality. There is, for example, a great deal of common ground between Western (Euro-American) and East Asian pedagogical practices. "Industrial" might be better replaced by "postindustrial" since WEIRD pedagogy is most evident in the so-called knowledge economy. "Rich" is misleading because the communities that have fully embraced WEIRD pedagogy are more likely to be middle class. And they aren't all democracies by any means; one finds WEIRD enclaves in every country in the world, regardless of politics.

PEDAGOGY AND CULTURE 3

> Nor did they explicitly and regularly check the child's understanding of the task. (de Haan 2001, 191)

> Teachers . . . would, before anything else, try to form the child's attitude to the activity. They would make clear that the child was supposed to be attentive to the teacher . . . in order for learning to take place, the child was going to be told what to do and the teacher was responsible for telling the child. (de Haan 2001, 186–187)

Follow-up interviews with community members augmented the experimental results. Mestizos with several years of schooling saw the Indigenous pattern in a negative light. They asserted that "Mazahua people were not interested in their children . . . they're indifferent towards them. They don't play with them, they don't do things with them, they would leave them alone the whole day. In fact, they do not *educate* their children.[2] [In contrast], Mazahua parents leave children to make their knowledge on their own [because they] are extremely intelligent. They learn *fast* (de Haan 1999, 74, emphasis added) . . . 'at one go' and no tests are needed as it is evident when the child has learnt something" (de Haan 1999, 114).

Informants touted the benefits of letting the child learn on their own, in terms of relieving parents of the necessity to spend time instructing them. For Mazahua villagers,

> The emphasis is not on how an individual performs but, rather, on what gets accomplished. This kind of reciprocity in favor of a collective effort is not so much a question of negotiating, or of turn taking, as it is an impulse to participate as fully as possible. It appears to reflect a social orientation growing out of an awareness of belonging to, participating in, and being part of a social entity. (Paradise and de Haan 2009, 196)

In a subsequent experiment, the task was to make origami figures. This would be a novel experience for the children. Bilingual Euro-American teachers were asked to teach children how to make an origami frog in the casual manner of a helpful "auntie" rather than as teacher. They were unable to

---

[2] A recent study reports the results of a survey of Marshall Island immigrant families in the United States charged with educating their students during the COVID-19 pandemic school closures. The Marshallese had not yet absorbed the WEIRD model of parenting and, therefore, lacked the skills and resources needed to "take over" from the school (Collet and Berman 2021).

4 LEARNING WITHOUT LESSONS

do this—even after extensive training—but instead turned the session into a "lesson" where "they attempted to control the children's attention, behavior and motivation" (Paradise et al. 2014, 134). Mexican teachers from village backgrounds had no difficulty with allowing the children to proceed largely on their own. The village teachers used very little verbalization, explicit direction, or praise, but instead allowed the children to take the initiative to observe and emulate their origami folding technique. The social dynamic was collaborative rather than hierarchical, with an expert instructing a novice. When the Mexican-heritage children got "stuck," they tended to look at the teacher's origami figure for guidance, while the US children looked to the teacher for help when they got stuck.

These studies introduce the central theme of the book: WEIRD children learn via lessons, and Indigenous children learn through their own initiatives using strategies that emerge spontaneously, including observation, overhearing, imitation, and play (Clegg et al. 2021).

Acknowledging the Elephant in the Room

This analysis will be guided by several organizing principles. An important part of the common lore of anthropology is that "other people have culture." That is, most people fail to recognize or appreciate that their lives are governed by habits, values, and expectations that are largely the product of history and culture. They fail to acknowledge that their own way of doing things is not necessarily universal or even widely shared. Academics are not immune. "The importance of culture on life span development is like the elephant in the room. At a certain level, we all know that culture is important, but most of us disregard it in our day-to-day theorizing and studying of developmental processes" (Coll 2004, 145).

Historically, *culture* has been the "noise" in studies of learning and development. Ideally, the "naive subjects" in a study should be shorn of prior knowledge (their culture) before the start of any investigation. Psychology has not, therefore, offered a pathway toward understanding how children acquire culture. Anthropologists, however, have generally conceded to psychology ownership of the *processes* involved in culture acquisition, limiting their contribution to descriptions of culture as the to-be-learned "content."

This *silo effect* can have enormous consequences for the construction of theory. In fact, as Henrich, Heine, and Norenzayan have demonstrated, much of what we consider "human" psychology comes from artificial lab research carried out with US undergraduates—"one of the worst subpopulations one could study for generalizing about *Homo sapiens*" (2010, 79).[3] Researchers tend to ignore possible cross-cultural variation and/or assume that WEIRD subjects are representative of the species (Killin and Pain 2022; Kline et al. 2018). However, I take the position that any attempt to construct a universal theory of childhood must not only sample more widely (Legare 2019) but be willing to entertain the possibility that the way in which, say, hunter-gatherer children learn their culture is reflective of a more "normal" and widespread pedagogy than the, by implication, "recently invented" WEIRD model (Whiten et al. 2003).

Indigenous pedagogy is deeply informed by the bedrock belief that children must be autonomous and their learning self-initiated. Parents tolerate young children's play with sharp knives because "that's how they learn" or "if they get cut, they'll be more careful." When children are forced to go to school, they must learn to "sit still," and they chafe at the loss of agency to an adult authority (Hays 2016). In non-WEIRD societies, the child is the agent in control of the learning process. As Alan Fiske (n.d.) notes, in the ethnographic record, there is "much less child-rearing than there is culture-seeking."

In WEIRD pedagogy, many trends are converging on the idea of a "core" knowledge base that all individuals—male, female, rich, poor, smart, and not-so-smart—must learn. Methods of teaching and frequent "standardized" testing are geared to achieving uniformity. Similarly, "parenting today is virtually synonymous with worry . . . we keenly feel our shortcomings, our inability to know what is best for our children" (Apple 2006, 1). A deliberate quest for uniformity in learning outcomes is much less evident in anthropologists' accounts (Gardner 2019). For example, "No Tobian (island in Micronesia) can master all traditional fishing techniques, for some are considered 'private property' [and] . . . the more difficult a technique, the fewer people that own it" (Johannes 1981, 89).

A corollary idea that permeates this volume is that pedagogy in the village is characterized by enormous redundancy. It is hard to imagine an individual learning calculus by watching someone else carry out calculations or from skimming a calculus textbook or inferring the calculus from the construction

---

[3] Forty years earlier, Urie Bronfenbrenner slammed research in child development as the "science of the strange behavior of children in strange situations with strange adults for the briefest period of time" (1979, 34).

6 LEARNING WITHOUT LESSONS

of a bridge. But, in the village, the child has many role models to observe and eavesdrop on. Learning the environment is accomplished through participant observation of gathering, gardening, fishing, and so on and attending to informative discussions among those processing the food (determining the distribution of newly butchered game) and cooking it. Individual exploration, play, and practice are additional avenues for learning. This redundancy contributes to the inherent diversity among individuals and flexibility in human communities that enabled the species to survive environmental change and occupy virtually every habitat on earth.

Helpful Constructs: Methodology

As an antidote to the "silo effect" mentioned earlier, this study—mirroring the approach of scholars dedicated to the study of childhood in culture—is interdisciplinary. As it happens, looking at childhood through the combined perspectives of cultural and linguistic anthropology, archaeology, developmental psychology, and history yields a much more nuanced and credible portrait of childhood. The interdisciplinary approach is especially valuable in work that is inductive or seeking to discover novelty as opposed to epistemology that aims to affirm previously established hypotheses. Chapter 4 owes much to recent archaeological work focused on children, and Chapter 6 draws largely on history (with some Dickens thrown in for color).

Interdisciplinarity aside, I rely primarily on the perspective of cultural anthropology, whose principal method is ethnography. Ethnography has some unique virtues that make ethnographic "data" particularly valuable. By gathering information as a participant observer, the ethnographer weaves together four strands of information. First, ethnographers describe what they're seeing—compiling a fulsome (often running to 400+ pages) observational log (complemented with photos and audio/video recordings) from which patterns can be detected. Second, by interviewing or engaging their informants in a discussion of what they've witnessed, they may gain an insider's (emic) perspective, which often renders foreign or exotic practices more intelligible to non-natives. Third, ethnographers record their own (etic) perspective. As a reader of ethnography, I pay particular attention to the anthropologist's "aha" moments when they are surprised or shocked by something that violates their own cultural model of childhood. Fourth, the anthropologist interested in looking beyond a single society can draw on an enormous archive of ethnographic accounts, referred to as the ethnographic record. Founded in 1949 at Yale, the Human Relations Area Files (HRAF) contain a significant and readily searchable portion of the ethnographic record, but, increasingly, a truly enormous volume of ethnographic accounts have been digitized and made readily available on the Internet. As an example, Box 3.7 lists eleven distinct anecdotal examples recorded by ethnographers on the topic "avoiding teaching." The eleven examples reflect great cultural and geographical diversity.

Helpful Constructs: Theory

Interest in the study of contrasting models of pedagogy has a long history. Margaret Mead (1964), for example, distinguished between "teaching cultures" as opposed to "learning cultures." Following up on several cross-cultural studies conducted in the 1960s, the discussion centered on the distinction between informal (the village) and formal (school) education. In formal education, "language becomes almost the exclusive means of exchanging information . . . when linguistic forms carry the full burden of communication, the amount of information available to the learner is restricted. Compare the many rich sources of information available to the child who learns by watching and doing" (Scribner and Cole 1973, 556). Greenfield and Lave (1982, 183) proposed a more detailed list of contrasts, such as:

Informal education

1. Embedded in daily life activities.
2. Learner is responsible for obtaining knowledge and skill.
3. Little or no explicit pedagogy or curriculum.

Formal education

1. Set apart from the context of everyday life.
2. Teacher is responsible for imparting knowledge and skill.
3. Learning by verbal interchange, questioning.

8   LEARNING WITHOUT LESSONS

In drawing on the ethnographic record for illustrative cases, I sought out detailed descriptions of cultural *practices*, "actions that are repeated, shared with others in a social group, invested with normative expectations . . . [and] provide the route by which children come to participate in a culture, allowing the culture to be 'reproduced' or 'transformed'" (Miller and Goodnow 1995, 7, 10). As an example, I coined the term "chore curriculum" (Lancy 2012; Chapter 5, this volume) to summarize a set of practices that facilitate the child's learning routine tasks. For example, chores can be broken down in various ways. Graduated sizes in tools, subtasks broken down by difficulty, tolerated "play breaks," strategic assistance offered to the novice, and many other routine and almost unconscious scaffolding tactics create a self-actuating zone of proximal development.

The description and interpretation of cultural practices is complemented and validated by careful elicitation of the *ethnotheory* (Harkness and Super 2006) offered by community members that provides an emic rationale for a particular practice—or its absence. For example, the apparent rarity of teaching in the ethnographic record is justified by ethnotheories that claim learning from lessons is inauthentic and flawed. Teaching usurps the child's autonomy and may be unnecessary as the child will eventually learn without it. The same pair of scholars authored another widely used construct, the *developmental niche* (Super and Harkness 1986). The niche reflects the interaction of ontogeny and culture in combining to foster learning and development. Chapter 4 on "Everyday Classrooms" draws on this construct.

The village origami teachers embraced "an ethnotheory labeled the *child-as-agent* perspective . . . in contrast to the *caregiver-as-agent* perspective" (Coppens et al. 2020, 13) held by Euro-American teachers. Children are often treated as free agents, and Bird-David traces this predisposition to infancy, where Nyaka (India) "babies . . . commonly fed themselves . . . they could actively suckle their mother's breast because of their constant bodily closeness to her. . . . Babies also wean themselves. . . . As toddlers, children are expected to help themselves to the family stew pot which sits at a height that they can reach" (Bird-David 2008, 538–539). Later, "young children could . . . be seen playing with large, sharp knives, with no one taking notice" (Bird-David 2008, 542). In WEIRD society, agency is granted sparingly, for the safety of the child but also so the parent can use small grants of agency as a form of bribery (Fasulo et al. 2007).

Cultural models are "taken-for-granted models of the world that are widely shared . . . by the members of a society and that play an enormous role in their

PEDAGOGY AND CULTURE   9

understanding of that world and their behavior in it" (Quinn and Holland 1987, 4). In an example that certainly applies here, Indigenous peoples generally share a model of childhood in which the child willingly offers assistance to others and strives to "fit in" to the community. A related view is to distinguish between "*collectivism* and *individualism*. Collectivist societies emphasize interdependence, group identity, interpersonal harmony, and achievement of shared goals. Individualist societies (WEIRD) emphasize independence, individual identity, personal assertion, and achievement of personal goals" (Halberstadt and Lozada 2011, 159; Keller 2007).

Another construct used by anthropologists is described as a "body of knowledge and practices produced by children for themselves or for their peers apart from the adult world known as *children's culture* [where] children rapidly acquire knowledge from different sources which they might then use to create new knowledge" (Gallois et al. 2017, 60, 71, emphasis added). In WEIRD society, "children's culture" looks quite different and might refer to the unique child spaces in the home; child-specific dining menu; unique digital display screens and entertainment personally selected by the child; private, child-oriented artifacts such as toys; exclusive child-focused activities, and so on. Chapter 3 reviews children's culture at length.

We can segue readily from children's culture to the idea that *culture is distributed.* This theory points out that culture can be seen as a body of information that is not uniformly transferred to each member of the rising generation. Rather, culture as a store of knowledge is loosely distributed over the entire community (Roberts 1964), its members, artifacts, and practices (Keller and Keller 1996). The twin theory from psychology reads, "In distributed cognition, a group of individuals shares a task in ways suggesting that the group as a whole be considered a cognitive organism" (Keil 2003, 372). Studies have shown, for example, that peak proficiency in complex skills such as hunting (Gurven et al. 2006) and the crafting of Arctic-worthy clothes (Gubser 1965) is limited to a few individuals who are thirty or older. If culture is distributed, this has implications for pedagogy.

Naveh argues that there is no " 'body of knowledge' to transfer to children because everything 'known' is specific to the person or persons and the situation. General instructions cannot be extracted. Hence, learning must be guided by individual initiative and interpersonal engagement, privileging knowledge based on personal experience" (Naveh 2016, 132).

As we'll see, children may have unique knowledge and skills because they exploit environmental resources that are ignored by their elders (Porcher

10 LEARNING WITHOUT LESSONS

et al. 2022). But this information can be drawn on in a crisis (Lancy 2015). Children are not just incomplete adults but unique creators and distributors of knowledge and skill.

A Note on Terminology

The greatest challenge in developing an outline of this work was deciding how to label the phenomena of interest. As the title suggests, I chose to highlight "lessons" to contrast with autonomous or self-guided learning (Lancy 2016a). "Pedagogy" is offered as an umbrella term that covers the entire gamut of facilities—human and material—that contribute to the child's learning and development. "Indigenous" emerged as a critical concept over several rivals, as I'll shortly explain.

From its prominent position in the title, the "Lesson" is a key concept throughout. I use it in lieu of teaching—which may seem like a more likely alternative—because it is less contentious. Teaching has become an important topic for research in anthropology, but it suffers from a multiplicity of very different definitions (Kline 2015; Gärdenfors and Högberg 2021). For example, "We prefer . . . a minimal definition of teaching: an individual modifies her/his behavior to enhance learning in another . . . Teaching cannot be a by-product of another activity" (Boyette and Hewlett 2018, 773). With this minimalist definition, the ensuing research (spot observation of children) suggests that teaching is ubiquitous (Boyette and Hewlett 2018). But minimalist definitions have come under criticism (Moore 2019, 49n) because they are "too general and not easily differentiated from every day social interaction" (Eskelson 2020, 33). The minimalist definition can be contrasted with more restricted definitions.

> Teaching is (1) an act of intentional communication in which (2) a knowledgeable individual (the "teacher") volunteers information for the benefit of one or more naive individuals (the "learners"), (3) with the intention of facilitating learning (e.g., the development of knowledge or skills) in the naive individuals. (4) The information provided by the knowledgeable individual is generalizable, or relevant to the identity of the group to which teacher and students belong and could serve as a platform for future insight or innovation by others. (Moore 2019, 41)

> If teaching is defined very broadly to include any behavior of one animal that serves to assist another animal's learning, teaching is relatively common in the animal kingdom. . . . But flexible and insightful forms of instruction in which one individual intends that another acquire a skill or piece of knowledge and adjusts its behavior contingent on the learner's progress in skill or knowledge would seem to be very rare. (Boesch and Tomasello 1998, 602)

Those who utilize more restrictive definitions in studying Indigenous pedagogy tend to record very little teaching. Bruner notes that in viewing hundreds of hours of ethnographic film shot among the !Kung and Netsilik foraging bands, he was struck by the total absence of teaching episodes: "One sees no explicit teaching" (1966a, 59). And in a study of traditional ecological knowledge (TEK[4]) in fishing communities on Buton Island (Sulawesi), Vermonden reported that "during two years of participant observation, I rarely observed oral transmission of fishing knowledge or techniques" (2009, 205).

Seeking an emic or native definition of teaching is fruitless. Most societies lack a term equivalent to teaching (Reichard 1934). For example, the "Aka [Congo Basin] do not have a specific expression for 'teaching,' they employ the term of '*mateya*' to refer to advice or guidance which accords with the Pygmy value of personal autonomy, implying that the child has a choice to follow the advice or guidance, or to refuse it" (Hewlett and Roulette 2016, 12). A second example: "The Old English word for to 'teach, instruct, guide' was more commonly *læran*, source of modern *learn* and *lore*" (Online Etymology Dictionary 2018). In fact, when anthropologists try to elicit a local term or terms to describe teaching, they are rebuffed with the emphatic declaration "We don't teach" (see Box 3.7). Truly, "teaching is a slippery concept" (Strauss and Ziv 2012, 187), which is why I opted for "lesson" as a less ambiguous term.

"Lessons" include a teacher who behaves in much the way that the Mexican teachers behaved in the case discussed at the beginning of this chapter. I had earlier composed a working definition (Lancy 2016b), which I draw on here:

---

[4] TEK is one of the cornerstones of Indigenous pedagogy as it encompasses the essential skills and knowledge that all community members will need to draw on. Think of it as the "three Rs" of the village curriculum.

12 LEARNING WITHOUT LESSONS

1. Lessons will not occur or are unlikely where the learner is able to acquire the requisite knowledge or skill in the absence of teaching.
2. Those who organize and conduct lessons incur costs in time lost from their regular activity and, possibly, materials as well. These costs must be offset by benefits to the teacher once the pupil(s) is/are successful (1 and 2 are from Thornton and Raihani 2008, 1823).
3. Lessons imply a specific skill or body of knowledge that will be transferred from teacher to pupil.
4. The teacher takes steps to secure the learner's intention to learn, verify that the "lesson" has been successful and take appropriate action if it has not (Hirst 1973).
5. The learner is aware of the teacher's intention and engages with or attends to the "lesson" (3–5 are from Olson 2008, 3).
6. The lesson focuses on a designated teacher, learner, and "content." The lesson "cannot be a by-product of another activity" (Boyette and Hewlett 2018, 773).
7. There is the assumption that the lesson incorporates eye contact, joint attention, and speech or gestures directed from teacher to pupil(s) (Shneidman and Woodward 2016).
8. There are standards or norms for the conduct of the lesson, the aim of the lesson, and the product or outcome.

Perhaps the reader has anticipated that a central argument will be that lessons are extremely common in WEIRD society and uncommon elsewhere.

"Pedagogy" as an organizing concept was rivaled by "education" and "socialization"; the latter is heavily used in discussions of child development in anthropology. I rejected education because it is too often linked or treated as synonymous with schooling, which would exclude 90 percent of the learning events reviewed in the book. I rejected socialization because of its connotation of a one-way, caretaker-initiated process. But pedagogy has a satisfying ambiguity and is not considered synonymous with schooling. Indeed, I find the following definition very satisfactory.

Pedagogy is the theory and practice of learning, and how this process influences, and is influenced by, the social, political and psychological development of learners. Pedagogy, taken as an academic discipline, is the study of how knowledge and skills are imparted in an educational context, and it considers the interactions that take place during learning. (Wikipedia 2023a)

The beauty of this very broad term is that it can comfortably accommodate learning situations as disparate as an algebra lesson and a group fishing expedition.

The last term that deserves some explication is "Indigenous." There are a variety of competing terms. We are discussing people who live in small, face-to-face communities; hence, "village" or "villagers" is sometimes used as shorthand. Other terms that have been used to conveniently label the communities of interest include "heritage," "traditional," "ethnic," "nonindustrial," "Aboriginal," and "premodern." "Primitive" and "tribal" were both popular at one time but are no longer considered appropriate. Most definitions of "Indigenous" stress the importance of stasis and continuity. For example, "indigenous peoples are culturally distinct ethnic groups whose members are directly descended from the earliest known inhabitants of a particular geographic region and, to some extent, maintain the language and culture of those original peoples" (Wikipedia 2023b).

Outline of the Volume

What follows is a summary of each of the remaining six chapters. The chapters are designed to be read in sequence but can be read in isolation without difficulty.

Chapter 2—Babies as Students?

Nowhere is the gulf between WEIRD and Indigenous pedagogy farther apart than in the treatment of infants. On the one hand, WEIRD babies are being cast in the role of pupils at an earlier and earlier age. Parents are anxious to optimize the child's development and are urged on by authorities and entrepreneurs selling training materials to construct "age-appropriate" lessons. On the other hand, Indigenous mothers, concerned for their baby's survival, take great pains to keep the infant in a womb-like environment with reduced stimulation and disturbance. Many of the taken-for-granted tactics for scaffolding the growth of speech, dexterity, and social interaction such as "baby talk" may be absent in Indigenous parenting. Hence, far more speech is directed at WEIRD babies who are, as a consequence, more often held *en face* as opposed to facing away from the caretaker.

14 LEARNING WITHOUT LESSONS

While WEIRD children may be treated as complete persons at birth, this recognition is usually delayed until the infant is capable of speech and independent locomotion in an Indigenous community. Nevertheless, untutored babies act like sponges, taking in information as shown by their ready imitation of facial expressions and speech. While the WEIRD baby is receiving lessons, her Indigenous counterpart is busy learning on her own. Unsurprisingly, researchers fail to find evidence of mothers playing with their infants and toddlers, while WEIRD mothers engage in extensive bouts of *educational* play.

Play grows in importance for Indigenous babies when they are old enough to pass to the care of an older sibling and join the typical juvenile playgroup. Sibcare is one of several practices that lighten a mother's burden so that she may return to work and prepare for the next birth. To this end, numerous societies conduct various exercises with older infants to accelerate sitting, standing, and walking. WEIRD parenting is all about acceleration, whether in weaning, locomotion, speech—especially vocabulary—or social interaction.

WEIRD parenting is predicated on relative parity in the status of children and adults; hence, much of infant-directed speech (IDS) is designed to approximate a conversation where the mother, for example, asks questions of the child that she knows they can answer. In Indigenous communities, the young are not so privileged. Their questions or requests are rebuffed. Speech directed at children is mostly aimed at getting them to do something helpful. Rather than speaking directly to the child, the adult may speak about the child to a third party, and it is up to the child to retrieve the message and behave accordingly. Rather than direct interaction between adults and children, the latter are supposed to observe the former and listen to their speech to others. The child must, in effect, design and execute their own lessons.

Another area where, at least in some Indigenous communities, parents accelerate development is in prosocial behavior, including sharing, etiquette (when interacting with adults), kinship structure, nomenclature, and interaction rules. The parent's objectives are to present a compliant child to the community, in hopes of finding part-time, volunteer caretakers, and to prevent the child from committing a faux pas. Elsewhere, parents maintain a laissez-faire attitude, and children learn proper manners in due course on their own. After all, children are anxious to "fit in."

The chapter concludes by asking the reader to consider whether all the lessons in the life of a WEIRD baby are necessary for successful development.

This is in light of the very successful development of Indigenous babies who are not prescribed a full menu of lessons.

Chapter 3—The Self-Starting Learner

The pedagogy that is detailed in Chapter 3 features the child's innate tendencies to observe carefully, to eavesdrop on conversations, to imitate others, and to play with and learn to use commonplace objects like tools. These inherited abilities are the foundation upon which Indigenous pedagogy is built. Systems of childcare, social relations, and subsistence are open and transparent. Communities freely provide access to raw materials children need to make sense of their world and to become helpful and accepted community members. Deliberate instruction is not, except under limited circumstances, considered necessary or efficacious.

From early infancy, children seem primed to rely on an inherited capacity to observe the flow of activity around them and seek out regularities. They acquire speech through eavesdropping on the conversations of others. Children are actually encouraged to "hang around" their elders, carefully watching their every move: "It's how they learn." When they grow tired of being spectators, they replicate, with friends, what they have observed in make-believe. And this, too, meets with approval. If the youngster is too young to work, they can, usefully, pretend to. The child's spontaneous initiatives are generally encouraged by the community. The visiting anthropologist will take note of various artifacts such as scaled-down or discarded tools, which children are encouraged to practice with. Archaeologists also find evidence of artifacts that functioned as toys at some point in their life span. Nearly everywhere, three-year-olds are granted limited rights to hold and comfort a baby sibling. This ready tolerance of children's desire to handle material that would, in WEIRD society, be prohibited grows out of the belief that learning occurs through doing.

From about six years of age, children transition from watching to participating. Eager to help out, children bid to participate in the routine work in the village, and most of these jobs can be broken into components, such as carrying and fetching, that are within the child's capacity. As these jobs proliferate and become more challenging, the child helper is also learning how to work collaboratively, the sine qua none of the Indigenous way of living. Praise is rare; the reward comes when an adult accepts the

16 LEARNING WITHOUT LESSONS

child's contribution to the task. Failure is not necessarily called out but leads to a new, less challenging assignment, or someone else steps up and redoes the work. Above all, care is taken to nurture the child's desire to be helpful and competent. Anthropologists have noted that much of the child's interaction with adults occurs in the course of shared work, not in play.

Numerous and varied illustrative cases from the ethnographic record will be drawn on to illuminate the child's "education" during this period.

Chapter 4—Everyday Classrooms

In Chapter 4, the focus is less on the child's individual learning processes and much more on the "developmental niche." "Everyday classrooms" implies routines that play out regularly in the village, which, incidentally, function as rich opportunities for learning. The "classroom" might be an irregular area in the village or camp that has been cleared of vegetation (thus reducing the incursion of snakes and insects). This area might serve as a gathering place for socializing adults and a temporary workshop where grain is spread to dry or fishing nets are repaired. At night it might be the scene of dancing around a bonfire. These exciting activities draw child spectators and eager helpers. The presence of adults, including those too old to forage or do fieldwork, provides vigilant sentinels alert to injury and mayhem. Young children and their sib-caretakers will spend the greater part of the day playing on and near this space, which the Kpelle call the "mother ground" and the Mbuti *bopi*.

A closely related developmental niche is the children's playgroup. These are ubiquitous in Indigenous societies and were once commonplace in industrialized societies, until anxiety regarding child abduction all but extinguished them. There are a number of features commonly part of the pedagogy of the playgroup. There's the physical space explicitly or implicitly allocated the role of playground. Younger and older children are bound together by complimentary needs. The older are naturally protective and authoritative, glad of an opportunity to act in a more mature role. This attitude is reinforced when the older sib is assigned sibcare duty by a parent. And the younger is drawn by the protection afforded by an older brother or sister and their willingness to serve as a role model to emulate. Because of the obligation to incorporate the very young into the flow of activity, play and games are not fiercely competitive. Older players may handicap themselves, and the goals of the game are set at the level of the youngest player.

PEDAGOGY AND CULTURE   17

Among the most commonly seen play activities in the playgroup are make-believe bouts. Unlike make-believe in WEIRD culture, one sees little fantasy or imagined characters and worlds. Rather, make-believe in the village inevitably involves a reenactment of common scenes throughout the village. Work activity is particularly rich as script material, and the oldest playgroup members take on the jobs of script composition and the assignment of roles to playgroup members. Again, the designated play area contributes to successful make-believe in several ways. It is a beehive of script-worthy activity, and adults in the vicinity might be persuaded to loan utensils as props. Failing that source, there will still be a motley collection of discarded tools, holed gourds, frayed rope, and broken furniture at the periphery or not far away.

The playgroup as everyday classroom is one of several sketched out in the remainder of the chapter. These include the family circle, where children get their initial opportunity to participate in activities that, heretofore, they have only been watching. The family circle is set in motion on mixed-age foraging excursions. Among the adaptations to make the excursion serve pedagogical ends is to slow the progression so smaller children can keep up. Public performances of various kinds—court sessions; ritual enactment such as a funeral; community gatherings featuring singing or storytelling; recounting of the day's hunting and gathering journeys—all provide learnable details of the larger culture. Children "take away" from these gatherings material to use in make-believe. The next classroom to be considered is the stone tool-making site, where recent excavations have revealed the routine presence of young, novice knappers. In general, we find that village workshops such as the blacksmith's forge, the potter's kiln, and the weaver's loom all provide opportunities for observation, overhearing, play with raw materials, and, for older children, informal apprenticeships.

Chapter 5—The Chore Curriculum

A major transition in the child's education occurs when play is gradually superseded by work. Play is appreciated as a means to keep children busy and out of the way. But virtually every skill is first encountered in play, and the "play stage" is seen as the essential first step in the chore curriculum. Once the child is perceived as making a real contribution to the family economy, others pay closer attention. Above all, the child for the first time will be *assigned* specific tasks. The reader will, no doubt, be surprised by the huge

18 LEARNING WITHOUT LESSONS

variety of "chores" undertaken by Indigenous children. And each task has its own curriculum or "ladder" of skills to master and then deploy. This chapter catalogs the varied inventory of child work and the learning process associated with each.

Aside from assigning chores to ensure the task fits the learner, scaled tools donated by parents or older siblings may also signal approval for the child to begin practicing the skill in earnest. The novice farmer, fisher, forager, or hunter may also be given opportunity and encouragement by being invited to join a work party. This boon is not granted lightly. Young hunters may wait years before they are considered sufficiently mature and discreet to accompany adults on a hunt. And they may play a support role (looking after the dogs, carrying provisions) but not yet join the chase. Other obstacles that might arise include gender and age. Foraging for tubers may be barred to boys. Another chore may be beyond the athletic ability of the learner, such as climbing coconut palms. However, the learner is given a great deal of leeway in terms of the pace of their development and the ultimate level of skill. No one is perfect.

The child is driven by two forces that motivate them to travel up the learning curve. These are the need to "fit in" and the burning desire to acquire knowledge and skill. Trying to secure a recognized place in the family economy is most evident in the child's ready volunteering to help others. Not only is there ample evidence of spontaneous helping in the ethnographic record, but numerous laboratory studies with children as young as fourteen months reveal an innate desire to help out.

These powerful needs are readily accommodated by assigning errands to the very young. Errand running is usually the child's first chore, and this is true across the spectrum of Indigenous communities. Errands can be readily graded in difficulty so that even toddlers can be sent to get water from the stream or well if provided with a small enough vessel. Aside from the obviously instrumental nature of errands, they are also valued as opportunities to plunge the child, like a debutant, into society. The errand allows the child to refine their growing store of polite phrases and understanding of the kinship system. Aside from the developmental value of errands, mothers will encourage their children to gather up and bring home any gossip or village news they might overhear.

In the transition from playing to working, young novices are typically paired with one or more mentors/role models. These are most likely older siblings, cousins, and neighbors. By the age of five or six, girls will spend a great deal of time observing and helping their mothers. And boys will be paired with somewhat older male relatives, as men do not welcome child apprentices, especially in hunting and fishing. Boys, at least until middle childhood, spend less time working and more time playing than girls of the same age, and, in fact, this transition reveals much about the child's future identity.

Moving from these general principles, the chapter proceeds to describe the chore curriculum as it plays out in a variety of societies. The survey includes children learning to become camel drovers on a Saharan caravan; a four-year-old Bamana boy trying to hoe a row of beans; a Western Apache boy diligently progressing—over several years—from hunting small birds and rodents to large ungulates; and Hadza four-year-olds beginning their foraging career by gathering nutritious baobab fruits that drop from the trees. Remarkably, careful measurement of caloric yields makes clear that the value of children's initial attempts is significant, even to the point of meeting their own nutritional needs.

At a somewhat later age, child novices are welcomed in the craft workshop. Using detailed descriptions of the craft curriculum, I am able to show the shared underlying principles or cultural models that structure the experience. For instance, in the pottery, a young girl will be encouraged to play with clay, shape crude pots, decorate vessels made by her mother, and, eventually, fire her fully mature, sale-worthy ceramics. The mother is the child's likely role model, but, in numerous cases, older girls take the initiative to observe and emulate the designs of other potters, and the same is true for weaving.

As the child moves through the chore curriculum, milestones are called out and celebrated. For example, a Netsilik (Arctic) girl's first-caught salmon and her brother's first-shot goose are acknowledged by the community. Note how chores are parceled out by gender. During the years from five to ten (middle childhood), the child acquires "sense." This transition is remarkably similar across Indigenous societies, even to a specific term in the language. Play is curtailed. Children have mastered their allotted chore inventory. Above all is the assumption of greater responsibility and the absence of close supervision. A growth spurt, rapid muscle development, and increased stamina complement these changes in character. If there are yet more challenging tasks to master, the older child is free to pursue or reject them. They are the architects of their own further development and may elect to specialize, selecting a willing role model and plotting their own learning strategy. Above all, the child is learning "on the job."

20 LEARNING WITHOUT LESSONS

Chapter 6—The Transition to Structured Learning

The primary theme of this work is that Indigenous children gain their education largely through informal, child-initiated pedagogy. But more structured, formal models of pedagogy are not completely absent from the village. A significant fraction of the world's Indigenous communities incorporates more school-like models of education. These include so-called bush schools, or initiation rites, and teacher-dominated apprenticeships in specialized skills such as ocean navigation and blacksmithing. In addition, the typical village now houses an elementary school, largely at the prodding of the United Nations campaign to foster universal primary schooling. It is important, however, to show how different these schools often are from the institutions serving WEIRD children.

The chapter opens with a brief survey of the pedagogical antecedents of the typical colonial-era public school. The earliest evidence we have for designated teachers and classrooms are the scribal training sites excavated in Egypt and Sumer from 5000 to 6000 years BP. The scene is uninviting. Students spend hours in mind-numbing copying of texts and rote memorization of terms. Teachers set lessons to be followed and severely punish students for mistakes or lack of diligence. This pattern continues throughout the centuries, even as schooling spreads and new subjects get added to the curriculum. Teachers cited ancient authorities to legitimize their practice: Aristotle called education the "partner of pain," and Menander (400 BCE) wrote: "He who is not beaten does not learn." Schooling sponsored by religious authorities was, if anything, more onerous.

We can find instances of this early coercive model of education among Indigenous peoples, particularly where sedentism and social hierarchy are well-established. In these communities, one may encounter two institutions: the initiation rite and the craft apprenticeship. Several elements in both apprenticeship and the initiation ritual are "school-like." First, all the participants are of roughly the same age and gender—a relative rarity for collective activity in the village. Second, they are all exposed to the same "curriculum." Third, physical punishments and threats of worse are integral to the initiation rites and the apprenticeship.

Craft apprenticeships typically incorporate both natural—learning largely through observation, imitation, and practice—and school-like pedagogy. The master stands as an authority figure who demands diligence and respect while offering little teaching or scaffolded support for novices. Onerous and unrelated work assignments (menial work in the master's home), verbal abuse, and corporal punishment are "standard" elements of pedagogy. As with schools, the apprentice's family must pay stiff fees to the master, while failure and noncompletion are commonplace.

The unsympathetic, teacher-centered pattern of early schools traveled among the baggage of the colonial powers as they spread "civilization" and religion around the globe. Anthropologists have provided a rich trove of accounts of pedagogy found in the earliest village schools. The elements noted for the earliest classrooms—rote learning, corporal punishment, rigid uniformity, abstract subjects, competition valued over cooperation—are all here in full. But while Western schools have evolved fairly successfully to produce workers for the changing economy, village children and their families are marginalized by the substandard schooling available to villagers as well as the lack of jobs for school leavers.

Hence resistance from students, who become sporadic attendees and dropouts, flourishes in small, rural communities and urban slums. More significant for this analysis is the evidence for a deeper—community—resistance based on the profound differences between the pedagogy of the village and the pedagogy of schooling and teachers.

However, despite widespread evidence of resistance and failure, the inevitable expansion of school access mandated by the agreement to provide universal primary education has contributed to modernization and infrastructure improvements in many small, rural communities, and at least a minority of students now find employment opportunities that require their school-learned skills. But the most dramatic evidence of change has been the repeated international survey finding that even a few years of schooling can "modernize" a woman's approach to fertility, child health, and support for her children's schooling.

Chapter 7—Global WEIRDing

The concluding chapter is, appropriately, forward focused. Although this book is about variety in children's mastering their culture, this chapter's emphasis is on growing uniformity. The title is meant to suggest that WEIRD notions of pedagogy, as many other aspects of WEIRD culture, are spreading rapidly around the world. The most obvious sign of this phenomenon is that a larger and larger proportion of the world's population is schooled.

22 LEARNING WITHOUT LESSONS

Aside from the expansion of schooling itself, teaching—good and bad—has escaped from the school and invaded formerly teacher-free settings. Hence the title of the chapter's first section is "Lesson Creep." Kindergarten has become the "new" first grade. Terms like "helicopter" and "lawnmower" parenting warn of the overwhelming increase in parental engagement with children's academic and social lives. Legions of mass-marketed parenting books and the blogosphere are crowded with exhortations to stimulate the child's development via lessons of various kinds "before it's too late." The family dinner hour, trips to the grocery store, cake baking, and household chores all become occasions for lessons that may have almost no instrumental connection to the task at hand. Free play in the neighborhood has ceded place to music and dance lessons, Kumon* tutoring, and organized sports.

Pushback against assembly-line, one-size-fits-all pedagogy is as old as Erasmus, writing in the sixteenth century that schools were "torture chambers." But there seems little likelihood the flow will be stemmed. Schooling is now linked to economic advancement, even in more remote, rural enclaves, and researchers are studying the processes involved as communities trend toward WEIRDness. WEIRD society and the less developed, less prosperous communities that live in its shadow are now subject to a ruthless Darwinian struggle. Children in the privileged group may suffer the effects of stress, depression, or worse. Children in less privileged communities will be enticed with the same goals and aspirations as their more thoroughly WEIRD counterparts while coping with much diminished resources. Valiant attempts to adapt school curricula to the local culture run aground on the great ridge that divides the pedagogical philosophy of the school from that of the formerly school-less community. For frustrated students, the psyche-saving response to consistent failure—by WEIRD standards—may be to opt out entirely.

The second topic in the chapter, "Lost Skills," follows directly from the first. If schooling is occupying a larger and larger portion of the child's time, it follows that children will have much less time to benefit from local, Indigenous pedagogy. While village children in middle childhood are expected to become responsible and mature community members and major contributors to their families, their "cosmopolitan" counterparts remain in a state of dependency and their care becomes more, not less, costly. From the work of Ochs and others, it seems that prosocial behaviors such as sharing and helping become attenuated, and pedagogy in the home takes on a lesson-like, discourse-heavy, academic character.

Another victim of WEIRDing is the drive to fit in, be helpful, and learn to work collaboratively. Parents who've received several years of successful, formal education transition to the WEIRD model of parenting. Children's offers to help, to do chores, and to act responsibly are spurned with the admonition to focus on schoolwork and their assignments. Children in school or doing homework will miss out on foraging expeditions and other work parties, leading to a loss of skills generally, but especially the loss of critical environmental knowledge. In the worst-case scenario, the village child is thrown into limbo, where poor schooling does not lead to steady employment and school leavers return to the village with a paucity of subsistence skills. This deficit is unlikely to be reversed by parents who do not believe in lessons.

The third topic in the chapter is labeled "The Schooled Mind." Here I review studies by cultural psychologists uncovering the effects of schooling on children's thinking and behavior. Barbara Rogoff and colleagues have led this search. Their research is focused on the decline or absence of cognitive and social skills due to schooling. Mexican villagers with little schooling exhibit wide-ranging attention, taking in many details from the natural and social environment, while more highly schooled WEIRD subjects focus more narrowly on the teacher and the details of the lesson. Influenced by the individualism of the school, WEIRD or nearly WEIRD children lose interest in learning through observation and are poor collaborators compared to their less acculturated counterparts. Another major shift takes place as the pedagogy of the village, dominated by direct, hands-on experiences, is replaced by lessons that are delivered primarily through speech and printed material.

Numerous lab studies with WEIRD students show that they cannot function autonomously. They follow the teacher's example or instructions and forgo any attempt to learn (about a novel toy) on their own through exploration and trial and error. WEIRD students are being taught to ignore the events unfolding around them, to avoid becoming "distracted." Meanwhile, unschooled village kids are very good observers and listeners and are adapted to process the steady stream of information that unfolds in public.

The fourth topic to consider is the future of research on Indigenous pedagogy. There is a sense of urgency in testing many WEIRD theories regarding children's learning. To do this requires locating communities that have not already made significant accommodation to the WEIRD model of parenting. The study of pedagogy in Indigenous communities has been significantly compromised by the spread of formal education. The challenge in the short run is to break down the many changes occurring in Indigenous communities and weigh their distinct impact on pedagogy. A community where children no longer participate in subsistence activity is, for the purpose of comparative analysis, already WEIRD. Many of the data-gathering tools that cross-cultural scholars have used may not yield meaningful data if subjects are too shy to answer fully.

The difficulties with empirical studies highlight the value of ethnography, where long-term participant observation allows one to collect real-life instances of the behaviors of interest. And there is the treasure trove referred to as the ethnographic record, where much of the material available for analysis was collected before the full impact of Global WEIRDing became so evident.

The final section of the chapter is devoted to a review of the major points made throughout the book. Many of these are presented as contrasting WEIRD and Indigenous practices.

2

Babies as Students?

> Infant education is much more important than you might expect. By interacting with your baby on a regular basis and taking your baby to infant classes, you can make sure that your child's education stays right on track.
>
> —The Learning Experience (2021)

> A [Dobe !Kung] child who is nursing has no awareness of things. Milk, that's all she knows. Otherwise, she has no sense. Even when she learns to sit, she still doesn't think about anything because her intelligence hasn't come to her yet. Where could she be taking her thoughts from? The only thought is nursing.
>
> —Shostak (1981), 113

Introduction

In Western, educated, industrialized, rich, democratic (WEIRD) society, schooling does not begin in first grade, nor kindergarten, nor even at birth. For at least some children, it begins in the womb. In this chapter, I call attention to the imperative for eager parent-teachers to begin preparing their child to assume the student role. This movement is driven, in part, by lab research with WEIRD infants, suggesting they are capable of learning at earlier ages than previously supposed (Featherstone 2017). Commercial enterprises have ratcheted up the pressure by marketing various aids to parent-teachers, including, for example, "Baby Signs"—allowing parents to fill the "wasted" months before baby speaks with vocabulary and attachment-enhancing American Sign Language (ASL) lessons (Acredolo and Goodwyn 2002).

This chapter reviews the exclusively WEIRD research on parent–infant interaction that leads scholars to claim *teaching* as the first and paramount means of socializing children (Strauss et al. 2002; Cšibra and Gergely 2009). Lessons can start prenatally and expand postnatally with the infant's

Learning Without Lessons. David F. Lancy, Oxford University Press. © Oxford University Press 2024.
DOI: 10.1093/oso/9780197645598.003.0002

26 LEARNING WITHOUT LESSONS

increasing capacity to learn. While WEIRD parents *claim* to be training their children to be independent, in fact they "strip the infant of true independence" (Gaskins 2006, 289). They do this because their first priority is to train the infant to accept the parent as the primary mediator of their every experience.

Following the review of research and popular opinion in the dominant society, I conduct a complementary analysis of literature on Indigenous communities, whose parenting ethnotheories consider children to be autonomous, self-starting learners, innocent of any great need for teaching. Mother–infant interaction may not include "baby talk" or "motherese"; infants may rarely be held *en face*; an infant's bid for attention (via pointing) may be ignored; and parents may not engage infants in interaction with objects (Solomon 2012). On the contrary, a widespread ethnotheory posits that "good" infant care requires frequent, quiet feeding followed by a restful interlude. Nearly continuous physical contact between the infant and others contrasts with the WEIRD pattern of more distal relations bridged by frequent infant-directed verbalization (LeVine 2014; Richman et al. 1992; Röttger-Rössler et al. 2015). This distinction has been neatly labeled as pediatric (Indigenous) versus pedagogic (WEIRD) child care (LeVine et al., 1994).[1]

WEIRD parent–child speech patterns are predicated on an assumption that the infant is a complete person from birth and that all the adult capacities are present in nascent form, to be stimulated and scaffolded by special speech forms such as baby talk and motherese. In contrast, many societies withhold fully human status, at least until the child is mobile and has acquired speech (Lancy 2014). Overall, very little didactic speech is directed to infants, but they are expected to attend to and learn from speech directed at others. The guiding ethnotheory targets an end state where the child develops a collectivist or interdependent character primed to "fit in" to the group, as contrasted with the WEIRD-worthy "individualist" who is socialized to fulfill her own exceptional destiny (Keller 2007). The parent–child interactions and speech patterns recorded by anthropologists show how societies shape children to fulfill these differing aspirations.

A significant number of societies in the ethnographic record endorse the accelerated training of infants in sitting, standing, and walking. This training

---

[1] A wonderful Indigenous version of this dichotomy was recorded in SW Madagascar. "That's how he grows up. Zagnahary [the creator god] makes his mind grow. As a mother, I just give him the breast" (Scheidecker 2023).

reflects the need to reduce the care burden posed by a not-yet-mobile child. A second pattern, found particularly in the South Pacific, might be called "social acceleration." During early childhood, actual lessons are used to accelerate the child's prosocial behavior: sharing of resources, knowledge of appropriate etiquette, kin terms, and polite speech. These efforts are aimed at rapidly integrating the child into the community, leading to the conferral of "personhood" (Maxwell West 1988). Volunteering to help out is likely a universal trait, which appears spontaneously in the first year. Child helpers may interfere with the work of others, so managing their contributions is a challenge that all non-WEIRD parents must face.

Education in the Womb and on the Lap

In China, fetal instruction (*Taijiao*) dates from the fourth century BCE. It was seen "as a means to influence the moral development of the child at the earliest possible opportunity" (Kinney 1995, 27). This childrearing philosophy spread throughout the educated classes and still holds sway. Korean mothers are expected to practice *T'aekyo*. A fundamental tenet is that the mother is a conduit from the outside world to the fetus. What she eats, thinks, sees, and hears are all transmitted to the fetus, so it is incumbent on her to avoid noxious or unpleasant experiences and seek out all that is beautiful and uplifting, such as white jade or a peacock (Kim and Choi 1994, 239–240). The Japanese practice of womb education (*Taikyoo*) suggests "the malleability of children's character during the early stages of life" (Uno 1991, 396). But the Japanese have modernized the pedagogy of womb education by introducing, for example, "English-language texts to be read aloud by the mother-to-be into a sort of resonating device strapped to her belly" (White 2002, 134).

Fetal instruction attracts WEIRD parents who are determined to optimize their child's development. Interviews suggest that "belly talk" is believed to jump-start the process of bonding between parents and their offspring (Han 2009, 13). Books, websites, and music CDs designed to enhance the fetus's intellectual and aesthetic tastes via the "Mozart effect" (Campbell 2002) have become a multi-million-dollar industry. However, there appear to be no actual long-term benefits for children subjected to Mozart while still in the womb (Lilienfeld et al. 2009, 48).

Numerous media producers sell aids to assist the anxious parent. BabyPlus[*] Prenatal Education System[*], where the "womb is the best classroom," is one

28 LEARNING WITHOUT LESSONS

example (BabyPlus.com). The system is touted on their website as a patented set of sound lessons, played during pregnancy, that "strengthen a baby's early cognitive development." Proponents of the device claim it leads to babies that are more interactive and responsive and *more ready for school* (Han 2020, 148). These claims have been thoroughly debunked (Wright and Karar 2010), yet the program has, nevertheless, spread to sixty-five countries, earning the owners $9 million annually.

Womb education does not appear in the ethnographic record because the fetus is not considered human (Maiden and Farwell 1997). "Inuit have no special term to denote a fetus in utero and by custom do not speak about it until after its birth. The fetus is never regarded as 'alive' until after it is born, so Inuit never think of it as a person" (Guemple 1979, 40). In the Sepik area (PNG) "unborn children were not regarded as human and were referred to as 'the belly'" (Kulick 1992, 98). It is somewhat surprising that childbirth does not immediately alter these perceptions. The newborn may still not be viewed as fully human.[2] In fact, in a survey of the ethnographic record, I found the majority delayed the granting of personhood until a later point in the life cycle, when the child's survival, worth, and "normal" human capacity (locomotion, speech, social interaction) were assured (Lancy 2014).

The first lesson after birth may be to promote recognition of the primary caretaker. Holding the baby en face and "making faces" as well as producing a panoply of sounds focuses the baby's attention on the caretaker. But the imagination and resources of the individual parent may appear inadequate, considering the "perils" of insufficient stimulation. As the venerable (begun in 1977) *Zero to Three* (2022) program warns, "We have three short years to build relationships, nurture brain development and solve the inequity issues that arise from the absence of quality early learning opportunities." An entire library of volumes devoted to educating the concerned parent has followed in the wake of *Zero to Three*. For example, Jill Stamm (2008) has written *Bright from the Start: The Simple, Science-Backed Way to Nurture Your Child's Developing Mind from Birth to Age 3*, where she "translates the latest neuroscience findings into clear explanations and practical suggestions for implementing brain enhancing activities." With guidance from "experts" (Harkness et al. 1992), the infant's parent can build an entire academic curriculum (Brunelle 2016; Hul 2019; Inouye 2011).

---

[2] Even naming may be delayed until the "person" emerges. In Indigenous communities, the child's name reflects social and kinship ties, whereas in WEIRD society, the name may be chosen for its novelty, signaling the child's uniqueness (Lancy 2017, 121–126).

BABIES AS STUDENTS? 29

Figure 2.1 Three-month-old Adley using pattern detection training material

Figure 2.1 depicts my three-month-old granddaughter looking at images in a pattern detection training kit.[3] This kit is one of dozens of "educational toys" developed for babies by expert designers at Lovevery® (Lovevery.com). At a hefty price, Lovevery® promises "Stage-based play essentials for your child's developing brain." Meanwhile, "the latest twist in infant instruction is lapware, computer activities designed for infants and toddlers, as young as

---

[3] This URL shows a video clip reflecting her opinion of this lesson: https://www.davidlancy.org/learning-without-lessons. Accessed January 31, 2023.

30 LEARNING WITHOUT LESSONS

6 months old, to be played while sitting on mom or dad's lap. These programs are promoted as *educational* software" (Bjorkland 2007a, 178).

Repeated references to "the developing brain," "neuroscience," and "cognitive development" suggest a misunderstanding of the underlying science. While research clearly shows rapid brain development in the early years, environmental influence—except in extremis—may be slight. The idea that brain growth can and should be *enhanced* via infant education is an unwarranted extrapolation from the research. David Bjorklund (2007a), in *Why Youth Is Not Wasted on the Young*, has championed the idea that neurological development occurs through processes shaped by millions of years of evolution, and the infant's developmental timetable is firmly established.

For example,

> Sensory limitations of many young animals reduce the amount of information infants must deal with, which facilitates their constructing a simplified and comprehensible world. The various sensory systems develop in a constant order for all vertebrates, with audition, for instance, developing before vision. This means that early-developing senses do not have to "compete" for neurons with later-developing senses. [Consequently], not all learning experiences are necessarily good for infants . . . [They may] be useless for infants who lack the requisite cognitive ability [and] may actually be detrimental to later learning and development. (Bjorklund 2007a, 90, 181)

Baby Talk

"In the U.S. today, new parents are advised on the importance of talking to their babies in order to develop their language abilities" (Faber and Mazlish 2002, 147). Those who would "school" their babies have a number of low-tech tools at their disposal. "Baby talk" is considered essential.

> When using Baby Talk, caregivers modify their speech by increasing its pitch, exaggerating its positive affect, slowing down its tempo, and speaking in short, syntactically simple sentences. Through such modifications and an extensive use of repetition, specialized lexicon, and diminutives and kinship terms, adult speech is phonologically, lexically, and grammatically transformed into BT. . . . Caregivers using BT also *accommodate* to the child in systematic ways. They engage in proto-conversational exchanges

BABIES AS STUDENTS? 31

even with newborns, interpreting infants' facial expressions, gestures, or vocalizations. In such interactions, the caregiver assumes the roles of both speaker and addressee, providing meaning and interpretation of the behaviors of the participants and of the discourse itself. (Solomon 2012, 122–123)

Baby talk is partnered with a number of other tactics for stimulating the infant. These include holding the child in an *en face* position to facilitate both verbal and nonverbal (making faces, peek-a-boo) communication. Tickling and other forms of tactile stimulation enhance the infant's engagement with the caretaker. Objects (rattles and other "age-appropriate" toys) are introduced in this dyadic relationship to maintain the infant's attention. This activity becomes a lesson in vocabulary as the objects are named and described. Other lessons focus on tactile and instrumental features. The interlocutor often uses pointing to call the child's attention to persons, events, or objects, and very young babies can point for the same purpose. This conglomerate of communication tactics has been referred to as the "education of the child's attention" (Ingold 2001, 139).

Parents are rewarded for their efforts by the infant's enthusiastic responses (Kärtner et al. 2010), which usually include an inherited and very early onset ability to imitate (Reissland 1988).[4] At two to three weeks, neonates can imitate facial expressions, and by six months, they imitate body movements (Meltzoff 2002, 24). Further studies document the child's early understanding of social relations (Callaghan et al. 2011). By three months, they can distinguish faces—familiar versus unfamiliar individuals—and detect various facial expressions. By five months, they decode them; and at seven months, they discriminate between more and less emotional expressions and respond appropriately (LaFreniere 2005, 192). At twelve months, they attend to and follow their mother's gaze (Okamoto-Barth et al. 2011). By eighteen months, infants reliably use other's facial expressions as a guide to their own behavior, reacting appropriately to expressions showing fear, joy, or indifference (Klinnert et al. 1983).

The central issue in these comparative accounts is whether the chicken or the egg came first. In the model of parenting and child development that has come to dominate WEIRD society, the baby's "precocious" tool kit for

---

[4] The critical importance of this ability in the child's acquisition of culture will be discussed in Chapter 3, "Learning via observation, eavesdropping/listening, and imitation."

32 LEARNING WITHOUT LESSONS

processing the stream of information that washes over him/her is, in large part, a product of parental intervention through lessons. An alternative view shared by infant cognition scholars (Gopnik et al. 2000) is that these lessons are largely superfluous; the child will gradually make sense of his/her physical and social environment without tutoring. "The specialized cognitive skills of children that underlie their innate ability to learn (as opposed to adults' more conscious and less reliable ability to teach) establishes the success of cultural reproduction as the child's achievement" (Langdon 2013, 174).

The development of speech is also viewed by WEIRD parents as requiring systematic instruction. Theorists claim that specific adult-initiated speech acts are essential to language learning. These include: "face-to-face interaction; a simplified baby-talk register (motherese); baby games like pattycake [and peek-a-boo] that teach turn taking and sequencing; and the use of direct address, eye contact [and pointing] as a way of securing [and/or directing] the child's attention" (Brown and Gaskins 2014, 199).

These views on the necessity for systematic instruction are clearly contradicted by various ethnographic accounts that point to the near total absence of lessons aimed at babies. One clear implication is to reaffirm the claim that WEIRD society is "one of the worst one could study for generalizing about *Homo sapiens*" (Henrich et al. 2010, 79). A broad sampling of these accounts makes clear the uniqueness of WEIRD views (see Box 2.1).

Several multisite, comparative studies of families found that the *en face* position, in which the mother holds the infant facing her, is common in middle-class homes but rare elsewhere, as is the tendency of the mother to talk to the infant (Field and Widmayer 1981; Tulkin 1977). In these studies, the varied Indigenous communities are more similar to each other than to the WEIRD outlier.

Further study with samples from Boston, Kenya, and Mexico indicate the importance of the mother's education in shaping her parenting. Mothers with more years of schooling (range = one to nine years) spend more time talking to and looking at their infant and less time holding him or her (Richman et al. 1992, 619). One obstacle to "nonessential" (interaction that does not involve feeding, cleaning, or calming) mother–infant interaction is the belief that the well-being of the infant (and mother as well) is best served by keeping the infant quiet and largely immobile. In the transition that results from a mother's experience as a student, the mandate to keep the infant calm

Box 2.1 The Untutored Baby

"A [Mazahua] baby or young child is almost constantly with his or her mother, yet rarely needs, demands or is given her full attention . . . moments of affection and closeness do not include intense one-on-one, face-to-face interaction; there is no capturing of attention or looking into one another's eyes in a holding way" (Paradise 1987, 82, 101).

Mapuche "adults rarely talk to young children using 'baby talk' or 'motherese'" (Murray et al. 2015, 391).

Gapun (Sepik area, PNG) "infants might be talked about, but not talked to, as they were considered lacking human sense or understanding" (Kulick 1992, 98).

"Hausa (Nigeria) mothers [do] not look at or talk to their babies—in accordance with a kin-avoidance code . . . known as *kunya* . . . mothers obey these rules, even while holding, cleaning and breast-feeding their babies" (LeVine 2004, 61).

Bonerate (Sulawesi) "mothers do not establish eye contact with their nurslings as they . . . are nursed quickly, without overt emotional expression either from the mother or from the child" (Broch 1990, 31).

"The Samoan cultural model of intentionality discouraged explicit conjecture on the motives behind others' actions. Consequently, caregivers usually tended not to provide an explicit gloss of unintelligible utterances of young children" (Schieffelin and Ochs 1986, 165).

"Young children are not assumed to be talking Warlpiri when they first utter expressions. Thus adults and older siblings do not expand or recast . . . children's early attempts to communicate. . . The Warlpiri, like other Australian Aboriginal groups, do not generally attempt to teach with direct verbal instruction. Rather the child acquires knowledge by observation and experience in real life situations" (Bavin 1991, 319).

Aka infants are held all the time and mothers are quite responsive, but vocalizations to infants and face-to-face interactions are quite infrequent compared to Euroamericans (Hewlett et al. 1998). "When adults are sitting, care providers place infants on their laps or between their legs *facing outward*" (Hewlett et al. 2000, 162, emphasis added) . . . Euroamerican adults were much more likely . . . to stimulate (e.g., tickle) and vocalize to

34 LEARNING WITHOUT LESSONS

their infants [who] were significantly more likely than Aka and Ngandu infants to smile, look at, and vocalize to their care providers" (Hewlett et al. 2000, 164).

"The Kaluli (PNG) speak of infant babbling as 'bird talk' and see this as part of nonspeaking infants' closeness to the animal and spirit world—something to be discouraged" (Lieven 1994, 59). "Babbling and other vocalizations were treated as nonreferential and unrelated to speech development; and there was no interpretation of these vocalizations by adults" (Solomon 2012, 129). They also were "surprised that American parents produced baby talk in the presence of young children and wondered how the children learned to speak proper language" (Schieffelin 1990, 173).

"in remote Senegalese villages [adults] reported that they avoided making eye contact or talking with their infants for fear that the baby might then be possessed by evil spirits . . . Parents also reported that an adult might be called 'crazy' if they talk to a baby, because 'nobody is there' " (Engle et al. 2007, 1514).

"I did not see Nayaka adults coo to babies, or talk with babies who cannot yet talk back, in a sort of play-dialogue (responding to the infants' imagined questions or asking them questions the infants are imagined to reply; or playing interactively with the infants in any other nonverbal way aimed to trigger an interactive response). Just as the infants initiate their own feeding, weaning, and cuddling, so they initiate two-way dialogues and interaction with others when they are ready and able to do so. From the perspective of child development research, such ethnographic observations are read as evidence that hunter-gatherer babies are strikingly autonomous agents from an early age" (Bird-David 2015, 94–95).

"adults rarely talk to young children in . . . urban Javanese communities because they . . . cannot yet understand the language" (Smith-Hefner 1988, 172–173).

Ese Eja (Amazonia) "children grow the way that crops do (*tiiani*); they need to be tended, protected, and, in a sense, cultivated" (Peluso 2015, 54).

"In Rome, the small child was characterized as 'being unable to speak' . . . for this is what the term *infans*, from which the word infant is derived, means" (Kleijueqgt 2009, 55).

> For the Tzeltal Maya, "interaction with infants is not a priority. . . . the chief goal of both mother and child caregivers is to soothe the infant and keep it calm, not to stimulate it" (Brown 2011, 37).
>
> "Soninke (Senegal) mothers do not usually talk to their children during childcare or diapering, which, in contrast, are rich exchange periods for French or American mothers" (Jamin 1994).
>
> In the poor black community of Trackton, babies are "listeners and observers in a stream of communication that flows about them but is not especially channeled or modified for them. Everyone talks *about* the baby, but rarely *to* the baby . . . When infants begin to utter sounds which can be interpreted as referring to items or events in the environment, these sounds receive no special attention" (Heath 1983, 75).

through body contact and frequent nursing may be replaced by a mandate to promote the child's readiness for schooling.

Calming versus Stimulating

"Gusii mothers in Kenya avert their eyes in response to mutual eye gaze with an excited infant, in part to keep their babies calm" (Kline et al. 2018, 55).[5] They represent an excellent exemplar of the "keep 'em quiet" ethnotheory. "Gusii mothers see themselves as protecting their babies, not as playing with or educating them. From their point of view, emotional excitement should be avoided, and verbal communication can wait until the child is capable of speech" (Richman et al. 1992, 618). Similar to Gusii famers, Jul'hoan (Botswana) foragers also show a much-reduced use of infant-directed speech compared to a US middle-class sample, which "probably reflects the fact that Jul'hoan mothers have less pedagogical motivation for facilitating the children's language development than do their Western middle-class counterparts" (Konner 1977, 18). Like the Gusii, Ju'hoan mothers respond promptly to infant cries but do not respond to the two-month social-smile milestone in ways Western mothers typically do (Bakeman et al. 1990). In

---

[5] Keeping the child isolated and in a semicomatose state through frequent nursing may seem extreme, but the myriad threats to the infant are validated in extremely high infant mortality rates associated with a subsistence-level lifestyle. Once the child has survived infancy, they are granted much greater freedom and autonomy (Lancy 2014).

36 LEARNING WITHOUT LESSONS

rural Iran, Friedl observed mothers quickly placing a frisky, vocalizing baby into a cradle to calm it down because "a happy (*rahat*, at ease) baby is quiet in voice and body" (1997, 100). The Javanese feel that a baby is extremely vulnerable, especially to sudden shock, which can lead to sickness or death. For if the baby were suddenly or severely disturbed by a loud noise, rough handling, strong taste, or physical discomfort, he would be *kagét*, "shocked, startled, upset, and . . . evil spirits (*barang alus*) . . . could enter and . . . cause him to be ill. All the customs of infant care can be seen as attempts to ward off this danger. The baby is handled in a relaxed, completely supportive, gentle, unemotional way" (Geertz 1961, 92).

Swaddling and the use of cradleboards and other devices that largely immobilize the infant are widespread cross-culturally. Aside from reducing the infant's demands for attention, swaddling protects them from environmental hazards as well as evil spirits (Martínez-Rodríguez 2009, 61). For example, among Pashtu (Pakistan) pastoralists,

> The baby is swaddled (*ghumdak kawal*) with a blanket (*tiltak*) that is wrapped around it twice and then fixed with strips of cloth (*sizni*). Swaddling continues for about one year. . . . Most of the time, the baby lays in its hammock, attached to the tent poles, its face covered with a dark cloth. When adults are busy outside the tent, the hammock is rocked gently with a string tied to it by children or neighbors who are not busy. (Casimir 2010, 15; see also Schölmerich et al. 1995)

From the historic record: "Swaddling was universally practiced because it kept the baby secure without the need for close supervision" (Calvert 1992, 24; see also Bai 2005, 11).

Although the research is limited, it does suggest that these Indigenous parenting practices are successful. Comparing eight-month-old infants on Vanuatu (Melanesia) with their North American, WEIRD counterparts, the latter were much more active and engaged (Aime et al. 2020). In an earlier study with three-month-olds, investigators systematically observed Eluama (Nigeria) and middle-class English caretakers faced with a fussy baby. "Eluama caretakers responded more often, more quickly and with physical contact rather than speech" (Whiten and Milner 1984, 39). The Nigerian response was much more effective at calming the baby.

Another striking contrast in infant care focuses on mother–infant play or its absence. Current "best practice" in WEIRD communities is to encourage

BABIES AS STUDENTS? 37

mothers and other family members to play with the infant using speech, sounds, facial expressions, and infant-appropriate toys. Such intensive interaction is posited to contribute to the establishment of "joint attention," upon which the teacher–pupil relationship and child language acquisition are based (Shneidman and Woodward 2016). As I will discuss, play and joint manipulation of objects is generally absent from Indigenous notions of infant care, but it is somewhat surprising to learn that the prevailing wisdom in the United States in 1914 declared (*Infant Care Bulletin of the Children's Bureau*) that

> playing with the baby was regarded as dangerous; it produced unwholesome pleasure and ruined the baby's nerves. Any playful handling of the baby was titillating, excessively exciting, deleterious. Play carried the overtones of feared erotic excitement . . . A young, delicate and nervous baby needs rest and quiet [and while] it is a great pleasure to hear the baby laugh and crow in apparent delight, but often the means used to produce the laughter, such as tickling, punching, or tossing, makes him irritable and restless. (Wolfenstein 1955, 172)

Mother–infant play gradually became accepted and, by 1940, a duty. Today, interviews with WEIRD mothers (and increasingly fathers) reveal the depth of their commitment to stimulate and entertain their infants. This is done through direct interaction, more distal speech, and the provision of "educational" toys (Thiessen et al. 2005). A typical quote from one study: "I talk to him, you know, throughout the day. Point stuff to him, tell him what it is. Do sounds" (Abella 2018, 126). This dedication may come at a price: "[It's been hard] balancing my life as not a mom, but just my own identity. I never realized how much I would miss socializing with friends and doing things that are not mom-related" (Abella 2018, 131).

In contrast to these views, parents in Indigenous societies, with few exceptions (Hewlett and Roulette 2016), do not engage in object play with infants and children. Attempts by cross-cultural psychologists to engage mothers and infants in play with novel objects have not been successful. On Vanuatu, parents have no template to follow in showing their infant how to play with a toy (Little et al. 2016, 1137). "!Kung adults do not make toys for babies . . . nor . . . encourage increasingly complex forms of object manipulation or object-focused language. Indeed, the folk view of development seems to emphasize a child's need for space to explore [because] *a n/tharo an/te* [he/she is teaching/learning him/herself]" (Bakeman et al. 1990, 796). Rural

Gujarati (India) women believe that a three-month-old baby does not need help to "interpret" toys, which serve "mainly in distracting a fussy or crying baby" (Keller 2007, 203).

Multiple accounts from field research indicate that, rather than serve as the infant's playmate, a conscientious mother will urge her infant/toddler to join siblings and peers in play (Scheidecker 2023). For the Amazonia-dwelling Runa, "childcare is often almost entirely delegated to older children" (Mezzenzana 2020, 549). Among the Bara (Madagascar), "to play, and to engage in other symmetrical ways with children, was considered inappropriate for adults . . . viewed as being childish, compromising one's dignity, and even morally transgressing the age-dependent social hierarchy that demanded asymmetrical ways of interacting" (Scheidecker 2023, 317). Indigenous Guatemalan "mothers laughed with embarrassment at the idea of entering into play with their toddlers, as this is the role of other children and occasionally grandparents. When a toddler is playing . . . it is time for a mother to get her work done" (Rogoff and Mosier 1993, 66).

Indigenous mothers, in fact, have to manage time efficiently, as they are in their peak years as workers and play a major role in food acquisition and processing. Then, too, high fertility rates mean that a mother will need to transfer her infant's care to an alloparent—grandmother, aunt, or older siblings—to devote attention to her next baby.

Child-Directed Speech

While the WEIRD program for parent-teachers calls for a generous quota of speech directed at infants, the portion allocated to toddlers is greater still. Parents begin early, constructing "conversations" with the child. They not only speak directly to the child, they assist him or her in formulating a response. Another highly recommended practice for WEIRD parents is "Serve and Return," which comes with a warning: "Because responsive relationships are both expected and essential, their absence is a serious threat to a child's development and well-being" (Center for the Developing Child 2022). The parent is urged to monitor the child's utterances and behaviors and treat them as "conversational gambits" to begin the volleying via words, objects, gestures, facial expressions, and so on. A mother who is too busy or distracted to take notice of and return her toddler's serve is jeopardizing the child's brain growth, according to authorities (Featherstone 2017).

BABIES AS STUDENTS? 39

Once a template for conversation is established, the parent can use it in creating opportunities for instruction. Vocabulary development is often the target of lessons. A well-known survey found a huge gap in the number of words used by WEIRD parents with their offspring as compared to samples from lower-class communities. This "gap" or discrepancy has been used to explain the depressed academic performance of "language deprived" students (Hart and Risley 1995). Another very common form of child-directed speech is rhetorical or "known answer" questioning, which "is precisely the style of communication valued in American schooling, where children are scaffolded to express their knowledge of the world by asking and responding to questions" (Kuchirko and Nayfeld 2020, 34).

The difficulty that scholars of child language face is that current theory regarding language development is based largely on research with WEIRD families. Many of the cornerstones of WEIRD theory and practice are largely absent in non-WEIRD communities.[6] Linguistic anthropologists frequently find that "infants and young children receive relatively little one-on-one directed spoken input from adults" (Cristia et al. 2019, 767). Parents do not ask questions of children nor expect to be questioned by them, and this applies equally to the working class in industrialized countries (Tizard and Hughes 1985).[7] In terms of Serve and Return, Brown presents a vivid account of an interchange in a Tzeltal Maya village between a mother and a twelve-month-old attempting to direct her mother's attention to a bird. But the mother's "response is minimal . . . and [she] does not treat this as an opportunity to teach the child words" (2011, 45).

The Nso of Cameroon are unlikely to display the *sensitive responsiveness* required of WEIRD parents, as the practice is based on the roughly equal status of the parent and child. "Indeed, this discourse style would undermine community preferences, common in many non-Western lifestyle groups, for infants to 'fit in' rather than 'stand out of' the everyday goings-on . . . this means that the responsibility to understand others falls to the infant, and not the other way around" (Keller et al. 2018, 1924). "The question-answer routine familiar in Western societies is not found in Walpiri society. The adult has knowledge, not the child, and questioning is not used as a teaching

---

[6] This generalization may extend to the historical record as "mother–child speech is rarely mentioned in Western history" (Traig 2019, 113).

[7] Next time you have some time to kill in an airport, observe family parties. In families that appear to fit the WEIRD stereotype, expect to see the adults pausing their activity or conversation to respond immediately to their child's question or request. In non-WEIRD families, expect to see children's bids for attention ignored—except an infant's cries.

40 LEARNING WITHOUT LESSONS

device. [In fact] the Walpiri child learns through experience and observation, rather than verbal teaching" (Bavin 1992, 321–322).

Aside from variation in the sheer amount of child-directed speech, the structure and intent of speech to children also vary. In Indigenous communities, child-directed speech generally flows in one direction as parents direct children to assist or carry out a chore (Abels et al. 2020). In a comparative study with one- and 1.5-year-olds, rural farmers in Mozambique used child-directed speech to issue imperatives, whereas their Dutch counterparts used "utterances with a cognitive intention" (Vogt et al. 2015, 341). Mazahua "children participate in . . . family . . . activities, [and] conversation and questions . . . usually occur for the sake of sharing necessary information . . . talk supports and is integral to the endeavor at hand rather than becoming the focus of a lesson" (Paradise and Rogoff 2009, 118).

"Lessons" per se are replaced by a trio of behaviors initiated by the child with full adult approval. This trio includes close observation of the behavior of others; eavesdropping or overhearing both casual and instrumental speech; and imitation with multiple trials as needed (Lee et al. 2020; more fully discussed in the next chapter). Note that child-directed speech of a pedagogical nature is considered largely unnecessary.

Overhearing

One by one, new studies are weakening arguments exalting infant-directed speech and child-directed speech as essential to the development of language and cognition. Prominent in this wave of research is overhearing (de León 2011). In one study, the authors measured the word count of speech overheard by, as well as directed at, the child. With this additional evidence, the vocabulary "gap" between middle- and working-class children narrowed substantially (Sperry et al. 2019). Joint attention between a caregiver and a child has often been assumed necessary for word learning. But children learn new words exclusively via overhearing, by as young as eighteen months (Gampe et al. 2012). Furthermore, it may be that relatively unrestricted village [children] "who routinely spend time in polyadic situations may be better at attending to and learning from overheard speech than children who spend most of their time alone with one adult" (Floor and Akhtar 2006, 78).

Learning via overhearing is also more compatible with Indigenous views on the transfer of knowledge. For a child to question an adult—perhaps as a prelude to seeking tutorial assistance—could be "considered immature and rude" (Paradise and Rogoff 2009, 121; Erchak 1977; Gauvain et al. 2013). Among the pastoralist Kyrgyz (Central Asia), one does not give "advice directly, but say it 'to the walls,' then people will be more likely to hear. There is a proverb that reflects this . . . 'if I speak to the *u'uk* (yurt roof poles), my son will listen to me' " (Bunn 1999, 78). Again and again, we can see that children must take the initiative to learn from others, paying particular attention to nondirective speech. "When a Minangkabau (Sumatra) child violates social standards in public, caregivers or peers immediately announce the misconduct to the [public, who react by] commenting on the misbehavior or starting to laugh. The child reacts with a *malu* (shame) display" (Röttger-Rössler et al. 2013, 270).

Overall, the attitude expressed in these events is the necessity for children to learn from others without the need for an instructor. Failure to pay attention or take responsibility provokes a moralizing response. And this is not an unreasonable expectation. Indigenous children—by virtue of their interacting with various caretakers and the freedom to visit neighbors—are immersed in a populous social world from birth (Tronick et al. 1987; see also Shneidman and Woodward 2016). And we know from lab studies that they are endowed with remarkable social skills, which allow them to detect patterns and meanings from the data their social world delivers. For example, by nine months, infants develop "groupness," the ability to "extract novel meanings during group-level interaction" (Bradley and Smithson 2017, 2).

While a "hands-off" approach serves Indigenous families well in socializing the young, we do see more direct intervention in some societies and in particular skill areas. In the next sections, I review practices that accelerate the child's sensorimotor and social development.

Accelerating Development

The infant's progress in learning its culture goes largely undetected. Instead, caretakers are more acutely aware of its failings. It cannot speak or understand speech; it cannot feed, dress, or clean itself. The sounds it makes and its uncontrolled body movements suggest that it is more animal than human, and, of course, its initial foray into self-locomotion—crawling—merely reinforces the notion that it is beast-like. Many societies are not overly troubled by this and wait patiently for the inevitable transformation. For example, among the

Mehinacu of Brazil, "when the child is about [one] and a half years old, one of his grandfathers gives him a haircut and a new name" (Gregor 1970, 242).

In other cases, there is a greater sense of urgency. The child's motor development may be "accelerated" (Remorini 2011). "Kogi (Columbia) children are . . . continuously prodded to advance their sensory–motor development" (Reichel-Dolmatoff 1976, 277). Nso (Cameroons) infants may be placed in a bucket or hole in the ground to facilitate sitting (Keller 2007, 120). A Ugandan baby's training begins at three months. It is bundled in a cloth and placed in a hole in the ground to support its spine "for about fifteen minutes a day, until able to sit unsupported" (Ainsworth 1967, 321). !Kung foragers accelerate sitting, standing, and walking because "in the traditional mobile subsistence pattern . . . children who cannot walk constitute major burdens" (Konner 1976, 290). More severe measures include the Zulu practice of placing the child on an ant's nest to motivate it to stand and walk (Krige 1965); Gau islanders (Fiji) giving a fourteen-month-old that is still not walking a chili-pepper enema (Toren 1990); and Baka foragers encouraging toddlers to keep trudging along the forest trail by poking them on the behind with a prickly seedpod (Higgens 1985, 101).

Infants are held under the arms and "walked" until they can walk or at least stand on their own. "A standing baby . . . makes less work for the mother" (Keller 2007, 124). Anthropologists also note the practice of adults "dandling" the baby on their lap while it pushes off (Takada 2005).[8] Activating this stepping reflex does enable walking at an earlier age (Zelazo et al. 1972).

> Wolof put great emphasis on the infant's interaction with a large array of potential caretakers, and standing and walking are accelerated through stretching exercises and massage to [hasten] the child's ability to self-locomote. [This skill] is the trigger for weaning [which] facilitates care by others [thus] unburdening the mother. Speech . . . directed to the child is designed "not to encourage early speaking [but to] make the child part of a complex set of social relationships." (Rabain-Jamin et al. 2003, 212)

> [Among the Amazonian Urarina] Training an infant to walk begins early [as] learning to walk is a milestone on the path to autonomy of singular significance . . . A child's first steps are also accorded greater recognition and importance by adults than its first words . . . Learning to walk is assisted by the use of a specialized aid, constructed by the father. (Walker 2013, 96)

---

[8] This type of activity to accelerate self-locomotion is widely practiced (Super 1976).

BABIES AS STUDENTS? 43

Weaning constitutes a second area of acceleration. While allowing the child to self-wean is not uncommon, "early"—long before the child might wean itself—weaning is widely reported. Commonly, weaning is accelerated when the mother applies hot pepper to her nipples, and this is reported to be quite effective (Culwick 1935; Whittemore 1989; Fouts 2004). Teasing and shaming are also commonly utilized to discourage nursing (Schieffelin 1986). Even if still nursing, the child learns to "serve itself."

> A hungry baby [Mazahua] boy . . . simply comes up to his mother's side and finds his away under her arm to her breast and nurses from below on his knees while her hands continue occupied. It is his initiative, and he finds the way . . . finishes and is off or, if tired and sleepy, she cradles him in her arms while she chats with someone nearby or . . . continues on with whatever it was she was doing. (Paradise 1987, 80)

These are examples of mothers "teaching" children skills that will eventually emerge without instruction, much as contemporary parents "teach" their babies to talk. Clearly the teachers are serving their own ends, not the child's (see Trivers 1974 on the general subject of parent–offspring conflict). Nevertheless, there may be an important life lesson embedded in this activity, namely, that the child must embrace independence and self-sufficiency—continuing its dependence on the mother will be strenuously discouraged.

Lessons in Kinship, Etiquette, and Sharing

Another target of acceleration occurs in the social domain. Diverse areas are targeted for acceleration, including politeness rituals, kin relationships (Guemple 1988), sharing, and other forms of culturally sanctioned, prosocial behaviors. Occasionally (examples follow), this intervention rises to the level of lessons. These practices are designed to protect the social standing of the family by ensuring the child conforms to rules of etiquette and deference (Fajans 1997, 54). Secondarily, the child is integrated into the family and community, which greatly facilitates alloparenting.[9] The illustrative cases in Box 2.2 target kin relations.[10]

---

[9] It is extremely common for childcare to be parceled out among family members, especially grandmothers and older female siblings. This process is referred to as "alloparenting."
[10] Here, too, children would probably learn the rules without intervention (e.g., kinship, Read 2001; social rank, Odden and Rochat 2004, Ochs and Schieffelin 2017; sharing, Boyette 2019).

Box 2.2 Lessons in Kinship

The Hopi—North American Puebloans—provide "deliberate instruction in kinship and community obligations" (Eggan 1956, 351).

"Tiwi children of Northern Australia learn about kinship through dance, whereby different moves and gestures are associated with different kinds of kin" (Mitchell and Jordan 2021, 165–166).

Warlpiri "acquire the forms and knowledge of the [kinship] system through constant exposure to the terms in social interaction, stories and ceremonies" (Bavin 1991, 339).

The Warlpiri also "use a stylized 'baby talk' with children . . . A number of the few lexical items specific to 'baby talk' are in the kin domain. For example, *mamiyi* used for *ngati* 'mother' and *lli!lli!* is used for 'father'. Children of 4 years demonstrate some awareness of this style; they use the register to their younger siblings in teasing situations, mimicking their attempts" (Bavin 1991, 327).

"Kinship is primarily transmitted from BaYaka (Congo) adults to children. This includes two kinship terms, *mbanda* and *ndoyi*, which are taught to young children through word play" (Sheina Lew-Levy, personal communication, March 25, 2021).

Inuit (Arctic) children "are drilled daily on their terms for relatives" (Guemple 1979, 43). "When visitors are present in one's own camp, children may be quizzed on their knowledge of their kin networks and their own places therein: 'Who is she to you?' 'Where [in this room] is your mother's sister?' 'Whose names do you have?'" (Briggs 1991, 270).

Kwara'ae (Solomon Islands) caregivers use "'repeating routines' . . . telling the child what to say, line by line. . . . Encoded in [these] routines is information on kin terms and relationships and on polite ways of conversing . . . important goal[s] . . . in a society where *enoenoanga* (delicacy) and *aroaroanga* (peacefulness) are key values . . . for maintaining harmony in the extended family and descent group" (Watson-Gegeo and Gegeo 1989, 62).

Mandinka (West Africa) adults deny providing any formal education in kinship reckoning, although informal education clearly consists of overheard conversations among adults. Adults may clarify for one another the identity of a specific *luntangho*, or stranger/guest, by repeating his or her clan name and origins, including kin associations with locally known consanguineal or affinal relations (Beverly And Whittemore 1993, 239).

Aside from helping infants and toddlers learn how to decode the local kinship system, many societies feel compelled to accelerate the acquisition of proper demeanor, correct etiquette, and deference to those of higher rank (see Box 2.3).

Box 2.3 Lessons in Social Behavior

Ngoni (Malawi) children are sent on errands, such as delivering a gift to other households. "These are lessons. . . . The child has to learn . . . the appropriate speech to be used for the appropriate relative. . . . He has to learn all the forms for presenting a gift and receiving a gift. All these things are very important . . . . The child is given the responsibility to learn through this task the accomplishments the society values" (Lee 1967, 56).

"Generally [Bamangwato] children were taught not to initiate verbal communication or ask questions of adults* . . . even if a child had been sent to deliver an urgent message, the child arrived . . . at the edge of a group of adults and stood or crouched silently until asked 'What is it?', and only then delivered his or her message. . . . Older children . . . were role models and reprimanded younger ones. If a child did interrupt or ask a question, adults ignored them, and if a child persisted, adults reprimanded him or her strongly" (Geiger and Alant 2005, 187).

"Among the Basotho of South Africa, mothers and older siblings prompt children in politeness . . . and proper terms of address" (Demuth 1986, 62–63).

The Japanese explicitly teach two-year-old children *aisatsu*, politeness routines (Burdelski 2006).

"The Javanese mother repeats 'polite' kin terms over and over and corrects her child's mistakes, urging it to observe proper etiquette. [Hence] children little more than a year old . . . go through a polite bow and say an approximation of the high word for good-by . . . a *prijaji* (aristocrat) child of five or six already has an extensive repertoire of graceful phrases and actions" (Geertz 1961, 100).

In the Mekong Delta of Vietnam, villagers collaborate in rigorous training of toddlers in polite speech and behavior vis-à-vis those older. Khánh (age three) is prompted to enact the deference ritual before leaving his neighbor's house. "He loudly and clearly uttered a respectful goodbye, using correct terms . . . he cheerfully bent his right knee and leaned his upper body slightly forward . . . the postural display of respect . . . Within 33 seconds, he had delivered the expected three-in-one deference ritual performance to each adult in the house: his neighbor's great-grandmother, grandfather, grandmother, aunt, aunt's friend, visiting researcher Fung, and her assistant. The order was not random but followed the hierarchical order among them" (Fung and Thu 2019, 282).

* That children should be "seen and not heard" is a common attitude. For example, "Mongolian etiquette (*yos*) requires not to attract attention to oneself and therefore renders the expression of personal feelings unwelcome." Exuberant toddlers are gently teased to curb their excesses (Michelet 2022, 5, 10).

A number of societies intervene early to promote sharing (Guemple 1979; Hogbin 1969; Lutz 1983; Read 1960). For example, Papel infants are given something desirable, such as a snack, and then are immediately told to pass it on to another, particularly a sibling (Einarsdottir 2004, 94). "Even small [Baining] babies are given items like a betel nut and are told to give it to someone else, who then thanks the baby" (Frye 2022, 38). The Kwara'ae also do this and "infants who cry or resist sharing are gently chided, teased, or laughed at, and told to share because 'he or she is your older or younger sibling'" (Watson-Gegeo and Gegeo 1989, 61). Among !Kung foragers, the grandmother most often takes on the task of teaching *hxaro*, their quite formal system of exchange and mutual support. The very young child is given beads and told which kinsmen to pass them on to (Bakeman et al. 1990, 796). It is certainly the case that sharing—especially of food—is a core value in many societies, and children are hastened into compliance (Dira and Hewlett 2018). But a related goal for lessons of this type is to make the child as attractive as possible to alloparents or foster parents.

As with the earlier examples of acceleration, there's no suggestion that children will not learn the appropriate prosocial behaviors with time (d'Andrade 1984; Fehr et al. 2008; Schmidt et al. 2011). There are many societies that highly value sharing and yet do not engage in this kind of enforced compliance and training. Comparative studies show that "children are sensitive to normative information as young as 1.5 years of age and they enforce norm conformity in others" (House et al. 2020, 36). Much of what Mandinka children learn about kinship is acquired through "social geography" (Beverly and Whittemore 1993).

As noted here, the success of the species has rested on *voluntary* compliance with social norms:

> Cultural evolution created cooperative groups. Such environments favored the evolution of a suite of new social instincts suited to life in such groups including a psychology that "expects" life to be structured by moral norms, and that is designed to learn and internalize such norms. New emotions evolved, like shame and guilt, which increase the chance that norms are followed. Individuals lacking the new social instincts more often violated prevailing norms and experienced adverse selection. (Boyd and Richerson 2006, 469)

Characteristically, in societies that explicitly promote prosocial behavior, the child is encouraged to behave correctly vis-à-vis the very individuals— older siblings, grandmothers, and other close kin—who are also likely recruits to serve as substitute caretakers (Weisner and Gallimore 1977). Willing and helpful alloparents free the mother to pursue other goals, including, prominently, another pregnancy and birth (Hrdy 2005, 2009). Children who are mobile and able to control their elimination (Gottlieb 2000, 86) and their emotions (Schieffelin 1986; Remorini 2012) can be marketed as desirable charges.[11].Training in "proper" behavior and speech is the functional equivalent of a cradleboard (Chisholm 1983, 72), where the primary goal is to "shape up" the infant/toddler in order to reduce the burden of its care.

From the preceding discussion, an emergent idea is that while children may be predisposed and prewired to strive to fit in and gain social membership, they may need some guidance and encouragement. While the infant's first choice of close companion would be its mother, she and other family members may prefer the infant attach to a grandmother or big sister. While the infant's attention may be focused on play, he may be redirected to participate in an affiliation ritual involving visiting kinsmen.

---

[11] Space limitations preclude any lengthy review of "child circulation." Suffice it to say, a very significant fraction of the world's Indigenous peoples embrace the idea that children will be moved from household to household to spread the costs and benefits of childcare equitably. It is often the child him/herself who initiates the move (Lancy 2022). Hence, every infant may be scrutinized by every community member as a future addition to their own household.

Managing Child Helpers

When ethnographers describe the lives of children in Indigenous communities, work figures prominently (Lancy 2018). It is customary for even very young children to volunteer to assist others who are carrying out some public task. In a typical rural village or camp, there is a lot of activity going on, which attracts the rapt attention of children. Children do not require much encouragement to participate. As developmental psychologist Felix Warneken (2015) convincingly demonstrates, fourteen-month-old infants are eager to offer meaningful assistance to others. The child exhibits a "drive" that is not dampened by the experimenter's addition of physical and other barriers.

In the village context, child volunteers are eager to "pitch in" (Paradise and Rogoff 2009; Lancy 2020) and participate in ongoing projects, whether house building, food processing, foraging, or caring for an infant. While explicit praise or reward is conspicuously absent from these scenarios, there are more fundamental benefits. First, the would-be helper is rewarded with various signs of acceptance and approval from family members:

> When a child became an active member of the family, performing small tasks and duties, it was looked upon as a promising future adult and included in the community. (Kaland 2008, 57)

> Nothing is more cheering for a Huaorani (Amazonia) parent than a three-year-old's decision to join a food gathering expedition. The young child . . . is praised for carrying his/her own *oto*. . . and bringing it back to the long-house filled with forest food . . . to share with co-residents. (Rival 2000, 116)

Second, since teaching is rarely employed to accelerate skill acquisition beyond the areas discussed in the previous section, the child must self-teach, using the opportunities available in the "everyday classroom" (Chapter 4).

> [Urarina] children learn at an extremely young age to "help" their parents, or at least to act in concert with them, well before they are capable of making any tangible contribution to the household . . . A baby girl, barely able to walk, will be seated by her mother's side and given a knife with which she will happily set about cutting discarded vegetable scraps and other refuse . . . Parents almost never provide direct instruction to their children; instead, they carefully set an example, which children learn to

follow. [Eventually,] the mother will expect her daughter to accompany her in the garden, weeding and planting, and the two will set about it together. (Walker 2013, 99, 105)

Infant volunteers are treated with respect—no one wants to sabotage a future worker—but they may need to be subtly redirected (Coppens et al. 2020, 2; Ochs and Kremer-Sadlik 2015, 732; Boyette and Lew-Levy 2021). A sharp knife may be exchanged for a dull one; a special area of the garden may be reserved for the emergent gardener; a scaled-down digging stick and assistance with moving rocks obstructing access to tubers will aid the junior forager; and an overconfident and obstreperous helper may be "brought up short" with a well-timed public shaming (Medaets 2016). "The aim of Runa child rearing is not to help a child 'flower' as in the upper middle-class American context . . . but rather to channel . . . individual will toward valuable sociality" (Mezzenzana 2020, 545).

Are All These Lessons Necessary?

Zero to Three is just one of many initiatives designed to motivate WEIRD parents to make every waking minute of the child's life a "teaching moment." But as Keller (2022) points out in her exposé of attachment theory,

[middle-class] German mothers now share upwards of 50% of the responsibility for the child's education, starting shortly after birth. The mother is now expected to serve also as social organizer, clinical counselor, early language and reading instructor, and principal playmate. As a result, they can get into a condition of complete physical and mental exhaustion, even psychiatric symptoms. (Keller 2022, 53)

Contrast this accelerating trend with another, summarized in the volume *The Scientist in the Crib* (Gopnik et al. 2000). Studies have established that babies automatically deploy a range of capacities that aid them in making sense of the world (Atran and Sperber 1991), including basic principles of physics, mathematics, biology, and psychology (Atran and Medin 2008; Bloch et al. 2001; Dehaene 1997; Norenzayan and Atran 2004). This catalog of capacities can also be mined for evidence of core knowledge systems (Carey and Spelke 1996) that function as "learning devices" (Baillargeon and Carey 2012, 58). As an alternative to Locke's *tabula rasa*—or the empty vessel waiting patiently to be filled by parents and teachers—infant cognition scholars posit the untutored emergence of key concepts and modules that facilitate learning about the world (MacDonald and Hershberger 2005, 25). As Bjorklund pithily notes, "children did not evolve to sit quietly at desks in age-segregated classrooms being instructed by unrelated and unfamiliar adults" (2007a, 120). And from the growing evidence of very early, spontaneously emerging information processing abilities, it looks like infants are primed to learn through direct, unmediated (by would-be teachers) engagement with the world.

In the next chapter, "The Self-Starting Learner," I lay out the core principles of Indigenous pedagogy and show how children proceed to learn their culture with minimal direct instruction.

3

The Self-Starting Learner

Children seem to be predisposed to rapidly and automatically acquire huge amounts of information from other people. They are, in a sense, "cultural sponges," soaking up knowledge from those around them.

—Mesoudi (2011), 15

Children between one and three are "imitation machines" in that their natural response to many situations is to do what others around them are doing.

—Tomasello (1999), 52

Introduction

In the previous chapter, Western, educated, industrialized, rich, democratic (WEIRD) parents are depicted as early and urgent teachers, beginning with the child's birth or earlier. A WEIRD parent's concern for jump-starting the child's academic thinking and corollary brain interconnectivity is an entirely novel human undertaking. Historically and cross-culturally, parents are concerned with keeping the infant healthy, but once survival is assured, the care of children devolves upon the family and community at-large. Weaned toddlers may spend little time in direct contact with their biological parents. The Indigenous child will, on its own initiative, attempt to join the community, mostly via offers to help out. Pitching in to assist in family endeavors puts the child in direct contact with the objects, ideas, and processes that form the basis for subsistence (Lancy 2018). They are expected to use their eyes and ears as conduits for gathering and processing vital information—information that will not be extracted by adults and reframed in lessons. This chapter is replete with descriptions of children learning in social settings where they are legitimate, if marginal, participants (Lave and Wenger

Learning Without Lessons. David F. Lancy, Oxford University Press. © Oxford University Press 2024.
DOI: 10.1093/oso/9780197645598.003.0003

52 LEARNING WITHOUT LESSONS

1991) as well as oral accounts gathered by ethnographers that reflect parental ethnotheories stressing the spontaneous, unguided nature of child learning and development (Lancy 2016).

I find the following account particularly apt to launch a discussion about self-starting learners. In the small village of Ikenwèn (Morocco), women make and sell argan oil and pottery.

> The women of the village do not like their daughters coming to disturb them in their work, until they turn about nine years old . . . younger girls who want to fire their clay toys must often find an ingenious solution to use the household oven (*taghouni*). When Khalija was young and her mother left the oven empty after baking bread, she slipped into the room where the oven was located and put her little utensils in the oven when it was still hot [and] sealed the oven opening with a large wet piece of fabric. About half an hour later the clay toys were fired. Similarly, when her mother asked her to empty the oven of charcoal, Khalija only half-emptied it and put her utensils into the oven [to fire them]. However, use of the household oven by the girls is quite rare. In most cases, the girls build their own oven, [which] faithfully reproduces the analogous oven built by the women. . . . It is by observing their mothers, by copying their gestures and activities [in play] that the girls learn to build and use a *taghouni*, and at the same time the processes for baking bread or clay modeled objects. (Fassoulas et al. 2020, 40)

The view that children must take the initiative (self-start) to learn their culture—and the consequent paucity of adult-organized lessons aimed at children—is supported by several core beliefs that are widely found in Indigenous communities (Lancy 2010). First, in small-scale, face-to-face communities, maintaining amiable social relations is vital; therefore, telling someone else what they should do, especially to their face, is unwelcome. And this laissez-faire attitude is extended to children (see Box 3.1).

A second widely held belief is that "parents do not presume to teach their children what they can as easily learn on their own" (Guemple 1979, 50). Noting the epigram that opened the chapter, children are endowed with marvelous tools for learning culture, which are activated virtually at birth. With only occasional exceptions, children take the initiative in identifying critical skills and ideas and finding ways to master them. Since they are usually successful, it would seem inefficient for an adult to take the initiative and organize lessons. Giovanna Bacchiddu (pre-press) declares that "in

THE SELF-STARTING LEARNER   53

Box 3.1 Avoiding Hierarchy

"Navahos abhor the idea or practice of controlling other beings in the course of everyday life" (Chisholm 1996, 178).

An egalitarian ethos [among Mbendjele] also contraindicates the inherently hierarchical act of teaching (Lewis 2008).

"In a learning situation [in rural Tahiti] . . . to tell anybody what to do, is intrusive and taken as a sign of unjustified adult mood-driven irritability and impatience" (Levy 1996, 129).

Aka "respect for an individual's autonomy is also a core cultural value . . . one does not impose his/her will, beliefs, or actions on others [including children]" (Hewlett and Hewlett 2013, 75).

"It is a feature of Kyrgyz 'education' not to give people advice directly, but to say it 'to the walls,' then people will be more likely to hear" (Bunn 1999, 78).

The !Kung have "an adverse reaction . . . to direct instruction. [They] can be irritated by . . . people who tell other people what to do or in any way set themselves above anyone else" (Blurton Jones and Konner 1976, 345).

---

two decades of ethnographic observation in [a remote village] on Chiloé Island (Chile), she had never seen a child asking for instruction or explanation."[1] She then proceeds to describe an occasion where a four-year-old girl, upon being finally allowed to peel potatoes for the family meal, "displayed her talent as a fast peeler, skillfully handling a sharp knife and managing a basketful of potatoes in minutes."

Third, of all the principles of Indigenous pedagogy, the most widely acknowledged is that children learn best from direct, hands-on experience.[2] "Actual hunting experience appears to be a prerequisite for the ability of [Baka] children to accumulate knowledge about hunting and gathering" (Sonoda 2016, 123). Many societies take the idea further and assert that one can *only* learn from direct experience (Heath 1983). Information gleaned

---

[1] Even when (Aka and Chabu) adolescents seek out "experts" to learn from, they choose "what to learn, thus learning was 'self-directed' " (Hewlett 2016, 205).

[2] The principled rejection of teaching extends to visiting ethnographers. "Orna and I, in trying to learn many elemental skills . . . received virtually no advice or instruction; people watched us founder without showing us how it is done" (Johnson 2003, 111).

54 LEARNING WITHOUT LESSONS

from another must be validated through personal replication, as every person's skill repertoire is idiosyncratic and subject to stylistic variation. Learning "secondhand" via the instruction of another leads to incomplete and inauthentic knowledge. Battiste, referring specifically to Native North Americans, claims that "the first principle of learning is a preference for experiential knowledge. Indigenous pedagogy values a person's ability to learn independently by observing, listening, and participating with a minimum of intervention or instruction" (Battiste 2002, 15). The Yukaghir are Siberian hunter-gatherers, and their ethnotheory of "good" parenting emphasizes the autonomy of the learner because to "be a hunter, you must know everything yourself [viz.] 'doing is learning and learning is doing'" (Willerslev 2007, 160, 162; Zarger 2011). Similarly, the Ju/wasi San assert that "tracking is not something that can be taught directly as much depends on the boy's ability to teach himself" (Liebenberg 1990, 70). For the Inuit, "there is a belief that orphans are exceptionally skilled because they were never helped as children" (Briggs 1991, 268). These anecdotal observations are supported by a large-scale comparative study of children's learning in nine foraging societies that showed how children's skill level was driven by the time logged exercising the skill. This suggests that children learn from practice, not instruction (Kramer 2021; Kramer and Greaves 2011).

Contrast this view with the massive and varied education infrastructure and many-year-long training of teachers in WEIRD society as the necessary foundation for children's learning. WEIRD children must turn to a parent or teacher to validate (affix a gold star, praise the "good job," award a "high grade") their efforts to learn. Efforts to learn must be held in check until the teacher has reiterated their authority, described the content to be learned, laid out the pedagogy to be followed, and set standards for the pupil's process and product.

Fourth, and in great contrast with WEIRD parenting, is the belief that learning often incurs risk to the child.[3] Numerous non-Indigenous ethnographers have revealed their own biases in their reactions to children's "playing with knives" (Lancy 2016). For example, Thomas Rhys Williams was accompanied by his spouse during his research on childhood among the Dusun in North Borneo:

---

[3] Jerome Bruner argued for the importance of unconstrained play with real tools because "in order for tool using to develop, it was essential to have a long period of optional, pressure-free opportunity for combinatorial activity. By its very nature, tool using (or the incorporation of objects into skilled activity) required a chance to achieve the kind of wide variation upon which [natural] selection could operate" (Bruner 1976, 38). In short, we wouldn't have such a large, diverse tool inventory today if kids had been prohibited from playing with things.

THE SELF-STARTING LEARNER   55

We were faced daily with Dusun parents raising their children in ways that violated the basic beliefs by which we were raised. . . . We consistently checked our . . . exclamations of concern or disgust . . . and [resisted] the temptation to take a "dangerous" object, such as a knife, from a toddler . . . knowing that in terms of the local culture, children are believed to die from accidents whether they play with knives or not and besides, as one Dusun father put it, "How can you learn to use a knife if you do not use it." (Williams 1969, 3)

Bonnie Hewlett recorded the views of her Aka informant Nali, who averred: "I don't like it when our children play with machetes, but if the baby decides to play, I leave it. And if the baby cuts themselves and if they see the blood, they themselves will decide not to play with the machete" (2013, 65). Lourdes de León offers a comparable perspective from the Zinacantec Maya. She had "never witnessed a boy being guided in how to chop or split wood, in spite of the risks involved. [She had] seen young children with knives, machetes, and other tools . . . experimenting on their own without adult intervention" (2015, 171).

Batek (Borneo) parents fostered self-reliance in their children in a number of ways. They let even the youngest of children explore their surroundings and try different skills and activities. They let children take risks—including using knives, making fires, and climbing trees—and they intervened only when they thought their children's activities far exceeded their abilities. When children cried, parents did not immediately rush to their aid. Rather, they sized up the situation and let children deal with most problems on their own. (Endicott and Endicott 2008, 124)

There are many "acceptable" risks associated with children's interaction with the environment as well. A Maasai (Tanzania) four-year-old waxed lyrical about the *Maerua crassifolia*, an evergreen:

The twigs are used as toothbrushes, and their leaves are boiled for use in local medicines. Children know the pragmatic values of the tree . . . based on their barefoot climbing experiences. A four-year-old boy explains, "It is full of fun, it smells very good, and it has strong but tender branches which lets me climb high easily. So, we can jump and swing with it. When sitting

56 LEARNING WITHOUT LESSONS

on the top, I can easily watch all my livestock and observe the birds and their nests." (Tian 2021, 77)

Fifth, in most folk or ethnotheories of child development, a key assumption is that children *want* to learn and deploy useful skills and information in order to "fit in." This view is acknowledged in child psychology literature as well: "Children are sensitive from a young age to their own interdependence with others in collaborative activities . . . and they value conformity to the group as a marker of group identity" (Tomasello 2009, 45–46).

The pedagogy that is detailed in Chapter 3 features the child's innate tendencies to observe carefully, eavesdrop on conversations, imitate others, and learn to use commonplace objects, including tools. These inherited abilities are the foundation upon which Indigenous pedagogy is built. Systems of childcare, social relations, and subsistence are open and transparent. Communities freely provide access to the raw material children need to make sense of their world and to become helpful and accepted community members. Deliberate instruction is not, except under limited circumstances, considered necessary or efficacious.

Learning via Observation, Eavesdropping/ Listening, and Imitation

From infancy, children rely on an innate capacity to carefully observe the world around them and seek out patterns or regularities. Unlike WEIRD society, where parents become language teachers at the birth of a child, in Indigenous communities, language is learned via eavesdropping, overhearing, or listening as a third party to other people's speech (Gampe et al. 2012; Sperry et al. 2020). Almost universally, societies not only tolerate children as spectators at any and all events—save perhaps potent ritual enactment—they invite and encourage them to accompany excursions that take them beyond the home and neighborhood. And the most compelling evidence that children are processing all this novelty is their inevitable effort to replicate or imitate what they have observed. This innate tendency to imitate others is readily accommodated by the community. In any maritime or riverine society, for example, there are child-sized canoes and paddles. Among forest dwellers, a would-be hunter practices with a smaller bow and arrows supplied by an older sibling. Would-be foragers dig for tubers with donated, made-to-size digging sticks. Three-year-olds are permitted to hold and "nurse" their infant siblings. Make-believe play is enhanced by the addition of loaned pots, and sibling caretakers carefully script make-believe roles to enable the full participation of their young charges (Lancy 2018).

In the West, "individualism," with its attendant "personal life," lowers a privacy screen that children penetrate at their peril. "Curiosity"—especially when displayed by children—may be frowned upon. But, as I have discovered, in small-scale, face-to-face societies, the onus is on the individual to suppress personal preferences. Attempting to shroud one's activities from scrutiny raises suspicion, as does calling undue attention to oneself. As a corollary, children have nearly unlimited access to social settings, behaviors, and artifacts, whether on "public" view or not. Children's freedom to indulge their evident curiosity is illustrated in the accounts in Box 3.2.

In fact, children are not just tolerated as spectators or eavesdroppers; such behavior has inherent pedagogical value (see Box 3.3).

Observation is often followed by imitation or emulation:

> Learning how to fish on Samoa occurs [through] observation coupled with emulation and experimentation. . . . Several of the older children observed (10–12 years of age) were moderately skilled fishermen who could successfully capture fish via one or more of these methods. When asked how they learned to do so, each indicated that they had at first observed the actions of a skilled fisherman and then had repeatedly tried to imitate their actions on their own, and with some practice began to successfully catch fish. (Odden and Rochat 2004, 44–45)

This combination of observation followed by imitation may appear—in make-believe play, for example—well before the child has the physical or mental capacity to fully replicate the observed behavior. Typically, the child undertakes some manner of imitation after a sometimes-lengthy delay. Extensive empirical study with WEIRD children has established that children as young as six months have the capacity for delayed imitation. Further, "Young children . . . also abstract the adult's goals . . . If an adult is unsuccessful in an attempt to complete a task, toddlers will copy the intended goals instead of the observed outcome" (Meltzoff and Williamson 2009, 481). Related studies with WEIRD samples have revealed another early-onset skill, namely, the ability of children to select the best from among a set of role models and focus their observation and imitation accordingly (Blakey et al. 2021). "Imitation of

58 LEARNING WITHOUT LESSONS

Box 3.2 Children Learning as Spectators

On Fiji, "any lively gathering in the house or village hall attracts small groups of children, who range themselves outside the building and peer at the proceedings through the chinks and crevices in the bamboo slats" (Toren 1988, 241).

BiYaka "children are almost constantly in the presence of at least one adult and have therefore almost ubiquitous opportunity for observational learning of adult subsistence behaviors. Furthermore, 'watching,' a behavior that is necessarily the commencing act of any visual observational learning, was a very high-frequency activity across all age groups" (Neuwelt-Truntzer 1981, 109).

Trobriand (PNG) "children hear of and witness much in the sexual life of their elders . . . [they] are allowed to listen to baldly sexual talk, and they understand perfectly well what is being discussed" (Malinowski 2008, 30–31).

Ganda (Uganda) "children over two years of age . . . sit politely, with their feet tucked under them out of sight, listening to the talk of their elders and speaking only when spoken to. If any young child becomes rambunctious and draws attention to himself, he is told to sit properly [and] be silent" (Ainsworth 1967, 12).

Bamana (Mali) children "can always listen to adults' conversations, yet they are urged to not interfere by posing questions or expressing opinions" (Polak 2012, 88).

Inuit "children should not ask questions; questions are considered silly. . . . Instead, they watch and practice. And then, having taught themselves, they are tested. . . . The proverb is: 'it is the fire that does the punishing'" (Briggs 1991, 269, 273).

Maori "children are permitted to eavesdrop on work-related conversations and they don't expect instruction" (Metge 1984, 9).

---

goal-directed action by preverbal infants is a selective, interpretative process, rather than a simple re-enactment of the means used by a demonstrator" (Gergely et al. 2002, 755; see also DiYanni and Kelemen 2008). However, children's tendency to overestimate their ability to imitate a model may confer an advantage: "as a result, they experiment with new tasks and are less perturbed by poor performance" (Bjorklund and Blasi 2005, 836).

Box 3.3 Principles of Indigenous Pedagogy

Mayan fathers say "boys learn by 'remembering what they see,' and 'being there in the cornfield and coming up to look'" (Fernández 2015, 68).

Piaroa (Amazon River basin) informants had no ready answer to questions regarding "how children learn about the environment, only referring to the fact that children come along on foraging trips. This suggests that the local learning process occurs in an unconscious, non-deliberate manner" (Zent 2001, 208).

"A Mazahua parent would never say '*ven, te voy a enseñar come se siembra*' (come, I will teach you how to sow). The child would learn this by observation. The grandfather then states that it is irrelevant whether a child is taught something or not. Children learn by themselves" (de Haan 1999, 74).

Nayaka children were rarely given formal instruction. Even when this was risky, they were left to learn for themselves by direct experience, by trial and error, and by joining the everyday activities of other children and adults. Very young children could, for instance, be seen playing with large, sharp knives, with no one taking notice (except for the anthropologist worried that they would harm themselves!) (Bird-David 2008, 542).

"In the conception of Quechua-speaking parents, *uyakuy* is a way to show 'respect' as it expresses the idea of 'listening for one's own benefit.' It implies 'minding' in the sense of paying attention to someone else" (García 2015, 149).

"One Japanese term for apprenticeship is *minari*, literally one who learns by observation" (Singleton 1989, 29).

A Venda potter is vehement that "We don't teach. When women make pots some [children and others] come to watch, then go and try" (Krause 1985, 95).

In Senegal, "young children are ubiquitous spectators at the metal working or blacksmith facility . . . it is clear that they acquire their skills through a combination of observation, play and the making of small pieces . . . This learning process results in a precocious proficiency" (Morice 1982, 517).

"My [Venezuelan Warao] informants consistently assured me: 'Nobody teaches a boy how to make a paddle or a canoe . . . boys learn from watching' . . . This work is carried out within the confines of the village and the children have been watching the craftsman for weeks. The boys are called frequently to the site to observe the process" (Wilbert 1976, 318).

60 LEARNING WITHOUT LESSONS

While the learner is urged to observe, listen, and copy, they are *not* expected to ask questions or to anticipate a verbal interchange with the role model. The Xikrin (Brazil) believe that the model should "remain silent, allowing the apprentice to pay better attention" (Cohn pre-press, 9).

As the Samoan fishing example indicates, the child is unlikely to be successful on the first attempt, so a period of trial and error, or practice, is necessary. An informative example from Dii (Cameroon) pottery-learning follows:

> The child usually sits next to her mother and watches her work. . . . The mother will intervene only to redirect the attention of the child and make comments like "Pay attention to what you do," "don't be so lazy," "don't waste the clay," "watch what I do." The child, initially, makes miniatures by extrapolating the method used by her mother to make full-sized pots. It implies the use of a trial-and-error technique, because the child has to figure out by herself how to interpret the model correctly. (Wallaert 2008, 188, 190)

A parallel case comes from Morocco:

> From the age of five, the male child is invited to join his father in the apiary. . . . At this stage . . . the small boy simply accompanies his father and observes his actions. "I learnt when I was a boy by watching what my father was doing" is a phrase that comes up again and again when talking to beekeepers about the origins of their beekeeping skills. . . . Slowly, the child begins to help his father when asked to. He might, for example, carefully pass him the required tool or instrument when asked—knives, smoker, newspaper, buckets . . . However, during this stage of the learning process, the child says almost nothing and his father explains nothing. Everything is learnt through observation. (Simenel et al. 2017, 6)

In this section, we've seen children getting their hands on and their heads around clay, pots, a kiln, fishing gear, marine life, a dugout canoe under construction, metal scraps, and finished products, among others. And it turns out that individuals, from an early age, can decode artifacts from examination, trial use, and observation of the artifacts in use by an expert.

Learning from Things

Objects hold particular fascination for the young. Six characteristics are striking in cross-cultural accounts of children's earliest encounters with "tools." First, toy tools that are strictly for play are uncommon, as children prefer the real thing (Fouts et al. 2016; Lew-Levy et al. 2022). Second, children are generally given free access to whatever arouses their interest, even to sharp knives, with nary a word of caution nor demonstration of "correct" handling. Third, children clearly learn a great deal from their free access to tools since "instructions" are embedded in the tool itself (Riede et al. 2022). Lab studies (e.g., Casler et al. 2009) show that very young children learn what tools are for via observation alone, with no need for instruction. Furthermore, by age four, the child will select the optimal tool for the task and spurn a suboptimal tool used by a demonstrator (Hernik and Çsibra 2009, 35). Sixth, children become competent tool users from an early age and successfully wield sharp machetes, adzes, arrows, digging sticks, and axes. We know this from the shocked reactions to this widespread phenomenon recorded in numerous ethnographers' accounts (Lancy 2016).

Several scholars have noted that a significant amount of cultural "information" is encoded in human artifacts (Portisch 2010, 710; Renfrew 1998; Vygotsky 1930/1978). These artifacts, particularly tools or the products shaped by tools, serve as an "external memory store" (Donald 1991, 308). That is, information on their function, history, and usability are embedded in the object itself. Most objects also reveal "affordances" that suggest *how* they should be used (Gibson 1982). A chair, for example, sends a pretty clear message: "You can sit on me." Not surprisingly, lab studies show that four-year-old subjects "were more likely to innovate on a tool that had visible affordances than one with concealed affordances" (Neldner et al. 2017, 335).

In contrast to expectations about adult teaching, an anecdote exemplifies how mixed-age learning occurs among the Savanna Pumé (Venezuela). Girls not uncommonly sit with female relatives while they weave, but this is not how girls take their first steps in becoming weavers. Rather, the basics of weaving are learned by young girls going to the trash middens and collecting simple forms of discarded basketry, which they slowly unweave and then reweave to recreate the piece (Kramer 2021, 21).

When a Bamana child plays with the ubiquitous short-handled hoe (Polak 2011, 103), there are only so many ways it can be effectively grasped. If he

62 LEARNING WITHOUT LESSONS

uses it to pierce the soil—as he has observed his siblings do—the number of possibilities is further reduced. Neither the grasping end of the handle nor the top side of the head makes much impression on the earth compared to the bottom edge. Ella Assaf and colleagues have found over 1,000 worked stone cores from a Lower Paleolithic site in Israel. The cores show evidence of having been worked by at least two individuals of different skill levels. She believes cores were exchanged so that "experienced knappers might have shared their knowledge, even if indirectly, by allocating previously shaped but not fully exploited cores to their inexperienced counterparts, who then used them as learning tools" (Assaf 2021, 1). This is an instance of "time gap apprenticeship." "Because the knowledge base of a community of practice is encoded in the products of that community, this encoding can be deciphered by others who have the intention of learning, even at a temporal remove from the original" (Kelly-Buccellati 2012, 212). In a parallel, contemporary practice among Aari (Ethiopia) potters, "the mother may start to make a pot and, after forming the basic shape, will pass it to their daughters to finish" (Kaneko 2014, 64–65). Each artifact may have recorded traces of information on how it was made and how it should be used, and children seem precocious decoders of this information.

One of the primary reasons that children in Indigenous communities are able to master the local tool/utensil inventory without teacher-led lessons is the simplicity and transparency of most artifacts. To take a fairly typical case[4]:

> The Wanka (Peru) household's tool kit is basic; the tools are homemade and simple enough to be widely available. . . . With four technounits (Oswalt 1976) each, the plow and the kiln are the most complex tools in the inventory. . . . Even the humblest household has a complete set of pottery-making tools, with the exception of a kiln . . . multipurpose tools are used in farming, pot making, and housekeeping. . . . Overall, the tool kit is simple and easily obtained. Many tools are found or scavenged objects, some are homemade, and few are bought. (Hagstrum 1999, 285, 287)

It is also worth noting that early humans got by with a single stone tool—the handaxe—for well over a million years (Mithen 1999, 494).

---

[4] Far rarer are societies like the Inuit (Eskimo), who have a robust tool kit, including numerous multicomponent tools (Boyd et al. 2011).

THE SELF-STARTING LEARNER   63

Multiple lab studies indicate that children have several important cognitive skills that facilitate learning to use tools. "Contrary to the view that babies are passive spectators bombarded with stimulation, from the earliest age infants are . . . explorers of their environment . . . manipulating, mouthing, listening, and looking at objects . . . to discover their properties and what they afford for action" (Rochat 1989, 871).

> Over the course of the first year, infants acquire a rich and varied repertoire of actions for manipulating objects. Moreover, infants apply these actions selectively, tailoring a particular kind of movement to an object's unique physical properties. For instance, by the middle of the second half-year, infants finger textured objects more than non-textured ones, shake or bang sounding objects more than non-sounding ones and press pliable objects more than non-pliable ones. (Bourgeois et al. 2005, 233)

In one lab study, young children were able to acquire relevant artifact categories from hands-off observation without any interaction with, or even close proximity to, a model (Elsner and Pauen 2007, 2069). In a more recent study, "children showed a remarkable capacity to parse the artifact world into discrete and stable functional categories. Between 2 and 3 years of age, children's behavior actively demonstrates their knowledge of the conventional use of many household objects" (Phillips et al. 2012, 2057). Another study in this vein showed even very young children learning from observation alone, while "providing an explicit demonstration ('look at how I do it') is not very useful [and, in fact] infants' attention is inhibited rather than enhanced [suggesting that] explicit teaching may not be the best way to help infants learn how to use a new tool" (Fagard et al. 2016, 1, 9).

Aside from studying tools and their uses, children handle them:

> Humans' propensity to manipulate objects starts almost as early as our infantile perceptual-motor abilities support it . . . 6- to 12-month-olds readily manipulate novel objects to explore their visible or haptic properties (e.g., squeezing soft objects or banging hard objects) . . . when infants first encounter an object, they will visually explore its surfaces, boundaries, textures, and markings. [In fact,] infants in face-to-face interactions with a parent are far more interested in their parent's object-handling than in their parent's face. (Deák 2014, 152–154)

64 LEARNING WITHOUT LESSONS

Beginning in late infancy, children are almost compelled to handle objects, including nonutilitarian items like rocks, pets, their food, and their mother's breast. And "handle" includes feel, manipulate, smell, taste, pound, and throw. While appearing to be random at first, the child's actions on the object seem increasingly purposeful. In one very well-known study, the authors traced the development of the ability to use a spoon. Sixteen infants (twelve to seventeen and eighteen to twenty-three months) were recorded using a spoon over a six-month span. The skill seems to be constructed in much the same way by different infants. There are predictable advances in refinement of movement, consistency, and overall efficiency. Infants persist in their "practice" for many months, in spite of the lack of reward in the form of successful use of the spoon to retrieve food and put it in their mouth (Connolly and Dalgleish 1989). The striking similarity across sixteen infants strongly suggests an inherited program for moving food to one's mouth. My impression from observation and the accounts of others points to a similar developmental trajectory for using a knife, axe, or machete (Lancy 2016).

It's no great leap to see an infant banging a stick on the ground transitioning to a toddler who is manifestly playing with objects—with or without an accompanying story line, as in make-believe. Many have argued that play is an important avenue in learning to use tools. Bjorklund and Gardiner study object play and "its possible role in helping children discover affordances of and between objects and how objects can be used as tools" (2010, 153). And empirical studies bear this out. In a study of three-year-olds, "for all participants, object-oriented play was significantly and positively related to tool use scores" (Schulz and Bonawitz 2007, 164). And, by way of contrast, if a teacher manages the child's interaction with tools, even in play, it constrains the child's exploration and experimentation.

David Bjorkland provides a clear summary of the child's readiness to make and use tools:

> Effective tool use in humans is nearly inevitable, but it is not based on an innate "tool use" adaptation unique to our species. Rather, infants have biases to manipulate objects, with the purpose of both seeing what objects can do (exploration) and what they can do with the objects (play). In the process, they discover affordances of the objects and develop action plans for using them. As children's basic cognitive abilities develop, their general tendency to see purpose in the objects and events in the world . . . make it increasingly likely that they will learn to use objects as culturally prescribed. (2016, 9)

To this point in our discussion, the learner has been kept at some distance from the model the child hopes to learn from by observing and listening to them. More direct engagement or outright participation in the activity may be desirable and even necessary. These encounters have been studied quite extensively in numerous rural communities in Mexico and Guatemala. Collectively, they are classed as learning by observing and pitching in (LOPI; Silva et al. 2015, 208).[5]

Learning Through "Pitching in"

A central goal of this volume is to make clear the points of distinction between learning in and outside of WEIRD society. In WEIRD society, for example, parents and other family members are virtually compelled to scaffold children's learning. This obligation has emerged and grown steadily over an extended period. Historically and cross-culturally, the child's first and primary teacher was her/himself. When the child inevitably sought to learn from another, they could not count on their target teacher or role model to cooperate willingly. Reichard describes a Navaho girl who learned to weave in spite of her mother's repulsing her interest (1934, 38), which paralleled a case from Truk (Micronesia) of an aspirant basket maker whose kin were unsupportive of her efforts to learn their skills (Gladwin and Sarason 1953, 414–415). In effect, the child-learner must cultivate the good will of potential role models, much as the novice in a craft apprenticeship (Chapter 6). "In Samoa, a child may dig up worms and donate them to a fisher in hopes of being invited along to observe the [fishing] process" (Odden 2007, 219).

This is, perhaps, one reason why Indigenous parents so assiduously promote the formation of social ties between their infants and other members of the family and community.

> From the moment a [Warlpiri] child is born . . . she will hear every day . . . for the next few years; "Look, your granny," "That's your big sister, your cousin, your auntie." In fact, they make up the bulk of verbal communication with babies and little children. (Musharbash 2011, 72)

---

[5] For a full exposition of the LOPI concept as developed by Barbara Rogoff and colleagues, see https://learningbyobservingandpitchingin.sites.ucsc.edu/overview/. Accessed April 10, 2023.

66 LEARNING WITHOUT LESSONS

Samoan . . . caregivers routinely prompted infants to notice . . . others. Infants were held face outward to witness . . . interactions nearby. Toddlers were fed facing others and prompted to notice and call out to people. (Ochs and Izquierdo 2009, 397)

In addition to the mother's efforts to provide the infant with social capital, by fourteen months, the child will be earning social capital on their own through offers to help out—by running an errand perhaps. This eagerness on the part of toddlers to help others appears to be a universal human trait, as verified by empirical studies of WEIRD toddlers (Warneken 2015) and a complementary survey of the ethnographic record (Lancy 2020). Vivid examples of a child "pitching in" have been recorded in studies of hunting and gathering communities in India and Ecuador.

Nayaka child helpers "gathered vessels or plantain leaves and brought them to where the meat was cut; they held a torch if the butchering took place at night; they held the animal's limbs to ease its cutting; they . . . monitored the equal distribution of meat chunks . . . and then carried the portions to the families." (Bird-David 2015, 96)

Huaorani children . . . become full members of the longhouse through their increased participation in ongoing social activities [and] by getting food and sharing it, by helping out in the making of blowguns, pots, or hammocks . . . adults never order children around; they do not command, coerce, or exercise any kind of physical or moral pressure, but simply suggest and ask. (Rival 2000, 115–116)

Aside from earning social capital, the child is also learning to collaborate.

Humans procure the vast majority of their food through collaborative efforts of one type or another . . . [and] there is evidence that children help more in a collaborative context than a non-collaborative context . . . [leading to a claim that there is] a fundamental human drive to collaborate with others to achieve joint and shared goals. (Tomasello and Vaish 2013, 238–239, 242)

In an interview study, Maya children "identified the use of sixteen medicinal plants used to cure common illnesses in their community . . . the most prevalent learning strategies were: observing adults using medicinal plants;

THE SELF-STARTING LEARNER   67

listening to related conversations during preparation; asking clarifying questions and collecting medicinal plants. Their own experience with illness was a source of knowledge. . . . Full integration into the community facilitated their acquisition of medicinal plant knowledge through a gradual learning process guided by their interest to help others." (Jiménez-Balam et al. 2019)

According to de Waal, humans are born with a drive to "fit in" or the "desire to be like others" (2001, 230). There's a premium for the learner in attending as closely to the social dynamics of the actors in a collaborative enterprise as to the mechanical details. From observational study of collaboration in Zincantecan Maya communities, "adults' goals were not to teach children but to accomplish the task at hand, with children strategically 'inserting' themselves into the ongoing work" (Alcalá et al. 2021, 197). Latinx children show *respeto* when they take pains to time their requests for inclusion or assistance carefully. Ideally, their intrusion fits "into the flow of the ongoing activity, to avoid interrupting or redirecting others' attention" (Ruvalcaba et al. 2015, 188). An example of such an insertion point occurs "when a parent, grandparent, or older sibling stops for a rest . . . the little ones pick up a hoe and attempt to imitate their elders" (Maretzki and Maretzki 1963, 510).

In the typical scenario where children are learning through a collaborative endeavor, "talk supports and is integral to the endeavor at hand rather than becoming the focus of a lesson" (Paradise and Rogoff 2009, 118):

[Correction may occur] when the child has made an error while productively working. It often occurs at the moment when the child needs to be more careful to avoid hurting him- or herself or causing damage to the objects and materials being used. Feedback can be direct or it can be subtle, such as making an adjustment to something the child has done and offered as complete. Praise is rare; [but] no response (no dismissal, explicit corrections, or adjustments of finished work) is seen as acceptance that the child has managed the job competently. (Gaskins 2015, 192)

Provision must also be made to handle a wannabe helper who is not yet capable of helping (Poelker and Gibbons 2019). Medaets describes the "Stop, you can't do it!" phenomenon in villages on the Tapajós River in Brazil. "In the Tapajós region, adult experts do not automatically welcome the novice as a co-participant and may actually disparage children's attempts to demonstrate their emerging skills" (Medaets 2016, 253). Responding negatively

68 LEARNING WITHOUT LESSONS

to a child's initial attempts at helping, however, may act as a goad, leading to greater self-reliance (Martínez-Pérez 2015, 116–117; Omura 2016, 267). And the Tapajós child will be welcomed as a participant at the successful conclusion of their self-instruction. The Maya equivalent is referred to as " 'strategic rejection,' [seen] as a way to provoke the child and increase their autonomous motivation, awareness of others, and sense of responsibility" (Coppens et al. 2020). To facilitate the novice's participation, some adjustments may be made, as, for example, when a young Bamana wannabe gardener is subtly positioned to work the soil while not disturbing others:

> Four-year-old Bafin has already grasped the meaning of sowing and is able to perform the various movements . . . he is entrusted with an old hoe as well as with some seeds so that he can gain some practice in this activity. However, . . . he has to be allocated a certain part of the field where he neither gets in the way of the others nor spoils the rows they have already sown. . . . As a rule, his rows have to be re-done. (Polak 2003, 126, 129)

One wants to avoid discouraging the child to such an extent that they lose their drive to help. For instance, repeatedly correcting the child or "doing over," according to an Indigenous mother in rural Mexico, undermines the child's development into a truly helpful child (Coppens et al. 2020). "Samoan children are never told they are 'too little,' 'too weak,' 'not old enough' to do anything. . . . If a child attempts something beyond its capacity it will be diverted, but not openly discouraged" (Mead 1967a, 235–236). Counterexamples of WEIRD parents discouraging their eager-to-help offspring are plentiful (Lancy 2022, 69–70). This comes from a middle class, urban Mexican family:

> A mother reported: "I'll walk into the bathroom and everything is all soapy, and she says to me 'I'm just cleaning.' I tell her, 'You know what? It's better that you don't clean anything for me, because I'm going to slip and fall in here.'" Mothers in the cosmopolitan community did not allow their children to take care of younger siblings, stating that childcare is the parent's responsibility alone, not the child's. One mother reported: "I tell her, 'Don't take roles that are not yours,' I tell her, 'Enjoy your childhood, you will be a mom one day.'" (Alcalá et al. 2014, 102, 104–105)

Consistent, negative feedback to eager helpers is successful at extinguishing the drive to pitch in, as many studies of WEIRD family life reveal self-centered, demanding, and decidedly unhelpful children (Lancy 2022, 69–70; Ochs and Kremer-Sadlik 2015, 773).

Selecting a Role Model

Asocial learning describes a rare situation where a child is able to figure out how to do something entirely on their own. Far more common is *social learning*, where the child learns from studying relevant behaviors of older, competent family and community members. There is wide agreement that "young children flexibly choose what, when and who to imitate. In a sense they choose their teachers and thus participate in their own learning and social development from infancy" (Lee et al. 2020, 29). And, without any explicit instruction or cuing, children as young as three years old "assume that what they see an adult doing is not just a random act but an instance of an established, normatively structured action type" (Schmidt et al. 2011, 535).

A major effort has been underway in recent years to inventory instances of social learning in Indigenous communities to ascertain the most likely candidates when children seek out role models. Somewhat surprisingly, there is a growing consensus that these models are same-age or somewhat older siblings and peers, not parents or grandparents (Röder 2018, 138). Studies of children learning about the natural environment have been particularly fruitful. Rebecca Zarger (2002a), working in a traditional Q'eqchi' Maya community, found that siblings pass along extensive information to one another about plants, including where to find them, their uses, and how to harvest or cultivate them. On the Caribbean island of Dominica, children's ethnobotanical knowledge appears to depend on the number of siblings available. Siblings are the prime sources of vegetable knowledge. However, "father presence in the household has no effect on children's plant recognition" (Quinlan et al. 2016, 445). In an interview study with Baka children, much of the child's knowledge of the local ecology was only shared among other children since they focused on different target species than adults (Gallois et al. 2017, 70). Among the Kalahari San, older children are readily available as role models for their juniors (Imamura and Akiyama 2016, 180).

70 LEARNING WITHOUT LESSONS

Unlike WEIRD society, where mothers are the primary caretakers and educators well into childhood, in an Indigenous community, the child spends most of its time in the company of other children. In a spot observation study among the Bara of Madagascar, toddlers are with their mothers 10 percent of waking time; the balance is spent with older children, as "the peer group obviously plays the dominant role for socializing small children" (Scheidecker 2016, 5). For the nomadic Pashtun, older siblings take over much of the care of infants after the first few weeks of life (Casimir 2010, 24). Marquesan "toddlers want to be with and be like older peers from whom they learn to take care of themselves, proper elimination, and the various household chores typically assigned to children" (Martini and Kirkpatrick 1992, 124). Sib caretaking occurs in the context of mixed-age and, often, mixed-gender play groups. A young child does not need to depend on his or her designated caretaker exclusively as the font of wisdom.

During middle childhood, a major shift occurs. Girls are, by this point, firmly attached to their mother as "junior partner," doing many of the chores normally assigned to married women, including infant care, harvesting or foraging, and meal preparation. Boys, however, are free from the domestic sphere (Bereczkei and Dunbar 1997) and use their freedom to range far and wide, spending most of the day combining work with play. Nevertheless, "Young Hadza (Tanzania) foragers [for example] are making substantial contributions by way of self-provisioning. The caloric contributions provided by both children and adolescents underwrite the cost of their care, possibly contributing to a mother's ability to successfully raise multiple dependents" (Crittenden 2016a, 161). Boys hang out mostly with older siblings, in part because fathers and older males are less accessible. Males are out of the village working in distant fields, working for wages at a logging camp or plantation, or hunting. Boys are considered a liability on hunting excursions, at least until they are no longer boys. A further obstacle in some societies is rigid division based on age and gender. Men may keep children (and women) at arm's length in order to preserve their standing with their peers. So girls spend their days in the company of and learning from older women, and boys stay with same-age and slightly older peers.

Adolescents often have great latitude in choosing a role model, especially in learning highly specialized skills such as spear hunting or pottery making. Interview studies with the Chabu of Ethiopia find both young men and young women exercising their prerogative to manage their own education. Men hunt, and boys progress up the ladder from play hunting to small-game capture to spear-hunting large mammals. When interviewed in adulthood, Chabu males remembered taking the initiative to join spear-hunting parties, when permitted, and learning from brothers, fathers, and other male relatives (Dira and Hewlett 2016, 77). Young Chabu women had even greater scope in self-apprenticing to older potters whose work is "modern" and in greater demand in the marketplace (Hewlett 2016, 209).

The autonomy granted to children in learning their culture is a major factor in promoting cultural change. Greenfield documents a transition that occurred over a forty-two-year period in the Highland Maya community of Nabenchuk. Earlier, girls had undergone a somewhat rigid apprenticeship, supervised by their mothers. But, as tourism increased, demand grew for new, more complex designs. These were readily picked up by younger, adolescent women from role models who were peers and more likely to have lived in or visited more metropolitan centers. Gradually, the opportunity to utilize new designs and benefit from market demand led girls to seek inspiration and guidance from weavers at-large rather than from their mothers (Greenfield 2004, 78–79; see also Greenfield and Lave 1982, 201). In the latest survey,

> intergenerational sociodemographic change—increased time in school, greater involvement in the money economy, and decreased family size— changed weaving apprenticeship, which, in turn, was related to changes in characteristics of learners. In 2012, weaving learners received more explanations, praise, and body instruction from their teachers. Learners, in turn, asked more questions. However, these changes came at a cost—the gradual loss of weaving as an everyday subsistence practice and art form. (Maynard et al. 2023)

Innovation

The idea that there might be two pedagogical strands the young might follow—one which leads to the preservation of tradition (Chapter 6) while the other leads to innovation (Rosado-May et al. 2020, 84)—is also documented in Argenti's study of Oku (Nigeria) wood carvers. In this case, young men could either join a very traditional apprenticeship, leading to eventual employment in the king's palace, or pick up the skills from observing woodcarvers at work and participating in informal workshops where several

72 LEARNING WITHOUT LESSONS

carvers share both tools and knowledge. Despite the informal pedagogy, the nonapprenticed *ghel kentshuf* (people of the chisel) "managed to carve with the same degree of skill as apprenticed carvers do . . . [further, they] were more innovative in their carving and were entrepreneurial in terms of finding new clients and markets for their work" (Argenti 2002, 498). Innovation may be inevitable, for "the artisan brings idiosyncratic ways of doing things, aesthetics, and so on to any task" (Wynn 1993, 399).

Numerous studies have uncovered evidence that children foraging in the absence of adults may discover and exploit resources that adults ignore. Note also that if adults and adolescents are not in the picture, children are probably learning how to forage from other children (see Box 3.4).
Somewhat surprisingly, crafts learning, especially pottery, may also afford innovation by learners, despite the presence of adult models (see Box 3.5).

Scenarios from ethnographic studies like these as well as descriptions of Indigenous children making up stories and fashioning the props to go with them are readily found (Chapter 5). Another cluster of studies calls attention to children's adaptation to cultural and environmental change (see Box 3.6). It is not too great a stretch to suggest that a child's ability to innovate or embrace change and innovation is enabled by tolerant attitudes toward curiosity, object handling, and risk taking (Sterelny 2021). And, as reviewed earlier in the chapter, all three are permitted or even encouraged outside WEIRD society. In WEIRD society, this "permissive" attitude is replaced by a blanket of adult-imposed restraints, which are eased only upon receipt of adult direction and instruction.

The result is the child's impaired ability to innovate. This is borne out in two lines of lab research. In the first, children must turn a pipe cleaner into a hook tool to retrieve a desirable toy. Studies with WEIRD samples indicated that this was too challenging for the majority of three- to seven-year-old subjects (Beck et al. 2011; Cutting et al. 2014). Anthropologist Sheina Lew-Levy and her coinvestigators, who study foraging bands, are skeptical about this research, critiquing the methodology and the implausibility of such a result given the nature of modern *Homo sapiens*. They assert that "innovative capabilities in childhood and adolescence may allow hunter-gatherer societies to continuously develop toolkits that are better suited to fluctuating environments" (Lew-Levy et al. 2020a, 2).

These findings suggest to me that children's tool use and invention must be grounded in the culture. The experimental situation must be representative of objects and problems they encounter in the community. Tool invention is

Box 3.4 Children as Autonomous Foragers

"Young foragers participate in a foraging activity that adults do not engage in. [They target] fledgling birds that have recently left the nest. Children prepare a stick . . . with the sticky pulp of an inedible berry called *rembo*. The *rembo* is used like a paste and spread on the stick, which is then placed in a small body of water, typically a watering hole. When the young weaver birds fly to the water to drink, several birds land on the stick, get stuck in the paste, and are then captured and consumed by the young foragers waiting at the water's edge. Children will spend several hours, and sometimes an entire afternoon, relaxing near watering holes and catching and roasting the birds. The watering holes are never far from camp, allowing children of all ages to participate" (Crittenden 2016, 168).

Mikea (Madagascar) children "have qualitatively different foraging strategies than older people . . . adults target mature *ovy* plants, which provide large tubers but with considerable digging effort. Children target young *ovy* plants, which provide small tubers with less digging. . . . For children, foraging is an extension of play that occurs outside camp . . . they learn at their own leisurely pace. Their objectives when foraging may be primarily social and recreational" (Tucker and Young 2005, 165–169).

"Children's foraging strategies may differ from adults in ways consistent with a goal to maximize efficiency now rather than in their adult futures . . . one striking thing about shell fishing is that children consistently do it differently than adults" (D. W. Bird and R. B. Bird 2000, 462–463).

Nukakau Island (PNG) children gather three types of shellfish for their own consumption, which adults neither gather nor eat. In fact, they laugh at the children pursuing low-quality food but who, nevertheless, catch a fair quantity of shellfish, cook them over a fire, and enjoy the fruits of their labor (Swadling and Chowning 1981).

"Mbya Guarani (Argentina) children older than 5 participate in excursions to gather fruits with peers . . . some of these areas are within the village, and others are located on the border between the village and the *colonos* (settlers) . . . excursions never involve adults. Children collect especially tangerines and oranges from the tallest trees, helping with sticks of different length, and once collected they consume them during the journey, and the remaining are brought to share with other members of their household" (Remorini 2016, 9).

> In the Lofoten Islands (Norway) cod fishery, when the fish are processed, the heads are granted to children, as young as six, who remove the tongues and sell them as a rare delicacy (Katzmann 2022).
>
> Kalahari San boys fashioned a ground-anchored slingshot from a pair of sticks, a discarded bicycle inner tube, and scavenged cloth and wire. Parked at the edge of a rare pool of water, the boys are very successful at shooting birds that arrive in flocks (Imamura and Akiyama 2016, 69).
>
> The Inuit have an imaginative ability to see multiple possibilities in materials, which enables them to make things out of unusual materials when the usual ones are not at hand and to use the "same" object for different purposes at different seasons, sometimes remaking it quite fundamentally to serve each purpose (Briggs 1991, 263; see also Pope et al. 2019).

not a skill that resides completely in the child's head. It is enabled by experience using actual tools and watching others use local tools in routine tasks.

In a related experiment, a child is taught numerous features of a multifaceted toy. As a result, those children—as compared to uninstructed control subjects—"performed fewer kinds of actions on the toy and discovered fewer of its other functions, than children who did not receive a pedagogical demonstration . . . and who explored broadly"[6] (Bonawitz et al. 2011, 328). As Bonawitz and colleagues explain, "teaching produces an inductive bias that constrains children's hypothesis space for better and for worse: in promoting rapid and efficient learning of target material, pedagogical instruction necessarily limits the range of hypotheses children consider" (2011, 323). In the absence of a teacher's oversight, "children's play with objects is typified by them using objects in novel and varied ways" (Pellegrini 2016, 98).

Insisting that the child attend to the behavior and speech of a teacher reduces their capacity to innovate and, as posited by Mark Pagel (see also Barnett 1953, 49), "Our capacity to be 'inventive' is just a way for generating varieties that social learning can sort through. Just so long as we have a way to generate a variety of outcomes for cultural evolution to act on, and an ability to recognize a good outcome when we see it, social learning can blindly do the rest" (Pagel 2012, 240).

---

[6] Earlier research had established that, from infancy, permitting the child the freedom to explore is positively correlated with later success in problem solving (Caruso 1993).

THE SELF-STARTING LEARNER   75

> ## Box 3.5 Children as Innovative Craftspersons
>
> "In prehistoric Huron (Canada) society . . . children were not only mechanically copying designs but were quite creative . . . a new decoration appears first on juvenile pots then later on adult pots, suggesting that decorations adopted during childhood are retained in adulthood" (Smith 2008, 71, 68).
>
> According to potters, each potter has their own style, even a young novice. This individuality in pot making is related to the Aari learning process, which initially involves the observation of experts (mothers) and, later, individual trial-and-error learning almost exclusively. "The latter trial-and-error stages allow individuals to diverge from their mothers and develop their own unique techniques . . . mothers seldom intervene verbally or physically in their daughters' pot-making process [which] encourages them . . . to create various kinds of pots" (Kaneko 2016, 225–226).
>
> "Many young Conambo (Ecuador) potters look for new ideas to broaden their stylistic repertoires . . . some modify their technological and decorative styles during extended visits to . . . other families in other places reachable by trekking the extensive trail system throughout the region or traveling by canoe along the river" (Bowser and Patton 2008, 125).
>
> "Once an [Iranian tribal] weaver begins to work on her own projects she often learns designs from women other than her mother . . . interviewees reported that they regularly compared and exchanged weaving designs with older sisters, aunts, sisters-in-law, and/or friends. Many women said that, for a reasonably skilled weaver, it is easy to memorize new designs just by looking at them" (Tehrani and Collard 2009, 289).

As I have tried to make clear, in societies where the dominant pedagogy emphasizes self-starting learners, teacher-organized and teacher-led lessons are scarce. One argument often given is that parents are too busy to teach children skills they will likely learn socially. But parents may recognize that using formal lessons may dampen the child's proclivity to explore, to experiment, and to innovate. It appears that children's attention to what the teacher wants "makes them worse at actually learning" (Gopnik 2016, 107).

Box 3.6 Children as Pioneers

Young Telefol women "have been quick to master the non-indigenous . . . method of working multicolored designs into the fabric of the *bilum* (string bag)" (MacKenzie 1991, 106).

Aboriginally, the Matses of Peru dwelt in the deep forests of Amazonia but gradually moved to more accessible sites along major watercourses. Matses boys were in the vanguard in exploring and exploiting riverine resources, fish in particular. Their rapidly acquired competence lowered the barrier for adult engagement with this unfamiliar and previously avoided ecology (Morelli 2011, 2023).

Clearly, vestiges of urbanization will find their way to the hinterlands, and adolescents are often the quickest to adapt and respond. "Settlements" provided for deep forest-dwelling tribal people in South America often incorporate medical facilities, schools, commercial outlets, and foreign religious institutions. Some Aché (Paraguay) were induced to settle on a reservation, and younger tribesmen adapted more rapidly to the changed circumstances. As a consequence, "the traditional power structure was turned upside down . . . young men [acquired] more wives and children than they had been able to acquire in the forest" (Hill and Hurtado 1996, 53).

"We Don't Teach"

The primary theme of this chapter is the child's amazing repertoire of inherited traits and abilities that enable rapid and efficient acquisition of culture. It seems to follow, logically, that there is little need for lessons, and, indeed, formal, directed instruction may be counterproductive.

In my own dissertation fieldwork in Liberia in 1971—which focused on how kids learn their culture—I was amazed at how rarely adults acted as a teacher or even acknowledged teaching as a legitimate part of their role. In one intensive study of a mother–daughter pair, I found that the onus was largely on the child to take the initiative. Nyenpu's mother, Sua, did not help, guide, or instruct her daughter. Parental views were far from Vygotskian and just the opposite of "pushy" parents, who may think that children can learn nothing important on their own.

THE SELF-STARTING LEARNER   77

Nyenpu first expressed an interest in net weaving when she was six; she only got as far as learning to twist the fibers into twine before she got discouraged and quit. This is her second time around and she has already thrown away three nets that began unsatisfactorily. Her mother says that Nyenpu won't learn it this time, but next time, in perhaps a year, she'll get it down. I was often told by my Kpelle informants that it's a waste of time to attempt to help a child learn "before they're ready" (Lancy 1996, 149).

We may be shocked by Sua's attitude, but I would argue that it is quite typical. For instance, take the Inuit (arctic hunter-gatherers), a society that is, in most respects, vastly different from the Kpelle (tropical forest forager/horticulturalists):

The Inuit consider it absurd to teach, scold, or get angry with children because they have not developed reason. Rather, they must be "accorded respect for their autonomy. If one teaches, scolds, or becomes angry at children and teenagers, one's own sense is called into question. Therefore, Inuit adults are virtually forbidden to teach or instruct children and teenagers directly, but rather are encouraged to help them learn spontaneously." (Omura 2016, 279)

I want to stress that parents not teaching is not simply a case of being neglectful or uninvolved in their offspring's development. Rather, the absence of lessons reflects a well-grounded pedagogy or folk model of learning (Harkness and Super 2006), as represented in forceful statements gathered by anthropologists from a wide range of societies. An extended example is taken from fieldwork with Nayaka hunter-gatherers.

Day after day a group of boys worked exclusively on perfecting their animal traps. This process involved much trial and error during which many seasoned adult trappers passed by the boys. None of the passersby approached the boys, not even once, nor did the boys come to ask for any advice or help from these adults. In fact, this example is quite representative as Nayaka men and women avoid any kind of direct teaching even between parents and children. (Naveh 2016, 127,128)

The cases in Box 3.7 illustrate the widely shared antipathy toward direct teaching (emphasis added).

78 LEARNING WITHOUT LESSONS

Box 3.7 Avoiding Teaching

Savanna Pumé children spend far *less than 1% of their time being instructed* (0.01% of 9390 in-camp scan observations for children aged 3–18), less than a minute per day (instruction includes an adult giving a directive, reprimand, explaining, teaching, or talking to a child) (Kramer 2021, 92).

Ingold speaks of the "extraordinary reluctance [of indigenous informants], infuriating to the anthropologist, to give advice or *instruction of any kind*" (1980, 274).

"Much of the [young Penan's] expertise will be gained through trial and error experience in play or while actually hunting, *not by direct instruction*" (Puri 2005, 281).

"By age six, Meriam [Torres Straits] children have become fairly efficient reef foragers. The learning process *involves little or no direct adult instruction*" (Bird and Bird 2002, 291).

"Directions cannot be called instructions in the sense that they are directed towards the child's learning process alone. In fact, directions seem to be primarily to get the [Mazahua] child [to] do the job right. Also, these directions are the same as those applied in normal work situations and those used for adults" (de Haan 1999, 108).

"One of my Nayaka friends, a man in his sixties, lost his usual patience when I kept asking how children will learn about the plants and animals, about finding things and directions in the forest, etc. He told me: 'No, no. *I never taught those things.* We only teach how to be together'" (Lavi 2022, 94).

"There is *no formal training* [among the Mbuti pygmies in Itruri Forest], but boys and girls alike learn all there is to be learned by simple emulation and by assisting their parents and elders in various tasks" (Turnbull 1965, 179).

"On Truk Island, with an economy based on fishing and gardening, there is *no. . . training* of children in our sense" (Bollig 1927, 96).

"On Borneo, Punan Bah children "are not encouraged to ask questions or to seek explanations on why things are the way they are . . . Adults see little point in any systematic teaching of small children, due to the belief that only from the age of about five when the souls stay put, will children have the ability to reason, and only from then on can one begin to admonish

> them with any hope of success. Still . . . adults rely more on setting children a good example *than on formal instruction*" (Nicolaisen 1988, 205–206).
>
> "If one asks a Chaga (Tanzania) where he got his knowledge, in nine cases out of ten, the reply is 'From nobody; *I taught it myself* '" (Raum 1940, 246–247).
>
> "In contrast to American parents, who seem to feel that knowledge is something like medicine—it's good for the child and must be crammed down his throat even if he does not like it—Rotuman *parents acted as if learning were inevitable* because the child *wants* to learn" (Howard 1970, 37).

Even in WEIRD society, not every parent is a competent teacher. Several studies have shown great variability in teaching ability across WEIRD communities (Marciszko et al. 2020). In a study of WEIRD parents teaching their children the game Chutes and Ladders, some parents used effective techniques, and others were quite ineffective. "Some provided no instruction, other than to correct children when they were wrong. Others did the computation for their children. Some insisted that children use a strategy, such as MIN, that they were not capable of using" (Bjorklund 2007a, 158). While WEIRD parents show great willingness to engage in play with their children and to "introduce" them to novel toys in experimental studies, their Indigenous counterparts show much less interest (Abels et al. 2017; Clegg et al. 2021). "Caregivers would let the child play independently when the novel objects were presented, while they returned to their chores" (Göncü et al. 2000, 322). As Indigenous people tend to view play as distracting the infant/child so that a mother can get her work done, the researcher's request that the mother play with the child seems like folly (Keller 2007, 203). Similar views are expressed by parents in the United States who do not belong to the WEIRD community. "Working-class and poor parents do not seem to feel obligated to attend to or follow up on children's [play activity]. In general, children's leisure activities are treated as pleasant but inconsequential and a separate world from those of adults" (Lareau 2003, 157).

Reading bedtime stories to one's children is one of the cornerstones of WEIRD parenting, and schools anxiously promote the practice to ensure that children get a "Head Start" as future readers. I conducted a study at an elementary school in Arizona, with the aim of documenting variability in parents reading with their primary-grade students. Mother–child pairs were selected from teacher nominations, which identified a range from advanced readers to those who were well "behind" their peers. The pairs were brought into an unused room in the school, furnished like a living room. A generous stack of books was piled casually on a coffee table. The pairs were told to select their own books to read and take turns reading; otherwise, they were uninstructed. The research assistant left, and the event was recorded for later analysis.

The mothers of fluent readers used a variety of very supportive strategies, and it was clear that joint storybook reading was very well established in the home. The "reluctant" reader pairs were sometimes painful to watch, as both mother and child struggled to form a strategy that would lead to success. Mothers controlled the process, selecting story-free "readers" rather than the livelier picture books, including several Caldecott winners. When it was their turn to read, they read in a monotone, without pausing to engage the child in the book. When the child read, the mother stopped them frequently to correct their "errors." The posture and demeanor of both suggested extreme discomfort (Bergin et al. 1994).

Similarly, "scaffolding" is the sine qua non of WEIRD parenting, but, here, too, a recent study of highly educated Swedish parents' scaffolding ability showed that a significant number were rated "not supportive" (Marciszko et al. 2020). Scaffolding was absent when parents and preschoolers were observed in a children's museum. To extract meaning from the exhibits required reading informational or directional signs. In two-thirds of observed instances, the parent failed to assist the child by reading the signs (Gelman et al. 1991).

Ethnographic studies of poor and working-class families in the United States echo findings from Indigenous communities. When queried, these parents accepted no responsibility for the child's education: "That's what teachers are for" (Lareau 2003, 157; see also Coll and Marks 2009, 90). In a large-scale study in the United States (Robinson and Harris 2014), the level of parents' academic involvement did not predict children's grades. In fact, "helping with homework" had a negative impact because parents lacked appropriate knowledge or teaching skills, and students were more successful on their own (Hoffman 2015).

In Indigenous communities around the globe, there is the shared notion that children possess the means to learn their culture without much intervention from those older and more competent. We have discussed inherited abilities that enable learning, willing role models, welcoming collaborators, and almost unlimited access to meaningful artifacts as distinct assets the learner can draw on. In the next chapter, we move from learning through an exchange among individuals and the activities they are engaged in, to a broader picture of the natural and built environments as offering convenient *developmental niches* (Super and Harkness 1986) for children's development.

4

Everyday Classrooms

> In the passage of human generations, each one contributes to the
> knowledgeability of the next not by handing down a corpus of dis-
> embodied, context-free information, but by setting up, through
> their activities, the environmental contexts within which successors
> develop their own . . . skills.
>
> —Ingold (2001), 142

Introduction

Among Batek foragers, a large family party goes into the forest canvassing for
medicinal plants, edible fruits, tubers, and small mammals. The excursion is
treated as a festive and playful occasion, with the very young welcome to participate. The personal experience of moving in the forest, monitoring one's
own skills, and training one's body is considered the best way of acquiring
knowledge. According to Tuck Po, "For children, these are their *everyday
classrooms*" (1997, 109, emphasis added). "Everyday classroom" is a shorthand expression that encompasses the diversity of settings where learning is
facilitated. These settings become classrooms when they, incidentally, function as developmental niches (Super and Harkness 1986), bringing together
tolerant experts and eager-to-learn novices. Children are free to observe, to
overhear, and to "meddle." From the point of view of a child learning the culture, everyday classrooms provide what Wimsatt and Griesmer label "infrastructure scaffolding" (2007, 66).

The basic ideas behind "everyday classrooms" and "infrastructure scaffolding" are that in every community, there are sites that seem to have exceptional value as places for learning. The activities at these sites endure over
time and are, to a great degree, predictable. Children are welcome to observe,
listen, and build a mental model of the phenomena to be learned. These sites
include a role model—someone carrying out tasks in an exemplary way,

Learning Without Lessons. David F. Lancy, Oxford University Press. © Oxford University Press 2024.
DOI: 10.1093/oso/9780197645598.003.0004

worthy of the learner's attention. A common example would be a young girl intently focused on her mother's treatment and care of an infant.

Such sites are littered with materials and objects that either stand in for or actually represent the raw materials and tools used by experts. For example, at stone toolmaking sites, children "practiced" on discarded cores or used poor-quality stone rejected by the experts. In at least some cases, young learners are given cast-off or made-to-scale tools, enhancing opportunities to learn. Tools, finished products, raw materials (clay, stone, wood, fibers), and discards like lithic debitage and pottery shards all contain information that can be extracted and applied to one's own self-instruction. Work sites typically include various auxiliary components that may be parceled out among young learners to enhance their sense of participation. Children are encouraged to demonstrate their keenness to learn by offering assistance, such as fetching, carrying, distributing completed products, looking after infant siblings, and so on. Sites primarily identified with play are close to home, are considered safe (the "mother ground" Lancy 1996), and largely replicate—in play—sites associated with work.

Unlike actual classrooms, "everyday classrooms" arise to fulfill other needs, unrelated to the education of children. Only minimal adjustments might be made—for example, slowing down the pace of a foraging excursion—to accommodate young learners. Everyday classrooms coincidentally align with children's inherited drive to learn autonomously. They obviate the time-consuming and nonproductive requirements for schools, lessons, and teachers, and provide obvious fitness benefits from an evolutionary perspective.

Learning in the Playgroup

Very shortly after children become mobile and/or are weaned, they transition to the care of older siblings who are responsible for their well-being. One of the minder's eventual responsibilities will be to facilitate the toddler's transition from her home base near the mother to the somewhat rowdy and relatively unfamiliar neighborhood playgroup (Tanaka 2022).

With the arrival of the next sibling, Mandinka infancy is over. Now, play begins and membership in a social group of peers is taken to be critical to *nyinandirangho*, the forgetting of the breast to which the toddler has had

84 LEARNING WITHOUT LESSONS

free access for nearly two years or more. As one mother put it, "Now she must turn to play." (Whittemore 1989, 92)

There's an almost universal tendency for village dwellers to grant children the autonomy to take charge of their own education. Nevertheless, there's also an unspoken assumption that siblings and peers are more congenial and appropriate role models than parents. For example,

> Kokwet (Kenya) mothers expressed *the view that children learned to talk more from each other than from their mothers* [who] claimed they did nothing to encourage their children's language development.... Naturalistic observations confirm the mothers' reports: by comparison with American studies, the frequency of the Kokwet mothers' speech to their two- to three-year-old children was remarkably low. (Super and Harkness 1986, 557, emphasis added)

Children's play bouts are simultaneously learning bouts—this is unlikely to be the case should adults try to behave as teachers. These roaming groups of autonomous learners are also considered to be creating a "children's culture." This culture is inherently frivolous and playful while also pursuing practical ends. Games are invented but so are novel ways of capturing food sources. That is, children are observed exploiting environmental niches and resources not exploited by adults.

The players gather in open spaces at the center of the community, where they can be casually supervised by the few (often elderly) adults working outside their homes. This very practical arrangement is referred to by the Kpelle (Liberia) as the "mother ground" (Lancy 1996, 84). The mother ground is cleared of vegetation, discouraging insect and reptilian intruders. This leaves a soil surface that is ideal for drawing and laying out various games, including versions of hopscotch. For the Kpelle, many of the games develop reasoning and mathematics skills and are graduated in complexity, thereby providing a ladder of difficulty for the novice to climb (Lancy 1996, 101–107).

Aside from casual supervision, the adults in the vicinity are busily pursuing their trades: food preparation, weaving nets and baskets, and stringing beads for sale. Children watch these activities carefully and then incorporate what they have seen into their make-believe play (Lancy 1996). Since the youngest are primarily looked after by older siblings, integrating the younger child into the flow of play activity, particularly make-believe, makes caretaking much easier (Maynard 2004a, 245). The younger child is less likely to wander off—drawing their caretaker away from the play activity—less likely to get bored, frustrated, or cranky, and less likely to seek comfort from the mother.

The Pala'wan (Philippines) equivalent of the mother ground is *lägwas*, an open, communal space among a cluster of homes:

> This open sky, clear and cleaned space, is the children's playground where kites can be made and flown, and tops can be thrown when the soil is dry.... Everyday objects and tools are accessible to all of the children: Nothing is forbidden to the touch or to handling which allows children to develop dexterity and awareness of sharpness at quite an early age, as no one interferes to prevent them their discoveries. (Revel et al. 2017, 5)

Children's play groups are

> autonomous.... They are separate, socially recognized institutions which are quite independent of parents, within which communal processes of development and learning take place.... The autonomous children's groups demonstrate that socialization is not necessarily limited to the nuclear family but can also take place largely in a peer group. (Röder 2018, 138)

The role model and "director" of play bouts may be one of the older children. Make-believe play is very common and is enlivened by the mixed ages and gender of playgroup members. This varied cast of characters is a boon to the typical "script," mainly incorporating what is on view in the community (Power 2000). Power, drawing on a large-scale survey, also noted that "Children's play in traditional cultures . . . rarely involves fantastic transformation . . . [or] character roles that the child will seldom, if ever, enact or encounter in life" (2000, 272). This is quite unlike Western, educated, industrialized, rich, democratic (WEIRD) children's play, which is infused with themes from books, videos, and toys. No one has yet traced the precise channels through which make-believe play episodes lead to the child's learning their culture, but we can come close to that ideal.

In "Becoming a Blacksmith in Gbarngasuakwelle," I described Kpelle children's amazingly detailed and faithful replication of the blacksmith's forge during an episode of make-believe. The blacksmith's compound was a lively gathering point in the village, consistently attracting a crowd of onlookers and gossips, young and old. Children could watch the action of the smiths

86 LEARNING WITHOUT LESSONS

and eavesdrop as village affairs were discussed. They thus built up a stock of script material that could be woven into their make-believe play. The boy playing the smith had obviously absorbed a great deal of the processes, both technical (he constructed reasonable replicas of bellows, anvil, and tongs) and social, assigning the roles of novice, wives, and helpers to his playmates. The terminology for tools, actions, and relationships used in the "script" was also a faithful rendition (Lancy 1980). While no claim can be made that playing at blacksmith constitutes preparation to become a blacksmith, the experience enables players to develop a more complete understanding of a cornerstone of the community. At the same time, one widely cited study did find clear relationships between "play pounding" (in a mortar and pestle) and play spear throwing, which were closely associated with later work grinding grain and hunting (Bock and Johnson 2004).

Tian has described an even more elaborate simulation that younger Maasai boys weave into a kind of board game, whose objective—like *Monopoly*—is to build up one's herd. The simulation encompasses the full gamut of livestock management:

> Children practiced livestock identification and grouping in this game. They identify and group the collected materials as different "herds" according to their type, size, color, and shape. . . . They gave names to their "oxen," which not only mimic cattle names from their homestead, but also use the ones they have heard from others. There were also occasions that children crawled on the ground and pretended to be "livestock" themselves. For instance, in session No. 6, except for two younger boys who acted as "herding boys," the other children put fresh cow dung on the bottom of their skirt and trousers, and crawled on the ground pretending to be a "bull" and "female cattle." During their play, they joyfully reviewed the livestock identification, classification, and grouping, which they have learned during daily chores. (Tian 2017a, 11)

An entire curriculum can be transmitted through the play group:

> In the Ngaanyatjarra Lands in remote Western Australia children play a guessing game . . . [whose] aim is to guess the identity of a referent by decoding a series of verbal and visual clues given by the game "leader." The task draws on shared knowledge of Ngaanyatjarra kinship networks and social geographies. (Ellis et al. 2017, 165)

EVERYDAY CLASSROOMS   87

Tools not only find their way into make-believe play, but they are also power-fully attractive in their own right—another developmental niche for learning one's culture:

> Kammu (Laos) boys develop expertise in fabricating hunting weapons and traps by creating toys that gradually evolve into the genuine articles. For example, "during the play the boys begin to try to build their own traps. They also like to build models of bigger traps, such as spear-traps." (Tayanin and Lindell 1991, 15)

> Nukak (Argentina) children make a wide array of small, poor-quality, but still quite functional tools, including bows, harpoons, blowpipes, and various kinds of vessels (gourd, basketry, ceramic). (Politis 2007)

Archaeologists have uncovered considerable evidence for children's attraction to objects in general and tools in particular. Recovery of small, crudely made artifacts assumed to be toys and/or child-produced testify to the presence of children as playful learners throughout many prehistoric sites (Uziel and Avissa Lewis 2013). Politis (2007) conducted a very interesting study using the tools of ethnoarchaeology. The investigator studied a living community but limited his perspective to material culture. He found, for example, that in a Nukak camp there are many discarded items that were not usable as tools but functioned well as toy tools. These artifacts are clustered in specific areas of the camp space, suggesting they were "owned" or claimed by children. Children's spaces also included satellite camps, adjacent to the main camp, adorned with simple tepees built and utilized by them.

Older children have greater freedom to explore beyond the mother ground, and it is extremely common to find mobile playgroups that alternate between games and work, such as playing tag while tending the herd; lustily chasing birds from ripening crops; and casually foraging for forest products, including fruits, edible tubers, small birds, mammals, and marine life. These parties may be gone from the hearth for the entire day and bring home to share any foodstuffs not consumed on the spot. In mixed-age groups, younger members are responsibly looked after by older members who, of equal importance, serve as conscientious role models and guides to the younger learners. Hunting parties of six- to fourteen-year-old boys are readily identified as everyday classrooms because it is obvious that they are the incubator for nascent hunting skills (Setalaphruk and Price 2007).

88 LEARNING WITHOUT LESSONS

Among the Hadza, boys go on hunting forays without adult supervision or guidance.[1] Daily practicing their hunting skill—they are given their first bow at age three—they are expert at hunting small mammals by thirteen. "Most of what they acquire they eat while out foraging" (Marlowe 2010, 158).

And, in Indigenous communities, generally, anthropologists are finding that culture is learned primarily in the company of peers, while parents play a much smaller role (Lew-Levy et al. 2021a; Maynard 2002; Rabain-Jamin, et al. 2003; see Chapter 3, this volume). Play gradually diminishes (earlier for girls than boys) as children concentrate on learning more directly from involvement in observing and essaying practical skills. Among the Pumé, "play time appears to be replaced with time spent foraging and doing in-camp tasks, both of which increase with age" (Kramer 2021, 106).

Learning in the Family Circle

I have earlier identified the "family circle" (Lancy 2022) as providing an excellent classroom. An example of the family circle as an environment for learning comes from a rural Taira village on Okinawa:

> Adults rely heavily on observation and imitation on the part of children; they seldom "teach" them to do things systematically. Parents were surprised and amused when questions such as "How do you teach children to transplant rice, harvest rice, or otherwise help in the fields?" were put to them. "We don't teach them; why they just learn by themselves," was the usual answer. . . . The relatively few restrictions placed on the young child are an important basis for learning. By being able to participate freely, children learn what is going on in their village from day to day (Maretzki and Maretzki 1963, 514). . . . Whatever adults are doing, children are present to watch their activities and overhear their conversations. Although parents do not seem to make any special efforts to have a child attend a function so that he might learn adult ways, they take their children to the fields, parties, public meetings, and rituals long before they consider them ready to absorb any learning. In the fields, children play among rows of vegetables. While rice is being transplanted, throngs of children sit on the dikes in the paddies,

---

[1] It is widely reported that sons don't accompany their fathers on the hunt. Baka "adult hunters only invite boys to accompany them on hunting expeditions once they have the dexterity and discretion needed for successful hunting" (Gallois et al. 2018, 452).

dangling their legs in the mud. They intently watch adults transplanting and weeding the paddies.... When a parent, grandparent, or older sibling stops for a rest to have a cup of tea, the little ones pick up a hoe and attempt to imitate their elders. (Maretzki and Maretzki 1963, 510)

Although young children are not taken to the mountains, in the village they watch adults sawing, splitting, and working the bamboo rings used in tying faggots.... They crouch with their mothers, who are busy with the laundry. It is not long before they pick up a small article of clothing and start soaping, rubbing, and rinsing just as their mothers do. (Maretzki and Maretzki 1963, 511–512)

Researchers studying language socialization find that infant caretakers do not engage in dyadic conversations with infants as WEIRD parents do. "Rather they routinely direct infants' attention to others in multiparty surroundings [the family circle] aligning them as onlookers, overhearers, and relayers of prompts, thereby immersing them in appropriate registers of adults and older siblings" (Ochs and Schieffelin 2017, 1).

We might say that the extraordinary capacity for social learning in the very young is exercised to its fullest extent in the family circle. Children can create a kind of mental Rolodex of the behavior and needs of other family members. They can create a blueprint of activities within the domestic sphere, fitting themselves into the flow of events and attempting to help out or mimic the actions of those older "as if" they were helping out.

According to Mitchell and Jordan (2021, 166), "Contemporary anthropological research on kinship emphasizes the importance of the everyday practices of living together for understanding relatedness, e.g., sleeping, sharing of food and other substances, dwelling together in houses. These habitual aspects of everyday life are doubtless highly significant in shaping emerging kinship concepts." In a typical village, living and working areas are intermingled. On display for curious eyes are food preparation, including butchering and cooking; house building, such as the erection of the family yurt; craftwork, such as basketmaking and, in an earlier period, stone toolmaking.

Medaets illustrates a congenial gathering in an Amazonian village, where a family of mixed ages is busy around the house with harvesting, processing, and roasting cassava into flour and tidying up. There are no fewer than eight children, aged four to fifteen, distributed across this scene, each one busy with a chore but also observing others (Medaets 2011, 3). Children are

90 LEARNING WITHOUT LESSONS

expected to pay attention to ongoing activity and attempt to fit in. This may involve an offer to assist or just quietly observe and listen. In doing so, the child is taking charge of their education in culture and also demonstrating a laudable desire to fit in.

For very small-scale, seminomadic groups, the mother ground play space is indistinguishable from the family circle. For example, Dobe !Kung

> move their camps periodically, the physical structures of the camps are rudimentary and few in number. For example, each nuclear family constructs its own grass hut. The huts are arranged in an elliptical pattern, spaced five to twelve feet apart and facing inward. Adults clear the bush around and a few feet in back of the huts and inside the public camp space. This creates a central yard, shared by all, and adults and children spend the great proportion of their time when they are in camp in full view of other people. . . . It is important to understand the absence of privacy and the permeability of nuclear family residential boundaries in this social setting. (Draper and Cashdan 1988, 342–343)

"Children play in the central open area at all camps [and, if available] a clearing with a vine swing" (Fisher and Strickland 1991, 222). Otherwise, the central open area is the venue for community life when not actively foraging. Socializing, food preparation and consumption, toolmaking and repair, and music and dance all occur in a very public arena, to which children have free access. It is very "well-fitted for learning about the social and ecological worlds" (Coward and Howard-Jones 2021, 90). As Donley-Reid notes, "architectural spaces (are) mnemonic devices" (1990, 115).

It is clear from Hewlett's description that the entire Aka camp—and this would certainly be true for other foraging bands (Turnbull 1978)—functions as the mother ground. He describes the campsite, with its maximum of twenty-five to thirty-five inhabitants, as "about the size of a large Euro-American living room" (Hewlett 1992, 225). In camp, even one-year-olds are free to roam widely within the perimeter and interact with whomever they wish. The camp is not "childproof"; no one panics if the baby handles knives or wanders into, say, a butchering site (Lancy 2022, 146).

The family circle often encompasses the foraging expedition. Whole families may be engaged in the quest for edible or medicinal plants. It is a jolly party with opportunities for gossip, play, and, of course, talk about the

EVERYDAY CLASSROOMS   91

environment, both its hazards and uses (Politis 2007, 178). Younger children are mostly avid spectators, observing, listening, and helping. Some Central African forest-dwelling hunter-gather communities, such as the Bofi, depend on net hunting. A net is strung across a promising stretch of forest, and "beaters," starting at a certain distance from the net, drive small mammals, such as duiker, into the net, where they are clubbed to death. Later, the catch is butchered to ease transport back to camp. Men, women, and children participate, and, as a group, they can obtain more food than individuals hunting singly (which men do). Children who are old enough to keep up with the hunters as they travel to the site are given one or more responsibilities, including setting up and holding the net, beating, preventing animals from escaping the net, and helping to carry the return load. As the extracts in Box 4.1 show, children play varied roles on foraging expeditions, allowing them to learn through participating.

Group fishing expeditions have many of the characteristics of group foraging in the forest. Mayangna and Miskito Nicaraguan forager-farmers use a variety of capture techniques to successfully locate and catch twenty-seven species of fish in their riverine environment. By tagging along and helping out, children rapidly acquire both fishing techniques as well as knowledge of the fish themselves.

> From an early age, children regularly observe the practice of fishing strategies, as they are frequently brought on excursions in dugout canoes with older relatives who fish. As youngsters, children often contribute by gathering and managing the fish caught by family members. . . . Adolescents . . . form fishing parties with same-aged friends and peers. . . . Overall, there are ample and diverse opportunities for both experiential and social learning about fish behavior. . . . As the Mayangna and Miskito learn about fish and fishing strategies, first via observations during childhood and then via experience as participants on fishing trips, they exhibit high levels of knowledge relatively early in life. (Koster et al. 2016, 114–117)

The foraging expedition as an "everyday classroom" is replete with opportunities to learn from the entire group and their interaction with the environment. At least some of this new information can be put to immediate practical use. However, the atmosphere is largely informal and play, song, and dance enliven the participants.

Box 4.1 Learning in the Forest

"Walking through the forest, men, women, and children . . . frequently check tree hollows and burrows for small prey and tree trunks for signs of lizards. . . . All net-hunt participants, but especially women and children, opportunistically gather insects, fruit, nuts, and plants whenever they have discovered" (Lupo and Schmitt 2002, 159).

"Ecological knowledge is often transmitted when Agta (Philippines) parents and children walk through the forest together . . . parents . . . may point out plants and animal tracks . . . [while] gazing at an object they are describing. All of this usually involves no or minimal verbal instruction" (Hagen et al. 2017, 395).

Samburu (Kenya) adolescents who engage in traditional activities, such as herding, incidentally gain traditional ecological knowledge (EK). Herding allows them to interact in the landscape with peers or elders who share knowledge about plants (Bruyere et al. 2016).

"During bush trips, older [Jul'hoansi] women often talk in much detail about the distribution of certain species they encounter along the way; they recollect stories about these species from their childhoods; or narrate properties of medicinal plants. . . . Children who accompany women on bush trips are exposed to their repetitive stories. . . . Narrating women, however, do not direct these stories as much at children, as at other adult accompanying women. . . . Children, nevertheless, . . . retell bush trip or hunting stories they have participated in or heard about in great detail" (Ninkova and Hays 2017, 10).

"The performance of subsistence activities is the keystone for Baka children to learn their ecological and cultural knowledge. The Baka (Cameroon) people often called the cultural knowledge and holistic wisdom gained, 'the school of [the] forest' (sikulù na bele)" (Sonoda et al. 2018, 161, 164).

Hadza "women gather in groups and can rely on each other to keep track of where they are and how to get from one place to the next. . . . Sharing navigational skill reduces the cost of errors to [individual] foragers" (Cashdan et al. 2012, 282).

As children accompany foraging parties, they acquire more general spatial and navigational skills. Empirical tests of these skills in three different societies show that, by seven, boys and girls are excellent navigators (Davis et al. 2021).

"Among the Pumé, children spend many daylight hours away from camp, playing and foraging. Groups of boys fish and hunt for small game. Girls gather fruit, berries, and firewood; dig for roots; and haul water from nearby wooded areas and streams. Mixed-sex groups of children as young as 3 and 4 forage for easily procured food at the edge of camp and cook it at their own fires.... However, [in traveling to] root patches and fruit groves [that] are several to many kilometers from camp, girls will normally accompany groups of women to gather these resources" (Kramer 2021, 9, 13).

At a Maasai village, girls as young as three join collecting parties of two to nine older girls. Searching within a 5 km radius of camp, the older girls expertly identify the various species of wood (twenty-four in total) and the preferred uses of each, such as heating, cooking and kraal construction. They must evaluate the dryness and use a sharp machete to cut the wood into packable lengths. No explicit teaching is offered; younger girls are to listen to, observe, and copy the more expert until they've mastered the task (Tian 2017b).

In a comparative study of societies where forest foraging is still practiced, the authors found that risk to the child is reduced by foraging in a *group* of children *closer* to the settlement, "leading to higher rates of food production than predicted by ecological risk" (Lew-Levy et al. 2021b, 10).

It is possible to map the geography of everyday classrooms. For example, Jarawa (Andaman) forest foragers see their world as a rough configuration of concentric circles, with camps at the center; play space and then work areas are located progressively farther out. As individuals grow and improve their knowledge and skill base, they may gradually expand their range of activity beyond the known trails of the "play zone" and outward into the peripheral "work zone" (Pandya 2016, 193).

"The *bopi*, or children's territory, lies a few yards from the Mbuti main camp.... While the children are playing in the *bopi*, [they are] safely out of the way yet close enough not to fall into danger" (Turnbull 1978, 128–129).

"Q'eqchi' Maya ... begin to learn the plants and animals in the immediate household environment first. Knowledge increases as experiences widen in scope during childhood. These expanding spheres of influence grow to encompass trips to the family farm, the forest, etc." (Zarger 2002b, 230).

The Child Spectator as Learner

Another everyday classroom encompasses adult gatherings where children act as nonparticipating spectators. These include, for example, court cases where the arbiter—the Kpelle Town Chief—speaks in an exhortatory manner, calling out the deep moral and cultural principles that have been violated in each case. Closely attentive child spectators readily learn these precepts (Lancy 1996). Ceremonies such as funerals and political gatherings are rich sources for learning the society's fundamental moral and social beliefs and always attract child spectators. "From birth onwards, [Nso] children become observant participants of routine practices, cultural festivities and ceremonies as they sit on laps or are carried on a caregiver's back, or run around the compound" (Yovsi 2014, 258). Among the Batek, much of the foundational knowledge for foraging is garnered by children while attending to the evening's recounting of the day's successes and failures (Tuck Po 1997). Boys are free to listen and learn as "real" hunters recount their experiences back in the village after the hunt (Blurton-Jones and Konner 1976, 338; Tayanin and Lindell 1991, 14; Hagen et al. 2017, 395; Sugiyama 2017, 7), even though—as noted for the Siberian Yukaghir—the hunters have no pedantic intent and make no adjustment for the rudimentary knowledge of the aspirant hunters (Willerslev 2007, 169).

Gatherings of a more entertaining sort are widespread and include scary and uplifting stories (Overing 1988), proverbs, jokes, song lyrics, gossip, and shadow-puppet theater:

> The shadow play has explicit religious and didactic value for all Balinese. . . . Children constitute the front rows of any audience, their attention being riveted on the servants who clown around and tell spicy, bawdy jokes. Young children, up to about ten or twelve years old, are drawn to any performance irrespective of the dramatic genre. . . . So the system of morality, together with the history and cosmology represented in the plays, is largely unconsciously adopted, and the molding of the individual to the social norms occurs imperceptibly and indirectly as a pleasurable "by-product" as it were of the cultural routine. (Hobart 1988, 118, 133)

On the occasion of a wedding, Maninka (Mali) villagers stage an elaborate dance:

The spatial setting is an amphitheater consisting of a ring of spectators and musicians who literally frame the situation and create a clear space to its interior . . . that serves as a dance floor . . . children and youth usually fill the ranks in the spectator ring. While standing at the sidelines of the performance arena, they . . . attentively follow the events in the arena. Sometimes they clap or move along with the main beat and sometimes they try out some dance steps themselves . . . [because] it's about imitating others. If you want to dance, you train yourself. There is no teaching of children by adults. The children themselves observe it and those who like it will then do it. (Polak and Doumbia 2022, 282, 284)

Akira Takada has documented at great length the process by which the youngest San toddlers progress from observer to full participant. Dance and music are introduced by adults during long nighttime gatherings. They are learned by older children through careful imitation. The performances are then replicated during daytime play bouts in the village, thereby affording the younger children the opportunity to learn them (Takada 2020, 179).

BaYaka utilize a pedagogy based on mockery, play, and public speaking. The means for correcting norm violations are subtle and nondirective. One such institution—*mòsámbò*—is designed to change behavior without limiting free will.[2] It is a noisy public-speaking protocol through which speakers remind others (especially children) of the social norms and values that have been violated (Bombjaková 2018). The fact that specific individuals are not called out diminishes the potential for conflict.

Firelight "stories are told in virtually all hunter-gatherer societies. . . . Such stories describe the workings of entire institutions in a small-scale society with little formal teaching" (Wiessner 2014, 14027). "The telling of stories among San is no watered-down nursery pastime but the substantial tale. Children are not barred from listening to the stories but the !Kung seem to have little interest in teaching the lore of their forefathers to the children" (Biesele 1976, 307).

However, by admitting the child into the sacred space implicated in these examples, much can be learned. The following collection of extracts (Box 4.2) illustrates this phenomenon.

The opportunity to learn extends beyond the role of spectator. As we have seen, children are inveterate mimics, and their make-believe play has

---

[2] Actually, variations on *mòsámbò* are ubiquitous among Pygmies (Turnbull 1961).

96 LEARNING WITHOUT LESSONS

Box 4.2 Learning as a Nonparticipant

"Children as young as six . . . begin to pick up the distinctive features characterizing people of rank and authority without any explicit instruction. This was particularly the case for distinctive behavioral aspects of common ritual events associated with chiefs that children could readily witness" (Odden and Rochat 2004, 46).

"A teaching practice may, in fact, cause very little learning. Conversely, a ritual activity, say, that is not aimed at causing learning may nevertheless greatly contribute to learning because it displays a good deal of socially relevant information in an intelligible form" (Atran and Sperber 1991, 41).

[Maninka] "adults deny providing any formal education in kinship reckoning, although informal education clearly consists of overheard conversations among adults. Adults may clarify for one another the identity of a specific *luntangho*, or stranger/guest, by repeating his or her clan name and origins, including kin associations with locally known consanguineal or affinal relations" (Beverly and Whittemore 1993, 239).

---

enormous capacity to reproduce what they've seen. The examples that follow in Box 4.3 reveal that after serving as an attentive spectator, the child recalls and replicates what has been learned, thus strengthening their mastery of the messages embedded in public performances.

These themes are readily taken up as precepts for normative behavior (Lancy 2022). Such public narratives can be viewed as curricula rooted in the pedagogy of autonomous, child-initiated learning. Or, as Gaskins notes, "observational learning shares two very important characteristics with play—intrinsic motivation and child-directedness. In addition, learning through observation can be invisible and unintentional, as in play, through repeated exposure to everyday events" (2014, 33).

In the next section, we take a brief digression. To this point, the scenarios we have examined have all been of living peoples in the ethnographic present, meaning that cases are described in the present tense even when the ethnography was completed a century ago. I was enticed to pursue the literature on the archaeology of childhood by a study I ran across, which was conducted in France. Pigeot describes a very well-preserved Neolithic site that struck me immediately as a kind of classroom, which, in turn, inspired me to notice other instances of everyday classrooms.

Box 4.3 Reenacting Ritual

"Talensi (Ghana) boys "hunt" for mice, and after they've played with their captives for a while, they "sacrifice" the "dog" on a miniature shrine and ask to be granted success in hunting" (Fortes 1938/1970, 68).

"BaYaka hunter-gatherer children imitate adults' forest spirit rituals in their ritual play (*mokondi massana*) . . . Adults can be present . . . but they rarely interfere" (Salali et al. 2019, 2).

Mehinacu (Brazil) "children produce an extremely accurate replication of the complete sequence of events from initial illness to the shaman's triumphant discovery of the culpable instrument of witchcraft" (Gregor 1988, 114).

"In the socialization of future healers in the Kalahari and in Fiji, the process begins as early as five, when little boys role-play the trance-inducing dance of the adult healer" (Katz 1981, 62).

Broch recorded five Bonerate girls between four and seven replicating a female possession-trance ritual. They took care to depict the act of walking on or stamping out "imaginary" embers. Only a few days earlier, "a real possession-trance ritual had been conducted in a neighboring village" (Broch 1990, 107).

Stone Toolmaking Sites as Classrooms

While this exposition is primarily constructed from studies of living peoples, the archaeological record is now seen, increasingly, as a valuable window on non-WEIRD childhoods (Lancy 2017a). For nonarchaeologists, it is surprising to learn how much can be inferred from scanty preserved remains from many thousands of years ago. Several studies suggest the strong possibility that everyday classrooms were available to children in the Stone Age (Castañeda 2018). We have ample evidence from physical remains (stone scatter from knapping areas) revealing a cluster (often roughly circular) of individuals ranging from experts to young children, who are identified as such by their crude products and use of discarded or poor-quality raw material. At a Middle Paleolithic site in Ethiopia, many tools or fragments tended to be rather small and absent signs of use—*practice* tools (Shea 2006, 212). But these studies also clearly show a pattern of improvement in the novice's

98 LEARNING WITHOUT LESSONS

products—the implication being that stone knapping sites may have been congenial environments for learning (Pigeot 1990; Assaf 2021). Studies in archaeology complement ethnographic evidence of children's play with objects, usually representing tools used in the community. Meaningful artifacts to explore and learn from are everywhere.

At the site of Etiolles (14,000 years BP), the work space was roughly circular, with the most productive workers in the center, nearest the hearth. Less proficient knappers were stationed at a corresponding distance from the center, with child novices at the periphery, where they could watch while "play" knapping but without getting in the way (Pigeot 1990, 132–133). A very similar distribution of knappers was excavated at Pincevent, a contemporaneous site also in France (Julien and Karlin 2015). Cunnar noted from a dart-making site in the Great Basin of the North American West (c. 5000 BP) that "the 'poor' preforms . . . are positioned in an arc around the excellent knapper [producing] a pattern of poor skill surrounding good and excellent products" (2015, 143). At a Neolithic site in Sweden, the debitage pattern showed an expert knapper remaining in place while less expert knappers seemed to change position (Högberg 2008), perhaps to get different vantage points on the expert. A late Paleolithic workshop in Denmark is referred to metaphorically as a "flint knapping school" (Fischer 1990).

In a very few contemporary communities, the "stone age" endures. Among the Grand Valley Dani in the western New Guinea Highlands, Hampton (1999) photographed a stone knapping "workshop." This was a semicircular ensemble of boys, ranging in age, each knapping at whatever level of skill they had reached, and a single adult knapper positioned at the apex.

At a Neolithic site in Spain, archaeologists posited that

> the work conducted at a flint mine implied the participation of the entire community providing novel social experiences for children and adolescents. They had the opportunity to move to a different location, mingle with members of other groups, and become integrated in the communal activity by means of peripheral tasks—such as the management of debris produced in extraction procedures and lithic reduction. [The site, consisting of] outcrops, quarries, and mines . . . represents the ideal "*class-room*" in which the younger generations could develop their skills as toolmakers and become initiated into the community. (Castañeda 2018, 721; emphasis added)

There is also consistent evidence that children moved through the workshop area and gathered larger, discarded stone tools to remove to more peripheral

EVERYDAY CLASSROOMS   99

"play" areas (Politis 2007). Here, they play with "real," if flawed, tools in clear view of experts making them (Hammond and Hammond 1981). This is very much in line with the theoretical proposal that children are "legitimate peripheral participants" (Lave and Wenger 1991) and, also, that "being a 'toy' is a potential characteristic of all objects in a child's environment" (Crawford 2009, 55; Politis 2007).

Another *cultural* adaptation that supports the novice's training is the provision of poorer quality material to practice on. Suitable, high-quality raw material may be difficult to obtain, and toolmaking inevitably produces a great quantity of waste material. Novices, therefore, may find or be given stone that can be worked but is otherwise unlikely to yield a usable tool. At an Upper Paleolithic site in the Netherlands, "children practiced on used-up cores abandoned by expert knappers" (Stapert 2007, 21)—a beautiful illustration of "infrastructure scaffolding" (Wimsatt and Griesemer 2007, 66).

Of course, we should interrogate these interpretations carefully. For example, were children singled out as needing special treatment? The answer may lie in Assaf's findings from Qesem Cave in Israel, dating to 420,000 years ago. They "suggest that the cave's inhabitants learned and shared knowledge about stone knapping and other adaptive skills throughout the recurrent human occupation of the cave" (2021, 1). Tools may have been traded back and forth and worked by more than one knapper. Experienced knappers might have thereby shared their knowledge, even if indirectly, by allocating previously shaped but not fully exploited cores to their inexperienced counterparts, who then used them as learning tools (Assaf 2021, 1). This seems to be a classic example of Wenger's (1999) *communities of practice*, where a social group shares a common interest and task. With this in mind, it is not hard to imagine children added to the mix with very little alteration in the community's routines, given their likely interest and fluid circumstances. Furthermore, we know from extensive lab study that children practice delayed imitation. They can observe a model and then, at a later time and place, replicate what they observed (Meltzoff and Williamson 2009, 481). However, lab studies with very young children suggest that "infants' attention is inhibited rather than enhanced by a demand to 'look at what I do' . . . explicit teaching may [therefore] not be the best way to help infants learn how to use a new tool" (Fagard et al. 2016, 1, 9).[3]

---

[3] The only non-WEIRD case of adults teaching infants how to use tools was recorded among the Aka by Barry Hewlett (1992, 234).

100 LEARNING WITHOUT LESSONS

Another question might be raised, namely whether children were physically capable of the strength, aim, and finesse to make progress in working stone (Grimm 2000). Hawcroft and Dennell (2000) designed an experimental study with 300 primary school students to measure their readiness for stone tool work. They measured strength, accuracy of aim, sequential design skill, and their ability to extract a given shape from a ball of solid matter. Abilities varied a great deal, but on every task, there were successful children and, universally, "there was . . . a significant improvement in accuracy as age increased" (Hawcroft and Dennell 2000, 96). As Jaffares cogently declares, as children "grow up in a world of tool users, tools became part of the developmental world of young Hominins" (2010, 517).

Learning in the Workshop

One of the major points of contrast between preindustrial and WEIRD societies is that creative work in the former case is conducted largely in public, whereas, in the second, manufacturing, including the processing of harvested crops, is conducted behind closed doors. Generally speaking, children are not welcome in "modern" workshops. For our purposes, a "workshop" is a designated area of the village where certain tasks are routinely carried out, often in groups. Children are usually welcome to observe, to play with cast-off materials, and are eager to respond to requests for assistance, especially to run errands. The workshop might be quite casual and suddenly appear when a quantity of meat or grain needs processing, only to disappear when the work is completed. Work spaces for pottery and weaving or a market stall may be more permanent, involving fixed infrastructure such as a kiln, a standing loom, or a market stand. These species of workshop provide opportunities for children to watch, to playfully imitate, and to "work" materials donated by the artisan, such as a ball of clay, a skein of yarn and toy loom, or their own scaled-down market stall.

Some work places are only partially open to children. This occurs, for instance, in a prohibition on children in proximity to a poison-arrow-making workshop (Blurton-Jones and Marlowe 2002). Many tasks are allocated to one sex only, so in a village where women are the potters, boys may be unwelcome in the pottery workshop. And vice-versa. In a fairly large number of societies, men reside separately from women and children. Boys are eager to be admitted to the sanctuary of the men's house or adolescent dormitory

EVERYDAY CLASSROOMS 101

and begin to learn from other males (Binkley 2006, 106). Kammu (Laos) boys make this transition at age five or six and will then learn from observing and listening to men making and repairing hunting and trapping equipment and retelling the oral history of the tribe. It is there more than in any other place that the boys will learn about their own culture (Tayanin and Lindell 1991, 14).

[Similarly], a Tapirapé (Brazil) boy became: *churangi* (young adolescent) [and] moved from the family dwelling to the *Takana* [which] was the place where adult men worked, and a boy had ample chance to watch them at it . . . he was supposed to learn the male manual arts—how to weave baskets, how to make a bow and straight arrows, how to fabricate the spirit masks that the men wore. . . . However, I never witnessed any express attempt . . . to teach a young boy such pursuits. (Wagley 1977, 149–150)[4]

The ethnographic study of children becoming potters is one of the richest areas of the literature on children learning in the workshop.[5] The principles that emerge from this research match up well with those deduced, more generally, from studying children's learning and contribution to the domestic economy (Lancy 2018, 2022). More importantly, I am struck by numerous parallels to what we have learned from lithic archaeology. First, both stone toolmaking and pottery making require a period of learning and practice to shape an object that matches a model. Second, just as Stone Age children seem to have learned a great deal from handling complete and unfinished tools as well as the by-products, aspirant potters may study broken potsherds to better understand the architecture and design of the vessel (Bunzel 1929; Kelly-Buccellati 2013). Third, archaeologists identify the work of child potters by size (smaller than standard), crudity, and characteristic error patterns, among others (Crown 2002; Králik et al. 2008; Langdon 2013)— the same criteria used in identifying novice stone toolmakers. Fourth, novice potters learn through focused observation of competent potters. Fifth, there are clear indications of development from novice to expert (Wallaert 2008).

---

[4] The Nunamiut Inuit display a closely parallel case (Gubser 1965).

[5] The learning of other crafts can be quite like pottery. In Penan basketmaking, for example, "baskets, motifs and knowledge are widely distributed throughout the community due to its predominantly egalitarian ethos, where most material objects, though claimed by someone, are freely shared, and where production takes place in the open for all to see and imitate if they wish" (Puri 2013, 289).

102 LEARNING WITHOUT LESSONS

> [Aari] daughters who are "ready" to make pots station themselves in front of their mothers so they can watch her every movement . . . the mother may start to make a pot and, after forming the basic shape, will pass it to their daughters to finish. . . . Girls progress—over about four years—from making the smallest, simplest pots to making increasingly larger and more complex pots. . . . Girls set their own pace and decide, on their own, which types to master and . . . make—once they've become competent. (Kaneko 2014, 64–65)

Sixth, pottery making, particularly by women, is conducted in the open, in a relaxed social gathering where even very young children are welcome. "If a woman has to stop to nurse her baby, another will often finish her pot for her, lest it get too dry" (Spindel 1989, 71; see also Köhler 2012). Seventh, children initially engage in pottery making via play, and this is condoned and encouraged by the expert: "A small girl plays with clay, making coils, pinch pots, and miniature animals while her mother builds coils into vessels" (Bowser and Patton 2008, 123). Eighth, there is very little evidence of direct instruction. Puebloan girls in the southwestern United States, for example, took the initiative to learn the craft, observing and imitating their mothers or other competent female relatives. Mature potters spared little time to serve as teachers. "Adults are quoted as stating that children understood the process more thoroughly when they learned through trial and error . . . [progress was] . . . largely driven by the child's interest and skill level" (Crown 2002, 109). Ninth, with only a few exceptions (e.g., formal apprenticeship, Lancy 2012; Wallaert 2008; Chapter 5, this volume), children are rarely compelled to learn nor punished for mistakes. This is true across the ethnographic record, even in societies that may use corporal punishment in other contexts.

Turning to pottery making in archaeological remains, how do we know that children were present and engaged? There are several approaches. First, numerous studies use fingerprints that have been baked into the vessel. Mellor, drawing on samples of thirteenth-century pottery, finds child-sized prints on pots, indicating they were allowed the unskilled task of "transporting freshly thrown vessels from the wheel to the drying area" (2014, 84). Further fingerprint evidence suggested that medieval children were engaged in "attaching the handles to the jugs" (Mellor 2014, 86). Kamp finds from a survey of historic pots in museum collections that "Measuring fingerprints left on them, one can determine that the youngest artisans may have been four years old"

EVERYDAY CLASSROOMS 103

(2002, 87). Dorland, studying collections of Late Woodland pottery, relies on fingernail impressions to establish age (2018).

Another strategy for detecting the involvement of children is to examine the products. Bagwell (2002) argues children's pots were small, poorly made, and served either as toys or as practice pieces or both. More detailed analysis reveals that children's pots exhibit "irregular wall thickness, unintentional asymmetry, manufacturing errors (e.g., drying cracks), omission of traditional steps in construction or decoration, awkward brush handling, irregular and inefficient line-work, sub-standard design, and juvenile fingerprints" (Grubbs et al. 2013, 176).

Studies of prehistoric pottery complement the many studies of contemporary potters. Photos and descriptions depict contemporary potters working in front of their homes or under a shelter, which is largely open. Other components of pottery making that are open to casual inspection include the kiln (which may be shared by several, usually related, potters); a covered drying area for newly made pots; storage facilities for tools used in the process, including objects for shaping, incising, and painting; and, last, the clay source, which may be some distance away.

In some cases, perhaps the majority, two or more women and girls work individually but in close enough proximity to facilitate conversation and mutual childcare. Aspirant potters are welcome to watch and may be given some clay to work:

> Pottery making in Sangopari (Côte d'Ivoire) society is elective and learned through an open, dynamic social process. Learning takes place in the open spaces used by potters.[6] This means several women may serve as models for girls. They, in turn, must take the initiative to observe patiently, to help with menial or routine aspects and to practice diligently. A woman will chase away inattentive or disruptive girls so she can get on with her own work. Women may occasionally offer direction but there is no explanation offered or instruction per se. (Köhler 2012, 128, 131)

From an Atzompa village in Southern Mexico and an Iroquois (Canada) village, we learn:

---

[6] Studies of Late Woodland-period Iroquois suggest that pottery making was a communal affair, and Dorland claims learning in a group with mixed skill levels improves skill acquisition in a learning-through-doing approach (Dorland and Ionico 2020, 24, 26). Iroquois "women made pots, often in a shared space, facilitating girls' learning from multiple role models" (Warrick 1984, 111).

104 LEARNING WITHOUT LESSONS

The role of the teacher is minimized, and learning is seen as consisting primarily of watching how an experienced potter works and trying to imitate her. One girl, who said that she had learned from her mother, went on to qualify her statement, explaining, "We aren't really taught by anyone, because we see it being done all around us from the time we are little." Similar remarks from others indicate the importance of observation. "One notices how it is done . . . I saw how my mother did it and began to work . . . I learned by watching." (Hendry 1992, 101)

There is a wide range of variability in pottery designs across households. The majority of women made pots, often in a shared space, facilitating girls' learning from multiple role models. Multiple longhouse excavations reveal an abundance of immature or crudely made pinch-pots representing the products of young girls. (Warrick 1984, 111)

There is a pervasive notion that one should not waste time attempting to teach someone a craft if they are not ready (Gosselain 2008). "Ready" means being old enough and strong enough to carry out the process, having picked it up through observing and imitating the "basics." And, most importantly, one must demonstrate high motivation to succeed. The future potter must invest in a long-term developmental process. This begins with a "play stage."

Aari (Ethiopia) potters bring their children to the work space, and mothers commonly give small portions of clay to their babies to play with when they cry. Through play, they become familiar with the materials used in pot making while their mothers are concentrating on work (Kaneko 2014). In her study of Puebloan ceramics in museum collections, Kamp found "'toy' figurines and vessels made of clay . . . the youngest artisans were about 4 years old" (2002, 87).

Aside from working with clay, the young potter "earns" the right to participate, even peripherally, by carrying out chores. A seven-year-old Dii (Cameroon) novice helps by fetching clay, water, or wood, thereby "learning the value of hard work" (Wallaert 2008, 188). Another rather menial task performed by novices is to move newly made pots into the shade (Köhler 2012, 131).

Young [Aari] potters also begin to develop their own styles, involving unique sequences of hand and finger movements, even as they are still mastering the basic techniques and concepts. . . . Each potter is said to have their own *aani* (lit. hand), which can be recognized and appreciated by potters and consumers alike. . . . Individuality in pot making is related to the Aari learning process [which] involves the observation of experts (mothers) and, later, individual trial and error learning [which] allows individuals to . . . develop their own unique techniques. (Kaneko 2016, 218, 225–226)

Everyday classrooms are ideal sites[7] in terms of affording pedagogical opportunities for eager-to-learn children. Child autonomy and self-initiated learning are bedrock principles of Indigenous pedagogy. But each case is different, both culturally (learning to hunt with traps requires different skills than spear hunting) and individually (not all children are equally diligent). Up to a point, everyday classrooms can accommodate this variability, but somewhere in the picture there will be older, wiser community members who, unobtrusively, exert influence and guidance to reward and motivate the learner. But take note: since there are no designated "teachers" in charge of the everyday classroom, no one is obligated to provide support for the learner, and overtures for guidance by the would-be apprentice may be soundly rebuffed (Edwards 2005; Reichard 1934).

Everyday classrooms are shaped by various forces: the need to make things, to gather food, to build shelters, to prepare family meals, and to work in a convivial social atmosphere. An interesting question, then, is to ask whether a particular instance has been in any way deliberately shaped to serve pedagogical ends or, alternatively, shaped by the force of eager, persistent learners. Unfortunately, such a process likely unfolds over a considerable time span and is, therefore, beyond the scope of a typical ethnography. In this and the previous two chapters, the focus has been primarily on novices, on the earliest stages of learning. I have provided a series of snapshots of scenes of activity in which the child may be playing various roles from passive onlooker to deep engagement. In the following chapter, I focus on the child as a worker making increasingly significant contributions to the domestic economy. As I hope to show, the prospect of the child becoming a productive contributor to the family engenders a process I have referred to as the "chore curriculum." Here curriculum suggests a subtle, underlying structure or schemata that facilitates a smooth developmental trajectory from the very young novice in early childhood to the reliable worker in middle childhood.

---

[7] I have not exhausted all examples of widely used everyday classrooms. Virtually every child will spend time learning and assisting in the food processing/kitchen area, for example.

5

The Chore Curriculum

Among the Iñupiaq, children provide critical support to the family through their labor. Young people embrace this opportunity to contribute: "They respect[ed] me, because I could do . . . my chores . . . without them telling me. That's my reward [but sometimes] I got reward[ed] with good meals."

—Sprott (2002), 229

Introduction

In my first attempt to review and synthesize the material on children's work, distinctive patterns emerged that crystalized into the expression "chore curriculum" (Lancy 1996, 149). In a second survey, further analysis refined and enhanced the value of the concept (Lancy 2008, 235–242). The term "chore" is somewhat self-evident, except that in contemporary society—at least since 1960 (Rutherford 2011)—we use it to characterize relatively minor tasks, completely peripheral to the "important" work that is done exclusively by adults. However, in the archives of ethnographers and historians (Fajans 1997; West and Petrik 1992), we find that children are expected to assist in a variety of critical areas of domestic and corporate production, including caring for infants, gardening, herding, and foraging (Gallois et al. 2015, 6; Kramer 2014, 52). However, there is a widely acknowledged distinction between the work that all children are *expected* to do (contingent upon age and gender) and realms of endeavor that are optional (contingent upon the child's interest and aptitude). A chore is any task that all or nearly all boys or all girls should master by a roughly agreed-upon age and carry out willingly and efficiently. Among the Kpelle, chores include running errands, fetching water and firewood, tending younger siblings, weeding in the fields, caring for livestock, daubing mud on the walls of houses under construction, sweeping out the compound, and so on (Lancy 1996). Gradually, more demanding and complex tasks emerge in the chore curriculum, consonant with the child's maturity and motivation. Among the universe of needed tasks, there are almost always one or two that are "just right" for a given child's age and strength. Furthermore, most realms of endeavor are conveniently and quite naturally graded in difficulty (Gaskins et al. 2007; Schildkrout 1990, 225).

Unlike many of the tasks that village children aspire to master, the chore inventory is more likely to be considered mandatory. The family functions as the unit of production, or the labor force, if you will. At some level, every member needs to contribute to this effort, contingent on their strength, size, and skill. And, as discussed in Chapter 2, even very young children are eager to "pitch in" and be helpful. This ideal workforce can be somewhat problematic. The Aka are cited as granting children great autonomy and choice in the activities that absorb their time. But the child's preferences may not coincide with family needs. The ubiquitous Aka sib-caretaker may suffer the loss of dinner or a cuff for refusing or failing to take care of a younger sibling (Boyette 2019, 488). But, as Barry Hewlett noted (personal communication, February 18, 2022), Aka children may simply ignore or refuse unwelcome chore assignments (see also Boyette and Lew-Levy 2021, 407–408).

Components of the Chore Curriculum

The term "curriculum" in chore curriculum conveys the idea that there is a discernible regularity to the process whereby children take the initiative to learn, master, and carry out their chores. Most importantly, chores are arranged along several dimensions: some require greater strength or motor skill, while others are assigned largely to girls or boys. There is a well-worn pathway that children reliably follow that leads to useful accomplishments in the short run and gradual development of more advanced skills and assumption of greater responsibility in the long run. Two central principles of the chore curriculum are the motivation of the child, which propels them up the learning gradient, and the nature of the task environment, which reduces the severity of that gradient by offering "steps" or stages. Several examples follow: "A . . . ladder of difficulty [can be] mapped out for young Agta (Philippines) fishers as they begin with shellfish in the shallows move up to small fish speared near the bank to deeper water fishing with a larger spear culminating in the giant mottled eel . . . and we have not observed verbal instruction" (Hagen et al. 2016, 404). Bajau (Indonesia) "sea gypsy" children, modeling the behavior of older peers, move from gathering shoreline

108 LEARNING WITHOUT LESSONS

resources such as crabs and trepangs to paddling small boats to likely fishing spots to free-diving to capture large fish with spear-guns (Kale and Araptarli 2021). We will examine these "ladders" and also consider what ensues when the child is not making the expected progress.

> Toy bows and arrows are typically given to small [Dobe !Kung] children, usually by siblings not much older than themselves. Stationary objects are their first targets. Soon moving ones, such as grasshoppers and beetles, are added. As boys get older, they improve their aim by throwing sticks and wooden spears. Their mastery of animal tracks, like their ability to iden- tify the hundreds of plant and animal species in the environment, is a slow process, acquired through practice and observation. . . . Around the age of twelve, boys are given their first quivers—with small bows and arrows—by their fathers, and begin to shoot birds and rabbits. They may also be taught to set snares. The next step is to accompany their fathers, uncles, and older brothers when they go out to hunt. . . . A boy is likely to kill his first large animal between the ages of fifteen and eighteen. The culture recognizes this event as a milestone and performs two separate ceremonies to celebrate. (Shostak 1981, 83–84)

A child may be steered away from undertaking tasks that are dangerous or difficult and directed to more appropriate endeavors, including play. Often, the guidance is simply to "watch and learn." The learning process depends on an eager, engaged learner and a reasonably competent role model— typically an older peer. The learner is expected to observe and attempt to replicate the chores undertaken by the model. Teaching, per se, is unusual, but guidance can be provided through teasing and shaming or by rebuffing the child's fledgling, unsuccessful forays (Medaets 2016). Explicit praise— "Good job!"—is extremely infrequent. The child's reward is to be included in group activity and to receive assignments of greater difficulty, much like a promotion.

While the academic or core curriculum found in schools is formal and imposed on students in a top-down process, the village chore curriculum is informal and emerges in the interaction of children's need to fit in and em- ulate those older, their developing cognitive and sensorimotor capacity, the division of labor within the family, and the nature of the tasks (chores) them- selves. A related and equally important contrast emerges as we compare the relative flexibility with respect to how well and how quickly the child masters a chore. "The Matsigenka (Lowland Peru) overtly do little to hasten a child's development. Their style is best described as a gradual raising of expectations" (Johnson 2003, 102). Mbendjele (Central African rainforest) "children are not judged by specific standards; they are not expected to grow in some prescribed desirable ways. Learning is to try your best and that is good enough" (Bombjaková 2018, 91). Great variability is expected, in contrast to modern schools where lesson uniformity and "staying on grade level" are paramount.

Another key element in the chore curriculum is the child's eagerness to learn and to "pitch in." Extensive research in experimental psychology (Warneken 2015) as well as cultural anthropology shows clearly that all children, regardless of culture, volunteer to help—without encouragement, explicit reward, or instruction (Lancy 2020). In the ethnographic literature, this is well illustrated in numerous cases of butchering. The process of butchering has the characteristics of an *everyday classroom*, conducted in full view of passersby, led by an expert and their helpers. Junior volunteers initially learn by observing and are then given a more active role. I observed just such a cohort butchering a large sea turtle in a coastal village in Madagascar, as well as several other vivid examples. Among the Runa of tropical Ecuador, a three-year-old came

> forward with water and a knife and assisted a neighbor to butcher a tapir . . . [When queried, his mother insisted] "You shouldn't have to ask for help" . . . In her mind, the anticipation and prompt acknowledgment of others' needs was not at all surprising, but rather the result of careful observation and an indication of "thought." (Mezzenzana 2020, 549)

Children quickly perceive the need for assistance:

> Nayaka (India) children assisted in the butchering and the division of the game: they gathered vessels or plantain leaves and brought them to where the meat was cut; they held a torch if the butchering took place at night; they held the animal's limbs to ease its cutting; they monitored the equal distribution of meat chunks between families, and then distributed the meat accordingly. (Bird-David 2015, 96)

In the remainder of this chapter, my goal is to catalog both the variety and regularity inherent in the chore curriculum.

110 LEARNING WITHOUT LESSONS

The Path to Mastery

Gerd Spittler's report on his study of Tuareg (Niger) nomadic pastoralists offers an extended example of the chore curriculum at work. For boys, the ultimate achievement is to pilot a camel caravan across a vast, empty desert. He notes that "there is no systematic instruction, no institutionalized apprenticeship" (Spittler 1998, 238). The curriculum begins in play. A girl or boy is given a baby goat or camel as a pet. Play evolves into care. By age three, a child will join a group of older children rounding up the herd for the evening and see they are corralled and fed. This is a daily chore and provides, as a bonus, the chance to learn the structure of the herd, their names, and their preferred grazing areas. Somewhat older boys will transition from goats to the more challenging camel herd. Their first chore will be to feed baby camels and prevent them from nursing, preserving the milk for humans.

At age ten, a boy leaves his home to join a Sahara caravan. Initially, not much is expected of him. His main responsibility is to pay close attention to what others are doing and saying. He proves his bona fides by helping to get water and wood, making the fire, holding the milking pot during milking, pegging out the young camels, and so on. At the age of thirteen, he shepherds camels by himself. He knows each animal well and can read tracks in the desert. Should he need guidance, he will seek it from older boys, not men, who might react with contempt. From here on, he continues to develop as a caravanner and, if sufficiently motivated and knowledgeable, may become a caravan leader (Spittler 1998).

A more modest but also vital assignment is learning to use a mortar and pestle—a task children have seen carried out adjacent to their house every night of the week. I observed (Lancy 1996) a group of Kpelle three- to four-year-old girls gathered in a circle. Each had a mound of sand and a stick, about a meter in length. Singing songs, they practiced driving their "pestles" into the mortar (sand pile). On other occasions, I observed a slightly older child using a wooden mortar and pestle, scaled to size. Rather than rice, the mortar contained weedy seed heads so that if an accident occurred, there would be no loss of food. I photographed a girl of about six years old pounding actual grain in an undersized mortar, in sync with an older girl, likely her sister, using the full-size mortar. Bril observed, "Girls are literally in synch with their role models. For example, studies demonstrate a young Malian girl's ability to match the rhythm and stroke of an older partner in joint pounding of grain in a mortar and pestle" (Bril 1986, 322).

THE CHORE CURRICULUM   111

Bamana children learning to use a short-handled hoe to prepare and plant millet furrows also proceed in stages. Polak identifies a key element in this process:

> Four-year-old Bafin has already grasped the meaning of sowing and is able to perform the various movements . . . he is entrusted with an old hoe as well as with some seeds so that he can gain some practice in this activity. However, . . . he has to be allocated a certain part of the field where he neither gets in the way of the others nor spoils the rows they have already sown. (Polak 2003, 126, 129)

Slight adjustments to the usual routines may be made to mitigate the effects of the child's inexperience.

With respect to learning hunting, a précis is available for the Western Apache. Children were kept from roaming beyond the camp until age eight but then quickly learned to shoot small game with sling or bow and arrow. They joined enthusiastically in communal quail drives. At twelve their tracking and hunting prowess yielded prey (rabbits, quail, wood rats), which they were proud to bring back to camp. For their first deer hunt, at fifteen or sixteen, a boy would be permitted to accompany an older male relative who acted as a role model. One earned the right to tag along (and observe) by fetching wood and water for the temporary hunting camp (Goodwin and Goodwin 1942, 475). Similarly, Inuit boys of ten were brought along on seal hunts to handle the dogs and to observe the hunt (Matthiasson 1979, 74). Omura offers a firsthand account of an Inuit hunting party.

> I accompanied them many times . . . skillful hunters rarely instruct teenagers directly or verbally on how to handle subsistencerelated tools such as rifles, harpoons, spears, nets, ropes . . . teenagers usually complete their tasks without any direction from more skilled hunters, instead judging from events what to do next. In most cases, they collaborate without saying anything, except for exchanging pleasant jokes [trusting] teenagers [will] learn . . . through observation or by trial and error while helping skillful hunters in subsistence activities. (Omura 2016, 279)

Even with change in the village economy, such as the introduction of cash crops, children's work remains crucial. For example, in the Guatemalan coffee industry, children make varied and critical contributions that vary with age

112 LEARNING WITHOUT LESSONS

and competence. The youngest plant seeds in small plastic bags to germinate new plants; they also collect coffee cherries that have fallen to the ground at harvest. Somewhat older children are responsible for weeding and spreading chalk. Twelve- to fifteen-year-old boys are responsible for spraying urea as a fertilizer and assisting with the trimming, which may involve climbing plants to lop off branches with a machete. All help with harvesting and sorting the cherries. Agile boys are only too happy to climb into the branches to collect fruit that adults cannot reach (Ruiz 2011, 169–171; see also de Suremain 2000). The principles of learning inherent to the chore curriculum readily transfer to a new industry.

In the following sections, connections between play and the chore curriculum are drawn, but the reader will have noted the contrast with postindustrial society, where play is heavily populated with imaginary characters, places, and activities. The underlying paradox is that, while it is clear from their exuberant and positive affect that village children are playing "for the fun of it," the activities, ideas, and artifacts that are often gathered to construct a play bout are borrowed wholesale from the work activity and social relations of familiar adults.

The Play Stage

The role of play in children's acquisition of their culture was discussed in the previous chapter but is particularly salient to the chore curriculum. Ethnographic descriptions of work activity enacted in make-believe and object play are rich and varied and even include archaeologists' reconstructions of childhood based on the discovery of miniature or crudely made artifacts or toys (Park 2006, 56–57). In the domestic sphere, we see children playing at food preparation, cooking, and feeding the family (Hogbin 1970, 137). In these vignettes, we occasionally get a glimpse of development over time in children's conceptualization of the world of work and of their place in it. In the following example, we see that the gender divide in work—men and women have differing assignments in the domestic economy—is initially established in make-believe play:

When [very young Kaoka-Guadalcanal] pretend to keep house they make no sexual distinction in the allocation of the tasks. Boys and girls together

THE CHORE CURRICULUM   113

erect the shelters, plait the mats, cook the food, and fetch the water. But within a year or so, although they continue to play in company, the members of each group restrict themselves to the work appropriate to their sex. The boys leave the cooking and water carrying to the girls, who, in turn, refuse to help with the building. (Hogbin 1969, 38)

On Wogeo Island (PNG), Hogbin observed this scene:

Wanai was now busily making mud pies and at this point begged Kalasika to build her an oven where these might be cooked. Gwa joined in the game, and, although no fire was kindled, the grubby mess was wrapped in leaves and put into the middle of a pile of stones. Wanai next made out that her water bottles were empty and told Naibula to fill them. "No, that's women's work," said Gwa. "We men don't touch such things. You go yourself." (Hogbin 1946, 276)

Another factor that contributes to the developmental and pedagogical value of the chore curriculum is the low threshold the child must cross in order to participate. Rather than learning the rudiments of cooking, fire, and food preparation (involving sharp knives) by plunging in—with the threat of spoiling the meal or hurting oneself—playfully "rehearsing" these activities enhances the likelihood of a successful debut in the actual kitchen. Goody (1992) describes a continuum from make-believe to "for real" food preparation in which older children model for younger ones, real but scaled-down pots may substitute for toy pots, and, if mother's willing, edible ingredients go into the pot rather than grass.

In all the cases listed in Box 5.1, adults provide resources and encouragement, signaling to the child that their play is culturally "approved" and that it contributes to the learning of critical skills. As described in the section that follows, adults may also convey their estimate of the child's progress via the donation of materials and by encouraging the child to "pitch in."

Running Errands

Margaret Mead, reporting on her first field study in Samoa, provides one of the earliest characterizations of the centrality of work in childhood.

Box 5.1 The Play Stage

"In Kusasi (Northern Ghana) pottery-making, the first contact with clay and pottery modeling . . . takes place in a ludic (play) context . . . some children play with clay and make objects which reproduce, symbolize and imitate activities carried out by adults. It is therefore an imitative process lacking explicit impositions by adults both in the final result and regarding the technical processes that children automatically generate to make them" (Trias et al., 2015, 94).

Inuit "girls make dolls out of scraps of skin and clothe them like real men and women. Their mothers encourage them, for it is in this way that they learn to sew and cut out patterns" (Jenness 1922, 219).

On Fais Island, Micronesia, an older family member "makes a precisely detailed meter-long outrigger canoe for a young boy who will spend many hours playing with it. Boys are also given scaled down fishing poles" (Rubenstein 1979, 185).

Hadza boys "get their first bows by about three years old and thereafter spend hours every day in target practice, often shooting at a gourd on the ground" (Marlowe 2010, 157).

In the Arctic, "boys and girls play at building snow houses . . . they borrow their parents' snow knives and make complete houses on a miniature scale" (Jenness 1922, 219).

Among the Chabu in the Ethiopian Highlands, boys are given scaled-down spears, are encouraged to engage in play hunting and listen to the stories told by hunters, and are urged "to go to the forest" (Dira and Hewlett 2016, 77).

Among the Siberian Khanty, children may build scale models—of buildings, skis, canoes, baskets, anoraks—before attempting a full-scale replication (Jordan 2014, 164).

The tiniest little staggerer has tasks to perform—to carry water, to borrow fire brands, to fetch leaves to stuff the pig . . . learning to run errands tactfully is one of the first lessons of childhood . . . these slighter tasks are laid aside for harder ones as soon as the child becomes strong enough or skilled enough. (Mead 1928, 633)

THE CHORE CURRICULUM   115

As a theme running throughout this text, an essential component of the domestic economy is that, aside from infants, *everyone contributes*. Sustaining home and community is the responsibility of every member. But, like the academic curriculum, the domestic economy can be viewed as a kind of job roster, where child workers are comfortably eased into tasks that are essential but also within their capability. Errand running is very frequently cited as "children's work."

Running errands nicely illustrates key characteristics of the chore curriculum. Children, at least when they are very young, have a powerful need to become competent (White 1959), fit in (de Waal 2001), strive for success (Weisfeld and Linkey 1985), be helpful (Rheingold 1982), and emulate those more senior (Bandura 1977). Children stand ready to accept responsibility (Edel 1957/1996), and the most elementary chore may be errand running. "Between eighteen and thirty months of age . . . the Guara (Venezuela) child begins to act independently as a messenger . . . Carrying water and firewood are the first daily chores regularly performed" (Ruddle and Chesterfield 1977, 31).

Fetching and carrying is naturally developmental. "Very young children (age 3) may start with one or two sticks of wood, or yams in a carry net, but by age 8 they are carrying firewood, water, produce and messages" (Zeller 1987, 544). A barely mobile toddler may be asked to carry a cup from its mother across an evening family circle to its father. The same toddler will tag along as an older sibling makes a longer delivery excursion, in effect, serving as an understudy. Errands can vary by length and territory; between close kin and relative strangers; can involve loads of varying size and fragility; or include an exchange of some kind, such as a market transaction. Adults match their assignments to the child's size and level of skill, and each new assignment ratifies (and motivates) the child's growing competence. Here is an example from Guatemala:

> The simplest and earliest task for which children are given actual responsibility is the running of errands, transporting objects to or from people's homes or going to a local shop for a few cents' worth of goods. Considerably more difficult are the errands to the maize fields or other errands that require the child to go outside the community. Selling various items in the community may range in complexity from approximately the status of an errand to the cognitively complex task of soliciting buyers from anywhere in the community and of making change. (Nerlove et al. 1974, 276)

116 LEARNING WITHOUT LESSONS

The stalwart little helper publicly advertises the quality of its upbringing and its worthiness as a potential foster child, enhancing the family reputation. For the Chewa, "to be 'sent' on such an errand is an opportunity for a child to enhance, as well as demonstrate, competence" (Serpell and Hatano 1997, 351–352). On the other hand, children are favored as errand runners "because adolescents or adults seen in proximity to a neighbor's house might be suspected of adultery, theft or witchcraft. And boys are favored because their virtue isn't as fragile as girls" (Lancy 2008, 238). Learning to become an errand runner comes naturally as children observe and replicate the process with only minor guidance from an older sibling role model.

Anthropologists often note with some degree of awe how early a child embarks on the chore curriculum, making a significant contribution to the domestic economy.[1] I have often observed youngsters, no older than five, carrying and looking after infants (see also Ottenberg 1968, 80; Kale and Aslan 2020, 11). In most Indigenous societies, very young children can be assigned tasks within their reach, such as errand running (see Box 5.2).

From Playing to Working

Girls may find that their freedom and opportunity to play is curtailed by their mother's need for a "helper at the nest" (Turke 1988). The mother becomes the model and supervisor of the girl's progress through the chore curriculum. As Riesman notes, by the time a young woman is pregnant, she has had years of watching her mother and others care for infants, and she herself has logged many hours of childcare under the watchful (and critical) eye of her mother and other senior female relatives (1992, 111). A Kpelle girl accompanies her mother to the garden, carrying a pail that has their lunch. At the field, she watches her mother hoe until given her own small hoe to try. She matches her mother's behavior, learning the moves through repeated practice and observation (Lancy 1996, 144). If a Mazahua mother has a market stall, her daughter will "pitch in" to assist her by trimming onions and tying them into bundles, using her mother's bundles as a model. She is eager to set up "her" stand and, once the mother's stand is established, does so using an abandoned piece of cardboard (Paradise and Rogoff 2009, 113).

---

[1] A wildly popular Japanese serial documentary follows very young (two- to six-year-old) children as they walk to the local supermarket from their middle-class homes. They travel along highway-side paths up to a kilometer each way, carrying a yellow warning flag to halt traffic at intersections. Since they can't read, they must memorize the shopping list, successfully navigate a large supermarket, and pay for their purchases. The program, called *Old Enough*, is available on Netflix, and a British version is in the works (Heritage 2022).

Box 5.2 The Errand Stage

On Raroia, a four-year-old, outfitted with suitably sized container, may make as many as ten trips a day carrying water from the community cistern to his home (Danielsson 1952, 121).

On Dominica Island, "children as young as five often run errands to find specific medicinal herbs from their home gardens, from neighbors, or even growing wild around the village" (Quinlan and Quinlan 2007, 173).

Among the Hadza, children's groups forage in the vicinity of camp while their parents are gone on longer expeditions. From four years of age, they successfully gather baobab fruits, tubers, and small birds and mammals, providing up to 25 percent of their daily diet (Marlowe 2010, 156; see also Tucker and Young 2005, 169).

Kramer, studying the Pumé (Venezuelan hunter-gatherers) found girls and boys of eleven or older gathering a significant portion of the family's food, while three- to six-year-olds were gathering usable amounts of fish, fruit, and tubers (2021, 18–19).

"The Martu are foragers in Australia's Western Desert. Desert-born adults recall a childhood spent foraging with other children to keep themselves fed" (Bird and Bird 2005, 135).

It is rarer to find boys paired so closely with their fathers. Children are often considered too boisterous to serve as companions on fishing (Broch 1990, 85) and hunting (Puri 2005, 233; Reyes-García et al. 2009, 283) expeditions. A Yanomami boy will not be welcomed on the hunt by his father until he is in his mid-teens and has already developed considerable expertise at tracking and knows the forest and its inhabitants intimately (Peters 1998, 90). Fathers are often absent from the homestead and unavailable as role models. Or, the nature of their work, such as felling trees to clear land for a farm, precludes a youngster from "pitching in."

Contrary to prevailing Western views on play, children may actually prefer to work when given the chance (Lew-Levy and Boyette 2018; Taggart et al. 2018). In fact, not all chores are foreshadowed in play. Little girls may be caring for an infant sibling in lieu of playing with a doll, for example (Broch 1990, 110), or assisting mother in a market stall in lieu of pretending to market (Paradise and Rogoff 2009, 113). The preference for work over play is widespread (see Box 5.3).

Box 5.3 Playing Becomes Working

Playing with a small gourd, a child learns to balance it on his head and is applauded when he goes to the watering place with the other children and brings it back with a little water in it. As he learns, he carries an increasing load, and gradually the play activity turns into a general contribution to the household water supply (Edel 1957/1996, 177).

"After watching Hadza 3- to 4-year-olds playing a while, one eventually realizes that children are not just playing but are actually digging small tubers and eating them . . . Foraging simply emerges gradually from playing . . . It involves a natural interest on the part of the young child watching older people forage and imitating them" (Marlowe 2010, 156).

"The extensive time Yucatec Mayan children spend in playing is not an indication they value play above work, but, rather, that their work abilities remain marginal and they turn to play when they are excluded from work... Thus, although play is a significant activity in children's lives, it is not the most highly valued even for children as young as four" (Gaskins et al. 2007, 193).

To guide and motivate the child, she/he may be given their own scaled-down collecting calabash, hoe, or machete. A Baining (PNG) five-year-old may be assigned his/her own garden plot, the harvest from which "belongs to" the gardener (Fajans 1997, 92; see also Hogbin 1970, 139–140).

In several Central African communities, systematic observation indicated that children preferred to use actual subsistence tools (e.g., machetes, knives, baskets, axes, nets) whenever available (Fouts et al. 2016, 687).

"Q'eqchi' children are encouraged to take on certain tasks only if adults think they are ready and able to do them properly. Until they reach that point, they are not usually assisted in the sense of 'scaffolding' or guided participation... by the time they get to the point of actually doing a certain task so that they make a real contribution, they are able to do so with little instruction because they have observed it so many times before" (Zarger 2002b, 120).

These findings from field studies have received support from recent US studies (Taggart et al. 2018). A sample of one hundred children, aged three to six, were asked to choose between pretend and real versions of nine different activities, and justifications for their choices were recorded. When given a choice, preschool-age children overwhelmingly preferred real activities to their pretend equivalents, 65 percent to 35 percent. Sixty-nine percent preferred to bake actual cookies rather than pretend to make cookies; 60 percent preferred to cut real vegetables with a paring knife; 66 percent preferred actual fishing; 74 percent preferred to feed a live baby, and so on. Children's preference for real activities appeared between three and four years of age, and then was constant through age six. Children said they preferred real activities because they are functional, useful, and provide novel experiences. When children preferred pretend activities, the most cited reasons were being afraid of the real, lack of ability, and lack of permission. I believe that the Western, educated, industrialized, rich, democratic (WEIRD) child-rearing model has misled parents (and professionals) into thinking that children prefer play over work, or that play is somehow more appropriate for them (Lancy 2017b).

Play in the village is much more focused and purposeful than play in post-industrial society. Our children are not necessarily moving toward a future profession. Their play may have no connection to solving practical problems either in the home or at school. In the village, play seems to follow a particular trajectory. However immature and crude the child's activity, the underlying raison d'être can be teased out of their actions and speech.

> At the age of five or six, Atzompa girls begin to take an interest in pottery making. . . . With a heap of stones and a few wisps of straw, they will go through the motions of glazing, stacking, firing, and unpacking the kiln, identifying the various steps as they manipulate their creations. . . . The clay itself, with its plastic qualities, can be an intriguing plaything. In one household I came across a child of six trying to make an *olla* like her mother's. She was happily engaged in smearing clay onto a mold and rolling out lumpy strips, which she asserted were to be the walls of her pot. . . . Children first learn to make tiny *apaxtles* or *cazuelas* and . . . progress will consist mainly of working up to the larger sizes. Their early products are apt to be lopsided and uneven, and it is usually two or three months before they can manufacture anything that is judged fit to be sold. (Hendry 1992, 101–102)

In a second illustration of this development from play to work, I was able to observe the "canoe curriculum." Ifaty village in SW Madagascar depends, primarily, on marine resources, and a modest-sized outrigger sailing canoe is the primary means of accessing such resources as well as marketing them.

120 LEARNING WITHOUT LESSONS

Virtually all adult males use such canoes almost daily. On the beach and in the shallows, I observed (almost simultaneously) the following: a two-year-old splashing alone in a tide pool, learning about water; three boys around age five clambering over a beached canoe, learning an agile dance from thwart to gunwale; two boys about seven, independently preparing and then sailing model canoes, making appropriate adjustments to sail angle and rudder; two boys of eight playing with an abandoned outrigger in the shallows—they climbed on, paddled it, capsized it, and took turns as captain and mate; when two young men began to rig and prepare to launch a full-size outrigger, the two boys paddled over to watch this unfold; and shortly after they sailed away, a boy of about ten came paddling in to shore in a half-size canoe. Based on previous and more thorough studies of the canoe curriculum (Pomponio 1992; Morelli 2013; Wilbert 1976), I am confident that these playful experiences prepare boys to become mariners with little need for any formal instruction.

Role Models

A widespread observation is that children are cared for by a variety of alloparents, and often these are older siblings. Again, as with so many chores, the young "child-minder" will transition to the role of playmate and organizer of play and games and then to an influential and competent role model in group or joint work activity. If I were discussing contemporary bourgeoisie society, this section might be labeled "Teachers." But, as analysis reveals (Lancy 2010a), active, child-centered *instruction* is quite rare outside contemporary WEIRD society. Rather, as children assume responsibility for learning their culture, they rely on those more expert to serve largely in the capacity of models (see Box 5.4). Again, contrary to contemporary views on what is "natural" (Lancy 2010b), the model is as likely to be an older sibling or peer as a parent, especially for boys (Weisner and Gallimore 1977).

There are probably several reasons for the choice of peers as role models. From an early age, children are placed under the care of older siblings who introduce them into the neighborhood playgroup (e.g., "Mayan toddlers learn primarily by observing and interacting with their sibling caretakers"—Maynard 2002, 978). At the threshold of the chore curriculum, children are far more likely to be in the company of peers than parents. Weisner notes that "children care for other children within *indirect chains of support*" (1996, 308,

THE CHORE CURRICULUM   121

Box 5.4 Peers as Role Models

By imitating their sib-caretakers, Marquesan "toddlers learn to run, feed and dress themselves, go outside to urinate and defecate, and help with household chores" (Martini and Kirkpatrick 1992, 124).

Fore children are expected to focus their attention as learners on older children, not adults. "If, for example, an older boy climbed a vine, a younger would tend to copy his movements in an attempt to do likewise" (Sorenson 1976, 198).

"Little [Bengali] girls accompany older girls in gathering, and they gradually learn the needed skills" (Rohner and Chaki-Sircar 1988, 33).

Meriam children from "age 6 forage in groups with older children, observing intently their prey choice and processing strategies through play and experimenting with various reef activities" (D. W. Bird and R. B. Bird 2002, 291).

"Young Q'eqchi' Maya (Belize) boys trap birds in the forest, providing a supplement to the protein intake of their families. They build traps from wood or sticks, in the shape of boxes. The birds come along in search of the seeds, bump the stick and are trapped. Knowledge of bird trapping is passed on from older to younger brothers" (Zarger 2002b 125).

---

emphasis added). That is, toddlers are managed by slightly older siblings, who are, in turn, guided by adolescents, while adults serve as rather distant "foremen" for the activity, concentrating primarily on their own more productive or profitable activity. This phenomenon is well illustrated in Polak's study of Bamana families engaged in bean cultivation (Polak 2003, 2011). Lab research with preschoolers in the United States suggests they "actively evaluate their teachers both for the knowledge they have and their ability to demonstrate it" (Bonawitz et al. 2011, 328). And there's considerable evidence that siblings are more patient and sympathetic mentors than adults (Maynard and Tovote 2010). A contrasting pair of anecdotes is very revealing. Raum observed a Chaga mother and her little daughter cutting grass to take home to feed the cattle. Tying the stalks into a bundle is difficult, but the "mother refuses requests for help by saying: 'Haven't you got hands like me?'" (1940, 199). Now consider a vignette of Pushtun children gathering and bundling shrubs (*buti*) to bring home.

Khodaydad, aged about ten years, showed and explained to his younger brother Walidad (aged about two and a half years) how to put *buti* together: He made up a small pile while Walidad squatted next to him and watched. Tying them together, he explained how to do it. Then he untied the bundle and bound it up again to show how it was done. Walidad then wanted to carry it home. His elder brother helped him shoulder it and his sister guided him home, and it was obvious that little Walidad was very proud of being able to accomplish the work. (Casimir 2010, 54)

Lew-Levy and colleagues have carried out observational studies of children foraging in groups of mixed-age juveniles. In two African societies, historically dependent on foraging, the BaYaka and Hadza both indicate high levels of learning from older siblings and playmates, especially in comparison to learning from adults (Lew-Levy et al. 2020; personal communication, February 11, 2019).

To conclude, I would stress that the onus is on the *learner* to actively seek knowledge and skill. The model is usually rather passive and may refuse to engage with the learner if they are perceived as lacking motivation and engagement. Hence, Bolin's description of learning to weave in the Andes is probably normative. "Children are not taught to spin or weave. Rather, they observe family members who have mastered these crafts and imitate them directly" (2006, 99). As Bolin suggests, the child likely draws on numerous models for guidance and inspiration, not just a single role model (see also Gosselain 2008, 153; Puri 2005, 280; Coy 1989b, 120; Aronson 1989).

Strategic Intervention

While lessons are a great rarity, the child's family is certainly aware of the learner's progress and may intervene, strategically, as a facilitator (see Box 5.5). For example, the "knowledge gained from [Meriam] adults about the reef and how to forage remains limited mainly to what is edible and what is dangerous" (D. W. Bird and R. B. Bird 2002, 291). "Sickles and knives are used expertly by many Taira 6-year-olds. Bandaged fingers and numerous little scars are evidence of learning and experimentation. Occasionally an adult will say, 'Hold the sickle this way so you don't get hurt'" (Maretzki and Maretzki 1963, 511). The path to mastery may be obstructed by the occasional "speed bump."

THE CHORE CURRICULUM   123

Box 5.5 Strategic Intervention

For Warao boys learning to make canoes, the sine qua non of survival, "there is not much verbal instruction . . . but the father does correct the hand of his son [and demonstrates] how to overcome the pain in his wrist from working with the adze" (Wilbert 1976, 323).

In Bamana (Mali) farming, some tasks are relatively easy to master, others, such as learning to plant millet seeds, may require an adult to demonstrate the correct procedure and relieve the boy's frustration (Polak 2011, 84–86).

"Nayaka [India] men and women avoid any kind of direct teaching, even between parents and children. [Boys] learn through observation of expert trappers and much trial and error but, on one occasion, ten-year-old Rajan was attempting, not too successfully, to replicate his father's trap. The father looked on benignly, and, without a word of criticism or instruction, took Rajan's trap apart and reassembled it so it would work properly" (Naveh 2016, 127–128).

Nine-year-old Hadza forager Abiba, digging to extract tubers, "encounters a large stone and struggles to get it out. . . . Without saying a word, her mother sits next to her and places a wedge stone under her digging stick . . . to lever the stone away . . . Abiba can now continue digging" (Boesch 2013, 145; see also Crittenden 2016, 67).

Conambo mothers may take their daughter's ill-formed ceramic vessel, reshape it, and hand it back to the child to decorate (Bowser and Patton 2008).

A Zinacantan weaver will "take over the weaving [from her daughter] at the more technically difficult parts of the process" (Greenfield 1984, 30).

"Verbal instruction was observed when mothers showed [Agta] girls how to distinguish plants with edible tubers from similar-looking plants, a difficult part of the learning process" (Hagen et al. 2017, 401).

Vermonden observed a Butonese novice having difficulty "attaching the last mesh of the *pani*, the 'wing' of the trap . . . This was corrected by a more experienced fisherman" (2009, 213).

124 LEARNING WITHOUT LESSONS

I would emphasize that direct intervention in a child's fledgling attempts is rare, in large part because Indigenous pedagogy, as I have indicated previously, stresses the need for children's autonomy. Also note that, compared to WEIRD practice, guidance or strategic intervention includes little or no verbalization by expert or learner.

Work and Identity

It is not enough to acknowledge that children are kept busy doing chores or that being helpful makes them "fit in." The very identity of the child may be largely defined in terms of the work that they do. Throughout human history, children have been seen as an investment. Parents have them and raise them so that their labor can support the household (Clark 1994; Kramer 2005) and, eventually, provide an old-age pension or social security (Horn and Martens 2009, 43). Among the severely impoverished Papel in Guinea-Bissau, infant mortality is extremely high; roughly one-third of all children born alive will die before they reach the age of five. In spite of these dire statistics, and the fact that women work extremely hard to eke out a bare survival, Jónína Einarsdóttir found that mothers were not interested in reducing their fertility; on the contrary, they wanted as many children as possible. They operated on the assumption that the more you have, the more likely there will be a few who survive and will "help with work, contribute to their emotional well-being, take care of them in old age, secure them a respectable funeral, and ease their entrance into the afterlife" (Einarsdóttir 2004, 86). A Kpelle mother asserts: "What makes a child good? If you ask her to bring water, she brings water. If you ask her to cook, she cooks, if you tell her to mind the baby, she does it. When you ask her to plant rice, she doesn't complain" (Lancy 1996, 76).

It is a foundational principle in many societies that the more a child contributes to the domestic economy through doing chores, the higher their social standing. As examples: "When a Nuer boy tethers the cattle and herds the goats . . . cleans the byres and spreads the dung to dry and collects it and carries it to the fires [then] *he is considered a person*" (Evans-Pritchard 1956, 146, emphasis added). Iatmul children's ability and willingness to work "increases both their standing and their independence" (Weiss 1993, cited in Leibel 2004, 83).

In some societies, the association between chores and identity is even more explicit. Among the Giriama, a two- to three-year-old is labeled, in effect, "water carrier." An eight-year-old girl is defined as a "maize pounder"; a boy of the same age is *muhoho murisa*, "herd boy" (Wenger 1989, 98). In premodern Russia, "our plowboy," "our herd boy," and "our nanny girl" were habitual terms parents used to address their children (Gorshkov 2009, 15). Among the Tchokwé, "children are identified through the roles they assume [for example] *kambumbu* are children . . . who help parents in the field or with fishing and hunting" (Honwana 2014, 41–42). The Savras recognize five stages in human development and name them according to the primary chores carried out at that age (Mohammad 1997).

Briggs argues that the Inuit have no developmental timetable. Progress is marked by the mastery of skills (a first duck egg collected, a pair of mittens made, a first ptarmigan or rabbit shot). These skills are not acquired at any particular age or stage but when the child decides to pursue them; success is duly acknowledged. Young people are considered ready for marriage not when they have reached a certain age but when they have acquired the necessary skills and can make a living (Briggs 1991, 269).

Aside from nomenclature that marks the child's developmental progression as a worker, we find a few examples of adults turning these transitions into minor rites of passage (see Box 5.6).

A brief digression: I had an epiphany as I wrote this chapter that nowhere in the ethnographic record had I run across any mention of parents or others attempting to increase a child's "self-esteem." Since the 1970s, self-esteem has been one of the cornerstones of the WEIRD parenting model. In an ethnographic study of self-esteem in the United States, parents described elaborate stratagems for buttressing their child's ego (Miller and Cho 2018). As should be clear from the discussion so far, in Indigenous communities, children acquire a full measure—no need for supplementary praise and reward—of affirmation and encouragement through diligent adherence to the chore curriculum. As recently as 1946, US authorities were urging parents to engage children in household chores. The rationale was as follows:

> The fundamental objective is to provide the child with a home, a family circle, of which he feels himself to be a cooperative member. . . . The more he plays on the home team—the more he runs errands for it, makes beds for it,

126 LEARNING WITHOUT LESSONS

Box 5.6 Noting Milestones in the Chore Curriculum

A Kaoka (Guadalcanal) boy's first pig (Hogbin 1969, 39).

"A peasant child from NE Brazil, upon reaching the age of eight, would receive the present of a hoe from his father. The hoe given to a child of this age was special for being smaller and lighter than one used by an adult . . . The receiving of one's first hoe in this way [is] a *rite of passage*" (Mayblin 2010, 34–35, emphasis is added).

A Netsilik (Arctic) girl's first-caught salmon and her brother's first goose are acknowledged by the community (Balikci 1970, 45).

Among the Saami of northern Europe, there are no rites of passage or acknowledgment of any kind for a growing girl until she completes her first pair of reindeer shoes or some other complex needlework (Pelto 1962).

"When an [Mbuti] boy kills his first 'real animal,' he is immediately acclaimed as a hunter . . . [and honored by cicatrization] . . . an operation performed . . . by one of the 'great hunters' " (Turnbull 1965, 257).

BiYaka "boys between the ages of five and eight are honored by a dance (*ekobo*) when they capture their first rodent" (Neuwelt-Truntzer 1981, 136).

"A Lapp boy receives his first leather belt and knife (and a fur edging to his winter hat) at the age of eight, when he is able to lead a reindeer ox to the pasture" (Itkonen and Minn 1948, 599).

> cooks for it, mows the lawn for it, really cooperates—the more it will mean to him. Therefore, he should not be spared chores. (Rutherford 2011, 93)

But chores have steadily declined, since the middle of the last century, as an important component of childhood (see Chapter 7), and (I'm proposing) no chores = low self-esteem.

Chores also play a major role in the differentiation of gender, especially before the appearance of secondary sex characteristics. Among the Kel Ewey Tuareg, goats are tended by boys and girls, but only boys tend camels (Spittler 1998). The Tarong equivalent of the camel, tended only by boys, is the *carabao* or water buffalo (Whiting and Edwards 1988, 224). In West Africa, weaving is the province of women among Akwete Igbo, and three-year-old girls are busy at pretend weaving, eventually picking up the skill through

THE CHORE CURRICULUM   127

watching and helping their mothers (Aronson 1989). For the Baulè, males weave, and boys acquire the skill through a lengthy, formal apprenticeship (Aronson 1989). Stereotypically, among Hadza foragers, girls forage and boys hunt (Marlowe 2010). Almost universally, girls are preferred as caretakers for younger siblings, and sons are conscripted for this chore only when a daughter is unavailable (Ember 1973, 425–426).[2] Indeed, it is common to see two clusters of children in open areas of the village or farm (e.g., the "mother ground," Lancy 1996, 9; Chapter 4, this volume). Girls gather together in a corner with their young charges, playing in a subdued fashion. Boys, however, roam more widely, engage in a panoply of games, some quite noisy and boisterous, and seem, generally, carefree (Read 1960, 82).

The Kerkenneh Islands are typical in transitioning girls into responsible roles well before boys: "By the age of four most little girls have some real responsibility in the household. Little boys are babied longer and are discouraged from imitating their mothers because that is women's work" (Platt 1988, 282). Indeed, boys in many societies are defined as much by their freedom from work, relative to girls, as by the specific work they do (Edwards 2005).

"Getting Sense" in Middle Childhood

Children before the age of five, roughly, are too immature to really absorb important lessons. However, a survey of fifty societies confirmed that there are two common transitions in children's development, at five to seven years and at puberty, when new duties are assigned (Rogoff et al. 1975). The ethnographic record is replete with references to this transition, usually in identifying a major change in the child's cognitive level. Here is how the Inuit express it:

> *Isuma* refers to consciousness, thought, reason, memory, will—to cerebral processes in general—and the possession of *isuma* is a major criterion of maturity. Saying that a person has *isuma* is equivalent to saying that she or he exercises good judgment, reason, and emotional control at all times, in addition to the skills appropriate to his or her age, gender, and role. Particularly important is control of anger, an emotion that ideally should never be admitted or acted on. The possessions of *isuma* entitles a person

---

[2] A significant exception to this generalization occurs in a few highly egalitarian foraging societies in Central Africa (Henry et al. 2005, 200).

128 LEARNING WITHOUT LESSONS

> to be treated as an autonomous, that is, self-governing, individual whose decisions and behavior should not be directed, in any way, outside the limits of the role requirements to which one is expected to conform. (Briggs 1991, 267)

In siSwati, the language spoken by the Swazi, the word for intelligence, *hlakaníphile*, is closely associated with the ability to complete tasks well after watching others complete the tasks (Booth 2002). "When the BaYaka child cooperates, it means he's intelligent [*mayele*]. A child who doesn't do it isn't intelligent yet" (Boyette and Lew-Levy 2021, 411). The child has reached a point in their development where they start to "get noticed" (Lancy and Grove 2011a) due to their evident intelligence or common sense, referred to among the Kipsigis as *ng'omnotet* (Harkness and Super 1985, 223); Ayoreo = *aiuketaotiguei* (Bugos and McCarthy 1984, 510); Sisala = *wijima* (Grindal 1972, 28); and Ifaluk Island = *repiy* (Lutz 1985), to name a few. "Intelligence in the village is associated with qualities like self-sufficiency, obedience, respect toward elders, attention to detail, willingness to work, and effective management of younger siblings and livestock" (Lancy 2020, 204; see also Wober 1972). Most, if not all, of these signs of maturity relate to the child as *worker*.

The onset of middle childhood marks an important transition in the child's identity. As Edel describes, Chiga children have been busy play/working and learning to do a variety of useful things. But around age seven or eight (earlier in some societies), the child falls into a routine of predictable, competent, essential work (see Box 5.7). Earlier, "any assumption of adult ways and attempts at adult skills or responsibilities is praised and applauded" (Edel 1957/1996, 178), but now they can be relied upon to do their chores without guidance, instruction, or scolding (Boyette and Lew-Levy 2021, 411).

Parental ethnotheories often take note of this transition (corresponding, incidentally, to Piaget's concrete operations) in children's behavior and ability. Play drops off; children have mastered the basic chore array; they assume greater responsibility in the domestic economy; and they carry out their work without guidance or prompting. A growth spurt, rapid muscle development, and increased stamina complement these changes in character. More challenging adult skills, like scaling tall trees to carefully remove honey from the hive, are pursued systematically. Children consciously adopt the role of novice, intently studying the work of others, persistently repeating and refining their efforts at foraging, hunting, and craftwork. Their diligence is rewarded by family and peers through the donation of materials and

Box 5.7 Children as Reliable Workers

She "may spend a long day working in the fields and come home to tend the fire and even to cook a simple meal, such as boiled corn or potatoes. She can carry her baby sister securely on her hip, and fetch firewood from a considerable distance without adult direction" (Edel 1957/1996, 177).

The Bakkarwal, nomadic pastoralists in Jammu and Kashmir, say that "*osh* comes to a human child increasingly from the age of seven or eight years [and] it is *osh* which enables a shepherd to tend his flocks well, day and night" (Rao 1998, 59).

"Essential to learning [among Paliyar] is a certain responsive posture. Those who seek knowledge need 'to listen (*etitθi*)' . . . This refers to an attentive frame of mind . . . and it should be in evidence by about age seven. . . . Many elders . . . hold that excessive talk, especially by youths, is not only undesirable, it 'can lead to forgetfulness'" (Gardner 2019, 188).

Tibetan children "look after herds of goats, sheep, dzo, and yaks in the mountains . . . a major responsibility since much of the wealth of nomadic families is invested in these animals. It can also be a very scary and lonely activity since wolves, snow leopards, and eagles regularly attack the sheep and goats. Using a slingshot to control the animals, boys at seven or eight years of age are considered to be effective herders" (Gielen 1993, 426).

---

strategic intervention to show the learner the way around obstacles. Above all, the child is learning "on the job" (Lancy and Grove 2011a).

Leading a Horse to Water

While this transformation in middle childhood occurs gradually and with little fanfare, the child may shy away from assuming greater responsibility and sacrificing personal autonomy in order to help where most needed. Truancy of this sort is often blamed on the parents, who are seen as failing to assign children responsibilities that are congruent with the identity of a "real worker" during middle childhood. For example, Giriama [Kenyan farmers] attach importance to providing children with duties that teach responsibility and mutuality. In their view, a mother who does not expect her children to

130 LEARNING WITHOUT LESSONS

help is remiss, even neglectful. A child so treated would inevitably emerge as an adult with few prospects and without the respect of the community (Wenger 1989, 93). Other cases of recalcitrance are noted in Box 5.8.

The chore curriculum, then, is remarkably successful in moving children from a state of dependency to one where they are both self-sufficient and contributors to the domestic economy. And this is accomplished with little intervention from an adult "teacher." What happens when a "student" reaches the end of the chore curriculum and "opts out?" Families vary in imposing sanctions on "laggards," with egalitarian societies being the most laissez-faire (Boyette and Lew-Levy 2021). Penalties range from the very mild, as when Mayan family members speak critically of a child who is cast in the role of "overhearer" (de León 2012) to more severe variations:

> Matsigenka children "who are disobedient or lazy are punished by being bathed in hot water or rubbed with an itch-inducing plant. Family and community members use various strategies to ensure children's contributions and participation in household tasks including public shaming. Additionally folk stories, involving *peranti* (lazy) characters who suffer dire consequences for their behavior, are told purposely." (Ochs and Izquierdo 2009, 395)

Box 5.8 Managing Young Workers

"A Gusii child who fails to carry out a chore may be ordered out of the house, implicitly refused food and shelter" (LeVine and LeVine 1963).

An Amhara adult may encourage a child to do its chores "by throwing clods of dirt or manure at him" (Levine 1965, 266).

"It is common for Q'eqchi' parents to remark that children are "lazy" and do not like to work hard. Most of the time this is said jokingly, but if said in earnest, this is one of the most disparaging things that can be said of a person" (Zarger 2002b, 127).

Mothers threaten to withhold food from Bengali girls who allow play to interfere with the completion of chores (Rohner and Chaki-Sicrar 1988).

"An Aka child's failure to care for an infant or toddler may lead to a denial of food or a blow from the infant's mother" (Boyette 2019, 488).

THE CHORE CURRICULUM   131

Overall, however, accounts of children *eagerly and successfully* doing chores are far more frequent than accounts of truants, and a large-scale, cross-cultural survey found that middle childhood is a period when the child's pro-social behavior becomes similar to adults' (House et al. 2020).

Variability in the Chore Curriculum

Unlike the academic curriculum, the village counterpart is much more varied and less standardized. Because the curriculum is tied to chores, changes in family composition, season of the year, and whether the learner is male or female all have a bearing. In a family with few children, some pressure might be applied to a young child to learn more rapidly or take on more mature tasks. In some cases, a shortage can be met by cross-gender role assignments. In a Luo-speaking community in Kenya, the shortage of daughters was community-wide, and Carol Ember discovered that "approximately half the boys in the community had been assigned 'feminine' work . . . because the ratio of boys to girls . . . was almost three to two . . . at the time of the study" (Ember 1973, 425–426).

Studies show that girls progress through the chore curriculum more rapidly than boys, who spend more time in play. Girls work alongside mothers and other female relatives in an atmosphere of mutual support and high activity, and they are given the opportunity to constantly expand their area of competence. Boys are not always welcome to join in male pursuits, so they must learn in the company of older boys. They are under much less pressure to make a direct contribution to the domestic economy. Then, too, the learning curve for boys beginning to hunt with bow and arrows or blowpipes and traps may be steeper than with comparable girls' chores. So their skills will develop more slowly (Kaplan 1997). The nature of subsistence is a factor. In a pastoralist community, boys will spend most days looking after livestock; while among hunter-gatherers, they have much greater freedom to construct an individualized curriculum that might involve trapping birds, extracting honey, climbing palm trees to gather fruit, and stalking small mammals.

I believe it is possible to derive some generalizations from this review. Equivalent—for the sake of argument—to our academic curriculum, the chore curriculum incorporates independent learning of commonplace tasks associated with subsistence and family life. Overwhelmingly, the child learner initiates the learning process. In most communities, the chore menu

132 LEARNING WITHOUT LESSONS

is quite extensive, which enables the child to undertake tasks appropriate to their level of expertise and gender. The child brings high motivation and inherited needs to be helpful and socially accepted to this project. Their principal learning strategy will be close observation of competent others, who are more likely to be somewhat older peers than adults. The child who wishes to take on the role of understudy, closely observing a role model, is usually welcome, especially if they display serious intent and commitment. The child is expected to learn useful skills but also figure out when to deploy those skills. Relatives may provide encouragement through gifting the child with a scaled-down or worn-out tool. On occasion, a sympathetic person may help the child over a barrier in their learning. A parent may direct the child to chores that are both needed and within the child's competence. Otherwise, relatively little investment is made in the learner, expecting that mastery will be achieved largely through careful observation and hands-on practice. Many would go further and argue that learning might be sabotaged by too much interference (e.g., attempts to teach) by another.

6

The Transition to Structured Learning

> The first injunction for those teaching children was to beat them to
> ensure their obedience.
>
> —Hanawalt (1993), 72

Introduction

While the dominant theme of this work is the learner-initiated, informal
pedagogy typical of small, Indigenous communities, I would be remiss not
to review the impact of more formal models of pedagogy. Drawing on history as well as anthropology, the origins of schooling are briefly summarized.
As the reader will see, the earliest pedagogy in the ancient and medieval
world is mirrored in important aspects of the schooling imposed on formerly classroom-less villages. Aside from the patterns of instruction, early
schools produced suffering, resistance, and opportunity. Schooling was/
is not seen as a universal good. Families resist what they see as harsh treatment of children and resent the loss of their labor. There are, further, two
institutions found abundantly in Indigenous communities—initiation rites
and apprenticeship—that carry an educational mandate. Both affect a great
many children and utilize pedagogy that is very much at odds with autonomous, child-initiated learning.

Pedagogy in the Victorian Era

The juxtaposition between pedagogy associated with schooling and teaching
and pedagogy embedded in a community's daily round of activities or
practices has a long history. But the dramatic contrast between the learning
environment of the school compared to that of home and community comes
into sharp focus during the Victorian era, circa 1850. This was a period of
dramatic social change, when children were less likely to be seen as "extra

Learning Without Lessons. David F. Lancy, Oxford University Press. © Oxford University Press 2024.
DOI: 10.1093/oso/9780197645598.003.0006

134 LEARNING WITHOUT LESSONS

hands" on the farm or as domestic laborers or factory workers who could earn a sparse but welcome wage. For members of the growing middle class, the value of their offspring was "set by smiles, dimples, and curls" rather than their "capacity for labor" (Zelizer 1985, 171). Compulsory schooling meant that, for good or ill, childhood now changed to accommodate this drastically new experience.

The works of Charles Dickens can be mined for vivid illustrations of this contrast. In *The Pickwick Papers*, we hear Sam Weller's (Mr. Pickwick's young man-of-all-work) father proudly claim credit for his son's perspicacity: "I took a good deal o' pains with his eddication, sir; let him run in the streets when he was very young and shift for hisself. It's the only way to make a boy sharp, sir" (Dickens 1836/1964, 306). Similarly, in *Our Mutual Friend*, Mr. Sloppy remarks to doll-dress maker Jenny Wren, while glancing at the great array of elaborate doll gowns on display: " 'You must have been taught a long time.' 'Never was taught a stitch, young man!' returned the dressmaker . . . 'Just gobbled and gobbled till I found out how to do it' " (Dickens 1865, 916). Or, if you prefer Tom Jones: "It is as possible for a man to know something without having been to school, as it is to have been at school and to know nothing" (Fielding 1749/1908, 282).

In these pithy quotes, there is a suggestion of pride in learning an occupation without the benefit of schooling, which was neither taken as a given for children nor universally desired. Aside from the significant additional cost, schooling was seen as having severe shortcomings.

> Teachers' academic abilities were limited. For instance, more than seven hundred "teachers" in 1851 could not sign their own names on their reports to educational authorities; they simply put a mark. . . . Rote memorization was the normal method for teaching . . . [Not surprisingly] children were heartily bored and remembered little of the material . . . [so] early schools often had difficulties with order. . . . One village school in 1880 had a single master and one pupil-teacher serving one hundred children. (Frost 2009, 35–39)

Again, from *Our Mutual Friend*:

> The school in which Charley Hexam had first learned from a book . . . was a miserable loft in an unsavory yard. Its atmosphere was oppressive and disagreeable; it was crowded, noisy and confusing; half the pupils dropped

THE TRANSITION TO STRUCTURED LEARNING   135

asleep. . . . The teachers, animated solely by good intentions, had no idea of execution, and a lamentable jumble was the upshot of their endeavors. (Dickens 1865, 258)

Charley's school may have seemed a paradise compared to Dotheboy's Hall, a private, for-profit boarding school where Nicolas Nickleby serves as a novice teacher. Headmaster Wackford Squeers, "that worthy pedagogue," is one of Dickens's most notorious villains, routinely beating and starving his pupils (Dickens 1839). Dotheboy's is synonymous with *Suffering* and *Resistance* as well. Historians have fully confirmed Dickens's characterization of the crude and coercive pedagogical practices in the nineteenth century. "Children were likely to look for any means of subverting or escaping from such regimes" (Cunningham 1995, 105). Parents, children, and reformers may have expressed their dissatisfaction, but change was unwelcome. Christopher Thomson opened a school at Tickhill, Yorkshire, in 1827, but he "acquired a reputation for not beating boys and for teaching poetry, a combination which put him out of business" (Jordan 1987, 178).

A great irony lies in the contrast between the way schooling is depicted in Dickens's fiction and in his own devastation when straitened family circumstances forced his removal from school. This traumatic event was soon followed by his employment—at age twelve—pasting labels on pots in a blacking factory for ten hours per day. "The future was snatched away, the dreams and visions of his youth thrown off" (Ackroyd 1990, 59). After all, he was male, the oldest of five children, and had already had quite a bit of schooling (Kaplan 1988). But for Dickens, schooling, despite its many shortcomings, represented *opportunity*. As a student, he could continue to pursue a life of the mind and, more practically, could aspire to secure white-collar employment.

As extreme as Dickens's vivid classroom scenes may seem to contemporary readers, they are not only representative of many, if not most, schools of the time, but the pedagogical principles on display can be traced back thousands of years.

The First Schools

The earliest appearance of formal education—classrooms, teachers, instructional materials, and consistent patterns of pedagogy—is associated with

136 LEARNING WITHOUT LESSONS

the world's oldest civilizations, Egypt and Sumer. By the third millennium BCE, both societies had evolved into populous, complex, wealthy empires with elaborate infrastructure and enormous public monuments, such as the pyramids of Giza. All these trappings of civilization had to be managed, necessitating comprehensive and widely understood records inscribed in the oldest known writing systems, cuneiform and hieroglyphics. This recordkeeping implied a bureaucracy employing an army of literate clerks, trained in classroom-like facilities (Williams 1972, 214). "The transmission of these skills from one generation of ruling elite and bureaucrats to the next generation required an institution of formal instruction, or school" (Eskelson 2020, 39). As in Dickens's time, schooling might enable a comfortable lifestyle, compared to, say, the peasants who toiled on the pyramids. To be a student was a privilege, and the earliest scribes were the offspring of such luminaries as governors, senior civil servants, and priests (Saggs 1987).

Much of the pedagogy that emerged during this period can still be found today.[1] The teacher was a stern figure of exalted standing. Lessons consisted primarily of rote memorization and copying of various standardized texts, lists, and figures, over and over until free of errors (Kelly-Buccellati 2012; Livingstone 2007). Training occurred in same-age, male cohorts gathered together and working through the curriculum in unison. Schooling material recovered from Middle Egyptian sites is "known by the title *Kemyt* . . . a collection of idioms and formulae which . . . reveal that it was *used as a textbook for a thousand years*" (Williams 1972, 217, emphasis added). "School tablets recovered from Nippur were largely standardized and are sometimes *known in hundreds of duplicates*" (Veldhuis 2011, 83, emphasis added). Fast-forward three millennia and little change is evident. In fifteenth-century Florence, a schoolbook was referred to as a *babuino* (baboon), "a reference to the fact that students learned to read by aping their teachers" (King 2021, 14).

Just learning to write legibly was a challenge, as the signs required great dexterity to execute. Mesopotamian scribes wrote on clay tablets (a classroom was referred to as "Tablet House") that could be erased, corrected, and reused; their Egyptian counterparts used broken pottery shards (*ostraca*) to practice on because papyrus was costly (Chiera 1938/1966). While a Mesopotamian scribe would use over 600 signs, there were 1,000 distinct Egyptian hieroglyphs.

---

[1] It is important to note that, even in "good" schools, the focus was always on the material to be learned, not the age, needs, or learning styles of pupils (Platt 2005).

THE TRANSITION TO STRUCTURED LEARNING 137

The earliest writing systems continued to be used for literature and sacred texts for several thousand years. Hence, scribes had to work with dead languages they had never used nor heard spoken, much like Latin being used as the prime written language while it was no longer used as a lingua franca. In the present, Indigenous school lessons (and texts) are often delivered in a foreign, colonial tongue rather than the students' mother tongue.

Kramer notes that early schools were "uninviting," lessons were dull, and discipline was harsh. One poor novice recorded: "My headmaster read my tablet, said: 'There is something missing,' caned me. 'Why didn't you speak Sumerian,' caned me. My teacher said: 'Your hand is unsatisfactory,' caned me . . . and so I began to hate the scribal art" (Kramer 1963, 238–239). An Egyptian proverb claims that aspirant scribes have ears on their backs, implying that they must be beaten regularly, or they will not listen.

> In Greek schools, corporal punishment was so widespread that the symbol used to represent education was the rod. In Rome, too, discipline and education were basically synonymous. Our word *discipline* derives from the Latin word for instruction. Roman teachers deployed a whole arsenal of weapons on their students, including the *virga* (birch switch), *flagellum* (whip), *scotia* (leather strap), and *ferula* (rod). (Traig 2019, 206)

Not surprisingly, scribal schools found the need to "encourage" resistant students via the carrot or stick. Novices had to copy texts extolling the profession, compared to others:

> The quarryman seeks for . . . every sort of hard stone. It is with his arms ruined and himself exhausted that he has brought things to completion. He sits down at the setting of the sun with his knees and his back cramped. . . . Be a scribe, that your limbs may be smooth and your hands languid, that you may go out dressed in white, being exalted. (Williams 1972, 218)

Another common theme was the exhortation to diligence, which appears in many school texts: "Don't be lazy, scribe, or you will be curbed at once. Do not set your mind on pleasures, or you will be a failure" (Williams 1972, 218).

The spread of schooling and the development of curricula did not faithfully track the development of society and attendant technology. The sophisticated architecture and engineering characteristics of the Roman Empire "were not formally taught in this period. Instead the knowledge necessary

138 LEARNING WITHOUT LESSONS

was passed on within the trades by direct example" (Corbeill 2001, 266). On the other hand, "the Romans used education . . . to reproduce social hierarchies within their own society. . . . The political function of pedagogy is . . . easily disguised" (Corbeill 2001, 282).

The social-sorting function of the earliest schools continued to grow in importance to create and strengthen class distinctions. Many of the mandatory subjects had no practical utility beyond separating the educated from the uneducated. In the Roman era, fluency in Greek was an important mark of distinction, only available to those who had been tutored in the language. Well into the nineteenth century CE, Latin played a similar role. In the early Middle Ages, a confessed murderer could avoid the hangman if literate—as a "benefit of clergy." It was not until the Renaissance and the rise of an extremely powerful merchant class that schools offered curricula of a strictly practical mien, including vernacular literacy and algebra. These schools utilized pedagogical principles that, at the time, must have seemed radical, namely:

> The subject matter . . . had to be divided into very small individual bits of knowledge. Teachers and textbooks taught by breaking a skill down into its smallest components, drilling them intensively, and then assembling the bits to make the whole. It was pedagogy based on the belief that if the student learned the pieces thoroughly, he would grasp the whole. Teacher and pupil had to comprehend perfectly every step of the process; intuitive leaps of learning were distrusted. (Grendler 1989, 409)

The gulf between the earliest pedagogical practices associated with schooling and the much older pedagogy rooted in routine cultural practices and untutored, unforced learning initiatives of village children is evident. The "everyday classroom" probably did not give birth to the "tablet house." I have earlier argued that the pedagogy of schooling may have its roots in the likely much older institution of apprenticeship (Lancy 2012). The two institutions have much in common. For example, both exhibit the rigid hierarchy that deprives learners of the freedom and autonomy formerly exercised in mastering critical skills and texts. And these controls are in part imposed to groom the apprentice/student for their subordinate social and political standing.

Studying apprentice masons in Mali, for example, Marchand learned that "the word for 'apprentice' in Djenné-Chiini is *maale-banya*—literally, 'the slave of the master'" (2009, 46); and Greek historian (first century CE) Dio Chrysostom "likens students to . . . slaves, citing their vulnerability to beatings from their teachers" (Connolly 2001, 368). In short, the agenda of the early schools and the craft workshops places economic gain and maintenance of social rank well above any efforts to improve student learning.

Apprenticeship

The lack of agreement among scholars on a definition of apprenticeship makes it a difficult topic to study. In Trevor Marchand's comprehensive ethnography of "apprenticeship" training for minaret builders in Yemen, he freely acknowledges that there is no native term to describe the phenomenon (Marchand 2001, 156; see also Trias et al. 2015, 94). Among those who study the pedagogy of apprenticeship, some consider it indistinct from informal learning in the community and completely unlike schooling (Greenfield and Lave 1982). Others (e.g., Gruber and Mandl 2001, 602–603) use the term to describe a relationship between teacher and pupil that doesn't at all resemble the master–apprentice relationship observed by anthropologists. Part of the confusion arises from the fact that elements found prominently in craft learning (Chapter 4), while not formally included in the apprenticeship, still serve as a kind of "preschool." In short, virtually all children who begin a formal apprenticeship will have been engaged in the craft on a playful basis for quite some time (Lancy 1980; Greenfield 2004).

In fact, anthropologists (and historians) consistently choose not to define apprenticeship; instead, they describe it as a conglomerate of discrete components (Coy 1989, 1–4). Here I will adopt Coy's strategy but also offer a definition that distinguishes this institution from similar but less formal means of craft learning, which I reviewed in Chapter 4.

> Apprenticeship will be defined as a formal, contractual relationship between a master and a novice of a specific duration, which is designed to serve two ends: to provide cheap labor by the apprentice and/or fees to support the master's enterprise; and to afford the apprentice an opportunity to learn and receive certification for mastery. (Lancy 2012, 113–114)

A key element that sets the apprenticeship apart is the existence of a paradox. On the one hand, a master craftsperson gains great value from their

140 LEARNING WITHOUT LESSONS

product. Hausa (Nigeria) weaver/farmers are much better off financially than those who only farm (Defenbaugh 1989, 164). The master is also the possessor of an establishment (the blacksmith's forge and tools, the potter's wheel and kiln, the weaver's loom plus equipment for spinning and dyeing) that must be set up and maintained. And, as I will show, the master commands an extensive "lore" that adds mystique and value to both the individual craftsperson and their products. For these reasons, the master must be loath to train up novices who will, eventually, turn into direct competitors or, worse, undermine the standing of the craft and its accomplished practioners via shoddy or substandard work. Many elements of the apprenticeship, including those I have labeled "counter-pedagogical," come together in solving this paradox.[2]

This implacable resistance to creating new competitors can create a poisonous atmosphere for the woeful apprentice.

The Chinese woodworking apprentice is in a veritable prison, bound to his master by contract . . . for three years [or] longer. . . . The demands made upon the apprentice were considerable. He led a Cinderella-like existence. . . . Seldom, if ever, . . . systematically instructed . . . he learned by observation and imitation, learning by doing . . . even the asking of a question is not allowed. . . . When he is seen making a mistake, no one sits down and talks it over with him. Immediately comes a kick or a slap to the face . . . master craftsmen reputedly concealed techniques from their apprentices, making sure that a newly graduated journey-man could not compete with them on equal terms. (Cooper 1988, 23–25)

Just as the earliest students were drawn from society's elite, craft learning from a master is restricted. One prominent gatekeeping mechanism is to limit access to one or another gender. "In Cameroon, women are potters, men blacksmiths" (Wallaert 2001, 473). Among the Akwete, only women may weave (Aronson 1989, 151); the reverse is true for the Tukolor (Dilley 1989, 185). Other barriers to craft participation may relate to clan (Spindel 1989, 71) or tribal membership. "Masons repeatedly assert that only boys

---

[2] Guilds arise to resolve the paradox once the community becomes large enough to support multiple workshops practicing the same craft. "One of the prime functions of a guild is to maintain a reasonable standard of work in the craft" (Lloyd 1953, 39). But in doing so "they crippled individual initiative and rejected innovation as unfair competition" (Mitterauer and Sieder 1997, 104).

THE TRANSITION TO STRUCTURED LEARNING   141

from the town's stock of building families will be taken on as apprentices and that the trade will remain dominated by the Bozo" (Marchand 2009, 154). To become an apprentice "in a Kanō atelier . . . membership in the samurai class was the normal prerequisite" (Jordan 1998, 49). In eighteenth- and nineteenth-century Europe, "entry to apprenticeship in certain occupations was to be denied to those who could not boast parents of the appropriate condition and status" (Aldrich 1999, 15; see also Barron 2007, 49).

> Kpeenbele Senufo (Cotê d'Ivoire) novice potters are allowed to take part in only three activities: burnishing pots, pounding shards for temper and bark for firing, and carrying pots to and from the place where they are fired. . . . Although they may know the pottery-making process . . . intimately, they are not allowed to become true apprentices until they marry. . . . This apprenticeship system ensures that the economic benefits from pottery remain firmly in the hands of the older potters. (Spindel 1989, 71)

A negative example from the more informal learning of ceramic production, sans apprenticeship, comes also from Cotê d'Ivoire (the Nyarafolo):

> In Sangopari Village it is unnecessary to belong to a specific endogamous social group to take up pottery, as it is open to everyone (Köhler 2012, 119) . . . no one sits down intentionally to pass on knowledge . . . instead experienced women simply act as role models. . . . Learners are not told how to do something, but what has to be done. Furthermore, why something should be done is also rarely explained (Köhler 2012, 131). . . . Passing on knowledge in Sangopari is an open and dynamic social process. Learning takes place in public spaces in the sphere of pottery-making women, and this means many women contribute towards learning. (Köhler 2012, 135)

A family that puts one of its offspring out to apprenticeship is making a significant investment since a fee must be paid up front, followed by periodic gifts to the master (Lloyd 1953). Furthermore, they are losing a member of the family work unit, whose output as an apprentice is taken by the master as his or her due. It is not uncommon for a craftsperson to place their own child with a distant kinsman or nonrelative (Laes 2015, 89), supposing that, as a parent with filial ties, they will not be able to impose the strict discipline, including corporal punishment, that is required. Esther Goody's characterization of Gonja weaving is representative.

142 LEARNING WITHOUT LESSONS

> In the Gonja weaving industry of Daboya (Ghana), weavers' sons are sent as foster children to learn from a skilled weaver. . . . When I asked why he wasn't teaching the boy himself, Bakweji curtly insisted that this wouldn't work. It would only lead to trouble between them . . . the son wouldn't give the father proper respect. (Goody 2006, 254)

The master occupies an exalted position in the community and in the workshop, requiring obeisance from the novice. Aside from an air of deference, the novice also pays homage through uncomplainingly carrying out various chores that have nothing to do with learning the craft, such as doing the master's family laundry (Jawando et al. 2012) or working on the master's farm (Lloyd 1953, 39). Even in the workshop, the novice will be assigned the lowliest menial tasks, such as bobbin winding (Dilley 1989, 187).

> During the first stage, which lasts almost two years, the Dowayo child is mainly a helping hand. She collects clay and fetches water and wood but does not fashion pots. The instructor seems to ignore her, and the student is not allowed to ask questions about the practice. This stage basically serves to forge the tenacity and motivation of the future potter. (Wallaert 2012, 29)

The most important pedagogical role played by the master throughout the apprenticeship is to serve as a model, to be closely observed and copied by the novice. Verbal instruction is rare. Among minaret builders, "curses and derogatory remarks were the most common form of communication from 'teacher' to 'learner' . . . as opposed to explanation . . . abuse served as a potent disciplinary tool, effectively reinforcing the existing hierarchy amongst the builders" (Marchand 2001, 144).

Douglas Brooks conducted a thorough ethnography of Japanese boatbuilding that included apprenticeships with five boatbuilders and interviews with many more. The masters did not provide an introduction but expected Brooks to learn through observation and imitation: "How I swung a hammer was not an issue of personal preference. . . . He had his way and he insisted it also be my way" (Brooks 2015, 130). Concerned that his lack of fluency in Japanese would be a handicap, he discovered, "I didn't need any Japanese because Mr. Fuji insisted on working in complete silence and offered no explanations whatsoever" (Brooks 2015, 79).

In Charles Keller's apprenticeship in a blacksmith's workshop, there was no learning activity or teaching by the master that was external to the workflow

THE TRANSITION TO STRUCTURED LEARNING   143

of the actual production process (Keller and Keller 1996, 5). An apprentice potter in ancient Greece progressed through "trial and error, patience, perseverance, and a gradual accumulation of skills" (Hasaki 2012, 188).

In Japan, the apprentice is *minari*, someone who learns from observation. The master potter will chastise the apprentice for posing a question since the answer would have been clear had he been more observant (Singleton 1989). In a contemporary Greek apprenticeship, questions by the apprentice were considered as a challenge to the master's authority (Herzfeld 1995, 138). The master is focused primarily on his or her own work and output, not the learner. The Mande blacksmith does not stop working to guide or teach, reasoning that the apprentice should "discover his own mistakes" (McNaughton 1988, 28).[3] Intervention is infrequent and strategic, designed to assist the apprentice over the most difficult speed bumps in the path of learning or prevent damage to material or equipment or both (Greenfield 2004; Lave 1982). Apprentice Dioula weavers are free to learn on their own, as long as their errors can be readily corrected and do not jeopardize the raw material. "In risky operations, such as the preparation of the warp, the expert takes over and the apprentice serves as observer-helper" (Tanon 1994, 36). When the master stops to correct the apprentice, he or she eschews verbal instruction in favor of physically shaping the learner's limbs and movements (Fowler 1977, 29). "Apprenticeship is essentially non-verbal. The apprentice learns by practice and failure" (Wynn 1993, 398).

Crafts can seem, at first glance, to be quite complex, but the process can be readily broken down into its constituent parts and actions, referred to in anthropology as the *chaîne opératoire*. It is often quite transparent, and novices are cycled through individual tasks, moving from least to most difficult. In Tukolor (Senegal) weaving, the first task to master is bobbin winding, and the last is setting up the loom. Several years will pass from mastering the first step to completing the last (Dilley 1989). Dii (Cameroon) novices, after a period performing menial service, are allowed to prepare the clay and make miniature pots, moving on to full-sized but utilitarian, undecorated pots, and finally to shaping and firing their own fully mature pots (Wallaert 2012). A Yoruba blacksmith's apprentice begins with fabricating small knives and then moves on to more substantial tools, like machetes and hoes, to the ultimate challenge: traps and guns (Obidi 1995).

---

[3] Argenti (2002) found that Oku woodcarvers who were self-taught were as skilled as their counterparts who had endured a lengthy apprenticeship.

144 LEARNING WITHOUT LESSONS

> Production processes [in a Monrovia, Liberia, tailor shop] have a logic and order to them, and these shape apprentice learning activities . . . it is more costly to make an error when cutting out a garment than when sewing it. Apprentices learn to sew garments before learning to cut out garments. . . . [They] work on small garments that can be made of scraps before items that take more, or more expensive fabrics. . . . [They] start on simple garments and gradually move on to more complicated ones. (Lave 1982, 181–183)

Of course, despite these safeguards, accidents will happen, and the apprentice can expect to be severely punished by the master or a journeyman for any error. An apprentice foundryman from fourth-century BCE Greece complained in a letter home that he was tied up, whipped, and "treated like dirt." A fifth-century BCE blackware skyphos shows a scene from a pottery workshop of an apprentice hung by his heels, presumably as correction (Jordan 2000, 101). In Dowayo pottery apprenticeship, spanking and forced eating of clay are used to ensure that the rules are respected. Humiliation is common because technical mistakes are treated as a challenge to the master's authority (Wallaert 2012, 29). "Before the neophyte [Mande blacksmith] can master techniques and form, he has to master pain. He begins at the bellows, where he spends many hours each day" (McNaughton 1988, 24).

In larger operations with many apprentices, the individual is granted less autonomy. Denying the apprentice the freedom to learn independently and at their own pace inevitably slows down their progress toward graduation, which, in many cases, appears deliberate. The artificial elongation of the learning sequence ensures the availability of the apprentice's virtually voluntary labor while preventing them from breaking away to become a competitor. Indeed, in a worst-case scenario, unscrupulous craftsmen in Togo accept a huge number of apprentices, take their fees, and exploit them as free laborers but prevent them from mastering the craft and becoming rivals (Marguerat 2000).

> Work [in the metal foundry] is fragmented to the extreme, and the worker, obliged to carry out one job only [until permitted to progress to another subtask, thus] has no hope of mastering or even of gaining an understanding of the entire production process—let alone its financial and commercial aspects. (Morice 1982, 518)

THE TRANSITION TO STRUCTURED LEARNING   145

Menial work, punishment, removal from family, and long hours with no break all serve to "weed out" novices. As the years pass, only the most determined and talented stay the distance. But there is a final and nearly insurmountable obstacle. One of the most interesting aspects of the apprenticeship is the understanding that the master's expertise is at least partly due to his or her knowledge of secrets or lore.

"Secrecy is endemic to Japanese boatbuilding. At the heart of the craft is knowledge of the dimensions, angles and ratios of the boats, which the boatbuilder must safeguard" (Brooks 2015, 10). The onus is on the apprentice to "steal" the opaque or hidden details of the boat's design, a practice termed *musumigeiko* (stealing lessons). McNaughton, who became an apprentice, refers to the Mande blacksmith profession as "floating on a sea of secret expertise" (1988, xvi). In Djenné, Mali, famous for its extraordinary mud architecture, "powerful 'secrets' shield masons and their teams of laborers from accidents and unseen malevolent forces. The secrets also guard the houses they build from damage or collapse and protect house owners" (Marchand 2009, 165).

> The [Tukolor] apprentice learns . . . the necessary skills in weaving . . . but also the mystical and religious aspects of craft lore [called *gandal*, which] can be used . . . to protect the weaver from spiritual forces associated with the craft and . . . as a means of defense against the malicious intention of other weavers. (Dilley 1989, 190, 195)

The secrets and lore are opaque, revealed grudgingly to those who are "submissive and patient" (Marchand 2009, 165). Sometimes, this knowledge has to be " 'stolen' through 'passive' listening, since the trainee's role . . . [did not include] the discourse of trade lore" (Marchand 2001, 119; see also Herzfeld 1995, 131; de Munck and Soly 2007, 15; Jordan 1998, 56). Perhaps we might think of these secrets as the "final exam." Once mastered, the apprentice becomes a steadfast member of the craft fraternity/sorority, committed to maintaining the craft's exclusivity.

The apprenticeship, in fact, may end with a formal graduation. From the Middle Ages, the end of apprenticeship was marked by a formal certificate and promotion to "journeyman." A blacksmith conducts the ceremony to "bless" the Dowayo potter, whose achievement is also marked by the gift of tools from the master (Wallaert 2012, 30; Argenti 2002, 509). The Tukolor master gives the completed apprentice the moving parts of the

146 LEARNING WITHOUT LESSONS

loom (Dilley 1989, 190). At a Yoruba blacksmith's graduation, "the master poured a libation to the god of iron, who, according to Yoruba belief, would bless the new craftsman abundantly" (Obidi 1995, 378). At the conclusion of the boatbuilder's apprenticeship, the "graduate" should make some changes or improvements to the master's design. "An innovation, no matter how small, was the final badge of independence from one's master" (Brooks 2015, 128).

As I argued earlier, the apprenticeship may have been a precursor to the first schools. Some of the pedagogical elements they share include the following: they have a social-standing admission test, thereby creating an exclusive cohort; the instructor is an exalted person who is to be obeyed and placated; the learner cannot act autonomously but must "stay within the lines"; the learner may be constrained to boring, repetitive activity that numbs body and mind; the teacher/master provides little formal instruction or even verbal feedback or guidance; the novice is sharply corrected and/or chastised, and punishment may be severe; learning takes place in a designated and distinct environment; some of the to-be-learned curriculum is opaque or decontextualized; and, after a considerable period of time, the students/apprentices who have persevered to mastery are "certified" and released to practice their rewarding trade.

The many commonalties between early schools and craft apprenticeships are to be expected, but it is somewhat surprising to find them occurring in initiation rites. But this is certainly the case, as I will show in the next section.

"Bush Schools"

In many societies, the passage from childhood to adolescence or adolescence to adulthood is through an initiation rite. Such rites are considered "rites of passage," a concept that also includes birth, a first haircut, first day of school, marriage, and funeral (van Gennep [1908] 1960). In more than half of the societies in the ethnographic record, young members must pass through an initiation process (Schlegel and Barry 1980, 698), and this proportion climbs to two-thirds if we include any type of ordeal such as circumcision (Schlegel and Barry 1991). These rites have sometimes been seen as similar to schooling, hence the popular name "bush school." However, an early survey argued that the pedagogy of the initiation rite resembled indoctrination

THE TRANSITION TO STRUCTURED LEARNING 147

rather than education (Lancy 1975). But indoctrination can be delivered in ways that are parallel to or at least resemble schools.[4]

What Are the Typical Pedagogical Tools?

While there is great variability in the structure and duration of initiation rites, and detailed descriptions are few, a survey of the ethnographic record reveals a number of general principles. First, initiates are set apart from the community and from their former selves. They may be literally removed from their homes (Dorjahn 1982, 40) and secluded in a strange place for an extended period (de Laguna 1965, 21). They will be distinguished from noninitiates by body decoration, special clothing, or other conspicuous marks. In the majority of cases, they are treated as a member of a cohort rather than as individuals. For the Gbusi, longhouse dwellers living in southwest Papua New Guinea (PNG),

> Rituals of status elevation are often prefaced by rites of humility, submission, or teasing before the aspirant assumes his or her new role. For the prospective Gebusi initiates, their in-between status was signified by bold stripes of yellow ocher, painted on them from head to foot. . . . [But] the initiates' biggest trial was to wear new wigs . . . tied in bulky bundles to narrow strands of . . . hair, [pulling] down mightily on the initiate's scalp. . . . All the while, the surrounding men crowded around the poor initiates, whooping and joking with abandon. (Knauft 2013, 84–85)

In this case, the markings signal the humiliation of the initiate; in others, permanent scars or tattoos are displayed with pride, signaling enhanced status. Abelam (agriculturalists of the Sepik Region, PNG) girls are "scarified at their first menstruation . . . standardized patterns are cut on their breasts, bellies, and upper arms" (Hauser-Schaublin 1995, 40).

While circumcision is a well-known and now controversial element of initiation, virtually all such rites involve some element of painful body mutilation, ranging, mildly, from tattooing (Markstrom 2008, 132) to scarification

---

[4] In the nineteenth century, street children were harried into "workhouse schools" designed to turn them into God-fearing, law-abiding, sober laborers. "The religious curriculum was clearly seen as having a beneficial effect, but writing was not taught, so that accusations that workhouse children were indoctrinated rather than educated may be sustainable" (Crompton 1997, 151–152).

148   LEARNING WITHOUT LESSONS

(Wagley 1977, 163) to the excision of the genitalia (Arnold 2006, 50).[5] The many and varied tribes found in PNG are particularly noted for the pain and utter terror associated with the process (Herdt 1990, 376). In numerous cases, the child is symbolically killed by a monstrous figure, disappears, and is then resurrected or reborn (Higgens 1985, 103). Among the Baktaman, swidden horticulturalists living in a remote area of the western highlands of PNG, "Water and fire are also used for torture, reinforcing the basic messages of [the] initiation: that those forces are powerful and dangerous; sacred knowledge is costly and must be paid for with hardship and its value thus confirmed" (Barth 1975, 66).

Among the Bimin-Kuskusmin of PNG, the initiate's nasal septum is pierced with a cassowary-bone dagger. Bleeding profusely, they are daubed with hot animal fat as they "struggle and shriek as large blisters form" (Poole 1982, 127). Severe physical punishment, then, appears as a second common pedagogical tool. In fact, as noted throughout the chapter, physical punishment, harassment, and privation are found in early schools and school-like institutions.

Extending beyond brief moments of fright and pain, many rites aim to break down the initiate to change how they see themselves and others. The wigs, body paint, and circumcision may be paired with severe tests of endurance. In addition to painful injury, other anxiety-inducing treatments include separation from one's home and physical ordeals, such as bathing in ice water or running until exhausted (Markstrom 2008, 131–132). Fiske and Rai (2015) argue that severe initiation rites are critical in the creation of a warrior class of youth, tightly bonded to each other through their shared ordeal.

> Powhatan (N. American) boys were trained from early in life to be stoic warriors who could withstand multiple hardships. Boys were initiated from ten to fifteen years of age . . . held deep in the forest . . . by older, initiated men, who subjected the boys to beating and forced them to ingest an intoxicating and dangerous plant. (Markstrom 2008, 161)

Liberian Kpelle preadolescents in same-sex cohorts were dramatically removed from the village by masked figures and sequestered for months or

---

[5] In a supremely ironic case in a Wagenia (Congo Brazzaville) village, Droogers (1980, 85) observed a group of boys carrying out a full-on reproduction of the boy's initiation ceremony culminating in a simulated circumcision.

THE TRANSITION TO STRUCTURED LEARNING   149

years in specially constructed villages in the bush (deep forest) to enforce a transition from "carefree" childhood to responsible adulthood (Erchak 1977). This forcible removal constitutes the "separation" stage in van Gennep's three-stage model of "Rites of Passage" (van Gennep 1908/1960). A similar fate awaited neighboring Temne boys: "From the time of capture . . . boys were in *kabangkalo* [where they] were scarified and [subject to] flogging, withholding [of] food, extra work, supporting a heavy weight for a long time and so on" (Dorjahn 1982, 39–40).

Gisu (Uganda) initiates are deemed worthy if they unflinchingly endure the "fierce, bitter and terrifying" *Imbalu* ordeal. But the boys can also display their ferocity and worth by dancing nonstop, day and night, while wearing an elaborate costume that includes "a headdress made from the skin of a colobus monkey and long tails decorated with cowrie shells which hang down his back and swirl in the dance" (Heald 1982, 20).

Another recurring pedagogical element in studies of initiation rites—with parallels in early scribal schools, craft apprenticeships, and village schools— is the unpackaging of ritual[6] and other closely guarded "secrets" (Hart and Pilling 1960; Werbner 2009, 448). One of the most thoroughly described male initiation rituals has been provided for the Baktaman (PNG). The initiation process is strung out over many years. Barth's analysis reveals that the initiation rites "aren't so much about transmitting cultural knowledge as senior males controlling those more junior" (Barth 1975, 219). Where the youth has, to this point, been able to learn from overhearing or observation in relative autonomy, the information conveyed in the initiation is secret and tightly controlled. "Much of the more highly valued information is cast in codes known only to a few members of the community" (Barth 1975, 18). But these codes are not taught directly. They are only hinted at and then "rendered false or grossly incomplete by further secrets. Even the central revelation of one initiation [stage]—e.g., 'the showing of the bones'—was [subsequently] shown to be . . . a hoax" (Barth 1975, 81). Shore comments, "We can assume from the available evidence that what they experience of the narrative at any given moment in their initiation is puzzling and disjointed at best" (1996, 248).

---

[6] Close cousins are Kuttab schools, which have been around a long time and are found wherever Islam has taken hold. Instruction consists primarily of reciting and ultimately memorizing the Qur'an, for which literacy is not essential. These schools aim to indoctrinate pupils in a specific moral code (Moore 2006, 113). Similar emphases on rigid discipline and memorization of texts are found in religious schools serving Hindu (Broyon 2004) and Coptic (Levine 1965, 267) students.

150 LEARNING WITHOUT LESSONS

> Since Kpelle elders stake a privileged claim to knowledge of *sale* [esoteric knowledge and medicines] and [local] history, they have the greatest concern in sustaining the barriers and boundaries which protect their knowledge from encroachment. The youth learn to honor these boundaries through [the initiation rites] which imbues them with fear and respect for the elders' ownership of knowledge and their prerogatives over its distribution (Murphy 1980, 199). . . . The persistent threat of beatings, poisonings, etc., for breaking the secrecy oath . . . creates an atmosphere of fear which is more important than the actual knowledge taught by the *zoo-na* (pl. of *zoo*) to the young initiates of the Poro and Sande "bush schools." (Murphy 1980, 200)

What is perhaps most interesting here is that, as noted with the "lore" that is embedded deeply in the craft apprenticeship, the pedagogy of initiation rites requires critical information to be deliberately rendered obscure and opaque. This is done to thwart the initiate's/apprentice's drive to gain full knowledge and the attendant authority. Mead referred to this sort of teaching as "functionless pedantry" (Mead 1964, 129), where learners are subjected to teaching not for the content or skill transmitted but to assert the teacher's dominant status.

As in school and in some apprenticeships, initiation rites end in a culminating event akin to a graduation ceremony, at the end of which the initiate displays visible signs of their successful endurance. For example, in communities in Amazonia, Mehinacu, and Canela nine-year-olds return to their families with their ears pierced to hold wooden plugs (Gregor 1970, 242; Crocker and Crocker 1994, 116), while Tapirapé boys acquire a prominent lip plug (Wagley 1977, 149). Young Tapirapé (Brazil) women, just prior to their first pregnancy, pass through a rite that concludes with decorative scarification:

> This traditionally consisted of a quarter-moon design on each cheek and a half-moon design under the chin . . . Only women who carried that design on their face were truly beautiful. The design was drawn in charcoal and then cut into the face with crisscross lacerations using the sharp incisor teeth of the agouti or paca. . . . Into these wounds ginipap juice was rubbed so that it would become permanently black. (Wagley 1977, 163)

Teeth are also often subject to modification. Adolescent Japanese girls of the Tokugawa (Edo) period had their teeth blackened (Sofue 1965, 156). Balinese children have their teeth filed and blackened during their coming-of-age ceremony (Covarrubias 1937), and Baka youth have their incisors filed to points. Though these rites may be fairly brief, "they are painful, require courage and fortitude, and give the successful initiate a sense of having left childhood behind" (Konner 2005, 51; Devin 2013).

As noted by Goldschmidt, "The dominant theme of the initiation is that of an ordeal—trial and proof of maturity" (1986, 95–96). Consequently, as in apprenticeships (Lancy 2012), parents may not be involved in their child's initiation (Hotvedt 1990). Initiation of youth is a community responsibility, in part because an overriding goal of the rites is to forcibly transform the youth into an adult or at least reorient their attention from immediate family and peers to elders in the community.

What Purposes Are Served?

Contrary to the impression created by the popular designation "bush school," initiation rites do *not* involve didactic instruction in everyday knowledge and skill. "Formal education in the initiations is minimal, as it is only occasionally desirable in everyday Afikpo (Nigeria) life. There really is no 'school in the bush,' the specific knowledge that the boys acquire is not extensive" (Ottenberg 1989, 237). During the Kpelle rites, initiates "usually know the most important practical skills, such as farming techniques, before joining. In many ways, they learn little that they did not already know. Rather, initiation intensifies respect for the elders and their apparent knowledge of the mystical powers of the secret society" (Murphy 1980, 200).

It is widely recognized in developmental psychology that "adolescents go through a period of social reorienting where the opinions of peers become more important than those of family members" (Blakemore and Mills 2014, 188). The existence of a distinct adolescent culture is acceptable in Western, educated, industrialized, rich, democratic (WEIRD) society, where the prolongation of the individual's student role postpones the onset of meaningful work and family formation. But, in most societies, there is the expectation that children should transition into more responsible roles at or before puberty (Lancy and Grove 2011a). Youth are to prepare themselves for becoming householders, spouses, and parents (see Box 6.1). This sets up a potential conflict that the initiation process addresses. Many accounts stress the importance of enforcing compliance and uniformity of behavior on youth who are used to enjoying a great deal of autonomy (Young 1985).

152 LEARNING WITHOUT LESSONS

Box 6.1 Conforming to Expectations

"During [Bonerate] circumcision rituals the novices are formally introduced to the ideal standards of conduct to which adults should conform" (Broch 1990, 137).

"Compliance with traditional wisdom enshrined in the formal songs and dances of Bemba elders is a sure sign that one 'understands'" (Maxwell 1983, 58).

For the Hopi of the southwestern United States, initiation could be quite severe. In Don Talayesva's autobiography, he confesses to being quite "naughty" as a boy. So, when he was initiated "with his age group . . . the Katsinas gave him extra blows with the sharp-spiked ocotillo whips to 'drive the evil from [his] mind, so that he may grow up to be a good and wise man'" (Simmons 1942, 80).

Bakkarwal youth must be forcibly weaned from the "bad influence" of the peer group (Rao 2006, 59).

"The enactment of 'respect' for elderhood and seniority, *tlotla bagolo*, is repeatedly, exaggeratedly dramatized during the ritual. . . . A Tswapong woman explained, it does not matter whether the elders are your parents or not. You will be taught that starting from today each and every elder is your parent; you should give her respect and love (*tlotlo le lerato*). An uninitiated woman is capable of passing without greeting . . . Now, when she has been initiated she will not do that" (Werbner 2009, 452).

Adolescents may need a degree of "re-packaging" to reorient them from the peer group to the larger community, to reinforce their respect for authority (Edel 1957/1996, 183) and to ready them for the responsibility of marriage (Richards 1956).

Among the Kaugel (PNG), young men who fail to fall into line and demonstrate the proper deference accorded to senior members of the tribe risk permanent bachelorhood since they can't possibly acquire on their own the enormous resources required to make an adequate bride-price payment (Bowers 1965).

THE TRANSITION TO STRUCTURED LEARNING   153

Two negative examples will also be instructive. Among small Aka Congo Basin hunter-gatherer communities, there are no initiation rites and no "generation gap."

> Adolescent . . . males and females consistently noted their parents as being the person they spent time with, felt closest to and turned to for comfort. . . . The function of the peer group seems to serve to reinforce and act as an extension of the relations of family. . . . Adolescents come and go as they please, begin sexual relations and select a mate without parental influence. (Bentz 2001, 27–28)

A second example, from Hadza savanna hunter-gatherers in Tanzania, displays a similar pattern. There is no initiation rite for males beyond a brief ceremony (*maito*) following a boy's first major kill (Marlowe 2010, 57). Instead,

> Teenagers look up to adults and get along well with their elders. This is at least partly due to the fact that adults do not try to control them and rarely express strong opinions about whom they should marry. . . . Since there is no wealth, men do not have the same leverage over their sons that they do in societies where marriage depends on the payment of bride-price or dowry. (Marlowe 2010, 55)

A related goal of many rites is to affirm the superior rank of senior adults compared to the newly initiated, and of males, more generally, over females. And this view of knowledge—as something grudgingly transmitted to youth in a way that protects and enhances the hegemony of seniors, male and female—is common (Brooks 2011, 207; Dorjahn 1982, 47).

For the Arapesh (Sepik Region, PNG), "initiation ceremonies [include] an ordeal followed by the novices being shown the secret paraphernalia . . . flutes, frims, paintings, statues, bullroarers" (Tuzin 1980, 26). Knowledge of these sacred artifacts and their uses was forbidden to women. Denying females access to powerful spirit forces aids in maintaining male hegemony.

Not surprisingly, this array of coercive and punishing tactics for socializing youth is quite effective. Hewlett (2016, 4), in explaining cultural change versus stasis, asserts that intracultural variation is reduced by the concerted efforts of multiple teachers all echoing the same lessons, such as those found in initiation ceremonies. However, the willingness of initiates to suffer through these arduous experiences is also accounted for by the rewards that follow completion. Opportunities are now available that were formerly denied, and

154 LEARNING WITHOUT LESSONS

Box 6.2 Welcoming Initiation

"Mardu [Aboriginal] boys have mixed feelings about their coming initiation. They are frightened of the ordeals they suspect lie ahead, yet they are also aware that others before them have survived. When their time approaches, they become understandably anxious to be inducted into the secret world of the men, to attain adulthood, and eventually to earn the right to marry" (Tonkinson 1991, 87).

Surviving the privations and tests of endurance and valor determines one's eligibility for marriage in most African pastoralist societies such as the Maasai (Spencer 1970) and Dinka (Deng 1972).

Ijo female initiates "eagerly looked forward to it as to a graduation ceremony into adulthood" (Hollos and Leis 1989, 125).

"Wunambal Aborigines learn the art of making spearheads from earliest youth, [but] they are not allowed until after the initiation ceremony has been performed to produce fully finished spearheads" (Moore 2015, 941).

Gbusi (PNG) initiates "would now be suddenly and imminently marriageable (Knauft 2013, 87) [and could anticipate receiving valuable gifts], especially prized hardwood bows and sheaves of elaborate arrows . . . Previously allowed to use only unpainted arrows for hunting, the initiates could now use painted and people-killing arrows in ritual display and, as need be, in warfare" (Knauft 2013, 89).

Among the Kamea (PNG), "It was inconceivable [until recently] for an uninitiated youth to take a wife. The men's cult taught young men how to behave in the presence of women and how to avoid being contaminated by the polluting sexual substances of their brides-to-be" (Bamford 2004, 42).

Fiske and Rai (2015) argue that severe initiation rites are critical in the creation of a warrior class of youth, tightly bonded to each other through their shared ordeal.

---

initiates "go willingly to be initiated, or even eagerly request it" (Fiske and Rai 2015, 180). BaYaka youth, for example, may "demand" to be initiated (Bombjaková 2018, 87). Box 6.2 provides a sampling of those opportunities. Although initiation rites continue into the modern era (Matavire 2017; Ricks 1997), they are coming under increasing attack from Christian missionaries,

THE TRANSITION TO STRUCTURED LEARNING   155

government authorities, and nongovernmental organizations (NGOs) dedicated to improving the lives of youth, especially girls. Initiation and other "pagan" practices have been suppressed and driven underground. Hence, young Kamea men can no longer advertise their initiated status by wearing a bone inserted through the nasal septum (Bamford 2004). Bumbita Arapesh youth may no longer experience initiation into the Tambaran cult. Denied access to the older men's secrets and spells, their ability "to produce thriving and abundant crops of yams," the staple food, will be impaired (Leavitt 1998, 186). Biersack warns: "What drops out of the picture with a loss of these practices is not just . . . ritual . . . but . . . the very social order that the ritual was meant to construct and maintain" (1998, 87). In response to this problem, there have been efforts to revive initiation rites (Solway 2017, 43).

To this point in the chapter, schooling and teaching are presented as "necessary evils," growing out of the needs of complex societies to manage information and citizens. However, teaching and school-like activities are found to a limited extent in at least some nonliterate, small-scale, face-to-face societies. The common denominator in the majority of such cases is a body of information that is inaccessible to the autonomous learner. Unlike so much of the "village curriculum," this information is not transparent and accessible to all but, rather, is hidden or "opaque."

The Opacity Problem

The ethnographic record is replete with vivid descriptions of children eagerly plunging into the learning and mastery of their culture. Endowed with a suite of instrumental skills, they can make sense of and learn to replicate most of the knowledge base that constitutes the cultural capital of their community. One such skill Hemingway prosaically referred to as a "crap detector" (Manning 1965) which scholars refer to as "epistemic vigilance." Sperber and colleagues identified this ability as "appearing in early childhood, arguably even in infancy" (Sperber et al. 2010, 373). It enables children to sort among individuals as sources of information, evaluate them by past performance and the overheard comments of others, and thereby reduce the risk of being misinformed. Epistemic vigilance joins a host of skills that, operating in consort, permit "children to become competent adults without the help of . . . teaching, [as] . . . learning is achieved as a by-product, in the course of interactions that have other purposes" (Atran and Sperber 1991, 39).

156 LEARNING WITHOUT LESSONS

But the ethnographic record *does* contain instances, however rare, of formal lessons designed and led by a teacher. I will detail a few interesting examples and then discuss what they have in common.

The Kogi are mountain-dwelling Indigenes in northeast Colombia who "Behind the drab façade of penury, lead a rich spiritual life" (Reichel-Dolmatoff 1976, 266). This all-pervading spiritual life is guided by native (non-Christian) priests (*Mámas*). The preparation of a prospective *Mámas* by senior priests begins in childhood and lasts until early adulthood. Formal instruction includes ritual, divination, memorization of sacred texts, and learning correct speech. Myths, songs, and spells must be memorized with correct intonation as well as coordinated body movements and minor gestures that accompany the performance. Failure or laxity leads to sleep and food deprivation or a beating. Novices "may be ordered to kneel on a handful of cotton seeds or on some small pieces of a broken pottery vessel" (Reichel-Dolmatoff 1976, 279). In contrast to the training of priests, the ordinary sub-sistence and craft skills required of the Kogi "are soon mastered by any child" (Reichel-Dolmatoff 1976, 281).

In the Ituri forest region of the Democratic Republic of Congo, the Lese people rely on cultivated plants and wild forest game obtained through ex-change with neighboring hunter-gatherers. Throughout this region, certain foods are broadly proscribed for certain individuals or families. "Over three hundred different types of reasons for avoiding foods were reported by the Lese. . . . For example, *kelikofu* [a type of hornbill] is bad for parents of children to eat, for when a child is sick, it shakes—just as the bird, when it comes out of its [nest] hole" (Aunger 2000, 452–453). These taboos are not freely talked about, so a child has no way of learning them through overhearing or log-ical deduction from behavior; they must be taught. "The same gender parent begins to opportunistically present the child with samples of a particular food item, with instruction that this item cannot be eaten. Often, some rationale is also provided" (Aunger 2000, 453). Jerome Lewis, who has studied learning among Central African forest foragers, makes clear that "teaching" is limited to these obscure taboos. Otherwise, children experience a "learner-motivated pedagogic process that does not depend on defining any individual [teacher] as a focus for learning important knowledge" (Lewis 2016, 147).

Among the West African Yoruba people, divination is of prime impor-tance to the smooth running of society. The process of becoming a *Babalawo* (diviner) is carefully structured to ensure the diviner learns the hundreds of sacred texts, all transmitted orally and committed to memory. While some

THE TRANSITION TO STRUCTURED LEARNING   157

aspects of divination can be learned through observing the diviner at work, "much of the teaching and learning occurs out of context. . . . As in typical classroom learning, the trainee is asked to memorize and learn material that has no natural context" (Akinnaso 1997, 371; see also Bascom 1969).

Another interesting case is described in *East Is a Big Bird*, a unique chronicle of life on a remote coral atoll in Micronesia. While virtually all male adults can sail an outrigger vessel among nearby islands, only a handful of master navigators can pilot a craft over great distances. A younger sailor who shows promise may "enroll" with one of the island's master navigators.

> Formal instruction begins on land. It demands that great masses of factual information be committed to memory. This information is detailed, specific, and potentially of life-or-death importance. It is taught by a senior navigator to one or several students, some young, some older. Often, they sit together in the canoe house, perhaps making little diagrams with pebbles on the sandy floor. This is a body of knowledge which is not kept secret, but . . . no one could possibly learn it except through the most painstaking and lengthy instruction, so no outsider could pick it up merely by occasional eavesdropping. Instead it is taught and memorized through endless reiteration and testing. (Gladwin 1970, 128, 131)

A final example comes from two studies of spear-hunting, among the Chabu (Ethiopia) and BaYaka (Congo). Because of the apparent complexity, boys are targeted for direct instruction on the subtleties of spear-hunting by senior relations (Dira and Hewlett 2016; Lew-Levy et al., 2020a).

These five examples of lessons, in the context of less complex, small-scale societies, have a number of elements in common, but all represent solutions to the opacity problem.[7] As Mead notes for the Manus, "the material environment offers no mechanical complexities such as elaborate machines, beyond the comprehension of the child . . . the simple principles upon which a Manus native builds and navigates his canoes, or builds his house, present no mysteries" (Mead 1967a, 235).

Among Aka Pygmy forest foragers, little girls observe and assist their mothers in building the family's new hut after the trek to a new hunting camp. At puberty, the girl, with no further instruction, builds and moves into her

---

[7] Note that experts do not always feel compelled to assist the learner with overcoming the opacity problem. Apprenticeship is a prime example where full mastery must include secrets which are jealously withheld and must be discovered by the apprentice.

own hut (Bentz 2001). This transparency in technology and social relations is a boon for the self-initiating learner and obviates the need for intervention by a teacher, explicit lessons, and so on. But the five cases just described show that "simple" societies may give birth to quite complex bodies of knowledge that are opaque to the uninitiated and difficult to access. Csibra and Gergely (2011), drawing on lab research with WEIRD subjects, call attention to opacity in arguing for the importance of early parent-infant teaching as anticipating a later need to teach the child all the elements of the culture. In my view, they overestimate the ubiquity of teaching as a means to overcome the opacity problem. As we have seen, there is little that is opaque in rural society. And, while the reverse is true in WEIRD society, Keil (2006) and Dunn (1988) have both found that a person's ignorance of how things work need not be an impediment to full social participation. People use locks, clocks, and zippers without being able to make them or explain how they work.

A thorough study of the opacity issue was conducted with Hadza bowyers. The bow and arrow is the Hadza's chief weapon for game hunting, upon which they depend for sustenance. In essence, the skilled bowyers cannot articulate how changing important dimensions of the bow will change the behavior of the bow. They show a deficit of *causal thinking*:

> Hadza bowyers consistently expressed beliefs about limb cross section that diverge from what is known about bow mechanics. . . . Study participants were asked why they believed a round cross-sectional shape to be best and 53% indicated that "it is the Hadza way," 32% stated that "this is the way the elders have instructed us," 10% expressed knowing through experience, and 5% stated that, although they believed round to be better, they did not have an explanation. (Harris et al. 2021, 1800)

A more persuasive theory parses the environment a child might need to adapt into two domains. Children deploy an "on-board," or inherited, suite of cognitive skills, such as epistemic vigilance, to figure out the natural and social worlds they are born into. Consider that "babies as young as 4 months already possess a 'theory of physics'" (Norenzayan and Atran 2004, 151). This is the "biologically primary domain" (Geary 2007, 3) and the basic learning processes and underlying cognitive skills children deploy would have appeared in the earliest hunter-gatherer children and continued to be adaptive to later-appearing pastoralist, farming, and early industrial societies (see Chapter 3). Language is found in the primary domain, and children acquire speech without much effort or instruction. In contrast:

THE TRANSITION TO STRUCTURED LEARNING   159

Academic learning involved . . . a suite of culture-specific biologically *secondary* domains, such as mathematics, and biologically secondary abilities and knowledge, such as the ability to phonetically decode written symbols[8] or to understand the base-10 structure of the formal mathematical number system (Geary 2007, 5, emphasis added) [leading to the necessity for] an evolutionarily novel context in which the cross-generational transmission of secondary abilities (e.g., writing) and knowledge (e.g., that a right angle = 90 degrees) is formalized. (Geary 2007, 53)[9]

However, as Bjorklund pithily observes, "Children did not evolve to sit quietly at desks in age-segregated classrooms being instructed by unrelated and unfamiliar adults" (2007b, 120). While no one would argue against the necessity of the three Rs, many children are distinctly uncomfortable spending hours each day confined to a school desk. I know I was. Hence, it makes sense that WEIRD parents might want to begin grooming their children from infancy to become good, compliant students (Csibra and Gergely 2011).

In the next section, we will follow the lives of children being introduced to those evolutionarily novel notions of quietly sitting in age-segregated classrooms while attending to the directions of a relative stranger. There is a rich trove of ethnographic accounts of this process as it is occurring around the world.

Village Schools

Episodically, between 1968 and 1971, I observed two village elementary schools "up-country" in Liberia. Unlike my own classroom experience in the 1950s and 1960s, these schools had more in common with the earliest schools, apprenticeship, and initiation rites. I argued that Liberian students were getting indoctrinated but not educated (Lancy 1975). While their progress in becoming literate and numerate was "hit or miss"—mostly the latter (Gay and Cole 1967, 35)—they readily accepted that schooling was the gateway to a life of ease and security as a white-collar or uniformed worker

---

[8] However, Serpell and Hatano (1997, 351–352) review three cases (the Vai in Liberia; the Cree in Canada; and the *kana* syllabary in Japan) where individuals routinely acquire literacy without formal instruction.

[9] This dichotomy has recently been confirmed from an unusual source. Studies show that as a result of COVID-19-driven school closures, student test results declined. However, the decline was much greater in math (very opaque) than reading (less so) (Mervosh 2022).

160 LEARNING WITHOUT LESSONS

in the city. Among the noteworthy attributes of these schools were the following:

> The use of English exclusively, a language that the Kpelle-speaking pupils had only a limited command of; absolute authority and hegemony of the teacher as government employee and sophisticated outsider; heavy reliance on rote memorization; overcrowding and near anarchy, interrupted only by frequent strikes on pupils' limbs; disdain for and harassment of girls; shortage of materials; and whatever academic skill pupils did acquire— such as limited literacy—had no utility outside the classroom. Parents, perhaps because of their own lack of schooling or their appreciation of the limited utility of poor schooling to significantly alter the child's (and, therefore, the family's) economic prospects, provided little support either before or during the child's school years—beyond the mandatory school fees and uniform. Indeed, the child was regularly kept from school should its assistance be required. (Lancy 2010, 93)

Few if any of the Kpelle students I observed realized their dream of salaried employment and became, instead, "school leavers." Universal primary schooling has created "an avalanche of failed aspirations throughout the third world" (LeVine and White 1986, 193). One can readily find parallel cases from North America (Deyhle 1991), Africa (Spittler 1998), Latin America (Macedo 2009), the Pacific region (Borofsky 1987), Papua New Guinea (Pomponio and Lancy 1986), and Asia (Montgomery 2001). No doubt much has changed since these observations were recorded, but several, more recent studies demonstrate the continuing pattern.

The Tsimané live in the Bolivian Amazon, where they practice a combination of gardening, hunting, and gathering. Children attend a nearby school, but "formal education should be classified as performing at the lower end of a graded 'educational continuum' relative to schools in industrialized countries" (Davis 2014, 2). The school day is relatively short, and there are frequent class cancellations; hence, "children between first and fifth grade attend 50% fewer hours . . . than their American peers" (Davis 2014, 3). Furthermore, teachers complain that Tsimané parents are unsupportive.

> If a child was chastised at school by the teacher, it was for a good reason, but the parents—instead of supporting the teacher's view—would encourage the child not to attend school again, if that was the kid's desire. . . . They do

THE TRANSITION TO STRUCTURED LEARNING   161

not usually reprimand their children [leading the teacher to declare] "these children are wild, and that is how they want to keep being." (Martínez-Rodríguez 2009, 74)

In Kayapó and Araweté [Brazil] communities, "the quality and amount (months/year) of schooling was low . . . teachers' absenteeism was high, schools had infrastructural problems, and students often missed school as they engaged in labor activities and rituals. . . . None of the children between 6 and 15 years old . . . were able to read or write" (Ruiz-Malén et al. 2013, 217). In lieu of schooling, children "spent their daylight time playing and undertaking subsistence work" (Ruiz-Malén et al. 2013, 213).

More recent follow-up research compared Tsimané children enrolled in schools of widely varied quality (measures like "Are basic writing materials (i.e., paper and pencils) provided to students by the school?") and found significant effects of quality on literacy, numeracy, and cognitive skill (Davis et al., 2021).

Nayaka (India) foragers are compelled to send their children to school but

the kind of schooling to which most Nayaka children have access does not provide them with tools to compete for higher education or more profitable jobs. The structural obstacles faced by those children in the context of the education system are so vast that it is almost impossible to break through them. With poorly equipped, poorly maintained, and poorly staffed schools and very frequent teachers' absenteeism and disrespectful treatment, what children learn best in most schools is to acknowledge their own inferior social status. (Naveh 2016, 14)

Living off the land in the Peruvian Amazon, Matses children demonstrate precocity in mastering their environment. Because the Matses had relocated from the interior forest to a more accessible riverside location (where schooling could be provided), the children, who rapidly adapted to the change, were far more at ease canoeing and fishing in the broad river than their parents. There is a painful contrast between the Matses children's mastery of their natural surroundings and their great discomfort and incompetence in the classroom:

The physical space of the classroom and the authoritarian teaching styles are aimed precisely at restraining movement while promoting quietness and

162 LEARNING WITHOUT LESSONS

stillness. The children are forced to sit down in silence, facing the teacher, with their legs trapped under the small desks and unable to turn around or they will be yelled at.[10] The classroom is not as sensorially rewarding as other daily environments such as the river. It is instead extremely boring and frightening (Morelli 2013, 291; 2012). Matses schools largely fail in their aim of providing the children with basic skills such as reading, writing and mathematics and helping them succeed in the nonindigenous world. (Morelli 2013, 281)

Unlike the Amazonian communities just described, compulsory schooling in the Arctic—enforced with fines—has been in place for many years. Children cannot opt out. The Yupiaq live in isolated communities, and children are expected to participate in hunting and fishing activities that are the mainstay of the economy. However, "schooling leads to disillusionment and alienation from the Yupiaq ways while instilling . . . aspirations for a world that is out of reach" (Kawagley 2006, 86). Ulukhaktok "children who previously spent their days helping parents with hunting, trapping, fishing, skin preparation, and general household chores now spend much of the day in an institutional setting learning skills unrelated, and sometimes antithetical, to those emphasized at home" (Condon 1987, 157).

From the 1950s (Marshall 1976) to the present (Takada 2020), the Ju|'hoan[11] speakers of Nyae Nyae have been studied as the last active hunters and gatherers in the Kalahari. Today children still learn to forage. And, aside from subsistence foraging, villagers earn fees as guides for trophy hunters and tourists and gather and sell medicinal plants to exporters. Since 1998, Jennifer Hays has studied childhood and schooling as it affects these people. There is no specific word for "teacher" in Ju|'hoan. The word used "today for 'school teacher' is *nxarokxao* which translates directly as 'owner of learning' " (Hays 2016, 37). This construct echoes one of the primary attributes of the craft or trade master, also the senior adults leading initiation rites. Knowledge is power, and those who own it exercise hegemony over those who lack it (Macedo 2009, 181).

---

[10] Joyce Kinkead, a colleague, supplied a more modern echo of these sentiments from *The Ladybird Book of Handwriting*: "The writer should be seated comfortably, feet flat on the floor and the desk sloping slightly. . . . The forefinger should rest on the pencil about one-and-a-half inches from the point, and should point into the paper at an angle of 45 degrees. . . . The ball point pen is most emphatically discouraged" (Gourdie 1968, 35).

[11] In earlier publications, these people were referred to as !Kung.

THE TRANSITION TO STRUCTURED LEARNING   163

After three years of local schooling in their native tongue, Nyae Nyae students must transfer to the government school at Tsumkwe. They live in a hostel. Few make it through the first year, and only one student in the past twenty-five years has gone as far as seventh grade. Hays identifies several reasons for this persistent "failure" (see Box 6.3).

For students from Nyae Nyae, the pedagogy of schooling has proved to be aversive and unattractive compared to the informal pedagogy characteristic of their community. In addition to numerous similar examples in the ethnographic record, the early history of rural/urban slum schools in the West tells a similar tale (see Box 6.4).

We have seen that Nyae Nyae parents, while not openly resisting schooling for their children, do little to deter them from following their own inclinations. However, in many Indigenous communities as well as poor and/ or rural families in the West, schooling is more actively opposed. In many cases, parental opposition to schooling arises from the need for children to perform critical, routine chores.

School–Village Conflict: School Versus Work

Perhaps the greatest contrast between WEIRD and non-WEIRD childhoods is in the area of work. From toddlerhood, children demonstrate their eagerness to "pitch in" and assist others in their work (Lancy 2020). In WEIRD society, these overtures may be discouraged. Elsewhere, helping is nurtured until—as young as five—the child becomes a cog in the routine machinery of the domestic economy (Lancy 2018). Whereas in non-WEIRD society, schooling may compete directly with work and work-themed play, in WEIRD society, schooling, which begins earlier and earlier in the child's life, effectively fills a vacuum (see Box 6.5).

Economics may play a prominent role in villagers' *acceptance* of schooling as well. Rather than spurning the school, parents and children alike may envision schooling as the gateway to a brighter future for graduates, such as easier work and material goods. And families can imagine generous remittances from their urban, salaried kin. One young aspirant told the anthropologists, "School children are seen as gentlemen; they have good manners . . . they are modern" (Sackey and Johannesen 2015, 455). Working in the Ministry of Education in Papua New Guinea in the 1970s, I witnessed great variability in villagers' enthusiasm toward schooling for their offspring. Ali Pomponio was

164 LEARNING WITHOUT LESSONS

Box 6.3 Nyae Nyae Resistance to Schooling

Mixed together with several other ethnic groups of greater means and status, the Nyae Nyae students find a hostile environment in Tsumkwe. They lack uniforms and other marks of upward mobility and are singled out for hazing.[*]

The principal explained that "they are not used to being told 'do this, do that' and they don't want to be treated like the others. . . . If they don't do their homework, they are supposed to get punished, but the [Nyae Nyae] kids, they don't like being punished" (Hays 2016, 50).

In contrast, "the characteristics of autonomy, tolerance of individual will, and lack of punitive discipline, are highlighted throughout the ethnographic literature on the Ju|'hoansi" (Hays 2016, 51).

The school authorities argue that parents " 'do not understand the value of education and do not force their children to go to school'; this is connected to a general lack of discipline: 'they have no rules' " (Hays 2016, 49).

The sporadic school attendance of Ju|'hoan youth is in keeping with their general approach to participation in daily activities. . . . For children who have been raised in a tolerant community that respects individual decisions about how they spend their time—and trusts them to make good decisions and to become competent adults—the transition to an environment where they are expected to be in the same place at the same time every day is met with *resistance*. This is one of many identifiable cultural discontinuities . . . that clearly play a role in the decision of Ju|'hoansi children not to attend Tsumkwe school" (Hays 2016, 53, emphasis added).

[*]*Pygmy* children in the Congo Basin suffer the same treatment by their non-pygmy peers (Raffaele 2003, 132).

---

conducting fieldwork in the Siassi Islands at the time, and we collaborated on a comparative study of several communities that had acquired schools relatively early or relatively late in PNG's history. As PNG was decolonized in the 1960s, there was a flood of new white-collar or "uniformed" jobs available to replace the departing expatriates.

In the Siassi Islands, parents had enjoyed a windfall from their children who were among the first to gain access to secondary education in the early 1960s and who did find ready employment in government jobs that were

THE TRANSITION TO STRUCTURED LEARNING   165

Box 6.4 Historical Resistance to Schooling

"In the Middle Ages . . . it was well known that children did not like to go to school and used every excuse not to" (Willemsen 2008, 35–36).

"Hardly the significant or defining experience of childhood, school life was remembered in most memoirs briefly, if at all, in the context of much fuller descriptions of free play and work with siblings and friends" (Fass 2016, 133).

For example, William White "was born in 1868 and grew up in Emporia, Kansas, at the edge of the open plains . . . and 'did chores cheerfully in the primitive, savage simplicity of childhood'" (Fass 2016, 115, cf. White 1946, 27). However, he "did not like schools, but that would not have differentiated William from most boys of his time, since the outdoors was much more alluring that the inside of a classroom" (Fass 2016, 115).

In nineteenth-century London, "children had to learn to accept the teacher's authority, to keep still during lessons, and not talk or move around without permission. These aims were not easily achieved: complaints of talkativeness and fidgeting, unruliness, disorder and inattention recur in the logbooks. The school room was organized for surveillance and discipline, with the children seated in rows ('facing mutely towards the source of knowledge')" (Davin 1996, 114).

---

opening up. But by 1979, the expense of sending children through to secondary school had climbed, while the returns had declined; graduates were no longer finding jobs (van Groningen 2023). Hence, enrollment in local elementary schools had dropped dramatically as parents recognized that schooling was no longer a good investment (Pomponio and Lancy 1986). They would achieve a greater return from their children if they kept them busy in gardens or collecting on the reef (Pomponio 1992). A similar sequence of stages can be found on Rotuman (Howard 1970, 63), Malaita (Watson-Gegeo and Gegeo 1992, 17), and Ponam Islands (Carrier 1981, 239), as well as in Africa (Grindal 1972, 92).

The Siassi Islanders and many other coastal communities were fortunate to catch this wave of opportunity. We found more remote Highland communities where children had only gained access to schooling in the 1970s. And the schools were drastically underfunded and mismanaged

166 LEARNING WITHOUT LESSONS

> ### Box 6.5 Conflict Between School and Work
>
> "German settlers in Pennsylvania opposed education on the ground that it would make children lazy and dissatisfied with farm work" (MacElroy 1917, 59).
>
> In Southern Morocco, a girl becomes a competent weaver with little or no investment; she just needs to pay attention to females who're weaving. Schooling is seen as requiring a much greater investment and is perceived as a "drain on female human resources for the household" (Naji 2012, 377).
>
> "Implementing Western-inspired schools into Mbendjele culture . . . can have negative effects not only on the children, but on the livelihood of the Mbendjele communities as a whole" (Bombjaková 2018, 283).
>
> Pastoralist Maasai children have fewer years of schooling than nonpastoralists: "Responsibilities of herding and caring for livestock typically begin at a very young age (6–7 years) and herding activities are generally difficult to combine with education because they occupy children for most of the day and may involve taking livestock far outside of villages" (Hedges et al. 2016, 8).
>
> On Romanum, a small volcanic island in Chuuk Lagoon, children care for younger siblings, harvest and process marine resources, husk and grate coconut, pound breadfruit, find firewood, and cook. Parents exert little effort to ensure children's school attendance (Spencer 2015).
>
> "Lu You called village schools *dongzxue*, or winter schools, because sons of farmers were sent there only in winter" (Bai 2005, 25).
>
> An eleven-year-old boy reports: "Immediately we hear that the [Cape Coast, Ghana] fishermen have arrived from the sea, we escape school to the shore to work" (Sackey and Johannesen 2015, 452).
>
> "School attendance of Baka children was very limited . . . children are still highly engaged in subsistence-related activities (i.e., hunting and gathering)" (Sonoda et al. 2018, 163).

(Little 2011). Nevertheless, Imbonggu parents willingly paid school fees and sent the majority of their sons to school. They were convinced that by attending the rudimentary (in every sense) school in the village, their sons would travel the *rot bilong mani* (road to riches) to a life of ease, just like the *whitpela.*[12] But by the beginning of the next decade, Imbonggu adults, now sadly wiser, angrily denounced the *bikhets* (big-heads)—school leavers who had returned to the village without jobs and without any appreciation for or tools to succeed in the village (Pomponio and Lancy 1986; Grove 2023).

Gapun (Sepik region, PNG) villagers experienced a similar transition. They went to the trouble and expense of building a school and lobbied for a teacher. They viewed the pedagogy of the school as analogous to the initiation rites that reveal powerful secrets to the initiates. They were powerless to help their children—beyond paying school fees—not having been schooled themselves. Families discovered that whatever secrets were imparted during primary school, they don't "open a road to the cargo"; their money-earning opportunities are no different than the unschooled (Kulick 1992, 180).

Much depends on the health of a nation's economy. With an expanding, dynamic economy like China's, schooling had provided opportunities for rural youth. Following the end of the Cultural Revolution, schooling took on a more practical mission, and villagers began to invest in children's schooling, which took precedence over other obligations like chores and religious ceremonies. Older, successful children were sent away for their secondary education. Following graduation and employment, they were expected to become the "'backbone of support' for their siblings who remained in the village" (Obendick 2013, 106). Migrating from the village to seek employment before completing one's education is now discouraged, and schoolteachers are held up as models for students to emulate (Stafford 1995). In Shandong, zeal for schooling—village students outscore urban students on national exams—comes from the desire to escape the stigma of being a peasant (Kipnis 2001, 17).

School–Village Conflict: Views on Teaching and Learning

Community resistance to schooling is also engendered by wide divergence in pedagogy. A *Mestizo* teacher condems the parents of her Mazahua pupils because they "were not interested in their children. . . . They don't play with them . . . leaving them alone the whole day. In fact, they do not *educate* their

---

[12] While village parents around the world seem eager to send their children off to earn their fortunes, studies of Native American communities in the United States present a very different picture. There, parents strenuously resist any notion that their children will use schooling as an "exit" strategy to move away from family and the reservation. This "resistance" is cited as one of the major causes of very low academic success among Native American students (Deyhle 1991, 294; Deyhle 1991; Condon 1987, 162). Other North American examples of resistance to the demands of the school ethos include the Amish (Hostetler and Huntington 1971/1992, 3) and Hopi (Simmons 1942, 100).

168 LEARNING WITHOUT LESSONS

children, but . . . leave them to make their knowledge on their own" (de Haan 1999, 74). These conflicting perspectives on the need for mothers to behave like teachers are echoed in numerous reports, including Cambodian immigrant mothers in the United States. "Most Cambodian parents believe that they should not be involved in their children's education" (Coll and Marks 2009, 90). Teachers in Germany with a high proportion of immigrant students despair at recruiting mothers as co-teachers (Keller 2021, 64).

From the earliest schools in Sumer to the present day, in remote rural schools, physical punishment is treated as an essential element of pedagogy. Teachers in Guinea believe *"Il faut suffrir pour apprendre"* = to learn, one must suffer (Anderson-Levitt 2005, 988), a philosophy shared with the apprenticeship. And while corporal punishment may be accepted in many societies (Ember and Ember 2005), it may be condemned in others. The Piaroa are forest foragers in the Guiana Highlands of Venezuela. Like many hunting and gathering societies, they "do not tolerate the display of physical violence, and children are never physically punished" (Overing 1988, 178). Hence, coercive tactics imposed on school children may be resisted by concerned parents.

In Tzotzil Maya communities in the Chiapas Highlands, schooling could be an ordeal:

> Children were severely punished for failure to learn their lessons well and for other infractions of the rules, such as the use of the mother tongue even before they had learned any Spanish. Often they were made to kneel on pebbles or fruit pits for lengthy periods of time in order that their lessons might penetrate; many teachers punctuated their instruction with a leather strap or a thorny switch. . . . Parents did all they could to save their children. . . . School-aged boys were dressed as girls . . . so that they might not be caught and forced into school. . . . Children were hidden in the forests, sometimes for days on end, so that the census-takers might not count them. Sad, indeed, was the fate of the child who had to attend school. (Modiano 1973, 87)

A parallel scenario played out for Native Americans in the Mountain West around 1875, when boarding schools were established at locations remote from the children's homes (Adams 2020).

> The Indian Bureau in 1944 lobbied hard to move Indian children into boarding schools because of their "healthful and cultural surroundings

THE TRANSITION TO STRUCTURED LEARNING   169

without the handicap of having to spend their out-of-school hours in tepees, shacks with dirt floors, and no windows . . . in surroundings where English is never spoken, where there is a complete lack of furniture and where there is sometimes an active antagonism or an abysmal indifference to the virtues of education." (Hansen 1979, 205)

The schools openly declared their aim to "sever the children from their culture," leading, ultimately, to the eradication of the Native tribes and assimilating them into the majority culture. They were punished for speaking their native tongue and practicing their faith, and they were forced to wear Western dress and much shorter hair. Punishment was so severe for the "little savages" that children frequently ran away or were removed by their parents. Poor diet and neglect led to high mortality among the students. Contrary to expectations, children did not learn "modern" farming practices to take back to their communities; their "free time" was taken up with maintaining the school, including cleaning, laundry, gardening, and various other chores. When parents resisted by threatening to remove their children or be compensated for their labor, "soldiers were called to forcibly enroll students." In the 1950s, the government started to close Native schools and students were integrated into public schools. But "Indigenous students were neglected and left to fail. In the 1970s, the dropout rate for the Ute tribe's students hit 90%" (Tanner et al. 2022).

A second area of potential conflict arises from the hierarchical relationship between the teacher and student and the notion that teaching and learning are unidirectional. The student can only learn from the teacher, and the teacher learns nothing from the student (see, e.g., Lavi 2022). This approach is antithetical to the Indigenous pedagogy found in many societies (Sackey and Johannesen 2015, 456). See the examples in Box 6.6.

Another inherent conflict can be found in the contrast between the Indigenous ethnotheory of child development—which prescribes observation and listening but little speaking in the presence of adults—and the public school's expectations of active verbal participation and interaction with the teacher (Morton 1996, 170). Consequently, when students behave according to the model of socialization embraced by their society, teachers consider them overly shy, stupid, or defiant (Philips 1983). See Box 6.7 for examples of nonverbal interaction in Indigenous learning.

The catalog of mismatches between the pedagogy of institutionalized public basic schooling (IPBS) (see Serpell and Hatano 1997) and the

Box 6.6 Sharing Knowledge

"The Yucatec Maya concept of *ikenal* specifies that any community members can tap into the knowledge of anybody else in the community" (Rosado-May et al. 2020, 86).

In Nayaka hunter-gatherer bands from the forests of South India, "sharing one's understandings is always done in a sensitive and careful manner [so as] not to convey their own understanding as the 'right one' in the sense of 'this is how it is' . . . [It] is said softly, often with a vocal tone that conveyed doubt" (Naveh 2014, 356).

In school, "those who show that they know the answer to the instructor's question first are rewarded with a praise. This encourages competition amongst the children and also promotes boastfulness. However, 'Showing what you know' behavior is understood as 'rude' from the Mbendjele cultural perspective" (Bombjaková 2018, 296). "As Mbúmà explained, in Mbendjele society, sharing knowledge . . . can be harmful if done inappropriately . . . and mustn't violate personal autonomy and egalitarian relations of those involved" (Bombjaková 2018, 100).

multiple pedagogies indigenous to the societies first exposed to schools in the postcolonial period could be readily extended. These are touched on in several other chapters. Schools and their attendant pedagogies do not arise spontaneously in the communities that lack them. There must be intervention from outside, either through NGO efforts or the civil government. In the late 1960s, the rural schools in Liberia were built with funds from USAID, and many were staffed by Peace Corps volunteers or graduates of long-established urban schools, not Kpelle-speaking locals. The schooling movement was boosted by the United Nations' efforts to promote development in the Global South, including mandating universal primary education. The United Nations set 2015 as the year when full participation in primary school was to be reached. But in 2021, 64 million children of primary age were not in school (UNICEF 2022). Decades earlier, scholars studying schools in developing nations raised the alarm: " 'Universal primary education' has captured the imagination of politicians and social planners. . . . Yet the project is confronted with a moral trap. . . . Stated in its simplest form, the trap is for the school to find itself in the business of producing failures" (Serpell 1993, 10).

THE TRANSITION TO STRUCTURED LEARNING   171

Box 6.7 The Paucity of Verbal Interaction

On Borneo, village children "are not encouraged to ask questions or to seek explanations on why things are the way they are. When they do so, they will usually be cut short with a remark like 'that is how it is,' or 'that is customary'" (Nicolaisen 1988, 206).

"There is amazingly little verbalization in the whole learning process. [Chiga] children seem never to ask 'why' questions, which are so much a feature of learning in our culture" (Edel 1957/1996, 178).

"Because Inuit children are present in many multi-age situations, they are exposed to a great deal of talk by older people. Yet, it became apparent in this study that they were neither expected to participate nor to ask questions of adults who were speaking together. If they did ask questions, the adults ignored them, leaving their questions unanswered" (Crago 1992, 494).

Mazahua "children participate in . . . family . . . activities [and] conversation and questions . . . usually occur for the sake of sharing necessary information . . . Talk supports and is integral to the endeavor at hand rather than becoming the focus of a lesson . . . Indeed, were the children to ask questions it would be considered immature and rude" (Paradise and Rogoff 2009, 118, 121).

In the Marquesas, "children defer to elders, initiate few topics of conversation, and take only brief speaking turns" (Martini and Kirkpatrick 1992, 203).

Bamana children rarely talk with adults, who are to be treated with deference and respect. "They can always listen to adults' conversations, yet they are urged to not interfere by posing questions or expressing opinions" (Polak 2012, 88).

Despite failure, authorities maintain a lemming-like commitment to universal schooling. Susan Shepler has spent more than a decade studying the lives of child soldiers in Sierra Leone. She calls out the irony:

The lack of opportunities for young people and the inherent structural violence of the education system lead to "a crisis of youth" that lead[s] to civil war. The proposed solution [for child veterans of the war] is to continue with

172   LEARNING WITHOUT LESSONS

the flawed ideologies of Western schooling and heal the young combatants with the almost magical application of education. Education has become the default solution for any problem of youth in the liberal Western framework. (Shepler 2014, 96)

But "mass schooling could be an instrument of emancipation as well as regimentation" (LeVine et al. 2012, 12), and I would like to end this chapter on a high note. There have been positive outcomes from the widespread implementation of IPBS, notwithstanding the mismatch in pedagogy.

Schooling and Opportunity

The sheer number of school places and the historic durability of schooling have enabled a steady stream of aspirants to persevere. Among the Mbendjele,

Children disliked attending school and some of them hid or ran further to the forest to avoid it. However, . . . some children enjoyed attending the school as they were self-motivated in learning reading and writing. This small group of children was dreaming of going to school in Impfondo, the Department capitol one day. (Bombjaková 2018, 292)

First-person accounts of those who succeed are inspiring. Birendra Giri, who eventually earned BS and MS degrees in the Netherlands, had heavy responsibilities in his subsistence-farming, Nepalese family, including animal husbandry and household chores normally assigned to girls. He walked 1.5 hours each way from his home to the closest school and did his homework after 8:00 p.m. When domestic duties prevented him from completing homework, he could expect a beating by the teacher "from palm to shoulder" (Giri 2007, 13).

A historical perspective reveals the inexorable expansion of schooling opportunities and spread of the Western or WEIRD culture so closely linked to IPBS (Cooperrider 2019). In the South Indian village of Totagadde, schooling was spurned by the elite as recently as 1964. But, gradually, community leaders sponsored education for their sons and then their daughters. There was a trickle-down effect to the lesser castes; so, by 2011, children of all castes attended school. Even low levels of schooling have enabled poor villagers to migrate to urban areas, where they find jobs with sufficient pay to send funds home to families still living in Totagadde. These funds, in turn,

THE TRANSITION TO STRUCTURED LEARNING   173

are invested in children's schooling. Or children are sent to live with urban relatives, thereby gaining access to better-quality education. But perhaps the greatest impact has been on women's lives. Over the last fifty years, completed fertility has declined from four offspring to two.

> Educated men demanded higher dowries or married educated women from other castes instead of uneducated local Brahmin women. This provided impetus for women's education. As women became more highly educated, dowry demands decreased. . . . By 1976, Brahmin girls were attending high school and with each decade, a higher level of education has become available for Brahmin women. (Ullrich 2017, 233–234)

A second longitudinal study was carried out in Kali-Loro, a village in south-central Java. Data from the latter years of Dutch rule indicate that a small proportion of the village was schooled. By the 1950s, only a small proportion did *not* receive primary schooling, and by the late 1970s, everyone attended. Enrollment in secondary schools also increased at the same pace. In a survey done in the early 1970s, children were still doing a full range of chores while attending school. The school system was in some ways adapted to the needs of households, which "depended on work inputs from their children. Primary school occupied only a few hours each school day and absences during busy periods such as the rice harvest were quite flexibly tolerated" (White 2012, 89).

Twenty years later, White observed many signs of modernization and improved living standards, primarily due to increased rice-crop yields. Family size had declined. Children below the age of thirteen were contributing little to the domestic economy. Secondary schooling remained attractive, in spite of being an

> unreliable conduit into the labour market. [Schooling represented an adherence to a] "modern lifestyle" . . . while farming itself is downgraded as an occupation. . . . Remaining in secondary school is a way to avoid the kinds of work that their parents do, and in that sense a way to postpone "real" work—to prolong the identification of self as student/youth . . . while waiting for a chance to leave the village. (White 2012, 94)

While a full twelve years of schooling may not dramatically alter the career prospects of Javanese village youth, even a few years of schooling may have

174 LEARNING WITHOUT LESSONS

a large impact on women and their offspring. Aggregating data from four countries (Mexico, Nepal, Zambia, Venezuela), LeVine and colleagues found that even a few years of schooling can "modernize" a woman's approach to her own fertility (reducing it), improve her ability to keep her offspring alive and healthy, and lead her to "internalize the teacher role from their experience in Western-type schools and use it as mothers" (LeVine et al. 2012, 139). "Indeed, the associations of women's schooling with demographic and health factors in the less developed countries during the late twentieth century are among the most thoroughly replicated empirical relationship in comparative social research" (LeVine et al. 2012, 21).

Schooling promotes a form of literacy that leads women to "tune in" to public health services and other components of the no-longer-opaque bureaucracy. "Academic literacy as we measured it had a strong and consistent effect on the auditory comprehension of radio messages requiring no reading." Furthermore, mothers were now able to produce an "intelligible illness narrative" when taking their child to the clinic (LeVine et al. 2012, 123).

It seems very likely that the "failure" of universal primary education to achieve a transformative effect in rural society might be ameliorated by ensuring effective schooling for girls. Likely outcomes include later marriage, lower fertility, participation in the monetary economy via employment, marketing, or craft production, and better ability to support their children's schooling. However, this transformation may be impeded by strenuous resistance from some quarters. For example, Kano is located in the heartland of Boko Haram:

> All Hausa married women in Kano—Habe or Fulani—live in *purdah* or seclusion (Schildkrout 1981, 83). . . . Any change in the activities of children, such as the change now occurring as a result of the government's campaign to enroll all children in primary school, profoundly affects the status of women. . . . The intensification of *purdah* which has occurred in northern Nigeria in the past few decades has probably placed an increasing burden on children, for it is the use of children in the domestic economy which makes *purdah* possible. (Schildkrout 1981, 84)

The explicit connection between women's schooling and subsequent emancipation is met by violent opposition from Muslim fundamentalists, as vividly detailed in Malala Yousafzai's (2013) autobiography. Unfortunately, the hard-won gains of Malala and her fellows are now threatened by the resurgence

THE TRANSITION TO STRUCTURED LEARNING   175

of the Taliban, who have blown up hundreds of girls' schools in Pakistan (Yousafzai 2013, 73) and blocked girls from attending beyond primary school in Afghanistan (Qazizai 2022).

The Impact of Schools and School-Like Pedagogy on Individuals and Communities

During the 1960s and 1970s, several research projects were undertaken to probe the effects of schooling on cognitive development. This relationship could only be pursued by studying otherwise normal children who had been exposed to little or no schooling. Inevitably, this meant research in rural, preindustrial, "tribal" communities. A firm connection was established, and several important works were published that argued for a distinction between informal (learning in the community) and formal education (learning in school). Greenfield and Lave, in their review of this literature, made the point that village pedagogy could certainly be labeled informal, but, with judicious probing, one could also discover instances of more formal means of instruction (Greenfield and Lave 1982, 182–183). My goal in this chapter has been to review an array of these more formal settings for learning in complex as well as small-scale, preindustrial societies to extricate their essential features. The focus on more formal institutions for teaching/learning offsets the earlier attention paid to informal pedagogy in the previous chapters.

Schooling is the earliest exemplar of formal education that we can reliably recover from the distant past. Students, selected from the social elite, are organized into cohorts (classes), meet in a designated space, are directed by an adult expert (teacher) previously unknown to them, and follow a set curriculum. The latter is highly routinized and relies heavily on copying and memorization. Verbal instruction by the teacher or his assistants is limited, but physical and verbal chastisement is frequent. Instruction is centered on the teacher and the to-be-learned skills, not the student, who is expected to "suffer" on the way to "graduation." While we don't find evidence of open resistance by students in antiquity, by the Middle Ages, schools, having changed little, were *expected* to produce rowdy behavior (Willemsen 2008, 124).

Apprenticeship is probably as old or older than schooling and might be found in more complex and populous communities across cultures and historical periods. The apprentice experiences many of the same conditions as early students. The regimen may be highly structured with an aloof and

176 LEARNING WITHOUT LESSONS

unsympathetic master. Physical pain and verbal abuse are to be expected as the apprentice foregoes the freedom to manage his or her learning. Often, the pace of development is retarded by the requirement that the apprentice "pay back" the master through long hours of menial and repetitive work. However, as in the autonomous learning practiced in the village at large, the actual apprenticeship may be preceded by a period of informal education, including a preparatory play stage, learning via observation and imitation, and learning from artifacts and processes via trial and error. Verbal instruction may be of minor importance in the apprenticeship as the expert primarily models correct procedure that the novice must imitate. The most striking aspect of the apprenticeship as a setting for learning is the use of various obstacles and disincentives that retard or prevent the apprentice from expeditiously achieving full mastery. Particularly elusive is the "lore," or secrets of the trade that are withheld. This counterpedagogy is designed to reduce competition from newly trained craftspersons.

Unfathomable "lore" is a key component of formal education in the initiation rite. Through mystification, severe physical privation, and painful surgery, the initiate is impressed with the power and authority of the senior adults and ritual leaders of the community. The rites stand in stark contrast to the learning environments found in the village. Children are grouped into cohorts rather than acting independently. They are exposed to a standardized curriculum that all pass through in unison; self-managed learning is absent. They are given painful and frightening lessons from relative (sometimes disguised) strangers rather than the casual and benign socialization of kin.

Although uncommon outside the apprenticeship or initiation rite, teaching and other attributes of formal education can be found scattered across the ethnographic record. The goal of these lessons may be highly variable, but one common denominator is that the concepts or skills to be transmitted to the novice are opaque. That is, it is felt necessary to actively instruct the novice diviner, priest, long-distance navigator, and so on, because they would not learn all that is necessary through observing and imitating the expert.

A final example will lead to an important insight. As noted earlier, the Ju|'hoansi are quite dismissive of any notion that hunting skills can be taught. One must learn to hunt through hands-on experiences and by carefully observing and listening to those who are more experienced. However, ethnographic filmmaker Derrick Wayne (2001) captured an exception to this rule. He filmed a young Ju|'hoansi man receiving deliberate instruction in bow hunting from senior hunters using a target. The situation was a source of considerable amusement to the spectators and was clearly an exceptional event. The lessons were staged because the man had been handicapped by an accident involving a poisoned arrow and had not learned to hunt in his youth. Now married and with a child on the way, band members sought to remedy the situation. The point here is that while teaching may be extremely uncommon before the advent of schooling, in any given community there may be some members with the knowledge and willingness to teach those who require it.

The last section of the chapter describes the impact of bringing universal primary schooling to communities with little or no prior history of formal education. Reviewing a number of cases, a pattern emerged of initial failure and resistance followed later by evidence of positive outcomes and greater acceptance. Another conclusion is that many of the attributes of the earliest schools, apprenticeship, and initiation rites can be found in the typical village school. The teachers may be imperious, unsympathetic, and punitive. The curricula rely heavily on repetition and rote memorization (Carpenter 2020). The child/pupil is under tight control with little scope for initiative, learning colaboratively, or freedom of movement. Not surprisingly, there is ample evidence for active and passive resistance on the part of students and their families. Two primary issues drive this resistance. First, where children are seen as part of the domestic labor force, schooling becomes a direct competitor for the child's time and allegiance. Parents' support for schooling is mediated by the child's value as a worker (leading to girls' lower enrollment) or the likelihood that a schooled child will have increased earning power. Second, resistance arises because the pedagogy of the school may be antithetical to the practices and beliefs prevailing in the village (Packer and Cole 2020, 17). Among the apparent conflicts are the following: the use of corporal punishment in schools; requiring children to labor on behalf of the teacher; denying the child the autonomy to learn in their own fashion and pace; and expecting unschooled parents to act as de facto teacher's aides.

A great deal of ground has been covered, but there's one important thread that runs through these various occasions for formal education in complex as well as small-scale, preindustrial societies. This thread is the role that these educational institutions play in establishing and maintaining the social hierarchy. It is evident from surviving texts that the trained "graduates" of scribal schools were the first "white-collar" workers who were explicitly exalted over those who labored. The apprenticeship is seen not only as a way

178 LEARNING WITHOUT LESSONS

to raise the laborer up to a respected artisan but is carried out in a way that severely restrains the apprentice's opportunities to exceed or outflank the senior practioners of the craft.

Initiation rites explicitly define and enforce the initiate's inferior relationship vis-à-vis more senior community members and, in some cases, affirm male dominance over women. A pedagogy tool shared by these institutions is the revelation—in a highly charged atmosphere—of potent secrets and lore. These act as a kind of currency that can be doled out or withheld (identified as taboo) to manipulate those whose knowledge is limited. And, last, the newly established schools in the Global South also distribute knowledge and authority sparingly, as if it were lore. Parents expect that when they pay to send their children to school, the teacher will reveal the secrets to economic success, defined as nice clothing, a bicycle or motorcycle, store-bought treats, and so on. But before long, it becomes clear that the schools that really deliver paying jobs and economic success are private and/or located in cities with correspondingly higher fees, beyond their means.

In the next chapter, I will review a growing body of research aimed at teasing out the long-term effects of schooling on individuals and communities. Effects can be large, changing the life trajectory of the educated, as happened with Brahmin girls in Totagadde. Lesser effects include a falling off in environmental knowledge. The effects may be quite subtle, such as altered cognitive processing. Examples include the tendency to overimitate and eschewing wide-ranging and enduring attention in favor of teacher-directed attention. The effects may be on social behavior, where formerly cooperative children become competitive after a few years of student-centered schooling. This has become a cutting-edge field with a great deal of recent work to be reviewed.

7

Global WEIRDing

While there is a growing agreement on the necessity of studies on non-Western, educated, industrialized, rich, democratic (WEIRD) populations, cultural practices in many areas, even in the remotest regions, are converging, owing to globalization. This process of cultural convergence has been appropriately coined "global WEIRDing. (Cooperrider 2019, cited in Salali et al. 2020, 2).

Introduction

This chapter focuses on communities in transition from sociocentric to child-centric models of childhood. In the traditional, small-scale society, children are expected to learn through their own initiative and act in a cooperative, respectful, and altruistic manner toward others. In modernizing communities, parents and children adopt some or all of the WEIRD formula, which includes high levels of parent-child speech and deliberate instruction, children's emancipation from social obligations (and chores), and high levels of indulgence of the child's preferences and desires (e.g., "childism" from Young-Bruehl 2012; "neontocracy" from Lancy 2022). This wholesale change in childhood is deemed necessary in order to allow time for the steadily increasing demands of schooling on the child's life. Global WEIRDing rests on a foundation of globalization, and among the specific corollaries of this change, studies have identified the following: mother's schooling beyond the primary grades; reduced family size; Western religious missions; improved economic circumstances; urbanization; and greater material resources.

There are four topics discussed in this last chapter. They are united by a concern with dynamic and changing aspects of pedagogy triggered by global WEIRDing. In the previous chapters, pedagogy is depicted as a relatively stable, well-rooted aspect of culture. Two very different models of pedagogy emerged: the self-initiated, autonomous learning of the village and the parent/teacher-dominated, lesson-based instruction of WEIRD society.

Learning Without Lessons. David F. Lancy, Oxford University Press. © Oxford University Press 2024.
DOI: 10.1093/oso/9780197645598.003.0007

180   LEARNING WITHOUT LESSONS

These two models are not separate and equal. The WEIRD model of good parenting and educating is taken as the ideal and is embraced by school and social welfare authorities around the globe (Scheidecker et al. 2023).

In the following section, "Lesson Creep," I show how the WEIRD model of childhood is changing, as much of a child's free time and leisure activities are captured and converted into highly structured lessons. The historic mix of childhood activities—play, chores, and school—is reshaped, with school-like activity overwhelming the others. I touch briefly on several areas of lesson creep. Obviously, schooling is moving rapidly into Indigenous communities that lack formal education. In addition, lessons are imposed on younger and younger children, even babies. Preschool and kindergarten, formerly dominated by play, are rapidly becoming more academic. After-school activities, including play, sports, and other extracurricular activities, are, increasingly, repackaged as lessons, with homework to complete, rules to be learned, steps to be followed, teachers/coaches to be attended to, and so on (Gray et al. 2023).

In the next topic, "Lost Skills," I survey areas of community life, especially those in which youth are involved, that have been affected by global WEIRDing. The first casualty of school attendance may be children's learning of practical, subsistence skills. School attendance occupies a large segment of the child's day, especially when taking into account travel time. Many Indigenous communities, in effect, dismiss the child from the domestic labor force, hoping they can parlay schooling into a paid job and support the family monetarily. The most damaging effect may be the loss of opportunities to go on foraging trips with neighbors and kin. As noted in Chapter 4, these outings function as "everyday classrooms." When children are in school—especially as distant boarders—they miss many learning opportunities, and their knowledge deficit will not be filled by parents and others offering to step up and organize lessons to replace lost traditional environmental knowledge (TEK). As families gain ground economically, one of the earliest casualties is the chore curriculum. A collateral impact may be a decline in the child's ability to work collaboratively and to learn through joint activity. It is not only rudimentary chores that are affected but centuries-old craft traditions. Young people associate crafts with a primitive past dominated by their elders. They are unsentimental about "heirlooms" and prefer the offerings in the city market. At the end of the section, I review attempts to introduce aspects of Indigenous knowledge and pedagogy in the village school.

GLOBAL WEIRDING   181

While some of the effects of increased engagement with schooling are quite predictable, others are more subtle and can only be teased out through more circumspect means of inquiry. This section is titled "The Schooled Mind." After just a few years of schooling, Indigenous people begin to show patterns of cognitive processing found in the West. Studies show that the schooled mind is less concerned with the utility of objects and strategies for their use; instead, the focus is on naming, categorizing, and placing such objects in an analytical framework. In school—and at home, if the parents have been schooled—the child will be the target of much more directed speech, and learning will occur in a language-rich, as opposed to a "hands-on," environment. Classroom processes emphasize individual achievement, and collaborative learning will be reduced. Another profound change is the shift from autonomous, child-initiated learning through observation and eavesdropping to learning via structured lessons led by a teacher. This change leads to a laser focus on the teacher as the repository of to-be-learned material.

In the concluding section, I review the challenges facing cross-cultural comparative researchers. "The Weirdest People in the World?" (Henrich et al. 2010) paper was an urgent call to take psychology's core theoretical propositions overseas to test their viability outside WEIRD society. Researchers were being exhorted to determine whether a particular pattern of results would be found in Indigenous communities or not, in which case, any claim of universality would be withdrawn. But, as I will show, global WEIRDing is rapidly shrinking the pool of communities that can serve as unacculturated comparison sites. New research strategies must be developed to cope with this problem.

Lesson Creep

Educationalization . . . is the art of making people ever more "stupid."
—Depaepe and Smeyers (2008), 383

WEIRD ideas about "parenting"[1] are paramount in establishing standards for parents, teachers, and education authorities around the globe (Kuchirko and

---

[1] "There is some debate about when the practice of parenting originated, but the word itself only came into common usage about forty years ago. . . . Before that, children weren't parented, but 'reared,' which did not require much anxious philosophical examination. You loved them; you did your best

182 LEARNING WITHOUT LESSONS

Nayfeld 2020). One of the most prominent of these ideas might be "You can't have too many lessons." In this section, I will offer a brief tour of areas where child-initiated learning and recreation opportunities have been turned into adult-controlled lessons.

I will start off with lessons to teach children what they could well learn without aid. "Baby Signs" is a recent "breakthrough," where parents teach American Sign Language to their preverbal offspring to accelerate their language development. "Considering how slowly babies learn even easy words like *ball* and *doggy*, let alone difficult words like *scared* or *elephant*, many months are lost that could be spent having rich and rewarding interactions, both for the child and the parent" (Acredolo and Goodwyn 2002, 3).

Other examples come from a growing body of research in WEIRD society that reveals educated parents are "teaching" children skills that they can readily learn on their own and have always done so (Shneidman and Goldin-Meadow 2012). Prominent examples include teaching children to speak (Clark 2005); teaching them how to do make-believe play (Vandermaas-Peeler et al. 2009; Haight and Miller 1993); how to play with peers (Budwig et al. 1986; Schütze et al. 1986; Waldfogel 2006); and how to play with dolls (Miller and Garvey 1984). When queried, "a few parents valued play as a source of amusement . . . [but most] believed that parental involvement in children's play maximizes learning outcomes and that parents are appropriate teachers for their children . . . adult involvement was key to unlocking the learning potential of children's play" (Fasoli 2014, 14). Parents are given special incentives to enrich fantasy play. After all, what parent would argue against *neuroscience*?

> Characters such as dragons, mermaids and pirates, and imagined situations such as caves, castles, oceans and pirate ships also give valuable experiences for children by enhancing vocabulary and strengthening language for thinking, improving communication skills and social development. We can now proceed with confidence given that *neuroscience* as well as educational psychology has established, without question, that such play is vital in brain development, particularly between the ages of about two-and-a-half to seven. (Featherstone 2017, 91, emphasis added)

---

to make sure they didn't die; but you didn't give a lot of thought to optimizing their cognitive development or nourishing their self-esteem" (Traig 2019, 1).

GLOBAL WEIRDING   183

The idea that play is too valuable developmentally to be left to children to manage has been adopted by educated parents around the world (Kärtner and von Suchodoletz 2021).[2] "The game begins at the earliest stages, even as the Korean parent chooses the baby's toys. Toys that stimulate the baby's left brain are considered the most desirable" (Cho 1995, 148).

From parent-led lessons targeted at specific skills, it is a small step to repurposing mothers as teachers and homes as schools (Popkewitz 2003).[3] Mariëtte de Haan writes of "the *pedagogization* of family life when parents feel the pressure to [organize] family activities [so they] are spent in educationally smart ways to maximize developmental outcomes for their children" (de Haan 2019, 31, emphasis added; Morelli et al. 2003; Sefton-Green 2015). Here is a brief excerpt from an authoritative and widely read prescription for repurposing a WEIRD home.

"How to Get Your Kids to Treat You Like Their Teacher"
Designate a School Area: In order for a child to listen to their parents teach, the parents must establish home as the new place to do schoolwork. Designate one area for schoolwork, and if possible, the area should not be the same place where the child typically plays. Getting a new table or desk that is similar to what a child would sit on in school can also be very beneficial.
Use a Timer: Work time needs to be clearly distinguished from break time, and a timer is the most effective way to do this. . . . Once they complete a work period without a reminder, reward them with enthusiastic praise and access to a preferred free-time activity. (Braff 2020)

WEIRD families in Japan go a step further[4]:

The home-study desk bought by most parents for their children symbolizes the hovering care and intensity of the mother's involvement: all models

---

[2] A review of twelve studies, in which young children were interviewed about what is or isn't play, concluded that children understood play to be an activity that took place with other children, with little or no involvement from adults (Goodhall and Atkinson 2019).
[3] "The estimated percentage of the school-age population that is homeschooled has doubled from 1999 to 2012" (Dotti-Sani and Treas 2016, 57).
[4] An illustrative contrast: in Poomkara village (S. India), "Children could be everywhere in the house but could claim none of the spaces as theirs. . . . Schoolbooks were often simply stuck under the palm roof and children's clothes hung on a rope. Children did their homework sitting on the same mat on which they slept at night. Even this mat was often shared with others" (Nieuwenhuys 2003, 103).

184 LEARNING WITHOUT LESSONS

have a high front and half-sides, cutting out distractions and enclosing the workspace in womb-like protection. There is a built-in study light, shelves, a clock, electric pencil sharpener and built-in calculator. [One] popular ... model included a push button connecting to a buzzer in the kitchen to summon mother for help or for a snack. (LeVine and White 1986, 123)

The kitchen has untapped lesson-generation opportunities (Finn and Vandermaas-Peeler 2013). A joint mother-child baking session is readily transformed into lessons focused "on literacy, and basic mathematical concepts and skills . . . the science of cooking, the sensation of taste and basic nutrition." However, the authors do mention that "a possible detrimental effect of an overly didactic parental focus during the cooking activity is that children may find the joint activity less fun or engaging" (Finn and Vandermaas-Peeler 2013, np). Can you imagine? And then there's the laundry. Not that WEIRD parents expect their children to actually do the laundry, but so many academic lessons can be built into the chore.

> *In this lesson, children will sort "laundry" by color, size, shape and clothing attribute*:
> Start sorting with just two *attributes*. Say: "Our first sort will be by size. You will have two baskets and you will be sorting your laundry into big and little piles. Can you give me an example of a piece of laundry that is big?" (Coat, towel, pants) "Yes. Go ahead and put your big laundry into one basket and the other basket will be for small laundry." "Can you give me an example of small laundry?" (Mittens, hand towels, underwear) Once their piles of laundry have been correctly sorted, tell the children to put all of their laundry back into a pile and get ready for the next sort. (Early Math Counts 2022)

Publicly funded programs like "Early Math Counts" that promote teaching at home via detailed lessons are now commonplace. In an example from the United Kingdom:

Parents are encouraged to experiment with everyday objects. . . . For instance, the [lesson] on light and sound contains a section on mirrors. Parents are asked to "go around the house with your child" comparing different mirrors; to 'talk to your child' to 'explain' that reflections in mirrors are reversed. A second type of activity is of the 'make and do' variety . . . in this case, there are instructions about how to make a kaleidoscope with your child using mirrors ... [other lessons] contain recipes for Victorian or Roman food, for example. (Buckingham and Scanlon 2003, 25)

But program evaluators uncover a great deal of resistance from working-class mothers: "You know, I'd never say to Peter, 'Ooh, you're learning about Romans, let's go in the kitchen and make some cakes.' That just wouldn't happen. You know, the practical side of it, we just wouldn't do it. Playing games and making cakes and all that sort of thing—no" (Buckingham and Scanlon 2003, 183).

As stressful and unwelcome as the conversion of homes to schools may be, the pandemic has shown how essential that has become for a child's successful education (Goldstein 2020). In recent years, international agencies have begun to promote patently WEIRD early child development (ECD) prescriptions in the Global South (Scheidecker et al. 2023; Ochs and Kremer-Sadlik 2021; Weber et al., 2017). Lego and UNICEF have combined to distribute "Early Childhood Development Kits," which are being introduced to parents in Bangladesh, Uganda, and Tanzania. The kits include various manufactured "toys" that are not representational but are meant to be incorporated into various parent-guided educational/play activities (Buechner 2022). Toys, as such, would have been absent in the typical Global South community until recently. Instead, children play with whatever is at hand, including cast-off tools and utensils, old fishing nets, bones, and corn cobs; imagination does the rest. As discussed in Chapter 3, children's play is valued for distracting them so they don't interfere with parents' work. Hence, the idea that an Indigenous mother would willingly take on the role of teacher/playmate is ludicrous. She is far more likely to interact with her children in work activity than in play (Callaghan et al. 2011).

Nevertheless, even without the aid of nongovernmental organizations, lessons are being disseminated from even the most rudimentary village school. There is growing evidence that Indigenous mothers with some years of schooling are adopting a more controlling and academic stance in their parenting practices (Köster et al. 2022, 439).[5] "Young Inuit mothers who had attended school were more likely than older Inuit mothers to involve

---

[5] From research on the island of Tanna, we can infer that this transition is not inevitable. Tannese mothers, despite completing primary and some secondary education, do not engage in direct instruction of their children, nor do they "teach" them the functions of a novel toy (Clegg et al. 2021).

186 LEARNING WITHOUT LESSONS

their children in classroom-style question-answer routines and labeling of objects, expecting this to be useful in preparing children for school" (Crago et al. 1993, 194). Zukow (1984), working in the Mexican state of Chiapas, found schooled mothers using a more didactic language-socialization style with their children. This pedagogical model commits the mother to a more interactive relationship with the preschool child. "In contrast with Mayan mothers with 0–2 grades of schooling, Mayan mothers with 12+ grades of schooling structured children's contributions mainly through the assignment of individual turn-taking and . . . asking known-answer and yes/no questions" (Chavajay 2006, 378).

> . . . evidence from Mexico, Venezuela, and Nepal indicates that experience in Western-type schools influences women's maternal behavior in a *pedagogical* direction. Pedagogical, in this context, means verbal responsiveness to and communicative engagement with preschool children and the tutoring of school-aged children; it can be interpreted as reflecting a process in which women internalize the teacher role from their experience in Western-type schools and use it as mothers. (LeVine et al. 2012, 139)

Parallel results were noted in studies of sib-caretakers. Zinacantec children with a few years of schooling used far more verbal discourse than previous generations and engaged in lesson-like interaction with their younger siblings. Schooled children also gave more explanations (Maynard 2004b, 530). In a Bakalanga village in Botswana, an episode of

> Playing "school" was recorded, where an older child would be the teacher and ask . . . a question such as "what is two plus two?" Once an older child had given the correct response, the teacher would turn to the youngest and command, "Say four!" This would frequently develop into a game of the teacher, the infant (and others) chanting the answer. (Geiger and Alant 2005, 187)

In the West, preschools are undergoing a gradual transformation from "before" schools to "preparatory" schools. Moving on from unstructured play as the *modus operandi*, preschools may now adopt a structured curriculum such as *Tools for the Mind*. Despite the nonsignificant results obtained in evaluating *Tools for the Mind* (Nesbitt and Farran 2021) and other academically oriented programs (Durkin et al. 2022), the trend continues unabated.

GLOBAL WEIRDING   187

In 1994, 500,000 children attended preschools in the United States; in 2003, 5 million were attending. A survey of preschools for the well-to-do found classes offered in Spanish and French, woodworking and tennis (Robbins 2006). The apogee of this movement to turn toddlers into students is private academic programs. "Age 3 is the sweet spot," said Joseph Nativo, chief financial officer for Kumon North America. "But if they're out of a diaper and can sit still with a Kumon instructor for 15 minutes, we will take them . . . as long as they can do 20 minutes of homework in math and reading every day, with their parents guiding and grading them" (Zernike 2011, np). In Korea, after-school academic "tutoring has almost become a form of child abuse" (Jeong 2019, 177).

Kindergarten dates to the late eighteenth century, founded with the aim of caring for children whose parents were employed. The original concept stressed what were considered "natural" activities for younger children: play, singing, dancing, unconstrained (e.g., no need to stay within lines) art, and an atmosphere of high interactivity among peers. But kindergarten— which has grown as rapidly as pre-K and expanded to a "whole day"—has been transformed in recent years. Not without controversy, kindergarten has become much more school-like, and "graduates" are expected to be able to read and write. "Instruction methods used in kindergarten now include workbooks, writing on lined paper, isolated skill development of letters and sounds and heavy emphasis on rote memory learning" (Russell 2011, 252).

Pushback against assembly-line, one-size-fits-all pedagogy is as old as Erasmus, writing in the sixteenth century. He wrote "that a constant element of enjoyment must be mingled with our studies so that we think of learning as a game rather than a form of drudgery. . . . Schools he lamented [were] torture-chambers; you hear nothing but the thudding of the stick, the swishing of the rod, howling and moaning, and shouts of brutal abuse" (Cunningham 1995, 44–45). Maria Montessori (1912) has, for over a hundred years, been the guilty conscience of educators. Ivan Illich (1971: xix), in *Deschooling Society*, lamented, "the attempt to expand the pedagogue's responsibility until it engulfs his pupils' lifetimes"; and John Holt (1981) championed "unschooling"—getting by without teachers, where learning is self-directed, interest driven, and natural.

Holt's philosophy is enacted in the Sudbury School, one of the most successful attempts at "unschooling." Since the first school was established in Sudbury, Massachusetts, in 1968, the basic model has been extended to sixty schools around the globe. Key elements in the Sudbury model are "(1) to make educational resources available in a supportive but non-intervening way, and (2) to create a milieu in which young people are expected to make their own educational decisions" (Gray and Chanoff 1986, 211). Given the great autonomy granted to students in choosing whether, what, and how they learn, an obvious question is "Are graduates prepared for economically viable futures?" Retrospective interviews were conducted with sixty-eight of the eighty-two graduates (in 1985). The authors conclude from the survey that "They have gone on to good colleges and good jobs. They have become, or are clearly en route to becoming, productive members of our society" (Gray and Chanoff 1986, 208–209). But Sudbury is a private school with tuition, affordable only to the upper echelon and, therefore, cannot easily be widely replicated.

Back in the public-school domain, recess has been eliminated altogether—to permit more time for lessons—or turned into a "curated" experience. A designated recess coach organizes children's activities and rapidly extinguishes spontaneous, rule-free play initiatives (Hu 2010). Efforts to "restore" recess have met with formidable obstacles (Global Recess Alliance 2022).

A similar fate has befallen the after-school period. Historically, this period belonged to children. I well remember the pleasure of outdoor exploration and play after school hours. Should I linger indoors on a frosty day, my mother would shoo me outside with the admonition "Go and get the stink blown off you." With the "curricularization of leisure" (Sefton-Green 2019, 194), this pattern is now exceptional. However, "the colonization of children's leisure is not being accomplished by school alone, but also by parents who are concerned with safety and optimizing their children's opportunities" (Nocon and Cole 2006, 102).

"Youth sports" were once epitomized by "pick-up" games of stick-ball, marbles, hopscotch, and so on, where the players themselves were the organizers, coaches, referees, and scorekeepers (Opie and Opie 1969). Without adult oversight, the children themselves had to develop the diplomatic skills to initiate and sustain satisfying contests (Lancy and Grove 2011b). But "the wholesale intervention of adults utterly transformed the informal world of traditional children's play" (Guttmann 2010, 147). Instead, " 'Little Leaguism' is threatening to wipe out the spontaneous culture of free play and games among American children" (Devereux 1976, 53). "The coach is given responsibility for instructing his players in the need for hard work, cooperation, competition, sportsmanship, and good citizenship, as well as teaching them the proper techniques for playing baseball" (Fine 1987, 61).

A common refrain as parents justify the value of, often costly,[6] extracurricular programs is their "educational" potential. Even programs that train girls to successfully compete in beauty pageants are lauded. "The idea that pageants can teach children specific skills that will help them be successful was brought up literally hundreds of times in interviews with pageant mothers" (Levey 2009, 206). In Western US ranching country, girls who love horses, riding, and rodeo are enrolled in Rodeo Queen clinics in order to "learn poise, makeup, how to give speeches, and model. It just makes more of a lady out of them" (Raitt and Lancy 1988, 277).

In spite of rapidly shrinking birth rates in countries that fit the WEIRD formula (Doepke and Zilibotti 2019), the amount of time mothers report that they spend in childcare has increased from 54 minutes/day in 1965 to 104 minutes/day in 2012. Father's childcare time quadrupled during the same period (Dotti-Sani and Treas 2016). Given the dramatic expansion of schooling of one sort or another,[7] we shouldn't have far to look for hypotheses explaining this demographic trend. Parents are spending time delivering lessons to their children or facilitating lessons taught by others.

> Most of the (WEIRD) children had to be driven to extracurricular activities several afternoons a week. They also needed help completing homework assignments due the following day. Children needed a "parent-manager" who kept tabs on where they had to be, when they had to be there, what they needed to bring with them, what homework assignment to prioritize, and how to pace one's progress on a long-term school project. In addition, parents needed to make sure that their kids got a snack to keep them going, did their homework correctly, and performed to the best of their abilities during their extra-curricular activities. (Kremer-Sadlik and Gutiérrez 2013, 130)

What do the children themselves think about adults managing their lives—for their own good? Survey results are quite consistent in revealing a very positive attitude about school and extracurriculars. A recent article on a COVID-inspired *New York Times* survey was titled "I Can't Believe I Am Going to Say This, but I Would Rather Be at School." Absent structured

---

[6] Parents in the United States are spending 10 to 25 percent of their income on their children's extracurricular pursuits (Dunn n.d.).

[7] An obvious indicator is the steady growth of home schooling and the tremendous spike in home-schooled children triggered by the pandemic (Grady 2022).

190 LEARNING WITHOUT LESSONS

activities, youth grow bored and apathetic since "It's harder to focus at home as there's no one to discipline you" (Dodd 2020, np). This informal survey is buttressed by a very substantial study that found that two-thirds of school-aged children in the United States participate in structured activity during nonschool hours.

> The overwhelming majority of students (85%) say kids who participate in organized activities such as a team or a club after school are "better off" than those who have a lot of time to themselves after school. . . . Half of the students surveyed (50%) say they were "bored and had nothing to do" when they weren't in school . . . and 3/4 agree that [this leads them] into trouble. (Duffett and Johnson 2004, 10)

My last example is taken from a recent social trend. Historically, Western schools have differentiated between "assigned" reading that had clear academic purpose and recreational or voluntary reading where students were free to select library books (mostly novels) to read at leisure. Voluntary reading has been highly valued, as evidenced by programs like National Reading Month and Million Book March (Reading Is Fundamental n.d.). However, in keeping with the movement to limit children's learning autonomously—without a teacher or parent's oversight—schools throughout the United States are now under siege from moral authorities eager to protect students from the harm caused by "inappropriate" literature. In a recent survey, 1,648 books had been banned in US schools following a successful petition, 1,000 in the state of Texas alone (Friedman and Johnson 2022).

In the next section, I address the question of what is lost or altered when the autonomous child is managed through the media of lessons and adult-organized activities. As lessons occupy more and more of children's time, what is taken away?

Lost Skills

Reports from anthropologists describe a continuous erosion of culture, in part or wholly attributable to the expansion of schooling and missionary activity (Brison 2009). Children are often attracted to all that is new and "superior." In Gapun village (PNG), despite adult displeasure, children stopped using the vernacular *Taiap* in favor of *Tok Pisin*, the lingua franca. The latter is the language used in town, school (along with English), and church (Kulick 1992, 8). Baka (Cameroon) adolescents, who have failed to convert their limited schooling into employment, "are drawn to bars where there's recorded music, dancing, and alcohol [which probably] displaces cultural activities such as the performance of tales, songs and traditional dances, many of which begin as night falls" (Gallois et al. 2015, 12). In the Solomon Islands, "young people . . . drop-outs without any marketable skills, come to town—lured by the 'lights' of Honiara's cinemas, shops, crowds, sports games, markets, etc." (Jourdan 1995, 211).

All too often in Indigenous communities, a Faustian bargain is enacted in which families relinquish the assistance of their youth in the hope that schooling will pay off monetarily. When, belatedly, this dream proves illusory, it is too late to remediate the failure and return to the chore curriculum.

The Decline of the Chore Curriculum

In the village of Kali Loro on Java, children are in school for longer periods and for more of the year compared to previous generations. They fail to participate in the family's subsistence activities, and without the farmer's skill set or the prospect of employment in the modern economy, they are left in limbo. Young men hang out in public and extort money from passersby, which they spend on video games, alcohol, narcotics, and pornography (White 2012, 95). White returned to Kali Loro over several decades and notes the gradual expansion of the school calendar, which necessitates a sharp reduction in time allocated to chores (White 2012). Rogoff and colleagues have documented this evolution occurring over three generations in the Guatemalan (Mayan) village of San Pedro. Among the many changes identified in children's lives, they note: "The increases in children's schooling across the generations have been accompanied by decreases in their contributions to family work" (Rogoff et al. 2005, 250).

A similar progression is documented for several Nahua-speaking communities in and around Guadalajara, Mexico. In the Indigenous community, children were deeply involved in self-guided learning and the practice of useful skills. They "pitched in" to help and were most welcome to do so. Indeed, a child who failed to show such behavior would be sanctioned. In the "cosmopolitan" community, where high levels of education had led to economic success, by contrast, "No children . . . were reported to take the initiative in family household work" (Alcalá et al. 2014, 104). Further, some mothers in the cosmopolitan community did not allow their children to take care of younger siblings, stating that childcare is the parent's responsibility alone, not the child's. One mother reported: "I tell her, 'Don't take roles that are not yours,' I tell her, 'Enjoy your childhood, you will be a mom one day'" (Alcalá et al. 2014, 105). This study was replicated in contrasting P'urhépecha (Mexico) communities. Virtually all the village children contributed to the household because "work is seen as something that dignifies human beings and makes one a member of the community" (Mejía-Arauz et al. 2015, 43). In the "cosmopolitan" community, however, "families report that children frequently engage in extracurricular activities in which they can develop artistic and sport skills" (Mejía-Arauz et al. 2015, 34).

Another change that, like language, affects the very fabric of society is decline in the ability to collaborate and learn through assisting others:

> Among the BaYaka Pygmies . . . one of the most important changes faced by children is schooling. [In] contrast with hunter-gatherer egalitarianism . . . the curricula of such schools promote hierarchy and utilize punishment for non-compliance. BaYaka adults normally avoid organizing and structuring children's time or deciding what they should be learning. (Sonoda et al. 2018, 163)

Hierarchy implies successes and failures. On the Pacific Island of Kosrae, learning in the village occurs continuously; while in the school, "there are set limits to the time in which any individual can display that he or she has learned. Without the open-ended provisions characteristic of [the community], school participants risk becoming nonparticipants. Their time can run out" (Michalchik 1997, 423). Hierarchy also suggests a shift to individualism as the ideal rather than collectivism (Cooperrider 2019).[8] We can expect that the strong drive for toddlers and children to "pitch in" and be helpful (Lancy 2020) will be attenuated.

---

[8] Teachers in two rural Mazahua communities have liberalized the learning environment, permitting students, while working as individuals, to share their ideas with classmates. "Certainly, some students were better at their lessons than others. . . . However, rather than being a quality that reflected upon herself as an individual, a student's relatively greater competence was directed toward supporting others" (Paradise and Robles 2016, 73).

Box 7.1 The Disappearance of Chores

In Norway, children's "household tasks are often tied to an allowance . . . referred to as 'week-salary' or 'month-salary.' The . . . children's contribution to the household is paid for by the parents [which indicates] that housework remains the responsibility of the parent" (Nilsen and Wærdahl 2014, 3).

In a study of thirty WEIRD families in Los Angeles, "no child routinely assumed responsibility for household tasks without being asked . . . the overall picture was one of effortful appeals by parents for help [who often] backtracked and did the task themselves. . . [becoming, in effect] a valet for the child" (Ochs and Izquierdo 2009, 399–400).

Among the Inuit, "children who previously spent their days helping parents with hunting, trapping, fishing, skin preparation, and general household chores now spend much of the day in an institutional setting learning skills unrelated, and sometimes antithetical, to those emphasized at home" (Condon 1987, 157).

In the modern Australian middle/upper class, children no longer work. When queried, children treat "the term *work* as having one meaning only: waged work outside the home. Work is something that one 'goes to' and that is done in exchange for money" (Bowes and Goodnow 1996, 302).

As lessons occupy a greater portion of the child's day, time allocated to chores declines. From being the norm, children's contributions to the family and community may become rare and subject to remuneration (see Box 7.1).

Withdrawing from the Natural Environment

The decline in skill learning associated with a reduction in children's chores is paralleled by a decline in the acquisition of TEK due to a reduction in foraging. Contrary to a common assumption, foraging is not limited to hunter-gatherers. Virtually all communities that live off the land, including pastoralists and subsistence farmers, engage in opportunistic hunting, fishing, and the gathering of wild foods and medicinal plants. The implication is that the majority of the world's Indigenous children will be taxed with the responsibility of learning to exploit the resources available in

194 LEARNING WITHOUT LESSONS

adjacent streams and bush. Globalization—especially schooling and missionary activity—imposes severe roadblocks for aspirant foragers (Cruz García 2006).

The most thorough study of how this is playing out is a retrospective analysis of the Western James Bay Cree of Subarctic Canada (Ohmagari and Berkes 1997). The Cree embrace the by-now familiar pedagogy of children learning through play with peers and helpful participation in the work of family and community members. As early as 1900, missionaries lobbied Cree parents to place their children in boarding schools, with the express purpose of assimilation. Their absence, especially from the forest camp during peak hunting and gathering seasons, robbed them of opportunities to master the environment. And this situation is not alleviated by the intervention of parents or others.

> Parents do not try to teach their children because they consider it an intrusion into someone else's life. Thus, if grown children wish to learn, it is expected that they would take the initiative themselves. . . . [But there is skepticism, as community members] consider that long years of schooling results in reduced attention span and patience, and loss of observational powers, generally impairing one's ability to learn in the bush. (Ohmagari and Berkes 1997, 215, 216)

More recent research on the loss of TEK has probed the knowledge of plants and animals—their identification, location, season, and harvest technique. Most of these studies indicate that increased schooling and market involvement are negatively associated with TEK (see Box 7.2).

Let me note one exception to this pattern of erosion of TEK as the usual consequence of schooling. The Menominee are Native Americans who occupy ancestral territory in Wisconsin and Michigan. The tribe still carries on several traditional foraging activities, including hunting and the gathering of wild rice. Parents use formal school-type instructional principles (querying children on plant names) with their accompanying children as they travel through the forest on field trips (Bang et al. 2016).

The Decline in Crafts Learning and Production

The loss of TEK is paralleled by the disappearance of craft traditions, in part due to schooling and employment in the modern economy (see Box 7.3).

Box 7.2 Truants from the Natural Classroom

"These changes in subsistence activities and ecological conditions may result in BaYaka growing up in towns and having fewer opportunities to observe and accompany adults during forest-related activities. This is especially important given that children acquire forest skills through observation, imitation and practice" (Salali et al. 2020, 10).

"School-going Agta boys . . . had no experience in hunting, whereas their non-school- going peers in Gabgab went on multiple-day hunting trips approximately twice a month" (Hagen et al. 2017, 408).

Jenu Kuruba "girls who spend diminished time in the bush and who do not learn traditional knowledge between 13 and 15 years of age have difficulty acquiring it later in life. It appears that something akin to a sensitive learning period might be occurring here—either culturally or psychologically" (Demps et al. 2012, 467).

"Compared with 2005, in 2017 fewer Hadza subadults left camp to forage, and overall, they targeted a smaller variety of wild foods, with the noticeable absence of wild honey, figs, and tubers. Participants in 2017 were significantly more likely to have attended school. [Nevertheless] some young foragers continue to be highly productive in collecting wild, undomesticated foods" (Pollom et al. 2020, 123).

"This study compared identification and knowledge of native plant species between Maasai boys enrolled in school with boys of similar age but primary responsibility as herders, called *moran*. On average, *moran* identified 38 species compared to 20 for students. . . . Further, *moran* shared nearly 18 correct facts about the plants, compared with ten for students" (Bruyere et al. 2016, 1).

Heckler (2001), working in three Amazonian (Piaroa-speaking, SW Venezuela) communities, found that the use of wild plant resources was decreasing dramatically. She also found that schooling had a negative impact on TEK—a finding replicated by another Piaroa scholar who writes: "Formal schooling and other intrusive knowledge forms and activities are competing and detracting from the learning of traditional environmental knowledge" (Zent 2001, 209).

"The process of modernization in Eastern Brazil, especially increasing access to formal education, appears to be incompatible with the retention of traditional domains of medical knowledge" (Voeks and Leony 2004, 294).

"Schooling may also have indirect effects by shaping mobility patterns. Among the Tsimanê, more schooling was associated with . . . worse performance on regional pointing accuracy . . . probably because spending time in school limited their outdoor spatial exploration relative to peers who did not attend school" (Davis and Cashdan 2019, 1).

Jenu Kuruba "children with more absences from school knew more about honey collecting than children who had fewer absences. . . . Missing five to six days of school each month may be a sufficient amount of time to increase honey collecting TEK for boys" (Demps et al. 2015, 33).

Box 7.3 The Decline in Crafts Learning

"None of the [Lurs] women weavers of nomadic-style tribal rugs and flat weaves used locally has young apprentices; their skills and products are considered old-fashioned" (Friedl 1997, 4).

"In some highland Maya communities, such as Chenalho and Mitontik, weaving is no longer universal among girls. These are communities in which schooling has come to be seen as a credentialing process that provides entrée to jobs, particularly teaching jobs" (Greenfield 2004, 86).

"The Kusasi girl combines her school time with the rest of her activities in the domestic sphere, including pottery production. This results in a delay in the acquisition of psychomotor frameworks associated with modelling and, occasionally, a final break with pottery production learning" (Trias et al. 2015, 96).

"A tradition of vocational inheritance, and equally the gradual loss of that masonry tradition, resonated deeply with the older members of the Djenné team whose sons, in some cases, were veering onto different paths of learning and livelihood" (Marchand 2014, 159).

On Bequia Island in the Grenadines, shipwrights build by "hand and eye," using their own knowledge and experience rather than printed plans or power tools. Young men have no interest in boatbuilding, so shipwrights can no longer find apprentices (Johnson 1984).

Can Indigenous Pedagogy Infiltrate the Village School?

The role of schooling in culture loss has not gone without protest. Some researchers working in South Indian communities "recommend exposure to TEK at school to improve TEK or neutralize the negative effects of formal education on TEK for children who go to school" (Demps et al. 2015, 28). But it is hard to imagine how to bridge the divide between "teacher-led lessons in the classroom" to learning through observing and pitching in (LOPI) on a family foraging outing in the bush. Agta researchers note that "the curriculum in class does not recognize, let alone promote, the value of Agta identity and Indigenous knowledge. [However,] the Department of Education (Philippines) has taken up the *Indigenous Peoples Education Initiative*, which aims to include indigenous knowledge in the school curriculum and to involve community elders in teaching" (Hagen et al. 2017, 408). But community elders rarely *teach* in their "natural habitat." The irony here is that the "best" teachers in any Indigenous community will be those who are more educated and acculturated and, hence, most likely to have suffered culture loss.

Although it takes wholehearted community support and supplemental funds, a very few Indigenous communities have succeeded in creating hybrid curricula (Suina and Smolkin 1994). The "culturally responsive" elements in these community-partnered schools include "ceremonial knowledge such as the *Kanuhwelatúksla* (Oneida Thanksgiving address); how to make water drums for social and ceremonial events, and how to conduct funerary rites; . . . Quechua songs . . . teach students about the histories and uses of the different Andean instruments and lyrics" (Huaman 2020, 265, 275). There is little evaluation of these programs, leaving open the question of whether knowledge and skill transmitted through lessons will have the same meaning and impact as traditional context-based social learning. And the "extra" lessons may be seen as reducing the time allocated to academic lessons (Tassinari and Cohn 2009: 150). At Niigaane school, "local parent pressures focused on the fear that children would not master English [and the] fear that children would not gain the skills viewed as necessary for financial survival in mainstream society" (Huaman 2020, 276). A comprehensive survey of culturally responsive schooling (CRS) is not encouraging.

> Although CRS has been advocated for at least the past forty years, we still see schools and classrooms that are failing to meet the needs of Indigenous students. . . . scholars have noted the limited nature of conclusive evidence

198 LEARNING WITHOUT LESSONS

supporting CRS for Indigenous youth . . . and very few studies make strong
claims about how students' academic performance is affected by efforts at
CRS. (Castagno et al. 2008, 942, 982)

These costly and heroic efforts to indigenize the curriculum tend to be isolated efforts (e.g., single schools), heavily dependent on supplemental funds
and extraordinary teachers (Lancy 1993; Lipka 1990). The programs close
after a few years for lack of funds, lack of qualified teachers, or lack of long-
term community support (Bombjaková et al. pre-press, 14). In the immediate
future, governments in the Global South will be investing less in indigenizing
schooling and more in programs that promise to help Indigenous students
succeed in a globalized economy.

In the section that follows, I will focus more specifically on cognitive and
social skills that appear to be influenced by schooling.

The Schooled Mind

groups differing in their amount of school-based experience or
every-day, work-related experience, approach the same task . . . in
very different ways.

—Cole (2005), 206–207

The primary goal of this volume has been to thoroughly describe children's
learning in societies where lessons are largely absent and to draw contrasts
with societies—going back several millennia—where schooling or using
lessons is the primary means to transmit knowledge to the rising generation.
But, as I have shown in this chapter, the pedagogy practiced in the last half-
century in WEIRD society continues to expand into heretofore lesson-free
environments. The entire world is now "schooled" at least to some degree. In
this section, I will touch on some of the effects of this massive transformation
on patterns of thinking and learning.

Practical versus Academic Intelligence

The pervasive spread of lesson-based cultural transmission has opened
fissures in the landscape of cognitive psychology. Various aspects of learning
and thinking assumed to be universal are now recognized as shaped by culture

GLOBAL WEIRDING 199

as well as evolution and human ontogeny (Henrich et al. 2010). Several of these fissures have been investigated. One example is "academic" versus "practical" intelligence. Rural adolescents surpassed urban adolescents in tests of practical adaptive intelligence (with items covering topics such as hunting, gathering, and location-finding), whereas the urban adolescents performed better on conventional measures of fluid and crystallized intelligence (Grigorenko et al. 2004, 186).

A parallel distinction has been made between "declarative" and "procedural" information (Thornton and Raihani 2008, 1823). Declarative information may be best conveyed by teaching or other top-down, highly structured processes, whereas procedural skills may be best acquired through a bottom-up, learner-initiated process (Bjorklund 2007, 192). For example, Wyndham's study of Raramuri ethnobotany found that even very young children may be knowledgeable about plants and their uses, while neither children nor most adults were particularly fluent when it came to plant names (2010, 87, 96). For Indigenous peoples, their model of how the world is organized is driven by immediate, practical concerns. This has been repeatedly demonstrated. Alexander Luria was an early contributor to this discussion.

Luria conducted interview-style testing of unschooled Uzbek peasants. In the first example we can see the informant reasoning from personal experience (or lack thereof) and an unwillingness to apply a general rule.

Problem posed: "In the Far North, where there is snow, all bears are white. Novaya Zemlya is in the far north and there is always snow there. What color are the bears?" Response: "We always speak of only what we see; we don't talk of what we haven't seen." (Luria 1976, 108)

In another problem, men and women were asked to sort and group various kinds and colors of weaving yarn (Uzbekistan is noted for its carpets). The male response was "men [not being weavers] don't know colors and call them all blue." The women refused to impose any grouping or organization—something educated Uzbeks did quite easily—exclaiming that "none of these are the same." (Luria 1976, 25, 27)

Instead of trying to select "similar" (*ukhshaidi*) objects, they proceeded to select "objects suitable for a specific purpose" . . . subjects did not interpret words as symbols of abstract categories usable for classifying objects. What mattered to them were strictly concrete ideas about practical schemes in which appropriate objects could be incorporated. (Luria 1976, 54)

200 LEARNING WITHOUT LESSONS

In a fishing community on Buton Island, Vermonden (2009) found directly parallel results, with fishers resistant to discussing marine life more generally; they eschewed speaking of types of fish or of considering different ways of grouping them. Their thinking was governed by their practice (true also for Penan hunters—Puri 2005, 280—and South American and African subsistence farmers—Henrich et al. 2010, 72). Not surprisingly, Vermonden writes: "Using structured interviews, I was able to elicit and record fishermen's extensive knowledge of fishes and, more generally, of the marine environment. [However,] during two years of participant observation, I rarely observed oral transmission of fishing knowledge or techniques" (Vermonden 2009, 205). Had Vermonden's informants been schooled, they might have used broader and more inclusive organizing principles, which required a more verbal and academic form of rhetoric.

Although there's evident variability, it is clear that Indigenous pedagogy is rooted in a particular understanding of the nature of knowledge. The Duna are a remote PNG tribe still using stone tools.

> Copying, and trial and error, rather than explicit teaching, are certainly the methods by which Duna learn about flaked stone. Duna men are not intellectualists and do not spend their time discussing the meaning of things. They assume that all people think the same way until faced with evidence to the contrary, in which case they remark: "well they're other men, their ways are something else." Duna men always insist on the particularistic nature of knowledge. What one man knows is not what another knows and, we suspect, the two cannot know the "same" thing. (White et al. 1977, 381)

In WEIRD society, the sheer volume of information transmitted through verbal, written, and pictorial media provokes cognitive change in students (Lancy 1983, 112–116). However, with one important exception (Bruner 1966b), most early theories of cognitive development in children failed to take into account the impact of schooling. Although Jean Piaget's theory of cognitive development is notably comprehensive and enduring, its universality was cast in doubt by researchers who tried replicating his Genevan results outside the West. Greenfield (1966, 234) found that Piaget's milestones for cognitive development in the "concrete operations" stage are met only by Wolof children with four or more years of schooling. This finding was extended and replicated by other investigators across numerous societies (e.g., Cole et al. 1971; Lancy 1983; Rogoff 1981) in the ensuing years.[9] Schooling (that endures for at least four to six years) shapes cognition in a variety of ways; but above all, it leads to a more analytic approach to information and problem solving. "Analytic thought involves a detachment of objects from contexts, a tendency to focus on objects' attributes, and a preference for using categorical rules to explain and predict behavior" (Henrich et al. 2010, 72).

In very recent work, Helen Davis and colleagues have taken a step beyond the school/village dichotomy. They are analyzing the impact of school *quality* in Tsimané communities, which, as we saw in Chapter 6, varies widely. The Tsimané live in communities with varying access to urban environments and "modern" society. Across Tsimané communities, the researchers identified schools of low (shorter school year, poor teacher preparation, low teacher/pupil ratio, no provision of paper and pencils, and so on), medium, and high quality. They found that school quality affected scores on a widely used measure of information processing as well as academic performance. "Reading and arithmetic ability varied by school quality: 88% of children in villages with low quality schools are illiterate vs. 65% and 57% of children in villages with medium and high-quality schools, respectively" (Davis et al. 2021 pre-press, 12).

The typical school lesson incorporates several pedagogical tools designed to promote analytical thinking. As examples, the language used in schools is profoundly different from that used in vernacular or colloquial conversation. A common rhetorical device in the classroom is for the teacher to ask a pupil a question that the teacher already knows the answer to. This is not done in normal discourse. Similarly, while speech directed at Indigenous children is pragmatic and goal-driven, in WEIRD households, parents provide preschoolers with decontextualized narrative, pretense, inquiry, and primed recall. This immersion in complex language prepares children for a predominantly academic childhood free of obligations in the domestic economy (Göncü et al. 2000; Rowe 2013).

Not only is the school's curriculum transmitted orally, it is also represented in written form. This is because "complex information transmitted through written instructions has lower rates of error than if it were transmitted

---

[9] A very recent review of this by-now massive literature confirms that many cognitive skills originally thought to be universal arise from adaptation to the requirements of formal education (Peng and Kievit 2020).

202 LEARNING WITHOUT LESSONS

verbally or if the recipient is able to only watch someone perform an activity" (Erkens and Lipo 2007, 247).

The Management of Attention

Schooling promotes numerous changes in the ways children relate to and learn from their environment. In Chapter 1, I described a critical study in Mexico that contrasted mothers' and teachers' approaches to "teaching" a child to make a market stall. The mothers' procedure was to encourage the children to pitch in and learn through assisting with construction. The teacher's first step was to corral the child's attention and impose a "lesson plan" on the proceedings. The construction of the stall became secondary to the correct enactment of a lesson in which the child must narrowly focus on the teacher. The alternative, characteristic of Indigenous society, is "wide-angled" or "open" attention to the myriad activities and conversations going on in the vicinity. For example, Efe Pygmy children spend the day among a plurality of individuals of varying age and sex (Tronick et al. 1987). Gaskins and Paradise (2010, 99–100) describe open attention as wide-angled and abiding. The first means that the individual is aware of and attends to a great deal of the environment at one time rather than attending to only one stimulus, such as the teacher. The second means that attention is sustained rather than episodic or short-term (Köster et al. 2018). Numerous examples of open attention can be gleaned from the ethnographic record. Hilger (1957, 50) was impressed by Araucanian children's keen eyesight, hearing, and powers of observation. Yukaghir hunters insist that, while you can learn by observing others, to become a proficient hunter you must hunt on your own: "Only then do you really start noticing the myriad of details around you" (Willerslev 2007, 169). Empirical testing confirmed that Inuit children possess extraordinarily high levels of visual memory (Kleinfeld 1971, 132).

A recent experimental study compared children from five communities in Guadalajara, ranging from very traditional (children contribute to domestic economy, low participation in schooling) to "Nouveau Cosmopolitan." The task set for the subjects was to replicate a model's construction of origami figures. The results affirmed that the greater the degree of acculturation, the more likely subjects (ages six to nine) were to focus narrowly on the model, while the more traditional subjects attended to and learned from their peers as well as the model and her origami figure (Mejía-Arauz et al. 2019). Several

GLOBAL WEIRDING   203

studies of this type, including an adult demonstrating how to make a toy (Silva et al. 2011), support the argument that "controlling children's attention to teach them contrasts with the Indigenous community-based learning tradition of structuring engagements in such a way that allows children to observe and contribute to ongoing activities" (Correa-Chávez et al. 2005, 675). For example, "If the child does not observe, a parent is likely to scold, 'Have you no eyes?' The expectation is that children take the initiative to observe, not wait for a lesson" (Rogoff et al. 2003, 193). A subsequent study explicitly looked at teaching and found that WEIRD children learned better from direct teaching situations, whereas "Yucatec Mayan children learned just as well from observing others' interactions" (Silva et al. 2015, 209). One might say that WEIRD children "zone out" when their attention is not captured by a teacher.[10] "Children from families with extensive schooling may rely more on having their attention directed by adults and muster less attention when no one is telling them to attend" (Silva et al. 2011, 909).

A related line of research featured younger (preschool age) children. Some subjects were taught the functions of a novel, multifaceted toy, while others were given a less-directed introduction. Then children were given time and freedom to play with the toy on their own. The nondirected group fully explored the toy, including undemonstrated functions. The "instructed" group limited their exploration of the toy to functions that had been demonstrated (Bonawitz et al. 2011). In a related study set in a children's museum, parents were asked to teach the workings of a novel causal structure to their children through free play. "Parents who were the most directive in their instruction had children who learned particular rules the best . . . but those children were the least engaged by the act of learning—they played with the causal toy for the least amount of time" (Medina and Sobel 2020, 24).

A brief digression: This anecdote is called "The Problem of the Clueless Snowboarder." A few years ago, on a ski trip, I was waiting to board the only Poma lift in Utah. Ahead of me in line was a group of teenage boys on snowboards. I noticed one young man whose back was to the lift-mounting point as he concentrated on talking with his friends. At his turn, he shuffled up to the mounting point, stopped, looked around, and said plaintively, "Who's gonna show me how to do this?" Meanwhile, as he fumbled, the

---

[10] John Gatto (1992, 8) writes in his bestseller *Dumbing Us Down: The Hidden Curriculum of Compulsory Schooling*: "Good students wait for a teacher to tell them what to do. It is the most important lesson."

204   LEARNING WITHOUT LESSONS

queue remained stationery for quite a bit. I would submit that our youth are in some danger of losing the ability or the motivation to learn through observation and overhearing. They are like domesticated sheep that are helpless to defend themselves, depending entirely on their human and canine guardians[11]. Anthropologist Martha Crago observed another illustration of the phenomenon in an Inuit community.

> One day when my eight-year-old daughter was watching some girls her age play a game in the house where we were staying, she turned to a woman who spoke English and said:
>> Anna: How do I play this game? Tell me what to do. What are the rules?
>> Inuk Mother: (gently) Watch them and you'll see how it goes.
>> Anna: I don't know how to learn by watching, can't you tell me?
>> Inuk Mother: You'll be able to know by watching. (Crago 1988, 211)

"Children who are used to the heavily explanatory, lesson-based approach of schooling may depend more on being told how to do things, even in a situation in which the needed information is available through observation of ongoing events" (Crago 1988, 192). Another scholar notes: "children who are used to experiencing scaffolding may actually rely on it more both because they expect it and because they have not developed the monitoring skills of children who are expected to be keen observers" (Akhtar 2005, 171).

Another brief digression: In WEIRD society, what happens when a child fails to attend to the teacher? A parent–teacher conference. But a parent can avoid this embarrassment by assiduously training their child in "self-regulation." Experts have lined out entire programs to intervene and shape the child's self-regulation. "To function well at school, both academically and socially, children need to regulate their behavior and emotions so that they can listen, sustain their attention and generally avoid disruptive or off-task behavior that may interfere with learning or disrupt relationships with their teachers and peers" (Morawska et al. 2019, 45). One area of emphasis urges the parent to routinize the child's life. "Children who are raised in home environments that are noisy and disorganized, [with] many simultaneous

---

[11] This is not a trivial issue. Eavesdrop on any conversation among college faculty and you will often hear them lament the timidity of students. They are so risk avoidant; they refuse to utilize the syllabus as a source of guidance. Nothing less than a face-to-face, verbal explanation from their professor is sufficient to reassure them of the A grade they are expecting.

GLOBAL WEIRDING 205

activities... [had poor] self-regulation later in school" (Morawska et al. 2019, 44). In contrast, Indigenous children are *expected* to develop self-regulation without intervention (see Chapter 5). The *normal* daily environment Indigenous children encounter *is* noisy, with many activities going on simultaneously. Children cope with the situation by deploying broad, inclusive attention to decode and learn from the "chaos."

Another fissure in the cognitive landscape is referred to as "overimitation." Lab studies have demonstrated that, from eighteen months, children will violate their own assessment of a learning opportunity by copying the essential steps in a procedure *and* nonessential moves added by the demonstrator. One explanation for this strange behavior points to the imperative to attend to and copy the teacher without question (Hoehl et al. 2019; Keupp et al. 2015). This seems a case of Margaret Mead's (1964, 129) "functionless pedantry," where the learner is subjected to teaching not for the content or skill transmitted but to assert the "teacher's dominant status." Interestingly, children under eighteen months—not yet schooled—behave rationally and elect to exclude the model's irrelevant actions (Gergely et al. 2002). Overimitation can be diminished or enhanced by varying the conditions. If the demonstrator remains present for the child's replication, overimitation is more likely than when the demonstrator leaves the lab (Nielsen and Blank 2011).[12] If the model explicitly acts like a teacher, overimitation is more pronounced (Buchsbaum et al. 2011).

Overimitation experiments have been replicated in several Indigenous communities, and subjects slavishly copied the model. The sole exception was Aka Pygmies from the Congo Basin. Unlike children in the other Indigenous communities, Aka subjects had not attended school, nor were they routinely instructed by their parents (Berl and Hewlett 2015). In a more recent study comparing German and Namibian Indigenous children, the latter "rely more on self-directed, observational learning and depend less on over-imitation" (Stengelin et al. 2019, 2634).

Attention management has also been examined from the teacher's perspective. WEIRD schooling—which sets the standard—has been referred to as "Assembly-Line Instruction, which places priority on teachers' management of students' attention, motivation, and behavior" (Paradise et al. 2014, 132). In this particular study, the investigator trained pairs of Euro-American

---

[12] I'm reminded of the chaos that typically ensued when a school teacher was temporarily absent from the classroom.

206 LEARNING WITHOUT LESSONS

and rural Mexican teachers to "teach children how to make an origami frog in the casual manner of a helpful 'auntie' rather than a teacher." The Euro-American teachers were unable to do this, even after extensive training; instead, they turned the session into a teacher-managed lesson. The Mexican teachers had no difficulty with allowing the children to proceed largely on their own. They used very little verbalization, explicit direction, or praise, but rather allowed the children to take the initiative to observe and emulate their origami-folding technique. The social dynamic was one of collaboration rather than the hierarchy of an expert instructing a novice (Paradise et al. 2014, 134–135). An interesting observation that emerged was that the Euro-American teachers felt that it was their responsibility to ensure the child's success, whereas the Mexican-heritage teachers did not share this obligation, feeling that the child was ultimately responsible (see also Clegg et al. 2021).

As discussed earlier in the chapter, lessons have escaped the classroom and, increasingly, characterize the way children learn everything:

> Adults structure young children's learning by managing children's attention, motivation, and involvement in ways that resemble lessons. For example, middle-class parents in the United States and Turkey were likely to try and engage toddlers in the parents' own agenda (which often involve a lesson) by means of mock excitement and praise and even by overruling the toddler's own expressed wishes. (Rogoff et al. 2003, 188)

Learning Collaboratively

A major theme in the analysis of learning without lessons is that learning occurs through social activity. Collaboration, as Keller notes, "has been a crucial necessity" in the evolution of the species. Helping others emerges in late infancy, and the helper is learning while contributing to the efforts of others. Schooling, however, has not typically promoted cooperative learning. Heidi Keller and colleagues utilized a lab simulation that placed a premium on a cooperative approach to problem solving. Their finding:

> German children from middle class families demonstrate amazingly low performance in cooperative tasks. . . . This seems to represent an alienation from the roots of socio-cognitive competencies during the evolution of humankind. . . . The development of social coordination has been a crucial

GLOBAL WEIRDING 207

necessity that allows humans to live in larger groups and thus become more effective in defending against predators and exploiting resources. (Keller et al. 2019, 127–128)

In an early comparative study on the Warm Springs Reservation in Oregon, Philips (1983) found that Native students were able to work collaboratively and without guidance. Their Anglo counterparts argued over turn-taking, who was "in charge" and, ultimately, were forced to rely on the teacher's instruction. In a Ghanaian village school serving fisher and farming communities, children were prohibited from taking the initiative and "any attempts to collaborate with friends were usually stifled by the teacher" (Sackey and Johannesen 2015, 456). In a long series of studies, Barbara Rogoff and colleagues examined the role schooling plays in the development of the ability to work collaboratively. In one study, village children who are expected to contribute to the collective efforts of their farming families,

> showed sophisticated blending of their agendas. They collaborated flu-
> idly, sharing leadership and smoothly exchanging roles, and anticipated
> each other's actions in accomplishing the task. In contrast . . . European
> American school children collaborated very little; they often divided the
> task, not sharing ideas but instead taking turns, excluding their partner, or
> one child simply bossing the other. (Rogoff et al. 2017, 880; see also Nielsen
> et al. 2016)

Learning collaboratively is not entirely absent from schools. In multigrade classrooms in rural Veracruz, the single teacher relies on older students to instruct the younger (Bryan and McLaughlin 2005). "Japanese elementary school classrooms often involve conversations in which children build on each other's ideas. Indeed, Japanese first graders take on responsibility, without direct management by an adult, for organizing the class to begin lessons, breaking into small groups to carry out and discuss science experiments, and running class meetings" (Rogoff et al. 2003, 187).

I think that growing up in a "teaching" as opposed to a "learning" culture (Mead 1964, 107) has enormous consequences for how children think and learn. Indigenous children, even those who are in school, may continue, through their heavy involvement in the domestic economy, to enjoy the benefits of a learning culture. Evolution has predisposed children to learn socially from a variety of role models in everyday settings (see Chapter 4). In

208 LEARNING WITHOUT LESSONS

contrast, WEIRD society implicitly embraces the idea that fully trained adult teachers should be the arbiters of all that is worth knowing and the "proper" methods for successfully educating the ignorant. Increasingly, WEIRD children have been relieved of any responsibility for their own education, because the culture favors indirect, second-hand knowledge that is selected, modified, packaged, and presented by others (Reed 1996).

The publication of "The Weirdest People in the World?" (Henrich et al. 2010) engendered calls for new initiatives to test the generalizability of empirical work on human behavior and cognition. There was and is recognition that only through multiple replications in non-WEIRD societies can the universality (suggesting a biological basis) of the behavior or reasoning process be verified. Unfortunately, as I will discuss in the concluding section, global WEIRDing is occurring at such a rapid pace that it is nearly impossible to find communities where WEIRD views and practices vis-à-vis children's lives are minimal. And this is especially true for hunting and gathering societies.

The Future of Cross-Cultural Comparative Research

> People in [WEIRD] societies consistently occupy the extreme end of the . . . distribution [making them] one of the worst subpopulations one could study for generalizing about *Homo sapiens*.
> —Henrich et al. (2010), 63, 65, 79

By now, I'm sure the reader has extracted the message that the future for a majority of the world's children is more and more lessons. The only children for whom that won't apply will be those living in extreme poverty. Their rescue will be affected by economic investment, not lessons. Hence, what follows in this penultimate section is not limited to the presence or absence of lessons but covers more generally the course that all scholars interested in the relationship between culture and behavior will follow.

I think it is safe to say that anthropologists who study childhood would not be the least surprised by the Henrich et al. declaration at the start of this section. At least since Margaret Mead's work in Samoa one hundred years ago, anthropologists have gathered data that would allow them to "veto" claims of universality made by WEIRD social science (LeVine 2007, 250). Mead (1928), in finding that Samoan adolescents did not experience the emotional conflict predicted by psychologist Granville Hall (1904) in his landmark work, exercised this veto. It meant that Hall's claim of universality for this adolescent trait was unsupportable. A modern example can be found in *Attachment Reconsidered: Cultural Perspectives on a Western Theory* (Quinn and Mageo 2013). But these "border crossings," until recently, have been comparatively rare. This is at least partly due to rhetorical and epistemological[13] barriers where lab scientists remain unaware and uninformed about relevant work by ethnographers. By and large, anthropologists and psychologists have stayed within disciplinary boundaries, even though cross-pollination can be very enlightening (Lancy 2020).

More recently, there has been an upsurge in interdisciplinary research as many have answered the call to evaluate empirical results obtained solely from WEIRD samples. Still, a pessimistic assessment claims that, in the last ten years, "the needle hasn't moved." The vast majority of psychological research is still carried out with samples drawn exclusively from the WEIRD population (Apicella et al. 2020). But while the needle may not be moving, anthropologists are recording how rapidly Indigenous cultures are changing (Chapter 7), especially where childhood is concerned. Given this dynamic, Clark Barrett (2020, 446) suggests that researchers stop repeating "rote procedures" and follow a more inductive approach, looking "more carefully at the scope of human phenomena we seek to understand."

Global WEIRDing increases the challenges faced by contemporary researchers. In cross-cultural studies aimed at testing the WEIRD theory of "overimitation," the authors (Nielsen et al. 2014) chose two sites, which were later questioned: "the San and Aboriginal Australians involved in these studies are no longer actively engaged in a way of life typical of hunter-gatherers or other small-scale cultures . . . they have had continuous exposure to Western ideas, values, and technology for many decades, and this life . . . has fundamentally altered their respective cultures" (Berl and Hewlett 2015, 3).

Short of discovering some mythical long-lost tribe (Nance 1988), researchers, in selecting a site, will need to assess the degree of acculturation

---

[13] As an example, lab science begins with a hypothesis and research design is dictated by the need to test the hypothesis. The process is deductive. In an ethnographic study, data are gathered on a general area of interest and, as notes are compiled, a search for patterns and apparent relationships ensues. This process is bottom-up or inductive. Historically, these naturalistic observations were dismissed as "anecdotatal." Meanwhile, deductive experiments and surveys are criticized as context-free and oblivious to the impact of culture on behavior. My perspective is that these boundaries can be overcome by a pragmatic strategy that judges data by its utility and not its purity.

(Gallois et al. 2015) and temper any claims their findings might suggest. Among the factors that may have an impact on children, directly or through the actions of family members, are the following: child's progress in school, including attendance; literacy; school quality; mother's education; expected participation in chores; sedentarization; fluency in the native tongue; family participation in the market economy; the degree of urbanization in the child's place of residence; and continuing practice of traditional religion versus mission impact. Another important point made by Brandl (2021) is the degree of heterogeneity in the community. A given community may be impossible to "grade" on all these dimensions because of local variability. Kramer provides an instructive example of the grading process:

> None of the Savanna Pumé study communities has a school, store, health clinic, electricity, well water, health care access, or can be reached by road. In the sample presented here from one Savanna Pumé band, no child has attended school, is literate, or speaks Spanish. Pumé maí is a child's first and only language. (Kramer 2021, 10)

There is a CATCH-22 lurking here as well. That is, assuming the researcher has found the veritable lost tribe, many of the contemporary tools of field research, such as interviewing, lab-style manipulation of objects, and video/audio-taping (Abels et al. 2017) yield data of dubious value. This is due to the naive informant's unfamiliarity, fear, or shyness in the presence of a foreign researcher, research tools, and procedures. A few examples are provided in Box 7.4.

The most direct way out of this dilemma is long-term ethnography. Over time, the ethnographer becomes a familiar figure who can communicate in the lingua franca. Ethnographic insight can then guide the framing of interview questions and the construction of tests. Community members become more comfortable with the researcher and are more amenable to being interviewed and filmed. Importantly, the ethnographer can augment or alter the project's objectives to take into account the community's needs (Kramer and Greaves 2022). Training in the ethnographic method is available at The Center for Applied Anthropology (Northern Kentucky University 2022). And, finally, one can mine ethnographic archives, such as the Human Relations Area Files (Yale University n.d.). This avoids many if not all of the acculturation issues.

Box 7.4 Indigenes Make Poor "Subjects"

Mayan "children ... who had attended school for a longer period had an easier time answering questions ... than their less-schooled counterparts" (Tovote and Maynard 2018, 38).

"A major problem with ... studies that have found that parents play a major role in cultural transmission, is their reliance on self-reports. Asking people from whom they learned a particular skill does not necessarily result in an accurate answer. Social psychologists have repeatedly demonstrated that people often have extremely poor insight into the causes of their own behavior" (Mesoudi 2011, 166–167).

"A system that fosters shyness around respected persons meant that my attempts to draw children into conversation were initially met with giggles and avoidance, if not outright fear" (Chapin 2014, 13–14).

With the least acculturated community, the Tainae, "it was unclear when an understanding of false belief emerges because it was almost impossible to persuade younger children to participate in the testing" (Vinden 1999, 40).

The Tao (Lanyu Island, Taiwan) "were difficult to interview because they felt this would provide an avenue for the Anito malicious spirits to spy on them" (Röttger-Rössler et al. 2015, 203).

The Final Tally

This summary is organized around a series of binary contrasts. On the one hand, we have the WEIRD model of lessons that are constructed in advance ("core curriculum") and directed by a teacher. On the other hand, there are discernible commonalities in practices, exclusive of structured lessons, that encourage and enhance learning in relatively unacculturated rural communities around the globe.

In WEIRD society, the division between learning in school and learning out of school has been reduced. Time spent parenting has dramatically increased even as the birth rate plummets, and much of this extra time is devoted to lessons. Free play is no longer a time for the child to evade adult oversight and enjoy peer interaction. Recess has been crowded out by increased "seat time." At home, parents feel obligated to manage children's play life

212 LEARNING WITHOUT LESSONS

to ensure that it is truly educational. For older children, pick-up games in the park are time wasters that are preferentially replaced by music lessons, homework, and organized sports. Most of the characteristics of school pedagogy have permeated the child's after-school life. Box 7.5 provides a partial list of the most noticeable differences between schooling and the pedagogy discernible in communities where Indigenous lifeways still predominate.

Box 7.5 Summarizing the Differences

While WEIRD parents are so eager to begin teaching their offspring that they pipe Mozart to the fetus and give vocabulary lessons to speechless babies, Indigenous parents isolate the baby, keeping it in a state of quiet rest to protect it from various threats, including witchcraft.

Popular tools employed with infant learners include dedicated speech (baby talk, motherese); games like peek-a-boo; tickling and other forms of tactile stimulation; and "age-appropriate, educational" toys. These various forms of stimulation would be considered potentially harmful in Indigenous communities. Talking to an infant who is yet two to three years from participation in a speech community would be seen as bizarre and a waste of time. Similarly, while WEIRD parents treat the infant's babbling as proto-speech worthy of response, villagers read babbling as a sign of delayed personhood—the infant is not yet a person.

In numerous societies, family members do engage in lessons designed to accelerate the child's independence. This may include exercises to strengthen the legs and encourage walking. In WEIRD society, the child may be carried or transported in a stroller long after they gain mobility. Prepping the child to become self-sufficient and thereby reduce the burden on caretakers is not a WEIRD priority.

Aside from locomotion, some cultures stress early integration of the infant into the community to spread the burden of care more widely. This leads to deliberate instruction in sharing and prosocial behavior as well as kinship relations and standards of etiquette and address. However, these teaching moments are very rare and have specific, limited objectives. Such concerns for the child's social integration into extended family and community are largely absent in the WEIRD model.

Not only do WEIRD parents play with their infants and young children, they ascribe educational merit to this practice. Indigenous people usually see value in children's play as a medium for learning but do not see a role for themselves—beyond donating "props" to facilitate learning through play.

Indigenous pedagogy involves relatively little verbal interaction. Explicit instruction delivered verbally is rare, and questions from the learner aren't necessarily welcome. In contrast, scholars find that WEIRD parents begin very early to shape the child's speech, including vocabulary lessons. By age four, these children have had an estimated 4 million words addressed to them.

In the village, youth have great autonomy, and learning bouts are self-initiated rather than teacher or caretaker initiated. Learning is woven into the flow of daily life versus being encapsulated in formal lessons.

The learner proceeds at her own pace, and the learning curve is jagged—in contrast to whole groups of learners being herded along at the same pace, yielding smooth learning curves superimposed one upon another.

Of all the principles of Indigenous pedagogy, perhaps the most widely acknowledged is that children learn best from direct, hands-on experience. The "Yukaghir (Siberian foragers) model of knowledge transferal could be described as "doing is learning and learning is doing" (Willerslev 2007, 162). Many societies take the idea further and assert that one can only learn from direct experience. Information from another must be validated through personal replication, as every person's skill repertoire is idiosyncratic and subject to stylistic variation. Contrast this with the standardized curricula and authority figures of contemporary schools.

Direct experience often comes about as a result of the child's need to be helpful and "fit in." The child helper is eased into ongoing work activity, allowing them opportunities to learn without explicit instruction. In WEIRD society, children as young as fourteen months bid for a helper's role but are often rebuffed and redirected to play or given a lesson.

Lessons have a distinct beginning and ending versus knowledge acquisition that continues indefinitely. Expertise in collecting medicinal plants, for instance, peaks in mature adulthood, likewise bow-hunting prowess.

Success in classroom learning is marked by praise and other forms of recognition versus the sole but sufficient reward of completing the task successfully.

The majority of knowledge and skills a village child acquires is directly accessible and transparent. For opaque subjects like mathematics, "figuring it out" may not work, necessitating teacher-led lessons (Geary 2007).

Schooling aims to transmit arbitrary symbol systems that will be used as tools for learning and thinking. In the village, children learn quite directly how to use particular tools in a limited tool inventory (Scribner and Cole 1973).

In the village, children learn from a large cast of role models, particularly peers. In school and in WEIRD homes, children are urged to "focus attention on the teacher." Peers are distracting.

Patterns of learning in Indigenous communities are embedded in parental ethnotheories that legitimate many impromptu and potentially dangerous child initiatives. Tolerance for risky endeavors (e.g., appropriating a hot kiln for one's use) is justified on the basis of children's necessary autonomy to truly comprehend and master new skills and the social condemnation of controlling and curbing another's actions—including children. Interdicting a child as they launch a self-initiated learning bout could have negative consequences in the long term.

A parent who feels compelled to redirect the child from potentially harmful or destructive acts may speak through a third party, as in, "My sister, does it look to you that your nephew is going to hurt himself badly?" Intervention of this type may be rare because even an injury can have pedagogical value. In WEIRD parenting, by contrast, children no longer have accidents, they suffer the consequences of "neglect."

In Indigenous villages, children are not to intrude in adult conversations or pose questions when someone is preoccupied with their own activity. Rather, they are expected to watch and listen to gather information needed to advance their learning. In WEIRD society, children are not expected to construct their own lessons from the words and actions of others. Hence, they are often isolated from adult conversations, interactions, work, private possessions, and so on.

Observation and listening often lead to imitation. From the infant's replication of another's facial expression to children's artful reenactment of work and socializing at the blacksmith's forge in make-believe play, imitation is essential to Indigenous pedagogy. The actors whose work is being imitated are generally quite sympathetic, permitting children to utilize scraps and worn tools in their fledgling efforts. On the subject of children as "natural" imitators, both psychology and anthropology are in accord.

In Indigenous society, inanimate objects are seen as having inherent pedagogical value. Handling tools, pottery, fabrics, foodstuffs, and so on all yield information to the curious. Significantly, adults and older siblings donate child-sized tools and cast-off materials without further elaboration. This suggests that the key to learning is not the participation of a teacher but the child's opportunity to handle and practice with authentic, functional objects. WEIRD society is much more likely to "protect" the child from potential injury—to the child or the object.

It is admittedly much easier to break down and learn to use the relatively simple technology of the village than modern technology, which is largely opaque. Digital devices are both simpler and easier to use than analog counterparts but are also much more difficult to comprehend and fix should something go wrong.

There is a significant portal for learning that opens up in late infancy. Prominent among the facilitative elements is the child's emergence as a determined helper. Occasional helping evolves quickly into the assumption of a suitably matched suite of chores, such as errand running. By participating collaboratively in routine work, the child is learning through observation, listening, and copying. Very occasionally, adults provide timely assistance, including verbal direction. Aside from growing in competence, the child is buoyed up for her or his efforts by the growing acceptance of the results. Indigenous children earn social capital through the quality and amount of work they contribute. WEIRD children start life with a full social bank account—because they're kids.

While all children are eager to be helpful and to "fit in," in Indigenous communities, the child must adjust to the situation or exit. WEIRD parents often repurpose a communal activity so that it serves the child's need to acquire academic knowledge; the initial task is paused while everyone takes advantage of a "teaching moment."

Not all children are welcome as participants, depending on their level of maturity. They may be publicly chastised for their presumption. This rejection is often seen as a goad that motivates aspirant helpers to pay closer attention, practice more frequently, or focus their efforts on nearly mastered tasks.

In WEIRD models of parenting, the parent or professional child caregiver is the role model of choice. But growing evidence suggests that, from early childhood, Indigenous children are more likely to "apprentice" to an older sibling than to an adolescent or adult. The juvenile role model displays entry-level skills that are within reach of the novice and, typically, the older sibling (cousin, neighbor) is already assigned to "mind" the younger. However, even in cases where the learner has targeted an adult practitioner, they must take the initiative and persuade the worker to permit them to closely observe and to donate discarded or waste material to practice on. Not all experts are willing to assist novices, so the child must develop an awareness of the most approachable and cooperative practitioners to serve as role models. One key trait of Indigenous pedagogy is that the child initiates the learning bout, not the designated role model.

The fact that learners "own" their own curriculum helps to explain the highly varied and innovative outcomes that emerge from Indigenous pedagogy. Reports from craft-learning clearly indicate that motivated novices seek out multiple role models to study, further diversifying and "modernizing" their products. In school, the teacher owns the curriculum, which today and in the past has been designed to achieve uniformity rather than innovation.

But even the self-starting learner may succumb to the desire to accelerate the process by seeking out direct instruction from an expert. Chapter 3, Box 3.7 provides several vivid examples of adults' aversion to assuming the role of teacher. That is, it's not just the child's desire for autonomy that reduces demands for lessons; experts express antipathy towards the role of teacher.

In WEIRD society, primary learning environments are highly engineered. The design of the classrooms, the furniture, the various analog and digital teaching tools, the training of teachers and aides are all subject to frequent evaluation and refinement. Indigenous pedagogy, less obviously, is shaped by local circumstances, including environmental and economic change. While opportunities for learning may abound, particular settings—dubbed "natural classrooms"—may provide especially fertile ground for learning. Chapter 4 details several examples, including the playgroup, the family foraging outing, and the craftsperson's workshop, among others. The key point is that in the village, natural classrooms are not shaped by the need to educate children. The opportunity to fulfill this important function occurs serendipitously with only slight modification to accommodate the needs and limitations of young learners.

The natural classroom idea is especially fruitful as a lens to study children's learning in the distant past. Excavations of several stone tool-making sites strongly suggest a pattern where experts served as suppliers of raw material and full visual access to the toolmaking process, thereby meeting the novice's needs.

Like "Natural Classroom," the phrase "Chore Curriculum" describes an important but critical species of scaffolding to subtly aid the child's acquisition of skill and knowledge. Indigenous children are expected to do chores or routine tasks that, collectively, make up the vital domestic economy. Children may enjoy considerable autonomy in choosing which chores will be carried out and when, but a child who refuses domestic service entirely is rare. Chores are either assigned or undertaken voluntarily, and they are often conducted by a paired older and younger sibling. These assignments and the accompaniment of an older role model constitute a potential curriculum. Through chore assignment, a developmental pathway from easier to harder tasks is constructed, in which the gradient of the learning curve is shallow. In fact, the journey begins in play/work, where children replicate in social and object play the tasks that will later be performed in earnest. When they are deemed ready, chore assignments take into account the skill, strength, and stamina of young workers, minimizing fatigue and loss of enthusiasm. Many work domains are inherently ranked by difficulty, such as marine gathering, with toddlers collecting shellfish in the shallows, 9-year-old veterans free-diving to spear large fish, and every level in between. Gender is worked into the curriculum as well. While most chores are gendered, these norms may be violated when a family member of the appropriate gender is unavailable.

While not universal, many Indigenous communities do include more structured and formal, school-like institutions. These include initiation rites and apprenticeships. Not surprisingly, the pedagogy more closely resembles that of early schools than of the informal pedagogy in the village. Both involve a set curriculum with limited autonomy for novices. Relations between the learner and the learned are characterized by extreme social inequality, which leads to a harsh and challenging learning environment. A critical component shared by initiation rites and apprenticeship is the use of lore or secrets, hiding critical information to undermine the initiate's confidence. In fact, neither type of institution is solely or even primarily concerned with educating the young; instead, the goal is to ensure that the youth are put in their place and show proper deference to community leaders.

With the global spread of schooling, scholars have revealed areas of conflict between Indigenous and WEIRD pedagogy. Among the major points of contention are the following: the student's loss of autonomy and opportunity to set their own curriculum; drastic reduction in sources of new knowledge, which now is limited to teachers and books; public schools are far more likely to use harsh language and corporal punishment than mentors in the community; the loss of opportunities to innovate and solve problems collaboratively; the replacement of active, hands-on learning by packaged lessons delivered through verbal and written means; the substitution of one's native language by a foreign tongue; and, where learning in the village automatically leads to meaningful participation in the domestic economy, school lessons are an exercise in futility.

In an ideal future scenario, one can imagine gradual improvement in the public schooling offered in Indigenous communities, which, in turn, will increase employability for successful students. This optimistic development ought to be coupled with policy changes that support and encourage communities to continue living off the land—should they choose—permitting youth to opt out of formal lessons. Rather than classrooms and urbanized teachers, these communities need extension agents who intervene strategically to help modernize food production while increasing sustainable yields.

References

Abella, Anna D. 2018. "The Time to Love: Ideologies of 'Good' Parenting at a Family Service Organization in the Southeastern United States." Unpublished PhD diss., University of South Florida, Tampa.

Abels, Monika, Zaira Papaligoura, Bettina Lamm, and Relindis D. Yovsi. 2017. "How Usual Is (Play as You Usually Would)? A Comparison of Naturalistic Mother–Infant Interactions with Videorecorded Play Sessions in Three Cultural Communities." *Child Development Research* 5: 1–8.

Abels, Monika, Andrew Kilale, and Paul Voght. 2020. "Speech Acts Addressed to Hadza Infants in Tanzania: Cross-Cultural Comparison, Speaker Age and Camp Livelihood." *First Language* 41(3): 294–313.

Ackroyd, Peter. 1990. *Dickens*. New York: HarperCollins.

Acredolo, Linda, and Susan Goodwyn. 2002. *Baby Signs: How to Talk with Your Baby Before Your Baby Can Talk*. Chicago: Contemporary Books.

Adams, David W. 2020. *Education for Extinction: American Indians and the Boarding School Experience, 1875–1928*. 2nd ed. Lawrence: University Press of Kansas.

Aime, Hilary, Philippe Rochat, and Tanya Broesch. 2020. "Cultural Differences in Infant Spontaneous Behavior: Evidence from a Small-Scale, Rural Island Society." *Infant and Child Development* 30(1): 1–10.

Ainsworth, Mary D. 1967. *Infancy in Uganda: Infant Care and the Growth of Love*. Baltimore, MD: Johns Hopkins Press.

Akhtar, Nameera. 2005. "Is Joint Attention Necessary for Early Word Learning?" In *The Development of Social Cognition and Communication*, edited by Catherine Tamis-LeMonda and Bruce D. Homer, pp. 165–179. Mahwah, NJ: Erlbaum.

Akinnaso, R. Niyi. 1997. "Schooling, Language, Knowledge in Literate and Nonliterate Societies." In *Cultures of Scholarship*, edited by Sarah C. Humphreys, pp. 339–386. Ann Arbor: The University of Michigan Press.

Alcalá, Lucía, Barbara Rogoff, Rebeca Mejía-Arauz, Andrew D. Coppens, and Amy L. Dexter. 2014. "Children's Initiative in Contributions to Family Work in Indigenous-heritage and Cosmopolitan Communities in Mexico." *Human Development* 57: 96–115.

Alcalá, Lucia, Maria D., C. Montejano, and Yuliana S. Fernandez. 2021. "How Yucatec Maya Children Learn to Help at Home." *Human Development* 65: 191–203.

Aldrich, Richard. 1999. "The Apprentice in History." In *Apprenticeship: Towards a New Paradigm of Learning*, edited by Patrick Ainley and Helen Rainbird, pp. 14–24. London: Kogan Page.

Anderson-Levitt, Katherine M. 2005. "The Schoolyard Gate: Schooling and Childhood in Global Perspective." *Journal of Social History* 38(4): 987–1006.

Apicella, Coren, Ara Norenzayan, and Joseph Henrich. 2020. "Beyond WEIRD: A Review of the Last Decade and a Look Ahead to the Global Laboratory of the Future." *Evolution and Human Behavior* 41: 319–329.

220 REFERENCES

Apple, Rima D. 2006. *Perfect Motherhood: Science and Childrearing in America*. New Brunswick, NJ: Rutgers University Press.

Argenti, Nicolas. 2002. "People of the Chisel: Apprenticeship, Youth, and Elites in Oku." *American Ethnologist* 29(3): 497–533.

Arnold, Mary Jo. 2006. "*Ndomo* Ritual and *Sogo bo* Play: Boy's Masquerading among the Bamana of Mali." In *Playful Performers: African Children's Masquerades*, edited by Simon Ottenberg and David A. Binkley, pp. 49–65. Brunswick, NJ: Transaction Publishers.

Aronson, Lisa. 1989. "To Weave or Not to Weave: Apprenticeship Rules among the Akwete Igbo of Nigeria and the Baulè, of the Ivory Coast." In *Apprenticeship: From Theory to Methods and Back Again*, edited by Michael W. Coy, pp. 149–162. Albany: SUNY Press.

Assaf, Ella. 2021. "Throughout the Generations: Learning Processes and Knowledge Transmission Mechanisms as Reflected in Lithic Assemblages of the Terminal Lower Paleolithic Levant." *Journal of Archaeological Science* (Reports) 35: 102772.

Atran, Scott, and Douglas Medin. 2008. *The Native Mind and the Cultural Construction of Nature*. Cambridge, MA: MIT Press.

Atran, Scott, and Dan Sperber. 1991. "Learning Without Teaching: Its Place in Culture " In *Culture, Schooling and Psychological Development*, edited by Liliana Tolchinsky Landsmann, pp. 39–55. Norwood, NJ: Ablex.

Aunger, Robert. 2000. "The Life History of Culture Learning in a Face-to-Face Society." *Ethos* 28(3): 445–481.

BabyPlus® Prenatal Education. "The Right Sounds at the Right Time." Accessed October 3, 2022. https://babyplus.com/

Bacchiddu, Giovanna. Pre-press. "'When I Grow Up, I Want to Peel Potatoes': Learning across Different Landscapes in Apiao, Chiloé, Chile." In *Theorizing Indigenous Children's Relations to the Environment: A Perspective from Lowland South America Cambridge Journal of Anthropology*, edited by Francesca Mezzenzana and Jan David Hauck.

Bagwell, Elizabeth A. 2002. "Ceramic Form and Skill: Attempting to Identify Child Producers at Pecos Pueblo, New Mexico." In *Children in the Prehistoric Puebloan Southwest*, edited by Katherine Kamp, pp. 90–107. Salt Lake City: University of Utah Press.

Bai, Limin. 2005. *Shaping the Ideal Child: Children and Their Primers in Late Imperial China*. Hong Kong: Chinese University Press.

Baillargeon, Renee, and Susan Carey. 2012. "Core Cognition and Beyond: The Acquisition of Physical and Numerical Knowledge." In *Early Childhood Development and Later Outcome*, edited by Sabina Pauen, pp. 33–65. Cambridge: Cambridge University Press.

Bakeman, Roger, Lauren B. Adamson, Melvin J. Konner, and Ronald G. Barr. 1990. "!Kung Infancy: The Social Context of Object Exploration." *Child Development* 61: 794–809.

Balikci, Asen. 1970. *The Netsilik Eskimo*. Garden City, NY: The Natural History Press.

Bamford, Sandra C. 2004. "Embodiments of Detachment: Engendering Agency in the Highlands of Papua New Guinea." In *Women as Unseen Characters*, edited by Pascale Bonnemère, pp. 34–56. Philadelphia: University of Pennsylvania Press.

Bandura, Albert. 1977. *Social Learning Theory*. Englewood Cliffs, NJ: Prentice Hall.

Bang, Megan, Ananda Marin, Doug L. Medin, and Karen Washinawatok. 2016. "Learning by Observing, Pitching In, and Being in Relations in the Natural World." In *Advances in Child Development and Behavior*, edited by Maricela Correa-Chavez, Rebeca Mejia-Arauz, and Barbara Rogoff, pp. 303–313. Oxford: Elsevier.

Barnett, Homer G. 1953. *Innovation: The Basis of Cultural Change*. New York: McGraw-Hill.

REFERENCES 221

Barrett, H. Clark. 2020. "Deciding What to Observe: Thoughts for a Post-WEIRD Generation." *Evolution and Human Behavior* 41: 445–453.

Barron, Caroline M. 2007. "The Child in Medieval London: The Legal Evidence." In *Essays on Medieval Childhood: Responses to Recent Debate*, edited by Joel T. Rosenthal, pp. 40–53. Donington, Lincolnshire, UK: Shaun Tyas.

Barth, Fredrik. 1975. *Ritual and Knowledge among the Baktaman of New Guinea.* New Haven, CT: Yale University Press.

Bascom, William Russell. 1969. *Ifá Divination: Communication between Gods and Men in West Africa.* Bloomington: Indiana University Press.

Battiste, Marie. 2002. *Indigenous Knowledge and Pedagogy in First Nations Education: A Literature Review with Recommendations.* Ottawa, ON: National Working Group on Education and the Minister of Indian Affairs Indian and Northern Affairs Canada (INAC).

Bavin, Edith L. 1991. "The Acquisition of Warlpiri Kin Terms." *Pragmatics* 1: 319–344.

Bavin, Edith L. 1992. "The Acquisition of Walpiri." In *The Cross-Linguistic Study of Language Acquisition*, Vol. 3, edited by Dan I. Slobin, pp. 309–372. Hillsdale, NJ: Lawrence Erlbaum Associates.

Beck, Sarah R., Ian A. Apperly, Jackie M. Chappell, Carlie Guthrie, and Nicola Cutting. 2011. "Making Tools Isn't Child's Play." *Cognition* 119: 301–306.

Bentz, Bonnie. 2001. "Adolescent Culture: An Exploration of the Socio-emotional Development of the Aka Adolescents of the Central African Republic." *Oriental Anthropologist* 1(2): 25–32.

Bereczkei, Tamas, and Robin I. M. Dunbar. 1997. "Female-Biased Reproductive Strategies in a Hungarian Gypsy Population." *Proceedings of the Royal Society of London*, Series B 264: 17–22.

Bergin, Christi, David F. Lancy, and Kelly D. Draper. 1994. "Parents' Interactions with Beginning Readers." In *Children's Emergent Literacy: From Research to Practice*, edited by David F. Lancy, pp. 53–78. Westport, CT: Praeger.

Berl, Richard E.W., and Barry S. Hewlett. 2015. "Cultural Variation in the Use of Overimitation by the Aka and Ngandu of the Congo Basin." *PLoS ONE* 10: e0120180.

Beverly, Elizabeth A., and Robert D. Whittemore. 1993. "Mandinka Children and the Geography of Well-Being." *Ethos* 21(3): 235–272.

Biersack, Aletta. 1998. "Horticulture and Hierarchy: The Youthful Beautification of the Body in the Paiela and Porgera Valleys." In *Adolescence in Pacific Island Societies*, edited by Gilbert H. Herdt and Stephen C. Leavitt, pp. 71–91. Pittsburgh: University of Pittsburgh Press.

Biesele, Megan. 1976. "Aspects of !Kung Folkore." In *Kalahari Hunter-Gatherers: Studies of the !Kung San and Their Neighbors*, edited by Richard B. Lee and Irven DeVore, pp. 302–324. Cambridge, MA: Harvard University Press.

Binkley, David A. 2006. "From Grasshoppers to Babende: The Socialization of Southern Kuba Boys to Masquerade." In *Playful Performers: African Children's Masquerades* edited by Simon Ottenberg and David A. Binkley, pp. 105–115. New Brunswick, NJ: Transaction Publishers.

Bird, Douglas W., and Rebecca Bliege Bird. 2002. "Children on the Reef: Slow Learning or Strategic Foraging?" *Human Nature* 13: 269–397.

Bird, Douglas W., and Rebecca B. Bird. 2005. "Martu Children's Hunting Strategies in the Western Desert, Australia." In *Hunter Gatherer Childhoods: Evolutionary, Developmental, and Cultural Perspectives*, edited by Barry S. Hewlett and Michael E. Lamb, pp. 129–146. New Brunswick, NJ: Aldine Transaction.

222 REFERENCES

Bird-David, Nurit. 2008. "Feeding Nayaka Children and English Readers: A Bifocal Ethnography of Parental Feeding in 'The Giving Environment.'" *Anthropological Quarterly* 81(3): 523–622. doi:10.1353/anq.0.0018

Bird-David, Nurit. 2015. "Modern Biases, Hunter-Gatherers' Children: On the Visibility of Children in Other Cultures." In *The Archaeology of Childhood: Interdisciplinary Perspectives on an Archaeological Enigma*, edited by Güner Coskunsu, pp. 91–103. Albany: SUNY Press.

Bird, Douglas W., and Rebecca Bliege Bird. 2000. "The Ethnoarchaeology of Juvenile Foragers: Shellfishing Strategies among Meriam Children." *Journal of Anthropological Archaeology* 19: 461–476.

Bjorklund, David F. 2007a. *Why Youth Is Not Wasted on the Young*. Malden, MA: Blackwell.

Bjorklund, David F. 2007b. "The Most Educable of Animals." In *Educating the Evolved Mind*, edited by Jerry S. Carlson and Joel R Levin, pp. 119–129. Charlotte, NC: Information Age Publishing.

Bjorkland, David F. 2016. "Incorporating Development into Evolutionary Psychology." *Evolutionary Psychology* 14(4): 1–14.

Bjorklund, David F., and Carlos Hernandez Blasi. 2005. "The Evolution of Language." In *Handbook of Evolutionary Psychology*, edited by David M. Buss, pp. 828–877. New York: Wiley.

Bjorklund, David F., and Amy K. Gardiner. 2010. "Object Play and Tool Use: Developmental and Evolutionary Perspectives." In *The Oxford Handbook of Play*, edited by Anthony Pellegrini, pp. 153–171. New York: Oxford University Press.

Blakemore, Sarah-Jayne, and Kathryn L. Mills. 2014. "Is Adolescence a Sensitive Period for Sociocultural Processing?" *Annual Review of Psychology* 65: 187–207. doi:10.1146/annurev-psych-010213-115202

Blakey, Kirsten H., Eva Rafetseder, Mark Atkinson, Elizabeth Renner, Fia Cowan-Forsythe, Shivani J. Sati, and Christine A. Caldwell. 2021. "Development of Strategic Social Information Seeking: Implications for Cumulative Culture." *PLOS ONE*, 16(8): e0256605. https://doi.org/10.1371/journal.pone.0256605

Bloch, Maurice E. F., Gregg E. A. Solomon, and Susan Carey. 2001. "Zafimaniry: An Understanding of What Is Passed on from Parents to Children: A Cross-Cultural Investigation." *Journal of Cognition and Culture* 1(1): 43–68.

Blurton-Jones, Nicholas G., and Melvin J. Konner. 1976. "!Kung Knowledge of Animal Behavior." In *Kalahari Hunter-Gatherers: Studies of the !Kung San and Their Neighbors*, edited by Richard B. Lee and Irven DeVore, pp. 325–348. Cambridge, MA: Harvard University Press.

Blurton-Jones, Nicholas G., and Frank W. Marlowe. 2002. "Selection for Delayed Maturity: Does It Take 20 Years to Learn to Hunt and Gather?" *Human Nature* 13(2): 199–238.

Bock, John, and Sara E. Johnson. 2004. "Play and Subsistence Ecology among the Okavango Delta Peoples of Botswana." *Human Nature* 15(1): 63–82.

Boesch, Christophe. 2013. *Wild Cultures: A Comparison between Chimpanzee and Human Cultures*. Cambridge: Cambridge University Press.

Boesch, Christophe, and Michael Tomasello. 1998. "Chimpanzee and Human Cultures." *Current Anthropology* 39(5): 591–614.

Bolin, Inge. 2006. *Growing Up in a Culture of Respect: Child Rearing in Highland Peru*. Austin: University of Texas Press.

Bollig, Laurentius. 1927. *The Inhabitants of the Truk Islands: Religion, Life and a Short Grammar of a Micronesian People*. Münster, Germany: Aschendorff.

REFERENCES 223

Bombjaková, Daša. 2018. "The Role of Public Speaking, Ridicule, and Play in Cultural Transmission among Mbendjele BaYaka Forest Hunter-Gatherers." Unpublished PhD diss., University College London.

Bombjaková, Daša, Sheina Lew-Levy, Romain Duda, Ghislain C. Loubelo, and Jerome Louis. Pre-press. "BaYaka Education: From the Forest to the ORA (Observer, Réflechir, Agir) Classroom." *Hunter-Gatherer Research*.

Bonawitz, Elizabeth, Patrick Shafto, Hyowon Gweon, Noah D. Goodman, Elizabeth Spelke, and Laura Schultz. 2011. "The Double-Edged Sword of Pedagogy: Instruction Limits Spontaneous Exploration and Discovery." *Cognition* 120: 322–330.

Booth, Margaret Z. 2002. "Swazi Concepts of Intelligence: The Universal Versus the Local." *Ethos* 30(4): 376–400.

Borofsky, Robert. 1987. *Making History: Pukapukan and Anthropological Constructions of Knowledge*. New York: Cambridge University Press.

Bourgeois, Kristine, Kwahar, Alexa W., Neal, S. Ashley, and Lockman, Jeffrey J. 2005. "Infant Manual Exploration of Objects, Surfaces and Their Interrelations." *Infancy* 8: 233–252.

Bowers, Nancy. 1965. "Permanent Bachelorhood in the Upper Kaugel Valley of Highland New Guinea." *Oceania* 36: 27–37.

Bowes, Jennifer M., and Jacqueline J. Goodnow. 1996. "Work for Home, School, or Labor Force: The Nature and Sources of Changes in Understanding." *Psychology Bulletin* 119: 300–321.

Bowser, Brenda J., and John Q. Patton. 2008. "Learning and Transmission of Pottery Style: Women's Life Histories and Communities of Practice in the Ecuadorian Amazon." In *Cultural Transmission and Material Culture: Breaking Down Boundaries*, edited by Miriam T. Stark, Brenda J. Bowser, and Lee Horne, pp. 105–129. Tucson: University of Arizona Press.

Boyd, Robert, and Peter J. Richerson. 2006. "Culture and the Evolution of the Human Social Instincts." In *Roots of Human Socialization: Culture, Cognition, and Interaction*, edited by Nick J. Einfield and Stephen C. Levinson, pp. 453–477. Oxford: Berg.

Boyd, Robert, Peter J. Richerson, and Joseph Henrich. 2011. "The Cultural Niche: Why Social Learning Is Essential for Human Adaptation." *PNAS* 108: 10918–10925.

Boyette, Adam H. 2019. "Autonomy, Cognitive Development and the Socialization of Cooperation in Foragers: Aka Children's Views of Sharing and Caring." *Hunter Gatherer Research* 3: 475–500.

Boyette, Adam H., and Barry H. Hewlett. 2018. "Teaching in hunter-gatherers." *Review Journal of Philosophy sand Psychology* 9: 771–797.

Boyette, Adam H., and Sheina Lew-Levy. 2021. "Socialization, Autonomy, and Cooperation: Insights from Task Assignment among the Egalitarian BaYaka." *Ethos* 48(3): 400–418. https://doi.org/10.1111/etho.12284

Bradley, Benjamin S., and Michael Smithson. 2017. "Groupness in Preverbal Infants: Proof of Concept." *Frontiers in Psychology* 8: 385. doi:10.3389/fpsyg.2017.00385

Braff, Danielle. 2020. "How to Get Your Kids to Treat You Like Their Teacher." *New York Times: Parenting*, April 21. nytimes.com/2020/04/21/parenting/coronavirus-home-schooling-children.html.

Brandl, Eva. 2021. "Theory of Mind and Teaching in ni-Vanuatu Children." Unpublished PhD diss., University College London.

Briggs, Jean L. 1991. "Expecting the Unexpected: Canadian Inuit Training for an Experimental Lifestyle." *Ethos* 19: 259–287.

224 REFERENCES

Bril, Blandine. 1986. "The Acquisition of an Everyday Technical Motor Skill: The Pounding of Cereals in Mali (Africa)." In *Themes in Motor Development*, edited by Harold Thomas, Anthony Whiting, and Michael G. Wade, pp. 315–326. Dordrecht: Martinus Nijhoff.

Brison, Karen J. 2009. "Shifting Conceptions of Self and Society in Fijian Kindergarten." *Ethos* 37(3): 314–333.

Broch, Harald B. 1990. *Growing Up Agreeably: Bonerate Childhood Observed*. Honolulu: University of Hawaii Press.

Bronfenbrenner, Urie. 1979. *The Ecology of Human Development*. Cambridge, MA: Harvard University Press.

Brooks, David. 2011. "Organization Within Disorder: The Present and Future of Young People in the Ngaanyatjarra Lands." In *Growing Up in Central Australia: New Anthropological Studies of Aboriginal Childhood and Adolescence*, edited by Ute Eickelkamp, pp. 183–212. Oxford: Berghahn Books.

Brooks, Douglas. 2015. *Japanese Wooden Boat Building*. Warren, CT: Floating World Editions.

Brown, Penelope. 2011. "The Cultural Organization of Attention." In *The Handbook of Language Socialization*, edited by Alessandro Duranti, Elinor Ochs, and Bambi B. Schieffelin, pp. 29–55. Chichester, UK: Blackwell.

Brown, Penelope, and Suzanne Gaskins. 2014. "Language Acquisition and Language Socialization." In *Cambridge Handbook of Linguistic Anthropology*, edited by Nicholas J. Enfield, Paul Kockelman, and Jack Sidnell, pp. 187–226. Cambridge: Cambridge University Press.

Broyon, Marie A. 2004. L'éducation sanskrite à Bénares, enjeu d'une socié qui oscille entre traditions et transition. Paper presented at a seminar on Learning Processes and Everyday Cognition: The Role of Play and Games, April 16, Charmey, Switzerland.

Brunelle, Lynn. 2016. *Big Science for Little People: 52 Activities to Help You and Your Child Discover the Wonders of Science*. An Official Geek Mama Guide. Boulder, CO: Roost Books.

Bruner, Jerome S. 1966a. *Toward a Theory of Instruction*. Cambridge, MA: Harvard University Press.

Bruner, Jerome S. 1966b. "On Cognitive Growth II." In *Studies in Cognitive Growth*, edited by Jerome S. Bruner, Rose R. Olver, and Patricia M. Greenfield, pp. 30–67. New York: Wiley.

Bruner, Jerome S. 1976. "Nature and Uses of Immaturity." In *Play—Its Role in Development and Evolution*, edited by Jerome S. Bruner, Alison Jolly, and Kathy Sylva, pp. 28–64. New York: Basic Books.

Bruyere, Brett L., Jonathan Trimarco, and Saruni Lemungesi. 2016. "A Comparison of Traditional Plant Knowledge between Students and Herders in Northern Kenya." *Journal of Ethnobiology and Ethnomedicine* 12(1): 48. doi:10.1186/s13002-016-0121-z

Bryan, Lynn A., and H. James McLaughlin. 2005. "Teaching and Learning in Rural Mexico: A Portrait of Student Responsibility in Everyday School Life." *Teaching and Teacher Education* 21: 33–48.

Buchsbaum, Daphna, Alison Gopnik, Thomas L. Griffiths, and Patrick Shafto. 2011. "Children's Imitation of Causal Action Sequences Is Influenced by Statistical and Pedagogical Evidence." *Cognition* 120: 331–341.

Buckingham, David, and Margaret Scanlon. 2003. *Education, Entertainment, and Learning in the Home*. Maidenhead, UK: Open University Press.

REFERENCES 225

Budwig, Nancy, Amy Strage, and Michael Bamberg. 1986. "The Construction of Joint Activities with an Age-Mate: The Transition from Caregiver–Child to Peer Play." In *Children's Worlds and Children's Language*, edited by Jenny Cook-Gumperz, William A. Corsaro, and Jürgen Streek, pp. 83–108. Berlin, Germany: Mouton de Gruyter.

Buechner, Maryann M. 2022. "What's Inside a UNICEF Early Childhood Development Kit?" *Forbes*, May 11. https://www.unicef.org/supply/early-childhood-developm ent-ecd-kit

Bugos, Peter E., Jr., and Lorraine M. McCarthy. 1984. "Ayoreo Infanticide: A Case Study." In *Infanticide: Comparative and Evolutionary Perspectives*, edited by Glen Hausfater and Sarah B. Hrdy, pp. 503–520. New York: Aldine De Gruyter.

Bunn, Stephanie. 1999. "The Nomad's Apprentice: Different Kinds of 'Apprenticeship' among Kyrgyz Nomads in Central Asia." In *Apprenticeship: Towards a New Paradigm of Learning*, edited by Patrick Ainley and Helen Rainbird, pp. 74–85. London: Kogan Page.

Bunzel, Ruth. 1929. *The Pueblo Potter, a Study of Creative Imagination in Primitive Art*. New York: Columbia University Press.

Burdelski, Matthew. 2006. "Language Socialization of Two-Year-Old Children in Kansai, Japan: The Family and Beyond." Unpublished PhD diss., University of California, Los Angeles.

Callaghan, Tarra, Henrike Holl, Hannes Rakoczy, Felix Warneken, Ulf Liszkowski, Tanya Behne, and Michael Tomasello. 2011. "Early Social Cognition in Three Cultural Contexts." *Monographs of the Society for Research in Child Development* 76(2): 1–142.

Calvert, Karin. 1992. *Children in the House: The Material Culture of Early Childhood, 1600–1900*. Boston: Northeastern University Press.

Campbell, Don. 2002. *The Mozart Effect for Children: Awakening Your Child's Mind, Health, and Creativity with Music*. New York: William Morrow.

Carey, Susan, and Elizabeth Spelke. 1996. "Science and Core Knowledge." *Philosophy of Science* 63: 515–533.

Carpenter, Kathie. 2020. *Life in a Cambodian Orphanage: A Childhood Journey for New Opportunities*. New Brunswick, NJ: Rutgers University Press.

Carrier, James G. 1981. "Labour Migration and Labour Export on Ponam Island." *Oceania* 51: 237–255.

Caruso, David A. 1993. "Dimensions of Quality in Infants' Exploratory Behavior: Relationships to Problem-Solving Ability." *Infant Behavior and Development* 46: 331–454.

Cashdan, Elizabeth, Frank W. Marlowe, Alyssa Crittenden, Claire Porter, and Brian M. Wood. 2012. "Sex Differences in Spatial Cognition among Hadza Foragers." *Evolution and Human Behavior* 33(4): 274–284.

Casimir, Michael J. 2010. *Growing Up in a Pastoral Society: Socialization among Pashtu Nomads*. Kolner Ethnologische Beitrage. Cologne: Druck & Bindung.

Casler, Krista, Treysi Terziyan, and Kimberly Greene. 2009. Toddlers View Artifact Function Normatively." *Cognitive Development* 24: 240–247.

Castagno, Angelina E., Bryan McKinley, and Jones Brayboy. 2008. "Culturally Responsive Schooling for Indigenous Youth: A Review of the Literature." *Review of Educational Research* 78(4): 941–993.

Castañeda, Nuria. 2018. "Apprenticeship in Early Neolithic Societies: The Transmission of Technological Knowledge at the Flint Mine of Casa Montero (Madrid, Spain), ca. 5300–5200 BCE." *Current Anthropology* 59(6): 716–740. doi:10.1086/700837

226 REFERENCES

Center for the Developing Child. 2022. "Serve and Return." Harvard University. Accessed December 14, 2022. https://developingchild.harvard.edu/science/key-concepts/serve-and-return/

Chapin, Bambi L. 2014. *Childhood in a Sri Lankan Village: Shaping Hierarchy and Desire*. New Brunswick, NJ: Rutgers University Press.

Chavajay, Pablo. 2006. "How Mayan Mothers with Different amounts of Schooling Organize a Problem-Solving Discussion with Children." *International Journal of Behavioral Development* 30(4): 371–382.

Chiera, Edward. (1938) 1966. *They Wrote on Clay: The Babylonian Tablets Speak Today*. Chicago: University of Chicago Press.

Chisholm, James S. 1983. *Navajo Infancy: An Ethological Study of Child Development*. New York: Aldine.

Chisholm, James S. 1996. "Learning Respect for Everything: Navaho Images of Development." In *Images of Childhood*, edited by C. Philip Hwang, Michael E. Lamb, and Irving E. Sigel, pp. 167–183. Mahwah, NJ: Erlbaum.

Cho, Hae-Joang. 1995. "Children in the Examination War in South Korea: A Cultural Analysis." In *Children and the Politics of Culture*, edited by Sharon Stephens, pp. 141–168. Princeton, NJ: Princeton University Press.

Clark, Eve V. 2005. *First Language Acquisition*. Cambridge: Cambridge University Press.

Clark, Gracia. 1994. *Onions Are My Husband: Survival and Accumulation by West African Market Women*. Chicago: University of Chicago Press.

Clegg, Jennifer M., Nicole J. Wen, P. Hartman, Adam Alcott, Elena C. Keltner, and Cristine H. Legare. 2021. "Teaching through Collaboration: Flexibility and Diversity in Caregiver–Child Interaction across Cultures." *Child Development* 92(1): e56–e75.

Cohn, Clarice. Pre-press. "Xikrin Children and the Bacajá River: Knowledge and Knowing from Others." In *Theorizing Indigenous Children's Relations to the Environment: A Perspective from Lowland South America, Cambridge Journal of Anthropology*, edited by Francesca Mezzenzana and Jan David Hauck.

Cole, Michael. 2005. "Cross-Cultural and Historical Perspectives on the Developmental Consequences of Education." *Human Development* 48: 195–216.

Cole, Michael, John A. Gay, Joe Glick, Don W. Sharp, Tom Ciborowski, Fred Frankel, John Kellemu, and David F. Lancy. 1971. *The Cultural Context of Learning and Thinking*. New York: Basic Books.

Coll, Cynthia G. 2004. "The Interpenetration of Culture and Biology in Human Development." *Research in Human Development* 1(3): 145–159.

Coll, Cynthia G., and Amy K. Marks. 2009. *Immigrant Stories: Ethnicity and Academics in Middle Childhood*. New York: Oxford University Press.

Collet, Vicki S., and Elise Berman. 2021. "Educators' Perspectives of the Marshallese Experience during Spring 2020 Remote Learning." *Review of Education, Pedagogy, and Cultural Studies* 41: 121–147. doi:10.1080/10714413.2021.1873005

Condon, Richard G. 1987. *Inuit Youth: Growth and Change in the Canadian Arctic*. New Brunswick, NJ: Rutgers University Press.

Connolly, Joy. 2001. "Problems of the Past in Imperial Greek Education." In *Education in Greek and Roman Antiquity*, edited by Yun Lee Too, pp. 340–372. Boston: Brill.

Connolly, Kevin, and Mary Dalgleish. 1989. "The Emergence of Tool-Using Skill in Infancy." *Developmental Psychology* 25: 894–912.

Cooper, Eugene. 1988. *Wood-Carvers of Hong Kong: Craft Production in the World Capitalist Periphery*. Prospect Heights, IL: Waveland Press.

REFERENCES   227

Cooperrider, Kensy. 2019. "What Happens to Cognitive Diversity When Everyone Is More WEIRD?" *Aeon*, January 23. Accessed December 17, 2022. https://aeon.co/ideas/what-happens-to-cognitive-diversity-when-everyone-is-more-weird

Coppens, Andrew D., Anna I. Corwin, and Lucia Alcalá. 2020. "Beyond Behavior: Linguistic Evidence of Cultural Variation in Parental Ethnotheories of Children's Prosocial Helping." *Frontiers of Psychology* 11: 307. doi:10.3389/fpsyg.2020.00307

Corbeill, Anthony. 2001. "Education in the Roman Republic: Creating Traditions." In *Education in Greek and Roman Antiquity*, edited by Yun Lee Too, pp. 261–287. Boston: Brill.

Correa-Chávez, Maricela, Barbara Rogoff, and Rebeca M. Mejía-Arauz. 2005. "Cultural Patterns in Attending to Two Events at Once." *Child Development* 76: 664–678.

Covarrubias, Miguel. 1937. *Island of Bali*. New York: Alfred A. Knopf.

Coward, Fiona, and Paul Howard-Jones. 2021. "Exploring Environmental Influences on Infant Development and Their Potential Role in Processes of Cultural Transmission and Long-Term Technological Change." *Childhood in the Past* 14(2): 80–101. doi:10.1080/17585716.2021.1956057

Coy, Michael W., ed. 1989a. *Apprenticeship: From Theory to Method and Back Again*. Albany: SUNY Press.

Coy, Michael W. 1989b. "From Theory." In *Apprenticeship: From Theory to Method and Back Again*, edited by Michael W. Coy, pp. 1–12. Albany: SUNY Press.

Crago, Martha B. 1988. "Cultural Context in the Communicative Interaction of Young Inuit Children." Unpublished PhD diss., McGill University.

Crago, Martha B. 1992. "Communicative Interaction and Second Language Acquisition: An Inuit Example." *TESOL Quarterly* 26: 487–505.

Crago, Martha B., Betsy Annahatak, and Lizzie Ningiuruvik. 1993. "Changing Patterns of Language Socialization in Inuit Homes." *Anthropology and Education Quarterly* 24: 205–223.

Crawford, Sally. 2009. "The Archaeology of Playthings: Theorizing a Toy Stage in the Biography of Objects." *Childhood in the Past* 2: 56–71.

Cristia, Alejandrina, Emmanuel Dupoux, Michael Gurven, and Jonathan Stieglitz. 2019. "Child-Directed Speech is Infrequent in Forager–Farmer Population: A Time Allocation Study." *Child Development* 90(3): 759–773.

Crittenden, Alyssa N. 2016a. "Children's Foraging and Play among the Hadza: The Evolutionary Significance of 'Work Play.'" In *Childhood: Origins, Evolution, & Implications*, edited by Courtney L. Meehan and Alyssa N. Crittenden, pp. 155–172. Santa Fe, NM: School for Advanced Research Press.

Crittenden, Alyssa N. 2016b. "To Share or Not to Share? Social Processes of Learning to Share Food among Hadza Hunter-Gatherer Children." In *Social Learning and Innovation in Contemporary Hunter-Gatherers: Evolutionary and Ethnographic Perspectives*, edited by Hideaki Terashima and Barry S. Hewlett, pp. 61–70. Tokyo: Springer.

Crocker, William, and Jean Crocker. 1994. *The Canela: Bonding through Kinship, Ritual and Sex*. New York: Harcourt, Brace.

Crompton, Frank. 1997. *Workhouse Children*. Stroud, UK: Sutton.

Crown, Patricia L. 2002. "Learning and Teaching in the Prehispanic American Southwest." In *Children in the Prehistoric Puebloan Southwest*, edited by Katheryn A. Kamp, pp. 108–124. Salt Lake City: University of Utah Press.

228 REFERENCES

Cruz García, Gisella S. 2006. "The Mother–Child Nexus. Knowledge and Valuation of Wild Food Plants in Wayanad, Western Ghats, India." *Journal of Ethnobiology and Ethnomedicine* 2: Article 39.

Cšibra, Gergely, and György Gergely. 2009. "Natural Pedagogy." *Trends in Cognitive Sciences* 13(4): 148–153. doi:10.1016/j.tics.2009. 01.005

Csibra, György, and György Gergely. 2011. "Natural Pedagogy as Evolutionary Adaptation." *Philosophical Transactions of the Royal Society of London. Series B, Biological Sciences* 366: 1149–1157.

Culwick, Arthur T. 1935. *Ubena of the Rivers.* London: Allen and Unwin.

Cunnar, Geoffrey E. 2015. "Discovering Latent Children in the Archaeological Record of the Great Basin." *Childhood in the Past: An International Journal* 8(2): 133–148. doi:10.1179/1758571615Z.00000000035

Cunningham, Hugh. 1995. *Children and Childhood in Western Society Since 1500.* White Plains, NY: Longman.

Cutting, Nicola, Ian A. Apperly, Jackie Chappell, and Sarah R. Beck. 2014. "Why Can't Children Piece Their Knowledge Together? The Puzzling Difficulty of Tool Innovation." *Journal of Experimental Child Psychology* 125: 110–117.

d'Andrade, Roy G. 1984. "Cultural Meaning Systems." In *Culture Theory: Essays on Mind, Self, and Emotion*, edited by Richard A. Shweder and Robert A. LeVine, pp. 88–119. Cambridge: Cambridge University Press.

Danielsson, Bengt. 1952. *The Happy Island.* Translated by F. H. Lyon. London: George Allen and Unwin.

Davin, Anna. 1996. *Growing Up Poor: Home, School and Street in London 1870–1914.* London: Rivers Oram Press.

Davis, Helen E. 2014. "Variable Education Exposure and Cognitive Task Performance among the Tsimané Forager-Horticulturalists." Unpublished PhD diss., The University of New Mexico.

Davis, Helen E., and Elizabeth Cashdan. 2019. "Spatial Cognition, Navigation, and Mobility among Children in a Forager-Horticulturalist Population, the Tsimané of Bolivia." *Cognitive Development* 52: 100800.

Davis, Helen E., Jonathan Stieglitz, Alberto M. Tayo, Hillard Kaplan, and Michael Gurven. 2020. "The Formal Schooling Niche: Longitudinal Evidence from Amazonia, Bolivia Demonstrates That Higher School Quality Augments Differences in Children's Abstract Reasoning." *PsyArXiv*, October 14. doi:10.31234/osf.io/d3sgq

Davis, Helen E., Jonathan Stack, and Elizabeth Cashdan. 2021. "Cultural Change Reduces Gender Differences in Mobility and Spatial Ability among Forager-Pastoralist Children, the TWA of Northern Namibia." *Human Nature* 32(5): 1–29.

de Haan, Mariëtte. 1999. *Learning as a Cultural Practice: How Children Learn in a Mexican Mazahua Community.* Amsterdam, Netherlands: Peeters Publishing.

de Haan, Mariëtte. 2001. "Intersubjectivity in Models of Learning and Teaching: Reflection from a Study of Teaching and Learning in a Mexican Mazahua Community." In *The Theory and Practice of Cultural-Historical Psychology*, edited by Seth Chaiklin, pp. 174–199. Aarhus, Denmark: Aarhus University Press.

de Haan, Mariëtte. 2019. "Can We De-pedagogize Society? Between 'Native' Learning and Pedagogy in Complex Societies." In *Learning Beyond the School: International Perspectives on the Schooled Society*, edited by Julian Sefton-Green and Ola Erstad, pp. 28–44. Abington, UK: Routledge.

REFERENCES 229

de Laguna, Frederica. 1965. "Childhood among the Yakutat Tlingit." In *Context and Meaning in Cultural Anthropology*, edited by Melford E. Spiro, pp. 3–23. New York: Free Press.

de León, Lourdes. 2011. "Language Socialization and Multiparty Participation Frameworks." In *The Handbook of Language Socialization*, edited by Alessandro Duranti, Elinor Ochs, and Bambi B. Schieffelin, pp. 81–111. Oxford: Blackwell.

de León, Lourdes. 2012. "'The j'Ikal is Coming!' Triadic Directives and Emotion in the Socialization of Zinacantec Mayan Children." In *Maya Daily Lives. Acta MesoAmericana*, edited by Philippe Nondédéo and Alain Breton, 24: 185–196. Markt Schwaben, Germany: Verlag Anton Saurwein.

de León, Lourdes. 2015. "Mayan Children's Creation of Learning Ecologies by Initiative and Cooperative Action." In *Children Learn by Observing and Contributing to Family and Community Endeavors: A Cultural Paradigm. Advances in Child Development and Behavior*, edited by Maricela Correa-Chávez, Rebeca Mejía-Arauz, and Barbara Rogoff, 49: 153–184. Cambridge, MA: Academic Press.

de Munck, Bert, and Hugo Soly. 2007. "'Learning on the Shop Floor' in Historical Perspective." In *Learning on the Shop Floor: Historical Perspectives on Apprenticeship*, edited by Bert de Munck, Steven L. Kaplan, and Hugo Soly, pp. 3–32. New York: Berghahn Books.

de Suremain, Charles-Édouard. 2000. "Coffee Beans and the Seeds of Labour: Child Labour on Guatemalan Plantations." In *The Exploited Child*, edited by Bernard Schlemmer, pp. 231–238. New York: Zed Books.

de Waal, Franz. 2001. *The Ape and the Sushi Master*. New York: Basic Books.

Deák, Gedeon O. 2014. "Development of Adaptive Tool-Use in Early Childhood: Sensorimotor, Social, and Conceptual Factors." *Advances in Child Development and Behavior* 46: 149–181.

Defenbaugh, Linda. 1989. "Hausa Weaving: Surviving Amid the Paradoxes." In *Apprenticeship: From Theory to Method and Back Again*, edited by Michael W. Coy, pp. 163–179. Albany: SUNY Press.

Dehaene, Stanislas. 1997. *The Number Sense: How the Mind Creates Mathematics*. Oxford: Oxford University Press.

Demps, Kathryn E., Jennifer Dougherty, García Zorondo-Rodríguez, Francisco Claude, and Victoria Reyes-García. 2012. "Social Learning across the Life Cycle: Cultural Knowledge Acquisition for Honey Collection among the Jenu Kuruba, India." *Evolution and Human Behavior* 33: 460–470.

Demps, Kathryn E., Jennifer Dougherty, Jenukalla M. G., Francisco Zorondo-Rodríguez, Victoria Reyes-García, and Claude García. 2015. "Schooling and Local Knowledge for Collecting Wild Honey in South India: Balancing Multifaceted Educations?" *Culture, Agriculture, Food and Environment* 37: 28–37. doi:10.1111/cuag.12045

Demuth, Katherine. 1986. "Prompting Routines in the Language Socialization of Basotho Children." In *Language Socialization across Cultures*, edited by Bambi B. Schiefflin and Elinor Ochs, pp. 51–79. Cambridge: Cambridge University Press.

Deng, Francis M. 1972. *The Dinka of the Sudan*. Prospect Heights, IL: Waveland Press.

Depaepe, Marc, and Paul Smeyers. 2008. "Educationalization as an Ongoing Modernization Process." *Educational Theory* 59: 379–389.

Devereux, Edward C. 1976. "Backyard versus Little League Baseball: The Impoverishment of Children's Games." In *Social Problems in Athletics*, edited by Daniel M. Landers, pp. 37–58. Urbana: University of Illinois Press.

230 REFERENCES

Devin, Luis. 2013. *La Foresta Ti Ha: Storia di un'iniziazione*. Castelvecchi, Italy: LIT Edizione.

Deyhle, Donna. 1991. "Empowerment and Cultural Conflict: Navajo Parents and the Schooling of Their Children." *Qualitative Studies in Education* 4: 277–297.

Deyhle, Donna. 1992. "Constructing Failure and Maintaining Cultural Identity: Navajo and Ute School Leavers." *Journal of American Indian Education* 31(2): 24–47.

Dickens, Charles. (1836) 1964. *The Pickwick Papers*. New York: New American Library.

Dickens, Charles. 1839. *Nicolas Nickleby*. London: Chapman and Hall.

Dickens, Charles. 1865. *Our Mutual Friend*. Philadelphia: T.B. Peterson & Bros.

Dilley, Roy M. 1989. "Secrets and Skills: Apprenticeship among Tukolor Weavers." In *Apprenticeship: From Theory to Method and Back Again*, edited by Michael W. Coy, pp. 181–198. Albany: SUNY Press.

Dira, Samuel Jilo, and Barry S. Hewlett. 2016. "Learning to Spear Hunt among Ethiopian Chabu Adolescent Hunter-Gatherers." In *Social Learning and Innovation in Contemporary Hunter-Gatherers: Evolutionary and Ethnographic Perspectives*, edited by Hideaki Terashima and Barry S. Hewlett, pp. 71–82. Tokyo: Springer.

Dira, Samuel J., and Barry S. Hewlett. 2018. "The Chabu Hunter-Gatherers of the Highland Forests of Southwestern Ethiopia." *Hunter-Gather Research* 3(2): 323–352.

DiYanni, Cara, and Deborah Kelemen. 2008. "Using a Bad Tool with Good Intention: Young Children's Imitation of Adults' Questionable Choices." *Journal of Experimental Child Psychology* 101: 241–261.

Dodd, Henry. 2020. "I Can't Believe I Am Going to Say This, but I Would Rather Be at School." *New York Times*, April 14. https://www.nytimes.com/2020/04/14/us/school-at-home-students-coronavirus.html

Doepke, Matthias, and Fabrizio Zilibotti. 2019. *Love, Money, and Parenting: How Economics Explains the Way We Raise Our Kids*. Princeton, NJ: Princeton University Press.

Donald, Merlin. 1991. *Origins of the Modern Mind: Three Stages in the Evolution of Culture and Cognition*. Cambridge, MA: Harvard University Press.

Donley-Reid, Linda W. 1990. "A Structuring Structure: The Swahili House." In *Domestic Architecture and the Use of Space: An Interdisciplinary Cross-Cultural Study*, edited by Susan Kent, pp. 114–126. Cambridge: Cambridge University Press.

Dorjahn, Vernon R. 1982. "The Initiation and Training of Temne Poro Members." In *African Religious Groups and Beliefs*, edited by Simon Ottenberg, pp. 35–62. Meerut, India: Archana.

Dorland, Steven G. H. 2018. "The Touch of a Child: An Analysis of Fingernail Impressions on Late Woodland Pottery to Identify Childhood Material Interactions." *Journal of Archaeological Science: Reports* 21: 298–304.

Dorland, Steven G. H., and Ionico, Daniel. 2020. "Learning from Each Other: A Communities of Practice Approach to Decorative Traditions of Northern Iroquoian Communities in the Late Woodland." *Journal of Archaeological Theory and Method* 28(1): 1–33.

Dotti-Sani, Giulia M., and Judith Treas. 2016. "Educational Gradients in Parents' Child-care Time across Countries, 1965–2012." *Journal of Marriage and Family* 78: 1083–1096.

Draper, Patricia, and Elizabeth Cashdan. 1988. "Technological Change and Child Behavior among the !Kung." *Ethnology* 27(4): 339–365. doi:10.2307/3773398

Droogers, André. 1980. *The Dangerous Journey*. The Hague: Mouton.

REFERENCES   231

Duffett, Ann, and Jean Johnson. 2004. *All Work and No Play: Listening to What KIDS and PARENTS Really Want from Out-of-School Time*. Washington, DC: Public Agenda.

Dunn, Cathy DeWitt. N.d. "The Cost of Extracurricular Activities." Dewitt and Dunn Financial Services. Accessed September 16, 2022. https://www.dewittanddunn.com/the-cost-of-extracurricular-activities/

Dunn, Judy. 1988. *The Beginnings of Social Understanding*. Cambridge, MA: Harvard University Press.

Durkin, Kelley, Mark W. Lipsey, Dale C. Farran, and Sarah E. Wiesen. 2022. "Effects of a Statewide Pre-Kindergarten Program on Children's Achievement and Behavior through Sixth Grade." *Developmental Psychology* 58(3): 470–484.

Early Math Counts. 2022. College of Education at the University of Illinois Chicago University and CME Group Foundation. Accessed September 16, 2022. https://earlymathcounts.org/lessons/laundry-sorting/

Edel, May M. (1957) 1996. *The Chiga of Uganda*. 2nd ed. New Brunswick, NJ: Transaction Publishers.

Edwards, Carolyn P. 2005. "Children's Play in Cross-Cultural Perspective: A New Look at the Six Culture Study." In *Play: An Interdisciplinary Synthesis*, edited by Felicia F. McMahon, Don E. Lytle, and Brian Sutton-Smith, pp. 81–96. Lanham, MD: University Press of America.

Eggan, Dorothy. 1956. "Instruction and Affect in Hopi Cultural Continuity." *Southwestern Journal of Anthropology* 12: 347–370.

Einarsdóttir, Jónína. 2004. *Tired of Weeping: Mother Love, Child Death, and Poverty in Guinea-Bissau*. Madison: University of Wisconsin Press.

Ellis, Elizabeth M., Jennifer A. Green, and Inge Kral. 2017. "Family in Mind: Socio-Spatial Knowledge in a Ngaanyatjarra Children's Game." *Research on Children and Social Interaction* 1(2): 164–198.

Elsner, Birgit, and Sabina Pauen. 2007. "Social Learning of Artefact Function in 12- and 15-Month-Olds." *European Journal of Developmental Psychology* 4: 80–99.

Ember, Carol R. 1973. "Feminine Task Assignment and the Social Behavior of Boys." *Ethos* 1: 424–439.

Ember, Carol R., and Melvin Ember. 2005. "Explaining Corporal Punishment of Children: A Cross-Cultural Study." *American Anthropologist* 107: 609–619.

Endicott, Kirk M., and Karen L. Endicott. 2008. *The Headman Was a Woman: The Gender Egalitarian Batek of Malaysia*. Long Grove, IL: Waveland Press.

Engle, Patrice L., Maureen M. Black, Jere R. Behrman, Meena Cabral de Mello, Paul J. Gertler, Lydia Kapiriri, and Mary E. Young. 2007. "Strategies to Avoid the Loss of Developmental Potential in More Than 200 Million Children in the Developing World." *The Lancet* 369: 229–242. https://doi.org/10.1016/s0140-6736(07), 60112-3

Erchak, Gerald M. 1977. *Full Respect: Kpelle Children in Adaptation*. New Haven, CT: Hraflex Books.

Erkens, Jelmer W., and Carl P. Lipo. 2007. "Cultural Transmission Theory and the Archaeological Record: Providing Context to Understanding Variation and Temporal Changes in Material Culture." *Journal of Archaeological Research* 15: 239–274.

Eskelson, Tyrel C. 2020. "How and Why Formal Education Originated in the Emergence of Civilization." *Journal of Education and Learning* 9: 29–47.

Evans-Pritchard, Edward E. 1956. *Nuer Religion*. Oxford: Clarendon Press.

Faber, Elaine, and Adele Mazlish. 2002. *How to Talk So Kids Will Listen and Listen So Kids Will Talk*. New York: HarperCollins.

232   REFERENCES

Fagard, Jacqueline, Lauriann Rat-Fischer, Rana Esseily, Eszter Somogyi, and J. K. O'Regan. 2016. "What Does It Take for an Infant to Learn How to Use a Tool by Observation?" *Frontiers in Psychology* 7: 1–11. https://doi.org/10.3389/fpsyg.2016.00267

Fajans, Jane. 1997. *They Make Themselves: Work and Play among the Baining of Papua New Guinea.* Chicago: University of Chicago Press.

Fasoli, Allison D. 2014. "To Play or Not to Play: Diverse Motives for Latino and Euro-American Parent–Child Play in a Children's Museum." *Infant and Child Development* 23: 605–621.

Fass, Paula S. 2016. *The End of American Childhood: A History of Parenting from Life on the Frontier to the Managed Child.* Princeton, NJ: Princeton University Press.

Fassoulas, Argyris, Jean-Pierre Rossie, and Haris Procopiou. 2020. "Children, Play, and Learning Tasks: From North African Clay Toys to Neolithic Figurines." *Ethnoarchaeology* 12(1): 36–62.

Fasulo, Alessandra, Heather Loyd, and Vicenzo Padiglione. 2007. "Children's Socialization into Cleaning Practices: A Cross-Cultural Perspective." *Discourse and Society* 18: 11–33.

Featherstone, Sally. 2017. *Making Sense of Neuroscience in the Early Years.* London: Bloomsbury.

Fehr, Ernst, Helen Bernhard, and Bettina Rockenbach. 2008. "Egalitarianism in Young Children." *Nature* 454: 1079–1084.

Fernández, David L. 2015. "Children's Everyday Learning by Assuming Responsibility for Others: Indigenous Practices as a Cultural Heritage across Generations." In *Children Learn by Observing and Contributing to Family and Community Endeavors: A Cultural Paradigm. Advances in Child Development and Behavior*, edited by Maricela Correa-Chávez, Rebeca Mejía-Arauz, and Barbara Rogoff, 49: 53–89. Cambridge, MA: Academic Press.

Field, Tiffany M., and Susan M. Widmayer. 1981. "Mother-Infant Interaction among Lower SES Black, Cuban, Puerto Rican and South American Immigrants." In *Culture and Early Interactions*, edited by Tiffany M. Field, Anita M. Sostek, Peter Vietze, and P. Herbert Leiderman, pp. 41–62. Hillsdale, NJ: Lawrence Erlbaum Associates.

Fielding, Henry. (1749) 1908. *The History of Tom Jones.* New York: E.P. Dutton.

Fine, Gary A. 1987. *With the Boys: Little League Baseball and Preadolescent Culture.* Chicago: University of Chicago Press.

Finn, Lauren, and Maureen Vandermaas-Peeler. 2013. "Young Children's Engagement and Learning Opportunities in a Cooking Activity with Parents and Older Siblings." *Early Childhood Research and Practice* 15(1). Accessed September 16, 2022. https://files.eric.ed.gov/fulltext/EJ1016154.pdf

Fischer, Anders. 1990. "A Late Palaeolithic 'School' of Flintknapping at Trollesgave, Denmark." *Acta Archaeologica* 60: 33–49.

Fisher, John W. Jr., and Helen C. Strickland. 1991. "Dwellings and Fireplaces: Keys to Efe Pygmy Campsite Structure." In *Ethnoarchaeological Approaches to Mobile Campsites: Hunter-Gatherer and Pastoralist Case Studies*, edited by Clive S. Gamble and William A. Boismier, pp. 215–236. Ann Arbor, MI: International Monographs in Prehistory.

Fiske, Alan P. N.d. "Learning a Culture the Way Informants Do: Observing, Imitating, and Participating" (unpublished manuscript). Accessed January 24, 2023. https://bec.ucla.edu/wp-content/uploads/sites/108/archive/papers/learning_culture.htm#:~:text=Learning%20A%20Culture%20The%20Way%20Informants%20Do%3A%20Ob

serving%2C,research%E2%80%94relies%20primarily%20on%20informa
nts%E2%80%99%20verbal%20descriptions%20or%20explanations

Fiske, Alan P., and Tage S. Rai. 2015. *Virtuous Violence*. Cambridge: Cambridge University Press.

Floor, Penelope, and Nameera Akhtar. 2006. "Can 18-Month-Old Infants Learn Words by Listening In on Conversations?" *Infancy* 9: 69–81.

Fortes, Meyer. 1938/1970. "Social and Psychological Aspects of Education in Taleland." In *From Child to Adult: Studies in the Anthropology of Education*, edited by John Middleton, pp. 14–74. Garden City, NY: Natural History Press.

Fouts, Hillary N. 2004. "Social Contexts of Weaning: The Importance of Cross-Cultural Studies." In *Childhood and Adolescence: Cross-Cultural Perspectives and Applications*, edited by Uwe P. Gielen and Jaipaul L. Roopnarine, pp. 133–148. Westport, CT: Praeger.

Fouts, Hillary N., Carin L. Neitzel, and Lauren R. Bader. 2016. "Work-Themed Play among Young Children in Foraging and Farming Communities in Central Africa." *Behaviour* 153: 663–691.

Fowler, Carol. 1977. *Daisy Hooee Nampeyo: The Story of an American Indian*. Minneapolis, MN: Dillon Press.

Friedl, Erika. 1997. *Children of Deh Koh: Young Life in an Iranian Village*. Syracuse, NY: Syracuse University Press.

Friedman, Jonathan, and Nadine Farid Johnson. 2022. "Banned in the USA: The Growing Movement to Censor Books in Schools." *Pen America*, September 19. Accessed December 27, 2022. https://pen.org/report/banned-usa-growing-movement-to-cen sor-books-in-schools

Frost, Ginger S. 2009. *Victorian Childhoods*. Westport, CT: Praeger.

Frye, Henrike. 2022. *Child-Directed Speech in Qaqet*. Canberra, Australia: ANU Press.

Fung, Heidi, and Mai T. Thu. 2019. "Cultivating Affection-Laden Hierarchy: Embodied Moral Socialization of Vòng Tay (Khoanh Tay) with Children in Southern Vietnam." *Ethos* 47: 281–306.

Gallois, Sandrine, Romaine Duda, Barry Hewlett, and Victoria Reyes-García. 2015. "Children's Daily Activities and Knowledge Acquisition: A Case Study among the Baka from Southeastern Cameroon." *Journal of Ethnobiology and Ethnomedicine* 11(86): 1–13.

Gallois, Sandrine, Romain Duda, and Victoria Reyes-García. 2017. "Local Ecological Knowledge among Baka Children: A Case of 'Children's Culture.'" *Journal of Ethnobiology and Ethnomedicine* 37(1): 60–80.

Gallois, Sandrine L., Miranda J. Lubbers, Barry Hewlett, and Victoria Reyes-García. 2018. "Social Networks and Knowledge Transmission Strategies among Baka Children, Southeastern Cameroon." *Human Nature* 29: 442–463.

Gampe, Anja, Kristin Liebal, and Michael Tomasello. 2012. "Eighteen-Month-Olds Learn Novel Words through Overhearing." *First Language* 32: 385–397.

García, Fernando A. 2015. "Respect and Autonomy in Children's Observation and Participation in Adults' Activities." In *Children Learn by Observing and Contributing to Family and Community Endeavors: A Cultural Paradigm*, Advances in Child Development and Behavior, edited by Maricela Correa-Chávez, Rebeca Mejía-Arauz, and Barbara Rogoff, 49: 137–151. Cambridge, MA: Academic Press.

Gärdenfors, Peter, and Anders Högberg. 2021. "Evolution of Intentional Teaching." In *The Oxford Handbook of Human Symbolic Evolution*, edited by Nathalie Gontier, Andy

234 REFERENCES

Lock, and Chris Sinha, pp. 1–25. Oxford: Oxford University Press. Online Publication Date: April 2021. doi:10.1093/oxfordhb/9780198813781.013.9

Gardner, Peter M. 2019. "Foragers with Limited Shared Knowledge." In *Towards a Broader View of Hunter-Gatherer Sharing*, edited by Noa Lavi and David Friesem, pp. 185–194. Cambridge: McDonald Institute for Archaeological Research, University of Cambridge.

Gaskins, Suzanne. 2006. "Cultural Perspectives on Infant-Caregiver Interaction." In *The Roots of Human Sociality: Culture, Cognition, and Human Interaction*, edited by Nicholas J. Enfield and Steven C. Levinson, pp. 279–298. Oxford: Berg Press.

Gaskins, Suzanne. 2014. "Children's Play as Cultural Activity." In *SAGE Handbook of Play and Learning in Early Childhood*, edited by Liz Brooker, Mindy Blaise and Susan Edwards, pp. 31–42. Thousand Oaks, CA: Sage.

Gaskins, Suzanne. 2015. "Childhood Practices across Cultures: Play and Household Work." In *The Oxford Handbook of Human Development and Culture: An Interdisciplinary Perspective*, edited by Lene A. Jensen, pp. 185–197. Oxford: Oxford University Press.

Gaskins, Suzanne, and Ruth Paradise. 2010. "Learning through observation in daily life." In The *Anthropology of Learning in Childhood*, edited by David F. Lancy, Suzanne Gaskins, and John Bock, pp. 85–117. Lanham, MD: Altamira Press.

Gaskins, Suzanne, Wendy Haight, and David F. Lancy. 2007. "The Cultural Construction of Play." In *Play and Development: Evolutionary, Sociocultural, and Functional Perspectives*, edited by Artin Göncü and Suzanne Gaskins, pp. 179–202. Mahwah, NJ: Erlbaum.

Gatto, John T. 1992. *Dumbing us Down: The Hidden Curriculum of Compulsory Schooling*. Philadelphia: New Society Publishers.

Gauvain, Mary, R. Lee Munroe, and Heidi Beebe. 2013. "Children's Questions in Cross-Cultural Perspective: A Four-Culture Study." *Journal of Cross-Cultural Research* 44 (7): 1–18.

Gay, John, and Michael Cole. 1967. *The New Mathematics and an Old Culture: A Study of Learning among the Kpelle*. New York: Holt, Rinehart and Winston.

Geary, David C. 2007. "Educating the Evolved Mind." In *Educating the Evolved Mind*, edited by Jerry S. Carlson and Joel R Levin, pp. 1–99. Charlotte, NC: Information Age Publishing.

Geertz, Hildred. 1961. *The Javanese Family: A Study of Kinship and Socialization*. New York: Free Press.

Geiger, Martha, and Erna Alant. 2005. "Child-Rearing Practices and Children's Communicative Interactions in a Village in Botswana." *Early Years: An International Research Journal* 25: 183–191.

Gelman, Rochel, Christine M. Massey, and Mary McManus. 1991. "Characterizing Supporting Environments for Cognitive Development: Lessons from Children in a Museum." In *Perspectives on Socially Shared Cognition*, edited by Lauren B. Resnick, John M. Levine, and Stephanie D. Teasley, pp. 226–256. Washington, DC: American Psychological Association.

Gergely, György, Harold Bekkering, and Ildikó Király. 2002. "Rational Imitation in Preverbal Infants." *Nature* 415: 755.

Gibson, Eleanor J. 1982. "The Concept of Affordances in Development: The Renascence of Functionalism." In *The Concept of Development*, edited by W. Andrew Collins, pp. 55–81. New York: Psychology Press.

REFERENCES 235

Gielen, Uwe P. 1993. "Traditional Tibetan Societies." In *International Handbook on Gender Roles*, edited by Leonore Loeb Adler, pp. 431–437. Westport, CT: Greenwood Press.

Giri, Birendra Raj. 2007. "An Autobiography of Child Work: A Reflexive Account." *Childhood Today* 1(2): 1–21.

Gladwin, Thomas. 1970. *East Is a Big Bird: Navigation and Logic on Puluwat Atoll*. Cambridge, MA: Harvard University Press.

Gladwin, Thomas, and Seymour B. Sarason. 1953. *Truk: Man in Paradise*. New York: Wenner-Gren Foundation.

Global Recess Alliance. 2022. "Statement on Recess." Accessed September 26, 2022. https://globalrecessalliance.org/recess-statement/

Goldschmidt, Walter. 1986. *The Sebei: A Study in Adaptation*. New York: Holt, Rinehart and Winston.

Goldstein, Dana. 2020. "The Class Divide: Remote Learning at 2 Schools, Private and Public." *New York Times*, May 9. Accessed January 6, 2023. https://www.nytimes.com/2020/05/09/us/coronavirus-public-private-school.html?action=click&module=RelatedLinks&pgtype=Article

Göncü, Artin, Jayanthi Mistry, and Christine Mosier. 2000. "Cultural Variations in the Play of Toddlers. *International Journal of Behavioral Development* 24(3): 321–329.

Goodhall, Natasha, and Cathy Atkinson. 2019. "How Do Children Distinguish between 'Play' and 'Work'? Conclusions from the Literature." *Early Child Development and Care* 189(10): 1695–1708.

Goodwin, Grenville, and Janice T. Goodwin. 1942. *The Social Organization of the Western Apache*. Chicago: University of Chicago Press.

Goody, Esther N. 1992. "From Play to Work: Adults and Peers as Scaffolders of Adult Role Skills in Northern Ghana." Paper given at 91st meeting, American Anthropological Association, San Francisco, December.

Goody, Esther N. 2006. "Dynamics of the Emergence of Sociocultural Institutional Practices." In *Technology, Literacy, and the Evolution of Society*, edited by David R. Olson and Michael Cole, pp. 241–264. Mahwah, NJ: Erlbaum.

Gopnik, Alison. 2016. *The Gardener and the Carpenter: What the New Science of Child Development Tells Us about the Relationship between Parents and Children*. New York: Farrar, Straus and Giroux.

Gopnik, Alison, Andrew N. Meltzoff, and Patricia K. Kuhl. 2000. *The Scientist in the Crib: What Early Learning Tells Us about the Mind*. New York: Harper.

Gorshkov, Boris B. 2009. *Russia's Factory Children: State, Society, and Law, 1800–1917*. Pittsburgh: University of Pittsburgh Press.

Gosselain, Olivier P. 2008. "Mother Bella Was Not a Bella: Inherited and Transformed Traditions in Southwestern Niger." In *Cultural Transmission and Material Culture: Breaking Down Boundaries*, edited by Miriam T. Start, Brenda J. Bowser, and Lee Horne, pp. 150–177. Tucson: The University of Arizona Press.

Gottlieb, Alma. 2000. "Luring Your Child into This Life: A Beng Path for Infant Care." In *A World of Babies: Imagined Childcare Guides for Seven Societies*, edited by Judy DeLoache and Alma Gottlieb, pp. 55–90. Cambridge, MA: Cambridge University Press.

Gourdie, Tom. 1968. *The Ladybird Book of Handwriting*. Longborough, UK: Willis & Hepworth.

Grady, Sarah. 2022. "National Household Education Survey and NCES Homeschooling Estimates." Institute of Education Sciences, conference presentation PowerPoint slideshow. Accessed September 16, 2022. https://www.hks.harvard.edu/sites/default/files/Taubman/PEPG/conference/homeschool-conference-slides-grady.pdf

Gray, Peter, and David Chanoff. 1986. "Democratic Schooling: What Happens to Young People Who Have Charge of Their Own Education?" *American Journal of Education* 94: 182–213.

Gray, Peter, David F. Lancy, and David F. Bjorklund. 2023. "Decline in Independent Activity as a Cause of Decline in Children's Mental Wellbeing: Summary of the Evidence." *The Journal of Pediatrics* 260: 1–8.

Greenfield, Patricia M. 1966. "On Culture and Conservation." In *Studies in Cognitive Growth*, edited by Jerome S. Bruner, Rose R. Olver, and Patricia M. Greenfield, pp. 225–256. New York: Wiley.

Greenfield, Patricia M. 1984. "A Theory of the Teacher in the Learning Activities of Everyday Life." In *Everyday Cognition: Its Development in Social Context*, edited by Barbara Rogoff and Jean Lave, pp. 117–138. Cambridge, MA: Harvard University Press.

Greenfield, Patricia M. 2004. *Weaving Generations Together: Evolving Creativity in the Maya of Chiapas*. Santa Fe, NM: SAR Press.

Greenfield, Patricia, and Jean Lave. 1982. "Cognitive Aspects of Informal Education." In *Cultural Perspectives on Child Development*, edited by Daniel A. Wagner and Harold W. Stevenson, pp. 181–207. San Francisco, CA: W. H. Freeman and Company.

Gregor, Thomas. 1970. "Exposure and Seclusion: A Study of Institutionalized Isolation among the Mehinacu Indians of Brazil." *Ethnology* 9(3): 234–250.

Gregor, Thomas. 1988. *Mehinacu: The Drama of Daily Life in a Brazilian Indian Village*. Chicago: University of Chicago Press.

Grendler, Paul R. 1989. *Schooling in Renaissance Italy*. Baltimore, MD: The Johns Hopkins University Press.

Grigorenko, Elena L., Elisa Meier, Jerry Lipka, Gerald Mohatt, Evelyn Yanez, and Robert J. Sternberg. 2004. "Academic and Practical Intelligence: A Case Study of the Yup'ik in Alaska." *Learning and Individual Differences* 14: 183–207.

Grimm, Linda. 2000. "Apprentice Flintknapping: Relating Material Culture and Social Practice in the Upper Paleolithic." In *Children and Material Culture*, edited by J. Soafer Derevenski, pp. 53–71. London: Routledge.

Grindal, Bruce T. 1972. *Growing Up in Two Worlds: Education and Transition among the Sisala of Northern Ghana*. New York: Holt, Rinehart, and Winston.

Grove, Cornelius N. 2023. *How Other Children Learn: What Five Traditional Societies Tell Us About Parenting and Learning*. Lanham, MD: Rowan & Littlefield.

Grubbs, Judith E., Tim Parkin, and Roslynne Bell, eds. 2013. *The Oxford Handbook of Childhood and Education in the Classical World*. Oxford: Oxford University Press.

Gruber, Hans G., and Heinz Mandl. 2001. "Apprenticeship and School Learning." In *International Encyclopedia of Social and Behavioral Sciences*, edited by Neil J. Smelser and Paul B. Baltes, pp. 601–644. New York: Elsevier.

Gubser, Nicholas J. 1965. *The Nunamiut Eskimos, Hunters of Caribou*. New Haven, CT: Yale University Press.

Guemple, D. Lee. 1979. "Inuit Socialization: A Study of Children as Social Actors in an Eskimo Community." In *Childhood and Adolescence in Canada*, edited by Ishwaran Karigoudar, pp. 39–71. Toronto: McGraw-Hill Ryerson.

Guemple, D. Lee. 1988. "Teaching Social Relations to Inuit Children." In *Hunters and Gatherers 2: Property, Power and Ideology*, edited by Tim Ingold, David Riches, and James Woodburn, pp. 131–149. Oxford: Berg.

REFERENCES 237

Gurven, Michael, Hillard Kaplan, and Maguin Gutierrez. 2006. "How Long Does It Take to Become a Proficient Hunter? Implications for the Evolution of Extended Development and Long Life Span." *Journal of Human Evolution* 51: 454–470.

Guttmann, Allen 2010. "The Progressive Era Appropriation of Children's Play." *Journal of the History of Childhood and Youth* 3: 147–151.

Hagen, Renée, Jan van der Ploeg, and Tessa Minter. 2017. "How Do Hunter-Gatherers Learn?: The Transmission of Indigenous Knowledge among the Agta of the Philippines." *Hunter-Gatherer Research* 2(4): 389–413.

Hagstrum, Melissa B. 1999. "The Goal of Domestic Autonomy among the Highland Peruvian Farmer-Potters: Home Economics of Rural Craft Specialists." In *Research in Economic Anthropology*, Vol. 20, edited by Barry L. Isaac, pp. 265–298. Stamford, CT: Jai Press.

Haight, Wendy L., and Peggy J. Miller. 1993. *Pretending at Home: Early Development in a Sociocultural Context*. Albany: SUNY Press.

Halberstadt, Amy G., and Fantasy T. Lozada. 2011. "Emotion Development in Infancy through the Lens of Culture." *Emotion Review* 3(2): 158–168.

Hall, Granville S. 1904. *Adolescence: Its Psychology and Its Relations to Physiology, Anthropology, Sociology, Sex, Crime, Religion, and Education*. New York: Appleton.

Hammond, Gawain, and Norman Hammond. 1981. "Child's Play: A Distorting Factor in Archaeological Distribution." *American Antiquity* 46: 634–636.

Hampton, O. W. "Bud." 1999. *Culture of Stone: Sacred and Profane Uses of Stone among the Dani*. College Station: Texas A&M University Press.

Han, Sallie. 2009. "Imagining Babies through Belly Talk." *Anthropology News* 50(2): 13.

Han, Sallie. 2020. "Mothering Tongues: Anthropological Perspectives on Language and the Mother–Infant Nexus." In *The Mother-Infant Nexus in Anthropology*, edited by Rebecca Gowland and Siân Halcrow, pp. 145–155. Cham, Switzerland: Springer.

Hanawalt, Barbara A. 1993. *Growing Up in Medieval London: The Experience of Childhood in History*. Oxford: Oxford University Press.

Hansen, Judith F. 1979. *Sociocultural Perspectives on Human Learning: An Introduction to Educational Anthropology*. Englewood Cliffs, NJ: Prentice-Hall.

Harkness, Sara, and Charles M. Super. 1985. "The Cultural Context of Gender Segregation in Children's Peer Groups." In *Child Development* 56: 219–224.

Harkness, Sara, and Charles Super. 2006. "Themes and Variations: Parental Ethnotheories in Western Cultures." In *Parenting Beliefs, Behaviors, and Parent–Child Relations: A Cross-Cultural Perspective*, edited by Kenneth H. Rubin and Ock Boon Chung, pp. 61–79. New York: Psychology Press.

Harkness, Sara, Charles M. Super, and Constance H. Keefer. 1992. "Learning to Be an American Parent: How Cultural Models Gain Directive Force." In *Human Motives and Cultural Models*, edited by Roy G. d'Andrade and Claudia Strauss, pp. 163–178. Cambridge, MA: Cambridge University Press.

Harris, Jacob A., Robert Boyd, and Brian M. Wood. 2021. "The Role of Causal Knowledge in the Evolution of Traditional Technology." *Current Biology* 31: 1798–1803.

Hart, Betty, and Todd R. Risley. 1995. *Meaningful Differences in Everyday Experiences of Young American Children*. Baltimore, MD: Brookes.

Hart, Charles W. M., and Arnold Pilling. 1960. *The Tiwi of North Australia*. New York: Holt, Rinehart and Winston.

Hasaki, Eleni. 2012. "Craft Apprenticeship in Ancient Greece: Reaching beyond the Masters." In *Archaeology and Apprenticeship: Body Knowledge, Identity, and*

238 REFERENCES

Communities of Practice, edited by Willeke Wendrich, pp. 171–202. Tucson: University of Arizona Press.

Hauser-Schaublin, Brigitta. 1995. "Puberty Rites, Women's Naven, and Initiation: Women's Rituals of Transition in Abelam and Iatmul Culture." In *Gender Rituals: Female Initiation in Melanesia*, edited by Nancy C. Lutkehaus and Paul B. Roscoe, pp. 33–53. London: Routledge.

Hawcroft, Jennie, and Robin Dennell. 2000. "Neandertal Cognitive Life History and Its Implications for Material Culture." In *Children and Material Culture*, edited by Joanna S. Derevenski, pp. 89–99. New York: Thames and Hudson.

Hays, Jennifer. 2016. "Who Owns Education? Schooling, Learning and Livelihood for the Nyae Nyae Ju|'hoansi." *Journal of Namibian Studies* 20: 37–61.

Heath, Shirley B. 1983. *Ways with Words*. Cambridge: Cambridge University Press.

Heald, Suzette. 1982. "The Making of Men: The Relevance of Vernacular Psychology to the Interpretation of a Gisu Ritual." *Africa* 52: 15–36.

Heath, Shirley B. 1983. *Ways with Words*. Cambridge: Cambridge University Press.

Heckler, Serena L. 2001. "The Ethnobotany of the Piaroa: Analysis of an Amazonian People in Transition." Unpublished PhD diss., Cornell University.

Hedges, Sophie, Monique Borgerhoff Mulder, Susan James, and David W. Lawson. 2016. "Sending Children to School: Rural Livelihoods and Parental Investment in Education in Northern Tanzania." *Evolution & Human Behavior* 37: 142–151.

Hendry, Jean C. 1992. *Atzompa: A Pottery Producing Village of Southern Mexico in the Mid-1950's*. Nashville, TN: Vanderbilt University.

Henrich, Joseph, Stephen J. Heine, and Ara Norenzayan. 2010. "The Weirdest People in the World?" *Behavioural and Brain Sciences* 33: 61–81.

Henry, Paula Ivey, Gilda A. Morelli, and Edward Z. Tronick. 2005. "Child Caretakers among Efe Foragers of the Ituri Forest." In *Hunter Gatherer Childhoods: Evolutionary, Developmental, and Cultural Perspectives*, edited by Barry S. Hewlett and Michael E. Lamb, pp. 191–213. New Brunswick, NJ: Aldine Transaction.

Herdt, Gilbert H. 1990. "Sambia Nosebleeding Rites and Male Proximity to Women." In *Cultural Psychology*, edited by James W. Stigler, Richard A. Shweder, and Gilbert H. Herdt, pp. 366–400. Cambridge: Cambridge University Press.

Heritage, Stewart. 2022. "*Old Enough*: The Japanese TV Show that Abandons Toddlers on Public Transport." *The Guardian*, April 7. Accessed December 17, 2022. https://www.theguardian.com/tv-and-radio/2022/apr/07/old-enough-the-japanese-tv-show-that-abandons-toddlers-on-public-transport

Hernik, Mikolaj, and Çsibra Gergeley. 2009. "Functional Understanding Facilitates Learning about Tools in Human Children." *Current Opinion in Neurobiology* 19: 34–38.

Herzfeld, Michael. 1995. "It Takes One to Know One: Collective Resentment and Mutual Recognition among Greeks in Local and Global Contexts." In *Counterworks: Managing the Diversity of Knowledge*, edited by Richard Fardon, pp. 124–142. London: Routledge.

Hewlett, Barry S. 1992. "The Parent-Infant Relationship and Social-Emotional Development among Aka Pygmies." In *Parent-Child Socialization in Diverse Cultures*, edited by Jaipaul L. Roopnarine and D. Bruce Carter, pp. 223–243. Norwood, NJ: Ablex.

Hewlett, Barry S. 2016. "Evolutionary Cultural Anthropology: Containing Ebola Outbreaks and Explaining Hunter-Gatherer Childhoods." *Current Anthropology* 57, Suppl. 13: S27–S37.

Hewlett, Barry S., and Casey J. Roulette. 2016. "Teaching in Hunter-/Gatherer Infancy." *Royal Society Open Science* 3(Jan. 1). https://doi.org/10.1098/rsos.150403

REFERENCES 239

Hewlett, Barry S., Michael E. Lamb, Donald Shannon, Birgit Leyendecker, and Helge Schölmerich. 1998. "Culture and Infancy among Central African Foragers and Farmers." *Developmental Psychology* 34(4): 653–661.

Hewlett, Barry S., Michael E. Lamb, Birgit Leydendecker, and Axel Schölmerich. 2000. "Parental Investment Strategies among Aka Foragers, Ngandu Farmers, and Euro-American Urban-Industrialists: An Anthropological Perspective." In *Adaptation and Human Behavior: An Anthropological Perspective*, edited by Lee Cronk, Napoleon Chagnon, and William Irons, pp. 155–179. New York: Aldine de Gruyter.

Hewlett, Bonnie L. 2013. "'Ekeloko' the Spirit to Create: Innovation and Social Learning among Aka Adolescents of the Central African Rainforest." In *Dynamics of Learning in Neanderthals and Modern Humans*, vol 1: *Cultural Perspectives*, edited by Akazawa Takeru, Nishiaki Yoshihiro, and Aoki Kenishi, pp. 187–195. Tokyo: Springer.

Hewlett, Bonnie L. 2016. "Innovation, Processes of Social Learning, and Modes of Cultural Transmission among the Chabu Adolescent Forager-Farmers of Ethiopia." In *Social Learning and Innovation in Contemporary Hunter-Gatherers: Evolutionary and Ethnographic Perspectives*, edited by Hideaki Terashima and Barry S. Hewlett, pp. 203–216. Tokyo: Springer.

Hewlett, Bonnie L., and Barry S. Hewlett. 2013. "Hunter-Gatherer Adolescence." In *Adolescent Identity*, edited by Bonnie L. Hewlett, pp. 73–101. New York: Routledge.

Higgens, Kathleen. 1985. "Ritual and Symbol in Baka Life History." *Anthropology and Humanism Quarterly* 10(4): 100–106.

Hilger, M. Inez. 1957. *Araucanian Child Life and Cultural Background*. Smithsonian Miscellaneous Collections, vol. 133. Washington, DC: Smithsonian Institution.

Hill, Kim, and A. Magdalena Hurtado. 1996. *Ache Life History: The Ecology and Demography of a Foraging People*. New York: Aldine de Gruyter.

Hirst, Paul H. 1973. "What Is Teaching?" In *The Philosophy of Education*, edited by Richard S. Peters, pp. 163–177. Oxford: Oxford University Press.

Hobart, Angela. 1988. "The Shadow Play and Operetta as Mediums of Education in Bali." In *Acquiring Culture: Cross Cultural Studies in Child Development*, edited by Gustav Jahoda and Ioan M. Lewis, pp. 113–144. London: Croom Helm.

Hoehl, Stephanie, Stefanie Keupp, Hanna Schleihauf, Nicola McGuigan, David Buttelmanne, and Andrew Whiten. 2019. "'Over-imitation': A Review and Appraisal of a Decade of Research." *Developmental Review* 51: 90–108. https://doi.org/10.1016/j.dr.2018.12.002

Hoffman, Jan. 2015. "Square Root of Kid's Math Anxiety: Their Parent's Help." *New York Times: Wellness*, August 24.

Högberg, Anders. 2008. "Playing with Flint: Tracing a Child's Imitation of Adult Work in a Lithic Assemblage." *Journal of Archaeological Method and Theory* 15(1): 112–131.

Hogbin, H. Ian. 1946. "A New Guinea Childhood: From Weaning Till the Eighth Year in Wogeo." *Oceania* 16: 275–296.

Hogbin, H. Ian. 1969. *A Guadalcanal Society: The Kaoka Speakers*. New York: Holt, Rinehart, and Winston.

Hogbin, H. Ian. 1970. "A New Guinea Childhood: From Weaning Till the Eighth Year in Wogeo." In *From Child to Adult*, edited by John Middleton, pp. 134–162. Garden City, NY: The Natural History Press.

Hollos, Marida C., and Philip E. Leis. 1989. *Becoming Nigerian in Ijo Society*. New Brunswick, NJ: Rutgers University Press.

Holt, John. 1981. *Teach Your Own: A Hopeful Path for Education*. New York: Delacorte.

240 REFERENCES

Honwana, Alcinda. 2014. "'Waithood': Youth Transitions and Social Change." In *Development and Equity: An Interdisciplinary Exploration*, edited by Dick Foeken, Ton Dietz, Leo Haan, and Linda Johnson, pp. 28–40. Leiden: Brill.

Horn, Cornelia B., and John W. Martens. 2009. *"Let the Little Children Come to Me": Childhood and Children in Early Christianity*. Washington, DC: The Catholic University Press.

Hotvedt, Mary E. 1990. "Emerging and Submerging Adolescent Sexuality: Culture and Sexual Orientation." In *Adolescence and Puberty*, edited by John Bancroft and June M. Reinisch, pp. 157–172. New York: Oxford University Press.

House, Bailey R., Patricia Kanngiesser, H. Clark Barrett, Tanya Broesch, Senay Cebioglu, Alyssa N. Crittenden, Alejandro Erut, Sheina Lew-Levy, Carla Sebastian-Enesco, Andrew M. Smith, Süheyla Yilmaz, and Joan B. Silk. 2020. "Universal Norm Psychology Leads to Societal Diversity in Prosocial Behaviour and Development." *Nature Human Behaviour* 4(1): 36–44.

Hostetler, John A., and Gertrude E. Huntington. 1971/1992. *Amish Children: Education in the Family, School, and the Community*, 2nd edition. Orlando, FL: Harcourt Brace Jovanovich.

Howard, Alan. 1970. *Learning to Be Rotuman*. New York: Teachers College Press.

Hrdy, Sarah B. 2005. "On Why It Takes a Village: Cooperative Breeders, Infant Needs, and the Future. In *Evolutionary Perspectives on Human Development*, 2nd ed., edited by Robert L. Burgess and Kevin MacDonald, pp. 167–188. Thousand Oaks, CA: Sage.

Hrdy, Sarah B. 2009. *Mothers and Others: The Evolutionary Origins of Mutual Understanding*. Cambridge, MA: Belknap.

Hu, Winnie. 2010. "Forget Goofing Around: Recess Has a New Boss." *New York Times*, March 14. http://www.nytimes.com/2010/03/15/education/15recess.html

Huaman, Elizabeth S. 2020. "Small Indigenous Schools: Indigenous Resurgence and Education in the Americas." *Anthropology and Education Quarterly* 51: 262–281.

Hul, Jean V. 2019. *The Artful Parent*. Boulder, CO: Roost Books.

Illich, Ivan. 1971. *Deschooling Society*. New York: Harper & Row.

Imamura, Kaoru, and Hiroyuki Akiyama. 2016. "How Hunter-Gatherers Have Learned to Hunt: Transmission of Hunting Methods and Techniques among the Central Kalahari San." *African Study Monographs, Supplementary Issue* 52: 61–76.

Ingold, Tim. 2001. "From the Transmission of Representations to the Education of Attention." In *The Debated Mind: Evolutionary Psychology versus Ethnography*, edited by Harvey Whitehouse, pp. 113–153. Oxford: Berg.

Inouye, Omi M. 2011. *Introductory Calculus for Infants*. Omi Online Omionline.ca

Itkonen, Toivo I., and Eeva K. Minn. 1948. *Lapps in Finland Up To 1945*. Vols. 1 and 2. Porvoo, Helsinki: Werner Söderström Osakeyhtiö.

Jaffares, Ben. 2010. "The Co-evolution of Tools and Minds: Cognition and Material Culture in the Hominin Lineage." *Phenomenology and the Cognitive Science* 9(4): 503–520.

Jamin, Jacqueline Rabain. 1994. "Language and Socialization of the Child in African Families Living in France." In *Cross-Cultural Roots of Minority Child Development*, edited by Patricia M. Greenfield and Roderick R. Cocking, pp. 147–167. Hillsdale, NJ: Lawrence Erlbaum Associates.

Jawando, Jubril O., Samuel Oluranti, and Bolawale Odunaike. 2012. "Apprenticeship Culture among Traditional Tailors in Atiba Local Government Area in Oyo State, South-Western, Nigeria." *Mediterranean Journal of Social Science* 3: 179–186.

REFERENCES 241

Jenness, Diamond. 1922. *The Life of the Copper Eskimos*. Report of the Canadian Arctic Expedition, 1913–1918, vol. 12(A). Ottawa, Canada: Canadian Government Publications.

Jeong, Hyeon-Seon. 2019. "Literacy Practices and Popular Media Culture in the 'Over-Schooled' Society." In *Learning Beyond the School: International Perspectives on the Schooled Society*, edited by Julian Sefton-Green and Ola Erstad, pp. 174–192. Abington, UK: Routledge.

Jiménez-Balam, Deira, Lucía Alcalá, and Dania Salgado. 2019. "Maya Children's Medicinal Plant Knowledge: Initiative and Agency in Their Learning Process." *Learning, Culture and Social Interaction* 22: 100333. https://doi.org/10.1016/j.lcsi.2019.100333

Johannes, Robert E. 1981. *Words of the Lagoon: Fishing and Marine Lore in the Palau District of Micronesia*. Berkeley: University of California Press.

Johnson, Allen. 2003. *Families of the Forest*. Berkeley: University of California Press.

Johnson, Norris B. 1984. "Sex, Color, and Rites of Passage in Ethnographic Research." *Human Organization* 43: 108–120.

Jordan, Brenda G. 1998. "Education in the Kano School in Nineteenth-Century Japan: Questions about the Copybook Method." In *Learning in Likely Places: Varieties of Apprenticeship in Japan*, edited by John Singleton, pp. 45–67. New York: Cambridge University Press.

Jordan, David R. 2000. "A Personal Letter Found in the Athenian Agora." *Hysperia* 69: 91–103.

Jordan, Peter D. 2014. *Technology as Human Social Tradition: Cultural Transmission among Hunter-Gatherers*. Berkeley: University of California Press.

Jordan, Thomas E. 1987. *Victorian Childhood: Themes and Variations*. Albany: SUNY Press.

Jourdan, Christine. 1995. "Masta Liu." In *Youth Cultures: A Cross-Cultural Perspective*, edited by Vered Amit-Talai and Helena Wulff, pp. 202–222. London: Routledge.

Julien, Michèle, and Claudine Karlin. 2015. "Un Automne à Pincevent: Le Campement Magdalénien du Niveau IV20." *Les Nouvelles de l'Archaéologie* 139: 5–11.

Kaland, Sigrid H. H. 2008. "Children and Society in the Viking Age." In *Children, Identity and the Past*, edited by Liv Helga and Melanie Wrigglesworth, pp. 51–67. Newcastle, UK: Cambridge Scholars.

Kale, Mustafa, and Hasan C. Araptarli. 2021. "Description of Children's Daily Life Participation Processes in the Sea Gypsies Community: Visual Narrative Technique." *Early Child Development and Care* 191: 1361–1375.

Kale, Mustafa, and Durmuş Aslan. 2020. "The Caregiving Practices of Nomadic Yuruk Turkmen Families for Their Children in Terms of Developmental Well-Being: An Ecocultural Perspective." *Early Child Development and Care* 191: 1376–1391. doi:10.1080/03004430.2020.1718123

Kamp, Katheryn A., ed. 2002. *Children in the Prehistoric Puebloan Southwest*. Salt Lake City: The University of Utah Press.

Kaneko, Morie. 2014. "'I Know How to Make Pots by Myself': Special Reference to Local Knowledge Transmission in Southwestern Ethiopia." *African Study Monographs*, Suppl. 48, March: 59–75.

Kaneko, Morie. 2016. "Variations in Shape, Local Classification, and the Establishment of a Chaîne Opératoire for Pot Making among Female Potters in Southwestern Ethiopia." In *Social Learning and Innovation in Contemporary Hunter-Gatherers: Evolutionary and Ethnographic Perspectives*, edited by Hideaki Terashima and Barry S. Hewlett, pp. 217–228. Tokyo: Springer.

242 REFERENCES

Kaplan, Fred. 1988. *Dickens: A Biography*. New York: William Morrow.

Kaplan, Hillard S. 1997. "The Evolution of the Human Life Course." In *Between Zeus and the Salmon: The Biodemography of Longevity*, edited by Kenneth. W. Wachter and Caleb E. Finch, pp. 175–211. Washington, DC: National Academy Press.

Kärtner, Joscha, and Antje von Suchodoletz. 2021. "The Role of Preacademic Activities and Adult-centeredness in Mother-Child Play in Educated Urban Middle-Class Families from Three Cultures." *Infant Behavior and Development* 64: e101600. doi:10.1016/j.infbeh.2021.101600

Kärtner, Joscha, Heidi Keller, and Relindis Yovsi. 2010. "Mother-Infant Interaction during the First 3 Months: The Emergence of Culture-Specific Contingency Patterns." *Child Development* 81: 540–554.

Katz, Richard. 1981. "Education is Transformation: Becoming a Healer among the !Kung and the Fijians." *Harvard Education Review* 51(1): 57–78.

Katzmann, Rebecca. 2022. "In Norway, Kids Slice Out Cod Tongues for Serious Money." *Smithsonian Magazine*, January. Accessed December 15, 2022. https://www.smithsonian mag.com/arts-culture/norway-kids-slice-cod-tongues-serious-money-180979245/

Kawagley, Ahgayuqaq O. 2006. *A Yupiaq Worldview. A Pathway to Ecology and Spirit*. 2nd ed. Long Grove, IL: Waveland Press.

Keil, Frank C. 2003. "Folk Science: Course Interpretations of a Complex Reality." *Trends in Cognitive Science* 7: 368–373.

Keil, Frank C. 2006. "Explanation and Understanding." *Annual Review of Psychology* 57: 227–254.

Keller, Charles M., and Janet Dixon Keller. 1996. *Cognition and Tool Use: The Blacksmith at Work*. New York: Cambridge University Press.

Keller, Heidi 2007. *Cultures of Infancy*. Mahwah, NJ: Erlbaum.

Keller, Heidi. 2021. *The Myth of Attachment Theory*. London: Routledge.

Keller, Heidi 2022. *The Myth of Attachment Theory*. London: Routledge.

Keller, Heidi, Kim Bard, Gilda Morelli, Nandita Chaudhary, Marga Vicedo, Mariano Rosbal-Coto, Gabriel Scheidecker, Marjorie Murray, and Alma Gottlieb. 2018. "The Myth of Universal Sensitive Responsiveness." *Child Development* 89: 1921–1928.

Keller, Heidi, Swantje Decker, and Paula Döge. 2019. "Together or Better Singular?" In *Children's Social Worlds in Cultural Context*, edited by Tia Tulvista, Deborah L. Best, and Judith L. Gibbons, pp. 117–131. Cham, Switzerland: Springer.

Kelly-Buccellati, Marilyn. 2012. "Apprenticeship and Learning from the Ancestors: The Case of Ancient Urkesh." In *Archaeology and Apprenticeship: Body Knowledge, Identity, and Communities of Practice*, edited by Willeke Wendrich, pp. 203–223. Tucson: University of Arizona Press.

Keupp, Stefanie, Tanya Behne, Joanna Zachow, Alina Kasbohm, and Hannes Rakoczy. 2015. "Over-Imitation Is Not Automatic: Context Sensitivity in Children's Overimitation and Action Interpretation of Causally Irrelevant Actions." *Journal of Experimental Child Psychology* 130: 163–175.

Killin, Anton, and Ross Pain. 2022. "How WEIRD Is Cognitive Archaeology? Engaging with the Challenge of Cultural Variation and Sample Diversity." *Review of Philosophy and Psychology* 14: 539–562, January 31. doi.org/10.1007/s13164-021-00611-z

Kim, Uichol, and So-Hyang Choi. 1994. Individualism, Collectivism, and Child Development: A Korean Perspective. In *Cross-Cultural Roots of Minority Child Development*, edited by Patricia M. Greenfield and Rodney R. Cocking, pp. 227–259. Hillsdale, NJ: Erlbaum.

REFERENCES 243

King, Ross. 2021. *The Bookseller of Florence*. New York: Atlantic Monthly Press.

Kinney, Anne B. 1995. "Dyed Silk: Han Notions of the Moral Development of Children." In *Chinese Views of Childhood*, edited by Anne B. Kinney, pp. 17–56. Honolulu: University of Hawai'i Press.

Kipnis, Andrew. 2001. "The Disturbing Educational Discipline of 'Peasants.'" *The China Journal* 46: 1–24.

Kleijueqgt, Marc. 2009. "Ancient Mediterranean World, Childhood and Adolescence." In *The Child: An Encyclopedic Companion*, edited by Richard A. Shweder et al., pp. 54–56. Chicago: The University of Chicago Press.

Kleinfeld, Judith. 1971. "Visual Memory in Village Eskimo and Urban Caucasian Children." *Arctic* 24(2): 132–138.

Kline, Michelle A. 2015. "How to Learn about Teaching: An Evolutionary Framework for the Study of Teaching Behavior in Humans and Other Animals." *Behavioral and Brain Sciences* 38, e31. doi:10.1017/S0140525X14000090

Kline, Michelle A., Rubeena Shamsudheen, and Tanya Broesch. 2018. "Variation is the Universal: Making Cultural Evolution Work in Developmental Psychology." *Philosophical Transactions of the Royal Society B* 373: 20170059. http://dx.doi.org/10.1098/rstb.2017.0059

Klinnert, Mary D., Joseph J. Campos, James F. Sorce, Robert N. Emde, and Marylin Svejda. 1983. "Emotions as Behavior Regulators: Social Referencing in Infancy." In *Emotion: Theory, Research, and Experience*, edited by Robert Plutchik and Henry Kellerman, pp. 57–86. New York: Academic Press.

Knauft, Bruce. 2013. *The Gebusi: Lives Transformed in a Rainforest World*. 3rd ed. New York: McGraw-Hill.

Köhler, Iris. 2012. "Learning and Children's Work in a Pottery-Making Environment in Northern Côte d'Ivoire." In *African Children at Work: Working and Learning in Growing Up*, edited by Gerd Spittler and Michael Bourdillon, pp. 113–141. Berlin: LitVerlag.

Konner, Melvin J. 1976. "Maternal Care, Infant Behavior and Development among the Kung." In *Studies of the !Kung San and Their Neighbors*, edited by Richard B. Lee and Irven DeVore, pp. 218–245. Cambridge, MA: Harvard University Press.

Konner, Melvin J. 1977. "Infancy among the Kalahari Desert San." In *Culture and Infancy: Variations in the Human Experience*, edited by P. Herbert Leiderman, Stephen R. Tulkin, and Anne Rosenfeld, pp. 287–328. New York: Academic Press.

Konner, Melvin. J. 2005. "Hunter-Gatherer Infancy and Childhood." In *Hunter-Gatherer Childhoods: Evolutionary, Developmental, and Cultural Perspectives*, edited by Barry S. Hewlett and Michael E. Lamb, pp. 19–64. New Brunswick, NJ: Aldine-Transaction.

Koster, Jeremy M., Orlando Bruno, and Jessica L. Burns. 2016. "Wisdom of the Elders? Ethnobiological Knowledge across the Lifespan." *Current Anthropology* 57: 113–121.

Köster, Moritz, Shoji Itakura, Yovsi Relindis, and Joscha Kârtner. 2018. "Visual Attention in 5-Year-Olds from Three Different Cultures." *PLoS ONE* 13(7): e0200239. doi:10.1371/journal.pone.0200239

Köster, Moritz, Marta Giner Torréns, Joscha Kärtner, Shoji Itakura, and Lilia Cavalcante. 2022. "Parental Teaching Behavior in Diverse Cultural Contexts." *Evolution and Human Behavior* 43: 432–441.

Králik, Miroslac, Petra Urbanová, and Martin Hložek. 2008. "Finger, Hand and Foot Imprints: The Evidence of Children on Archaeological Artefacts." In *Children, Identity and the Past*, edited by Liv Helga Dommasnes and Melanie Wrigglesworth, pp. 1–15. Newcastle, UK: Cambridge Scholars Publishing.

244 REFERENCES

Kramer, Karen L. 2005. *Maya Children: Helpers on the Farm*. Cambridge, MA: Harvard University Press.

Kramer, Karen L. 2014. "Why What Juveniles Do Matters in the Evolution of Cooperative Breeding." *Human Nature* 25: 49–65.

Kramer, Karen L. 2021. "Childhood Teaching and Learning among Savanna Pumé Hunter-Gatherers." *Human Nature* 32(1): 87–114.

Kramer, Karen L., and Russell D. Greaves. 2011. "Juvenile Subsistence Effort, Activity Levels, and Growth Patterns." *Human Nature* 22: 303–326.

Kramer, Karen L., and Russell D. Greaves. 2022. "The Savvy Hunter-Gatherer. Self-Determination, Humanist Perspectives and Scientific Views from Savanna Pumé Foragers of the Venezuelan llanos." Paper given at the 13th Annual CHAGS conference, Dublin, February 28.

Kramer, Samuel N. 1963. *The Sumerians: Their History, Culture and Character*. Chicago: University of Chicago Press.

Krause, Richard A. 1985. *The Clay Sleeps: An Ethnoarchaeological Study of Three African Potters*. Birmingham: University of Alabama Press.

Kremer-Sadlik, Tamar, and Kris Gutiérrez. 2013. "Homework and Recreation." In *Fast Forward Families: Home, Work and Relationships*, edited by Elinor Ochs and Tamar Kremer-Sadlik, pp. 130–150. Los Angeles: University of California Press.

Krige, Eileen J. 1965. *The Social System of the Zulus*. Pietermaritzburg, South Africa: Shuter and Shooter.

Kuchirko, Yana, and Irena Nayfeld. 2020. "Language Gap: Cultural Assumptions and Ideologies." In *International Approaches to Bridging the Language Gap*, edited by Cristina A. Huertas-Abril and Maria E. Gómez-Parra, pp. 32–53. Hershey, PA: IGI Global.

Kulick, Don. 1992. *Language Shift and Cultural Reproduction: Socialization, Self, and Syncretism in a Papua New Guinea Village*. New York: Cambridge University Press.

Laes, Christian. 2015. "Children and Their Occupations in the City of Rome (300–700 CE)." In *Children and Family in Late Antiquity: Life, Death and Interaction*, edited by Christian Laes, Katariina Mustakallio Laes, and Ville Vuolanto, pp. 79–110. Leuven, Netherlands: Peeters Publishing.

LaFreniere, Peter. 2005. "Human Emotions as Multipurpose Adaptations: An Evolutionary Perspective on the Development of Fear." In *Evolutionary Perspectives on Human Development*, 2nd ed., edited by Robert L. Burgess and Kevin MacDonald, pp. 189–205. Thousand Oaks, CA: Sage.

Lancy, David F. 1975. "The Social Organization of Learning: Initiation Rituals and Public Schools." *Human Organization* 34: 371–380.

Lancy, David F. 1980. "Becoming a Blacksmith in Gbarngasuakwelle." *Anthropology and Education Quarterly* 11: 266–274

Lancy, David F. 1983. *Cross-Cultural Studies in Cognition and Mathematics*. New York: Academic Press.

Lancy, David F. 1993. *Qualitative Research in Education: An Introduction to the Major Traditions*. White Plains, NY: Longman.

Lancy, David F. 1996. *Playing on the Mother Ground: Cultural Routines for Children's Development*. New York: Guilford.

Lancy, David F. 2008. *The Anthropology of Childhood: Cherubs, Chattel, Changelings* Cambridge: Cambridge University Press.

REFERENCES 245

Lancy, David F. 2010a. "Learning 'From Nobody': The Limited Role of Teaching in Folk Models of Children's Development." *Childhood in the Past* 3: 79–106.

Lancy, David F. 2010b. "When Nurture Becomes Nature: Ethnocentrism in Studies of Human Development." *Behavioral and Brain Sciences* 33: 39–40.

Lancy, David F. 2012. "First You Must Master Pain:' The Nature and Purpose of Apprenticeship." *Society for the Anthropology of Work Review* 33(2): 113–126.

Lancy, David F. 2014. "'Babies Aren't Persons': A Survey of Delayed Personhood." In *Different Faces of Attachment: Cultural Variations of a Universal Human Need*, edited by Hiltrud Otto and Heidi Keller, pp. 66–109. Cambridge: Cambridge University Press.

Lancy, David F. 2015. "Children as a Reserve Labor Force." *Current Anthropology* 56: 545–568.

Lancy, David F. 2016a. "Playing with Knives: The Socialization of Self-Initiated Learners." *Child Development* 87(3): 654–665.

Lancy, David F. 2016b. "Teaching: Natural or Cultural?" In *Evolutionary Perspectives on Education and Child Development*, edited by Dan Berch and David Geary, pp. 32–65. Heidelberg: Springer.

Lancy, David F. 2017a. "Homo Faber Juvenalis: A Multidisciplinary Survey of Children as Tool Makers/Users." *Childhood in the Past* 10(1): 1–19.

Lancy, David F. 2017b. *Raising Children: Surprising Insights from Other Cultures*. Cambridge: Cambridge University Press.

Lancy, David F. 2018. *Anthropological Perspectives on Children as Helpers, Workers, Artisans and Laborers*. New York: Palgrave-Macmillan.

Lancy, David F. 2020. *Child Helpers: A Multidisciplinary Perspective*. Cambridge: Cambridge University Press.

Lancy, David F. 2022. *The Anthropology of Childhood: Cherubs, Chattel, Changelings*. 3rd ed. Cambridge: Cambridge University Press.

Lancy, David F., and M. Annette Grove. 2011a. "Getting Noticed: Middle Childhood in Cross-Cultural Perspective." *Human Nature* 22: 281–302.

Lancy, David F., and M. Annette Grove. 2011b. "Marbles and Machiavelli: The Role of Game Play in Children's Social Development." *American Journal of Play* 3: 489–499.

Langdon, Susan. 2013. "Children as Early Learners and Producers in Early Greece." In *The Oxford Handbook of Childhood and Education in the Classical World*, edited by E. Grubbs, Tim Parkin, and Roslynne Bell, pp. 172–194. Oxford: Oxford University Press.

Lareau, Annette. 2003. *Unequal Childhoods: Class, Race, and Family Life*. Berkeley: University of California Press.

Lave, Jean. 1982. "A Comparative Approach to Educational Forms and Learning Processes." *Anthropology and Education Quarterly* 132: 181–187.

Lave, Jean, and Etienne Wenger. 1991. *Situated Learning: Legitimate Peripheral Participation*. Cambridge: Cambridge University Press.

Lavi, Noa. 2022. "We Only Teach Them How to Be Together: Parenting, Child Development, and Engagement with Formal Education among the Nayaka in South India." *Anthropology and Education Quarterly* 53: 84–102.

The Learning Experience. 2021. "A Guide to Infant Education: What It Is and When to Start." Bipper Media. Accessed November 11, 2021. https://bippermedia.com/a-guide-to-infant-education-what-it-is-and-when-to-start/

Leavitt, Stephen C. 1998. "The *Bikhet* Mystique: Masculine Identity and Patterns of Rebellion among Bumbita Adolescent Males." In *Adolescence in Pacific Island Societies*,

246 REFERENCES

edited by Gilbert H. Herdt and Stephen Leavitt, pp. 173–194. Pittsburgh: University of Pittsburgh Press.

Lee, Carol D., Andrew N. Meltzoff, and Patricia Kuhl. 2020. "The Braid of Human Learning and Development." In *Handbook of the Cultural Foundations of Learning*, edited by Na'ilah S. Nasir, Carol D. Lee, Roy Pea, and Maxine McKinney de Royston, pp. 24–43. New York: Routledge.

Lee, Dorothy. 1967. "A Socio-Anthropological View of Independent Learning." In *The Theory and Nature of Independent Learning*, edited by Gerald T. Gleason, pp. 51–64. Scranton, PA: International Textbook.

Legare, Christine H. 2019. "The Development of Cumulative Cultural Learning." *Annual Review of Developmental Psychology* 1: 119–147.

Leibel, Manfred. 2004. *A Will of Their Own: Cross Cultural Perspectives on Working Children*. London: ZED Books.

Levey, Hilary. 2009. "Pageant Princesses and Math Whizzes: Understanding Children's Activities as a Form of Children's Work." *Childhood* 16(2): 195–212.

Levine, Donald N. 1965. *Wax and Gold: Tradition and Innovation in Ethiopian Culture*. Chicago: University of Chicago Press.

LeVine, Robert A. 2004. "Challenging Expert Knowledge: Findings from an African Study of Infant Care and Development." In *Childhood and Adolescence: Cross-Cultural Perspectives and Applications*, edited by Uwe P. Gielen and Jaipaul Roopnarine, pp. 149–165. Westport, CT: Praeger.

LeVine, Robert A. 2007. "Ethnographic Studies of Childhood: A Historical Overview." *American Anthropologist* 109: 247–260.

LeVine, Robert A. 2014. "Attachment Theory as Cultural Ideology." In *Different Faces of Attachment: Cultural Variations of a Universal Human Need*, edited by Hiltrud Otto and Heidi Keller, pp. 50–65. Cambridge: Cambridge University Press.

LeVine, Robert A., and Barbara B. LeVine. 1963. "Nyansongo: A Gusii Community in Kenya." In *Six Cultures: Studies of Child Rearing*, edited by Beatrice Blyth Whiting, pp. 15–202. New York: John Wiley & Sons.

LeVine, Robert A., and Merrie I. White. 1986. *Human Conditions*. New York: Routledge.

LeVine, Robert A., Suzanne Dixon, Sarah LeVine, Amy Richman, P. Herbert Leiderman, Constance H. Keefer, and T. Berry Brazelton. 1994. *Child Care and Culture: Lessons from Africa*. Cambridge: Cambridge University Press.

LeVine, Robert A., Sarah LeVine, Beatrice Schnell-Anzola, Meredith L. Rowe, and Emily Dexter. 2012. *Literacy and Mothering: How Women's Schooling Changes the Lives of the World's Children*. New York: Oxford University Press.

Levy, Robert I. 1996. "Essential Contrasts: Differences in Parental Ideas about Learners and Teaching in Tahiti and Nepal." In *Parents' Cultural Belief Systems: Their Origins, Expressions, and Consequences*, edited by Sara Harkness and Charles M. Super, pp. 123–142. New York: Guilford Press.

Lewis, Jerome. 2008. "Ekila: Blood Bodies, Egalitarian Societies." *Journal of the Royal Anthropological Institute* 14: 297–315.

Lewis, Jerome. 2016. "Play, Music, and Taboo in the Reproduction of an Egalitarian Society." In *Social Learning and Innovation in Contemporary Hunter-Gatherers: Evolutionary and Ethnographic Perspectives*, edited by Hideaki Terashima and Barry S. Hewlett, pp. 147–158. Tokyo: Springer.

Lew-Levy, Sheina, and Adam H. Boyette. 2018. "Evidence for the Adaptive Learning Function of Work and Work-Themed Play among Aka Forager and Ngandu Farmer

Children from the Congo Basin." *Human Nature* 29: 157–185. doi:10.17863/CAM.15690

Lew-Levy, Sheina, Stephen M. Boyette, Adam H. Kissler, Alyssa N. Crittenden, Ibrahim Mabullae, and Barry S. Hewlett. 2020a. "Who Teaches Children to Forage? Exploring the Primacy of Child-to-Child Teaching among Hadza and BaYaka Hunter-Gatherers of Tanzania and Congo." *Evolution and Human Behavior* 41: 12–22.

Lew-Levy, Sheina, Annemieke Milks, Noa Lavi, Sarah Pope, and David Friesem. 2020b. "Where Innovations Flourish: An Ethnographic and Archaeological Overview of Hunter–Gatherer Learning Contexts." *Evolutionary Human Sciences* 2: 1–23, e31.

Lew-Levy, Sheina, Stephen Kissler, Adam H. Boyette, Alyssa Crittenden, Ibrahim A. Mabulla, and Barry Hewlett. 2021a. "Who Teaches Children to Forage? Exploring the Primacy of Child-to-Child Teaching among Hadza and BaYaka Hunter-Gatherers of Tanzania and Congo." *Evolution and Human Behavior* 41: 12–22.

Lew-Levy, Sheina, Rachel Reckin, Stephen M. Kissler, Ilaria Pretelli, Adam H. Boyette, Alyssa N. Crittenden, Renée Hagen, Randall Haas, Karen Kramer, Jeremy Koster, Matthew J. O'Brien, Koji Sonoda, Todd A. Surovell, Jonathan Stieglitz, Bram Tucker, Noa Lavi, Kate Eliis-Davies, and Helen Elizabeth Davis. 2021b. "Cross-Cultural Variation in Child and Adolescent Time Allocation to Work and Play in Twelve Hunter-Gatherer and Mixed-Subsistence Societies." *Human Nature*. doi:10.1038/s41598-022-12217-1

Lew-Levy, Sheina, Marc M. Andersen, Noa Lavi, and Felix Riede. 2022a. "Hunter-Gatherer Children's Object Play and Tool Use: An Ethnohistorical Analysis." *Frontiers in Psychology* 13: Article 824983. doi:10.3389/fpsyg.2022.824983

Lew-Levy Sheina, Daša Bombjaková, Annemieke Milks, Francy Kiabiya Ntamboudila, Michelle Anne Kline, and Tanya Broesch. 2022b. "Costly Teaching Contributes to the Acquisition of Spear Hunting Skill among BaYaka Forager Adolescents." *Proceedings of the Royal Society B* 289: 20220164. https://doi.org/10.1098/rspb.2022.0164

Liebenberg, Louis. 1990. *The Art of Tracking*. Cape Town, South Africa: Creda Press.

Lieven, Elena V. M. 1994. "Crosslinguistic and Cross-Cultural Aspects of Language Addressed to Children." In *Input and Interaction in Language Acquisition*, edited by Clare Gallaway and Brian J. Richards, pp. 56–73. Cambridge: Cambridge University Press.

Lilienfeld, Scott O., Steven J. Lynn, John Ruscio, and Barry L. Beyerstein. 2009. *50 Great Myths of Popular Psychology: Shattering Widespread Misconceptions about Human Behavior*. New York: Wiley Blackwell.

Lipka, Jerry. 1990. "Integrating Cultural Form and Content in One Yup'ik Eskimo Classroom: A Case Study." *Canadian Journal of Education* 17(2): 18–32.

Little, Christopher A. J. 2011. "How Asabano Children Learn; or, Formal Schooling amongst Informal Learners." *Oceania* 81: 146–166.

Little, Emily E., Leslie J. Carver, and Cristine H. Legare. 2016. "Cultural Variation in Triadic Infant–Caregiver Object Exploration." *Child Development* 87(4): 1130–1145.

Livingstone, Alasdair. 2007. "The Pitter-Patter of Tiny Feet in Clay." In *Children, Childhood and Society*, edited by Sally Crawford and Gillian Shepherd, pp. 15–28. Oxford: Archaeopress.

Lloyd, Peter. 1953. "Craft Organization in Yoruba Towns." *Africa* 23(1): 30–44.

Lovevery.com. "The Play Kits." Accessed October 3, 2022. https://lovevery.com/products/the-play-kits

Lupo, Karen D., and Dave N. Schmitt. 2002. "Upper Paleolithic Net-Hunting, Small Prey Exploitation, and Women's Work Effort: A View from the Ethnographic and

248 REFERENCES

Ethnoarchaeological Record of the Congo Basin." *Journal of Archaeological Method and Theory* 9(2): 147–179.

Luria, Alexander R. 1976. *Cognitive Development: Its Cultural and Social Foundations.* Cambridge, MA: Harvard University Press.

Lutz, Catherine A. 1983. "Parental Goals, Ethnopsychology, and the Development of Emotional Meaning." *Ethos* 11: 246–262.

Lutz, Catherine A. 1985. "Cultural Patterns and Individual Differences in the Child's Emotional Meaning System." In *The Socialization of Emotions*, edited by Michael Lewis and Carolyn Saarni, pp. 37–54. New York: Plenum.

MacDonald, Kevin, and Scott L. Hershberger. 2005. "Theoretical Issues in the Study of Evolution and Development." In *Evolutionary Perspectives on Human Development*, 2nd ed., edited by Robert L. Burgess and Kevin MacDonald, pp. 21–72. Thousand Oaks, CA: Sage.

Macedo, Silvia L. 2009. "Indigenous School Policies and Politics: The Sociopolitical Relationship of Wayãpi Amerindians to Brazilian and French Guyana Schooling." *Anthropology and Education Quarterly* 40(2): 170–186.

MacElroy, Mary H. 1917. *Work and Play in Colonial Days.* New York: Macmillan.

MacKenzie, Maureen A. 1991. *Androgynous Objects: String Bags and Gender in Central New Guinea.* Reading, PA: Harwood.

Maiden, Ann Hubbell, and Edie Farwell. 1997. *The Tibetan Art of Parenting: From before Conception through Early Childhood.* Boston: Wisdom Publications.

Malinowski, Bronislaw. 2008. "Childhood in the Trobriand Island, Melanesia." In *Anthropology and Child Development: A Cross-Cultural Reader*, edited by Robert A. LeVine and Rebecca S. New, pp. 28–33. Malden, MA: Blackwell.

Manning, Robert. 1965. "Hemingway in Cuba." *The Atlantic*, August.

Marchand, Trevor H. J. 2001. *Minaret Building and Apprenticeship in Yemen.* Richmond, VA: Curzon Press.

Marchand, Trevor H. J. 2009. *The Masons of Djenné.* Bloomington: Indiana University Press.

Marchand, Trevor H. J. 2014. "For the Love of Masonry: Djenné Craftsmen in Turbulent Times." *Journal of African Cultural Studies* 26: 155–172.

Marciszko, Carin, Linda Forssman, Ben Kenward, Marcus Lindskog, Mari Fransson, and Gustaf Gredebäck. 2020. "The Social Foundation of Executive Function." *Developmental Science* 23: e12924. https://doi.org/10.1111/desc.12924

Maretzki, Thomas W., and Hatsumi Maretzki. 1963. "Taira: An Okinawan Village." In *Six Cultures: Studies of Child Rearing*, edited by Beatrice Blyth Whiting, pp. 367–539. New York: John Wiley & Sons.

Marguerat, Yves. 2000. "The Exploitation of Apprentices in Togo." In *The Exploited Child*, edited by Bernard Schlemmer, pp. 239–247. New York: Zed Books.

Markstrom, Carol A. 2008. *Empowerment of North American Indian Girls: Ritual Expressions at Puberty.* Lincoln: University of Nebraska Press.

Marlowe, Frank W. 2010. *The Hadza: Hunter-Gatherers of Tanzania.* Berkeley: University of California Press.

Marshall, Lorna J. 1976. *The !Kung of Nyae Nyae.* Cambridge, MA: Harvard University Press.

Martínez-Pérez, Margarita. 2015. "Adults' Orientation of Children—And Children's Initiative to Pitch in—To Everyday Adult Activities in a Tsotsil Maya Community." *Advances in Child Development and Behavior* 49: 113–135.

REFERENCES 249

Martínez-Rodríguez, Maria R. 2009. "Ethnobotanical Knowledge Acquisition among Tsimane' Children in the Bolivian Amazon." PhD diss., University of Georgia, Athens.

Martini, Mary, and John Kirkpatrick. 1981. "Early Interaction in the Marquesas Islands." In *Culture and Early Interactions*, edited by Tiffany M. Field, Anita M. Sostek, Peter Vietze, and P. Herbert Leiderman, pp. 189–215. Hillsdale, NJ: Lawrence Erlbaum.

Martini, Mary, and John Kirkpatrick. 1992. "Parenting in Polynesia: A View from the Marquesas." In *Parent-Child Socialization in Diverse Cultures*, edited by Jaipaul L. Roopnarine and D. Bruce Carter, pp. 199–222. Norwood, NJ: Ablex.

Matavire, Mac. 2017. "South Africa Circumcision Ritual: A Dangerous Route to Manhood." *Medical Xpress*, July 23. Accessed December 17, 2022. https://medicalxpr ess.com/news/2017-07-safrica-circumcision-ritual-dangerous-route.html

Matthiasson, John S. 1979. "But Teacher, Why Can't I Be a Hunter: Inuit Adolescence as a Double-Blind Situation." In *Childhood and Adolescence in Canada*, edited by Ishwaran Karigoudar, pp. 72–82. Toronto: McGraw-Hill Ryerson.

Maxwell, Kevin B. 1983. *Bemba Myth and Ritual: The Impact of Literacy on an Oral Culture*. New York: Peter Lang.

Maxwell West, Mary. 1988. "Parental Values and Behavior in the Outer Fiji Islands." In *Parental Behaviour in Diverse Societies*, edited by Robert LeVine, Patrice M. Miller, and Mary Maxwell West. *New Directions for Child Development* 40: 13–26.

Mayblin, Maya. 2010. "Learning Courage: Child Labour as Moral Practice in Northeast Brazil." *Ethnos: Journal of Anthropology* 75(1): 23–48.

Maynard, Ashley E. 2002. "Cultural Teaching: The Development of Teaching Skills in Maya Sibling Interactions." *Child Development* 73: 969–982.

Maynard, Ashley E. 2004a. "Sibling Interactions." In *Childhood and Adolescence: Cross-Cultural Perspectives and Applications*, edited by Uwe P. Gielen and Jaipaul Roopnarine, pp. 229–252. Westport, CT: Praeger.

Maynard, Ashley E. 2004b. "Cultures of Teaching in Childhood: Formal Schooling and Maya Sibling Teaching at Home." *Cognitive Development* 19: 517–535.

Maynard, Ashley, and Katherine E. Tovote. 2010. "Learning from Other Children." In *The Anthropology of Learning in Childhood*, edited by David F. Lancy, Suzanne Gaskins, and John Bock, pp. 181–205. Lanham, MD: Alta–Mira Press.

Maynard, Ashley E., Patricia M. Greenfield, Carla P. Childs, and Michael Weinstock. 2023. "Social Change, Cultural Evolution, Weaving Apprenticeship, and Development: Informal Education across Three Generations and 42 Years in a Maya Community." *Applied Developmental Science*. https://doi.org/10.1080/10888 691.2022.2151445

McNaughton, Peter R. 1988. *The Mande Blacksmiths: Knowledge, Power and Art in West Africa*. Bloomington: Indiana University Press.

Mead, Margaret. 1928. "Samoan Children at Work and Play." *Natural History* 28: 626–636.

Mead, Margaret. (1928) 1961. *Coming of Age in Samoa*. New York: New American Library.

Mead, Margaret. 1964. *Continuities and Discontinuities in Cultural Evolution*. New Haven, CT: Yale University Press.

Mead, Margaret. 1967. "An Investigation of the Thought of Primitive Children, with Special Reference to Animism." In *Personalities and Cultures: Readings in Psychological Anthropology*, edited by Robert Hunt, pp. 213–237. Garden City, NY: The Natural History Press.

Medaets, Chantal V. 2011. "'Tu garante?' Reflections on the Transmission Practices and Learning in the Lower Tapajós, Brazilian Amazon." Paper presented at the 34th annual meeting of ANPEd (Brazilian Educational Research and Post-Graduate Association), October.

Medaets, Chantal V. 2016. "Despite Adults: Learning Experiences on the Tapajós River Banks." *Ethos* 44: 248–268.

Medina, Carol, and David M. Sobel. 2020. "Caregiver-Child Interaction Influences Causal Learning in a Structured Play Setting." *Journal of Experimental Child Psychology* 189: 104678. doi:10.1016/j.jecp.2019.104678

Mejía-Arauz, Rebeca, Maricela Correa-Chávez, Ulrike K. Ohrt, and Itzel Aceves-Azuara. 2015. "Collaborative Work or Individual Chores: The Role of Family Social Organization in Children's Learning to Collaborate and Develop Initiative." In *Children Learn by Observing and Contributing to Family and Community Endeavors: A Cultural Paradigm. Advances in Child Development and Behavior*, edited by Maricela Correa-Chávez, Rebeca Mejía-Arauz, and Barbara Rogoff, Vol. 49, pp. 25–51. Cambridge, MA: Academic Press.

Mejía-Arauz, Rebeca, Amy L. Dexter, Barbara Rogoff, and Itzel Aceves-Azuara. 2019. "Children's Management of Attention as Cultural Practice." In *Children's Social Worlds in Cultural Context*, edited by Tia Tulvista, Deborah L. Best, and Judith L. Gibbons, pp. 23–39. Cham, Switzerland: Springer.

Mellor, Maureen. 2014. "Seeing the Medieval Child: Evidence from Household and Craft." In *Medieval Childhood: Archaeological Approaches*, edited by D. M. Hadley and K. A. Hemer, pp. 75–94. Philadelphia, PA: Oxbow Books.

Meltzoff, Andrew N. 2002. "Elements of a Developmental Theory of Imitation." In *The Imitative Mind: Development, Evolution and Brain Bases*, edited by Andrew N. Meltzoff, Wolfgang Prinz, and George Butterworth, pp. 19–41. Cambridge: Cambridge University Press.

Meltzoff, Andrew N., and Rebecca A. Williamson. 2009. "Imitation." In *The Child: An Encyclopedic Companion*, edited by Richard A. Shweder et al., pp. 480–481. Chicago: The University of Chicago Press.

Mervosh, Sarah. 2022. "Pandemic Learning Loss." *New York Times*, November 28. Accessed May 12, 2022. https://www.nytimes.com/2022/11/28/briefing/pandemic-learning-loss.html

Mesoudi, Alex. 2011. *Cultural Evolution: How Darwinian Theory Can Explain Human Culture and Synthesize the Social Sciences*. Chicago: University of Chicago Press.

Metge, Joan. 1984. *Learning and Teaching: He Tikanga Maori*. Wellington: NZ Ministry of Education.

Mezzenzana, Francesca. 2020. "Between Will and Thought: Individualism and Social Responsiveness in Amazonian Child-Rearing." *American Anthropologist* 122: 540–553.

Michalchik, Vera S. 1997. "The Display of Cultural Knowledge in Cultural Transmission: Models of Participation from the Pacific Island of Kosrae." In *Education and Cultural Process: Anthropological Approaches*, edited by George D. Spindler, pp. 393–426. Prospect Heights, IL: Waveland Press.

Michelet, Aude. 2022. "Shared Secrecy: Teasing, Attachment, and Children's Emotional Management in Rural Southern Mongolia." *Journal of the Royal Anthropological Institute* 28: 240–259.

Miller, Peggy J., and Grace E. Cho. 2018. *Self Esteem in Time and Place: How American Families Imagine, Enact, and Personalize a Cultural Ideal*. New York: Oxford University Press.

REFERENCES   251

Miller, Peggy, and Catherine Garvey. 1984. "Mother–Baby Role Play: Its Origins in Social Support." In *Symbolic Play: The Development of Social Understanding*, edited by Inge Bretherton, pp. 101–130. Orlando, FL: Academic Press.

Miller, Peggy J., and Jacqueline J. Goodnow. 1995. "Cultural Practices: Toward an Integration of Culture and Development." In *Cultural Practices as Contexts for Development: New Directions for Adult and Continuing Education*, edited by Jacqueline J. Goodnow, Peggy J. Miller, and Frank Kessel, pp. 5–16. San Francisco, CA: Jossey-Bass.

Mitchell, Alice, and Fiona M. Jordan. 2021. "The Ontogeny of Kinship Categorization." *Journal of Cognition and Culture* 21: 152–177.

Mithen, Steven. 1999. "Imitation and Cultural Change: A View from the Stone Age, with Specific Reference to the Manufacture of Handaxes." In *Mammalian Social Learning: Comparative and Ecological Perspectives*, edited by Hilary O. Box and Kathleen R. Gibson, pp. 389–399. Cambridge: Cambridge University Press.

Mitterauer, Michael, and Reinhard Sieder. 1997. *The European Family: Patriarchy to Partnership from the Middle Ages to the Present*. Chicago: University of Chicago Press.

Modiano, Nancy. 1973. *Indian Education in the Chiapas Highlands*. New York: Holt, Rinehart, and Winston.

Mohammad, P. H. 1997. "Child Rearing and Socialization among the Savaras." *Man and Life* 23(4): 173–182.

Montessori, Maria. 1912. *The Montessori Method*. New York: Frederick H. Stokes.

Montgomery, Heather. 2001. *Modern Babylon: Prostituting Children in Thailand*. Oxford: Berghahn Books.

Moore, Leslie C. 2006. "Learning by Heart in Qur'anic and Public Schools in Northern Cameroon." *Social Analysis: The International Journal of Cultural and Social Practice* 50: 109–126.

Moore, Mark W. 2015. "Bifacial Flintknapping in the Northwest Kimberley, Western Australia." *Journal of Archaeological Method and Theory* 22(3): 913–951.

Moore, Richard. 2019. "Pedagogy and Social Learning in Human Development." In *The Routledge Handbook of the Social Mind*, edited by Julian Kiverstein, pp. 35–52. New York: Routledge.

Morawska, Alina, Cassandra K. Dittman, and Julie C. Rusby. 2019. "Promoting Self-Regulation in Young Children: The Role of Parenting Interventions." *Clinical Child and Family Psychology Review* 22(1): 43–51.

Morelli, Camilla. 2011. "Learning to Sit Still: The Physical Implications of Schooling for Matses Children in the Peruvian Amazon." Paper presented at the workshop on Schooling in Anthropology: Learning the "Modern Way," December 5, Brunel University.

Morelli, Camilla. 2012. "Teaching in the Rainforest: Exploring Matses Children's Affective Engagement and Multisensory Experiences in the Classroom Environment." *Teaching Anthropology* 2(2): 53–65.

Morelli, Camilla. 2013. "The River Echoes with Laughter: How Children's Ways-of-Knowing Transform the World and Future Horizons of Matses People in Peruvian Amazonia." Unpublished PhD diss., University of Manchester.

Morelli, Camilla. 2023. *Children of the Rainforest*. New Brunswick, NJ: Rutgers University Press.

Morelli, Gilda A., Barbara Rogoff, and Cathy Angelillo. 2003. "Cultural Variation in Young Children's Access to Work or Involvement in Specialized Child-Focused Activities." *International Journal of Behavioral Development* 27(3): 264–274.

252 REFERENCES

Morice, Alain. 1982. "Underpaid Child Labour and Social Reproduction: Apprenticeship in Kaolack, Senegal." *Development and Change* 13: 515–526.

Morton, Helen L. 1996. *Becoming Tongan: An Ethnography of Childhood.* Honolulu: University of Hawai'i Press.

Murphy, William P. 1980. "Secret Knowledge as Property and Power in Kpelle Society: Elders Versus Youth." *Africa* 50: 193–207.

Murray, Marjorie, Sofia Bowen, Nicole Segura, and Marisol Verdugo. 2015. "Apprehending Volition in Early Socialization: Raising 'Little Persons' among Rural Mapuche Families." *Ethos* 43: 376–401.

Musharbash, Yasmine. 2011. "Warungka: Becoming and Unbecoming a Warlpiri Person." In *Growing Up in Central Australia: New Anthropological Studies of Aboriginal Childhood and Adolescence*, edited by Ute Eickelkamp, pp. 63–81. Oxford: Berghahn Books.

Naji, Myriem. 2012. "Learning to Weave the Threads of Honor: Understanding the Value of Female Schooling in Southern Morocco." *Anthropology and Education Quarterly* 43: 372–384.

Nance, John. 1988. *The Gentle Tasaday: A Stone Age People in the Philippine Rain Forest.* Biddeford, ME: Godine.

Naveh, Danny. 2014. "Knowing and Learning among Nayaka Hunter-Gatherers." *The Eastern Anthropologist* 67: 345–362.

Naveh, Danny. 2016. "Social and Epistemological Dimensions of Learning among Nayaka Hunter-Gatherers." In *Social Learning and Innovation in Contemporary Hunter-Gatherers: Evolutionary and Ethnographic Perspectives*, edited by Hideaki Terashima and Barry S. Hewlett, pp. 125–134. Tokyo: Springer.

Neldner, Karri, Ilana Mushin, and Mark Nielsen. 2017. "Young Children's Tool Innovation across Culture: Affordance Visibility Matters." *Cognition* 168: 335–343.

Nerlove, Sarah B., John M. Roberts, Robert E. Klein, Charles Yarbrough, and Jean-Pierre Habicht. 1974. "Natural Indicators of Cognitive Development: An Observational Study of Rural Guatemalan Children." *Ethos* 2: 265–295.

Nesbitt, Kimberly T., and Dale C. Farran. 2021. "Effects of Prekindergarten Curricula: Tools of the Mind as a Case Study." *Monographs of the Society for Research in Child Development* 86(1): 340. doi:10.1111/mono.12425

Neuwelt-Truntzer, Sandra. 1981. "Ecological Influences on the Physical, Behavioral, and Cognitive Development of Pygmy Children." Unpublished PhD diss., University of Chicago.

Nicolaisen, Ida. 1988. "Concepts in Learning among the Punan Bah of Sarawak." In *Acquiring Culture: Cross-Cultural Studies in Child Development*, edited by Gustav Jahoda and Ioan M. Lewis, pp. 193–221. New York: Croom Helm.

Nielsen, Mark, and Cornelia Blank. 2011. "Imitation in Young Children: When Who Gets Copied Is More Important than What Gets Copied." *Developmental Psychology* 47: 1050–1053.

Nielsen, Mark, Ilana Mushin, Keyan Tomaselli, and Andrew Whiten. 2014. "Where Culture Takes Hold: 'Overimitation' and Its Flexible Deployment in Western, Aboriginal and Bushmen Children." *Child Development* 85(6): 2169–2184.

Nielsen Mark, Ilana Mushin, Keyan Tomaselli, and Andrew Whiten. 2016. "Imitation, Collaboration, and Their Interaction among Western and Indigenous Australian Preschool Children." *Child Development* 87: 795–806.

Nieuwenhuys, Olga. 2003. "Growing Up between Places of Work and Non-Places of Childhood: The Uneasy Relationship." In *Children's Places: Cross-Cultural Perspectives*, edited by Karen Fog Olwig and Eva Gullov, pp. 99–118. New York: Routledge.

REFERENCES 253

Nilsen, Ann C. E., and Randi Wærdahl. 2014. "Gender Differences in Norwegian Children's Work at Home." *Childhood* 22: 53–66.

Ninkova, Velina, and Jennifer Hays. 2017. "'Walking in Your Grandfather's Footsteps': Kinship and Knowledge Transmission among the Jul'hoansi (Namibia)." *Anthropochildren* 7 (Jan.): 1–17. doi:10.25518/2034-8517.2842

Nocon, Honorine, and Michael Cole. 2006. "School's Invasion of 'After-School': Colonization, Rationalization, or Expansion of Access?" In *Learning in Places: The Informal Education Reader*, edited by Zvi Bekerman, Nicholas C. Burbules, and Diana Silberman Keller, pp. 99–121. New York: Peter Lang Publishing.

Norenzayan, Ara, and Scott Atran. 2004. "Cognitive and Emotional Processes in the Cultural Transmission of Natural and Nonnatural Beliefs." In *The Psychological Foundations of Culture*, edited by Mark Schaller and Christian S. Crandall, pp. 149–169. Mahwah, NJ: Lawrence Erlbaum.

Northern Kentucky University. 2022. "Ethnographic Field School: Center for Applied Anthropology." Accessed February 2, 2023. https://pop.nku.edu/academics/artsci/about/centers/cfaa/ethnographic-field-school.html

Obendick, Helena. 2013. "When Siblings Determine Your 'Fate.'" In *The Anthropology of Sibling Relations*, edited by Erdmute Alber, Cati Coe, and Tatjana Thelen, pp. 97–121. New York: Palgrave Macmillan.

Obidi, Samuel S. 1995. "Skill Acquisition Through Indigenous Apprenticeship: A Case Study of the Yoruba Blacksmith in Nigeria." *Comparative Education* 31(3): 369–383.

Ochs, Elinor, and Carolina Izquierdo. 2009. "Responsibility in Childhood: Three Developmental Trajectories." *Ethos* 37: 391–413.

Ochs, Elinor, and Tamar Kremer-Sadlik. 2015. "Discursive Underpinnings of Family Coordination." In *The Handbook of Discourse Analysis*, Vol. 1–34, edited by Deborah Schiffrin, Deborah Tannen, and Heidi E. Hamilton, pp. 728–751. Berlin: Springer. doi:10.1002/9781118584194.ch34

Ochs, Elinor, and Bambi B. Schieffelin. 2017. "Language Socialization: An Historical Overview." In *Language Socialization. Encyclopedia of Language and Education*, Vol. 3, edited by Patricia A. Duff and Stephen May, pp. 1–13. Cham, Switzerland: Springer.

Odden, Harold L. 2007. "The Acquisition of Cultural Knowledge of Hierarchy by Samoan Children." Unpublished PhD diss., Department of Anthropology, Emory University.

Odden, Harold L., and Philippe Rochat. 2004. "Observational Learning and Enculturation." *Educational and Child Psychology* 21(2): 39–50.

Ohmagari, Kayo, and Fikret Berkes. 1997. "Transmission of Indigenous Knowledge and Bush Skills among the Western James Bay Cree Women of Subarctic Canada." *Human Ecology* 23(2): 197–222.

Okamoto-Barth, Sanae, Chris Moore, Jochen Barth, Francys Subiaul, and Daniel J. Povinelli. 2011. "Carryover Effect of Joint Attention to Repeated Events in Chimpanzees and Young Children." *Developmental Science* 14: 440–452.

Olson, David R. 2008. "Some Preliminaries to the Natural History of Pedagogy." In *Fostering Change in Institutions, Environments, and People*, edited by David C. Berliner and Haggai Kupermintz, pp. 1–14, Mahwah, NJ: Erlbaum.

Omura, Keiichi. 2016. "Socio-Cultural Cultivation of Positive Attitudes toward Learning: Considering Differences in Learning Ability between Neanderthals and Modern Humans from Examining Inuit Children's Learning Process." In *Social Learning and Innovation in Contemporary Hunter-Gatherers: Evolutionary and*

254 REFERENCES

Ethnographic Perspectives, edited by Hideaki Terashima and Barry S. Hewlett, pp. 267–284. Tokyo: Springer.

Online Etymology Dictionary. 2018. "Teach (v)." Updated September 29, 2018. Accessed January 17, 2023. https://www.etymonline.com/word/teach

Opie, Iona, and Peter Opie. 1969. *Children's Games in Street and Playground.* Oxford: Clarendon Press.

Oswalt, Wendall H. 1976. *An Anthropological Analysis of Food-Getting Technology.* New York: Wiley.

Ottenberg, Simon. 1968. *Double Descent in an African Society: The Afikpo Village-Group.* Seattle: University of Washington Press.

Ottenberg, Simon. 1989. *Boyhood Rituals in an African Society: An Interpretation.* Seattle: University of Washington Press.

Overing, Joanna. 1988. "Personal Autonomy and the Domestication of the Self in Piaroa Society." In *Acquiring Culture: Cross Cultural Studies in Child Development*, edited by Gustav Jahoda and Ioan M. Lewis, pp. 169–192. London: Croom Helm.

Packer, Martin, and Michael Cole. 2020. "The Institutional Foundations of Human Evolution, Ontogenesis and Learning." In *Handbook of the Cultural Foundations of Learning*, edited by Na'ilah S. Nasir, Carol D. Lee, Roy Pea, and Maxine McKinney de Royston, pp. 3–23. New York: Routledge.

Pagel, Mark. 2012. *Wired for Culture: Origins of the Human Social Mind.* New York: W. W. Norton and Company.

Pandya, Vishvajit. 2016. "When Hunter-Gathers Gather but Do Not Hunt: Jarawa Children's Changing World." In *Social Learning and Innovation in Contemporary Hunter-Gatherers: Evolutionary and Ethnographic Perspectives*, edited by Hideaki Terashima and Barry S. Hewlett, pp. 187–202. Tokyo: Springer.

Paradise, Ruth M. 1987. "Learning through Social Interaction: The Experience and Development of the Mazahua Self in the Context of the Market." Unpublished PhD diss., University of Pennsylvania.

Paradise, Ruth, and de Haan Mariëtte. 2009. "Responsibility and Reciprocity: Social Organization of Mazahua Learning Practices." *Anthropology and Education Quarterly* 40(2): 187–204.

Paradise, Ruth, and Adriana Robles. 2016. "Two Mazahua (Mexican) Communities: Introducing a Collective Orientation into Everyday School Life." *European Journal of Psychology of Education* 31: 61–77.

Paradise, Ruth, and Barbara Rogoff. 2009. "Side by Side: Learning by Observing and Pitching In." *Ethos* 37: 102–138.

Paradise, Ruth, Rebeca Mejía-Arauz, Katie G. Silva, Amy L. Dexter, and Barbara Rogoff. 2014. "'One, Two, Three, Eyes on Me!': Adults Attempting Control versus Guiding in Support of Initiative." *Human Development* 57: 131–149.

Park, Robert W. 2006. "Growing Up North: Exploring the Archaeology of Childhood in the Thule and Dorset Cultures of Arctic Canada." *Archeological Papers of the American Anthropological Association* 15: 53–64.

Pellegrini, Anthony D. 2016. "Object Use in Childhood: Development and Possible Functions." In *Evolutionary Perspectives on Child Development and Education*, edited by David C. Geary, and Daniel B. Berch, pp. 95–115. Heidelberg, Germany: Springer.

Pelto, Pertti, J. 1962. *Individualism in Skolt Lapp Society.* Helsinki: Suomen Muinaismuistoyhdistys.

Peluso, Daniela. 2015. "Children's Instrumentality and Agency in Amazonia." *Tipití: Journal of the Society for the Anthropology of Lowland South America* 13(1): 44–62.

REFERENCES 255

Peng, Peng, and Rogier A. Kievit. 2020. "The Development of Academic Achievement and Cognitive Abilities: A Bidirectional Perspective." *Child Development Perspectives* 14: 15–20.

Peters, John F. 1998. *Life among the Yanomami: The Story of Change among the Xilixana on the Mucajai River in Brazil.* Orchard Park, NY: Broadview Press.

Philips, Susan U. 1983. *The Invisible Culture: Communication in Classroom and Community on the Warm Springs Indian Reservation.* Long Grove, IL: Waveland Press.

Phillips, Brenda, Rebecca Seston, and Deborah Kelemen. 2012. "Learning about Tool Categories via Eavesdropping." *Child Development* 83: 2057–2072.

Pigeot, Nicole. 1990. "Technical and Social Actors: Flint Knapping Specialists at Magdalenian Etiolles." *Archaeological Review from Cambridge* 9: 126–141.

Platt, Brian. 2005. "Japanese Childhood, Modern Childhood: The Nation-State, the School, and 19th-Century Globalization." *Journal of Social History* 38: 965–985.

Platt, Katherine. 1988. "Cognitive Development and Sex Roles of the Kerkennah Islands of Tunisia." In *Acquiring Culture: Cross Cultural Studies in Child Development*, edited by Gustav Jahoda and Ioan M. Lewis, pp. 271–287. London: Croom Helm.

Poelker, Katelyn E., and Judith L. Gibbons. 2019. "Sharing and Caring: Prosocial Behavior in Young Children around the World." In *Children's Social Worlds in Cultural Context*, edited by Tia Tulvista, Deborah L. Best, and Judith L. Gibbons, pp. 89–102. Cham, Switzerland: Springer.

Polak, Barbara. 2003. "Little Peasants: On the Importance of Reliability in Child Labour." In *Le travail en Afrique noire: Representations et pratiques a l'epoque contemporaine*, edited by Hélène d'Almeida-Topor, Monique Lakroum, and Gerd Spittler, pp. 125–136. Paris: Karthala.

Polak, Barbara. 2011. "Die Könige der Feldarbeit." Unpublished PhD diss., Kulturwissenschaftlichen Fakultät der Universität Bayreuth.

Polak, Barbara. 2012. "Peasants in the Making: Bamana Children at Work." In *African Children at Work: Working and Learning in Growing Up*, edited by Gerd Spittler and Michael Bourdillon, pp. 87–112. Berlin: LitVerlag.

Polak, Rainer, and Noumouké Doumbia. 2022. "Learning to Dance in Rural Mali." In *Dance and Economy, Dance Transmission: Proceedings of the 31st Symposium of the International Council for Traditional Music (ICTM) Study Group on Ethnochoreology*, edited by Dalia Urbanavičienė and Anne von Bibra Wharton, pp. 282–290. Vilnius, Lithuania: Academy of Music and Theatre.

Politis, Gustavo G., translated by Benjamin Alberti. 2007. *Nukak: Ethnoarchaeology of an Amazonian People.* Walnut Creek, CA: University College London Institute of Archaeology Publications.

Pollom, Trevor R., Kristen N. Herlosky, Ibrahim A. Mabullaand, Alyssa N. Crittenden. 2020. "Changes in Juvenile Hadza Foraging Behavior during Subsistence Transition." *Human Nature* 31: 123–140.

Pomponio, Alice. 1992. *Seagulls Don't Fly into the Bush.* Belmont, CA: Wadsworth.

Pomponio, Alice, and David F. Lancy. 1986. "A Pen or a Bush Knife: School, Work and Personal Investment in Papua New Guinea." *Anthropology and Education Quarterly* 17: 40–61.

Poole, Fitz-John P. 1982. "The Ritual Forging of Identity: Aspects of Person and Self in Bimin-Kuskusmin Male Initiation." In *Rituals of Manhood: Male Initiation in Papua New Guinea*, edited by Gilbert H. Herdt, pp. 99–154. Berkeley: University of California Press.

256 REFERENCES

Pope, Sarah M., Joel Fagot, Adrien Meguerditchian, David. A. Washburn, and William D. Hopkins. 2019. "Enhanced Cognitive Flexibility in the Seminomadic Himba." *Journal of Cross-Cultural Psychology* 50(1): 47–62.

Popkewitz, Thomas S. 2003. "Governing the Child and Pedagogicalization of the Parent: Historical Excursus into the Present." In *Governing Children, Families, and Education: Restructuring the Welfare State*, edited by Marianne N. Bloch, Kerstin Holmlund, Ingeborg Moquvist, and Thomas S. Popkewitz, pp. 35–61. New York: Palgrave Macmillan.

Porcher, Vincent, Stephanie M. Carrière, Sandrine Gallois, Herizo Randriambanona, Verohanitra M. Rafidison, and Victoria Reyes-Garcia. 2022. "Growing up in the Betsileo Landscape: Children's Wild Edible Plants Knowledge in Madagascar." *Plos One* 17(2): e0264147. doi:10.1371/journal.pone.0264147

Portisch, Anna O. 2010. "The Craft of Skillful Learning: Kazakh Women's Everyday Craft Practices in Western Mongolia." *Journal of the Royal Anthropological Institute*, Supplement, 16: 62–79.

Power, Thomas G. 2000. *Play and Exploration in Children and Animals*. Mahwah, NJ: Erlbaum.

Puri, Rajindra K. 2005. *Deadly Dances in the Bornean Rainforest: Hunting Knowledge of the Punan Benalui*. Leiden: KITLV Press.

Puri, Rajindra K. 2013. "Transmitting Penan Basketry Knowledge and Practice." In *Understanding Cultural Transmission: A Critical Anthropological Synthesis*, edited by Roy Ellen, Stephen J. Lycett, and Sarah E. Johns, pp. 266–299. Oxford: Berghahn Books.

Qazizai, Fazelminallah. 2022. "Taliban Reverses Decision, Barring Afghan Girls from Attending School Beyond 6th Grade." *NPR: All Things Considered*, March 23. Accessed May 12, 2022. https://www.npr.org/2022/03/23/1088202759/taliban-afghanistan-girls-school

Quinlan, Marsha, and Robert Quinlan. 2007. "Modernization and Medicinal Plant Knowledge in a Caribbean Horticultural Village." *Medical Anthropology Quarterly* 21: 169–192.

Quinlan, Marsha B., Robert J. Quinlan, Sarah K. Council, and Jennifer W. Roulette. 2016. "Children's Acquisition of Ethnobotanical Knowledge in a Caribbean Horticultural Village." *Journal of Ethnobiology* 36(2): 433–456.

Quinn, Naomi, and Dorothy Holland. 1987. "Culture and Cognition." In *Cultural Models of Language and Thought*, edited by Dorothy Holland and Naomi Quinn, pp. 3–40. New York: Cambridge University Press.

Quinn, Naomi, and Jeanette M. Mageo, eds. 2013. *Attachment Reconsidered: Cultural Perspectives on a Western Theory*. New York: Palgrave Macmillan.

Rabain-Jamin, Jacquelin, Ashley E. Maynard, and Patricia M. Greenfield. 2003. "Implications of Sibling Caretaking for Sibling Relations and Teaching in Two Cultures." *Ethos* 31: 204–231.

Raffaele, Paul. 2003. *The Last Tribes on Earth: Journeys among the World's Most Threatened Cultures*. Sydney, Australia: Pan Macmillan.

Raitt, Margaret, and David F. Lancy. 1988. "Rhinestone Cowgirl: The Education of a Rodeo Queen." *Play and Culture* 1(4): 267–281.

Rao, Aparna. 1998. *Autonomy: Life Cycle, Gender, and Status among Himalayan Pastoralists*. Oxford: Berghahn Books.

Rao, Aparna. 2006. "The Acquisition of Manners, Morals and Knowledge: Growing Into and Out of Bakkarwal Society." In *The Education of Nomadic Peoples: Current Issues, Future Prospects*, edited by Caroline Dyer, pp. 53–76. Oxford: Berghan.

REFERENCES 257

Raum, Otto F. 1940. *Chaga Childhood*. Oxford: Oxford University Press.

Read, Dwight W. 2001. "Formal Analysis of Kinship Terminologies and Its Relationship to What Constitutes Kinship." *Mathematical Anthropology and Cultural Theory* 1: 239–267.

Read, Margaret. 1960. *Children of Their Fathers: Growing Up among the Ngoni of Malawi*. New Haven, CT: Yale University Press.

Reading Is Fundamental. N.d. "Million Book March." Accessed December 27, 2022. https://www.rif.org/millionbookmarch

Reed, Edward S. 1996. *The Necessity of Experience*. New Haven, CT: Yale University Press.

Reichard, Gladys. 1934. *Spider Woman: A Story of Navaho Weavers and Chanters*. New York: Macmillan.

Reichel-Dolmatoff, Gerardo. 1976. "Training for the Priesthood among the Kogi of Columbia." In *Enculturation in Latin America*, edited by Johannes Wilbert, pp. 265–288. Los Angeles: UCLA Latin American Center Publications.

Reissland, Nadja. 1988. "Neonatal Imitation in the First Hour of Life: Observation in Rural Nepal." *Developmental Psychology* 24(4): 464–469.

Remorini, Carolina. 2011. "Becoming a Person from the Mbya Guarani Perspective." Unpublished MS thesis, National University of La Plata, Argentina.

Remorini, Carolina. 2012. "Childrearing and the Shaping of Children's Emotional Experiences and Expressions in Two Argentinian Communities." *Global Studies of Childhood* 2(2): 144–157.

Remorini, Carolina. 2016. "Children's Skills, Expectations and Challenges Facing Changing Environments: An Ethnographic Study in Mbya Guarani Communities (Argentina)." In *Indigenous Peoples: Perspectives, Cultural Roles and Health Care Disparities*, edited by Jessica Morton, pp. 31–70. Hauppage, NY: Nova Science Publishers.

Renfrew, Colin. 1998. "Mind and Matter: Cognitive Archaeology and External Storage." In *Cognition and Material Culture: The Archaeology of Symbolic Storage*, edited by Colin Renfrew and Chris Scarre, pp. 1–6. Oxford: Oxbow Books.

Revel, Nicole A., Hermine Xhauflair, and Norlita Colili. 2017. "Childhood in Pala'wan Highlands Forest, the Känakan (Philippines)." *Anthropochildren* 7: 1–27. Accessed December 16, 2022. https://popups.uliege.be/2034-8517/index.php?id=2812&file=1

Reyes-García, Victoria, James Broesch, Laura Calvet-Mir, Nuria Fuentes-Peláez, Thomas W. McDade, Sorush Parsa, Susan Tanner, Thomás Huanca, William R. Leonard, and Maria R. Martínez-Rodríguez. 2009. "Cultural Transmission of Ethnobotanical Knowledge and Skills: An Empirical Analysis from an Amerindian Society." *Evolution and Human Behavior* 30: 274–285.

Rheingold, Harriet. 1982. "Little Children's Participation in the Work of Adults, a Nascent Prosocial Behavior." *Child Development* 53: 114–125.

Richards, Audrey I. 1956. *Chisungu*. London: Faber and Faber.

Richman, Amy, Patrice Miller, and Robert A. LeVine. 1992. "Cultural and Educational Variations in Maternal Responsiveness." *Developmental Psychology* 28: 614–621.

Ricks, Thomas E. 1997. *Making the Corps*. New York: Touchstone.

Riede, Felix, Sheina Lew-Levy, Niels N. Johannsen, Noa Lavi, and Marc M. Andersen. 2022. "Toys as Teachers: A Cross-Cultural Analysis of Object Use and Enskillment in Hunter–Gatherer Societies." *Journal of Archaeological Method and Theory* 30: 32–63. https://doi.org/10.1007/s10816-022-09593-3

Riesman, Paul. 1992. *First Find Yourself a Good Mother*. New Brunswick, NJ: Rutgers University Press.

258 REFERENCES

Rival, Laura M. 2000. "Formal Schooling and the Production of Modern Citizens in the Ecuadorian Amazon." In *Schooling the Symbolic Animal: Social and Cultural Dimensions of Education*, edited by Bradley A.U. Levinson, pp. 108–122. Lanham, MA: Rowman & Littlefield.

Robbins, Alexandra. 2006. *The Overachievers: The Secret Lives of Driven Kids.* New York: Hyperion.

Roberts, John M. 1964. "The Self-Management of Cultures." In *Explorations in Cultural Anthropology*, edited by Ward H. Goodenough, pp. 433–454. New York: McGraw–Hill.

Rochat, Phillipe. 1989. "Object manipulation and exploration in 2- to 5-month-old infants." *Developmental Psychology* 25: 871–884.

Robinson, Keith, and Angel L. Harris. 2014. *The Broken Compass: Parental Involvement with Children's Education.* Cambridge, MA: Harvard University Press.

Röder, Brigitte. 2018. "Prehistoric Households and Childhood." In *The Oxford Handbook of the Archaeology of Childhood*, edited by S. Crawford, D. M. Hadley, and G. Shepherd, pp. 123–147. Oxford: Oxford University Press.

Rogoff, Barbara. 1981. "Schooling and the Development of Cognitive Skills." In *The Handbook of Cross-Cultural Psychology*, edited by Harry Triandis and Alistair Heron, pp. 233–294. Boston: Allyn and Bacon.

Rogoff, Barbara, and Christine Mosier. 1993. "Guided Participation in San Pedro and Salt Lake." *Monographs of the Society for Research in Child Development* 58(8): 59–101. doi:10.1111/j.1540-5834.1993.tb00436.x

Rogoff, Barbara, Martha J. Sellers, Sergio Pirotta, Nathan Fox, and Sheldon H. White. 1975. "Age of Assignment of Roles and Responsibilities to Children." *Human Development* 18: 353–369.

Rogoff, Barbara, Ruth Paradise, Rebeca M. Arauz, Maricela Correa-Chávez, and Cathy Angelillo. 2003. "Firsthand Learning through Intent Participation." *Annual Review of Psychology* 54: 175–203.

Rogoff, Barbara, Maricela Correa-Chávez, and Marta Navichoc Cotuc. 2005. "A Cultural/Historical View of Schooling in Human Development." In *Developmental Psychology and Social Change: Research, History, and Policy*, edited by David B. Pillemer and Sheldon H. White, pp. 225–263. Cambridge: Cambridge University Press.

Rogoff, Barbara, Andrew D. Coppens, Lucía Alcalá, Itzel Aceves-Azuara, Omar Ruvalcaba, Angélica López, and Andrew Dayton. 2017. "Noticing Learners' Strengths through Cultural Research." *Perspectives on Psychological Science* 12: 876–888.

Rohner, Ronald P., and Manjusri Chaki-Sircar. 1988. *Women and Children in a Bengali Village.* Hanover, NH: University Press of New England.

Rosado-May, Francisco, Luis Urrieta Jr., Andrew Dayton, and Barbara Rogoff. 2020. "Innovation as a Key Feature of Indigenous Ways of Learning." In *Handbook of the Cultural Foundations of Learning*, edited by Na'ilah S. Nasir, Carol D. Lee, Roy Pea, and Maxine McKinney de Royston, pp. 79–96. New York: Routledge.

Röttger-Rössler, Birgitt, Gabriel Scheidecker, Legerecht Funk, and Manfred Holodynski. 2015. "Learning (by) Feeling: A Cross-Cultural Comparison of the Socialization and Development of Emotions." *Ethos* 43(2): 187–220.

Rowe, Meredith L. 2013. "Decontextualized Language Input and Preschoolers' Vocabulary Development." *Seminar in Speech and Language* 34(4): 260–266. doi:10.1055/s-0033-1353444

Rubenstein, Donald H. 1979. *An Ethnography of Micronesian Childhood: Context of Socialization on Fais Island.* Unpublished PhD dissertation, Stanford University.

REFERENCES   259

Ruddle, Kenneth, and Ray Chesterfield. 1977. *Education for Traditional Food Procurement in the Orinoco Delta*. Los Angeles: University of California Press.

Ruiz, Luisa F. M. 2011. "Coffee in Guatemala." In *Hazardous Child Labour in Latin America*, edited by G. Kristoffel Lieten, pp. 165–189. London: Springer.

Ruiz-Malén, Isabel, Carla Morsello, Victoria Reyes-García, and Renate B. Marcondes De Faria. 2013. "Children's Use of Time and Traditional Ecological Learning: A Case Study in Two Amazonian Indigenous Societies." *Learning and Individual Differences* 27: 213–222.

Russell, Jennifer L. 2011. "From Child's Garden to Academic Press: The Role of Shifting Institutional Logics in Redefining Kindergarten Education." *American Educational Research Journal* 48: 236–267.

Rutherford, Markella. 2011. *Adult Supervision Required*. New Brunswick, NJ: Rutgers University Press.

Ruvalcaba, Omar, Barbara Rogoff, Angélica López, Maricella Correa-Chávez, and Kris Gutiérrez. 2015. "Children's Avoidance of Interrupting Others' Activities in Requesting Help: Cultural Aspects of Considerateness." *Advances in Child Development and Behavior* 49: 185–205.

Sackey, Enoch T., and Berit O. Johannesen. 2015. "Earning Identity and Respect Through Work: A Study of Children Involved in Fishing and Farming Practices in Cape Coast, Ghana." *Childhood* 22: 447–459.

Saggs, Henry W. F. 1987. *Everyday Life in Babylonia and Assyria*. New York: Hippocrene Books.

Salali, Gul D., Nikhil Chaudhary, Jairo Bouer, James Thompson, Lucio Vinicius, and Andrea Bamberg Migliano. 2019. "Development of Social Learning and Play in BaYaka Hunter-Gatherers of Congo." *Nature Scientific Reports* 9, Article number 11080, July 31. Accessed December 16, 2022. https://www.nature.com/articles/s41598-019-47515-8?fbclid= IwAR2uEkfUSG_AQr6_vqbCzD6PKtaSaMe0d0TH1hGL71fdFQ1fL5sOuqvammA

Salali, Gul D., Mark Dyble, Nikhil Chaudhary, Gaurav Sikka, Inez Derkx, Sarai M. Keestra, Daniel Smith, James Thompson, Lucio Vinicius, and Andrea B. Migliano. 2020. "Global WEIRDing: Transitions in Wild Plant Knowledge and Treatment Preferences in Congo Hunter-Gatherers." *Evolutionary Human Sciences* 2(e24): 1–14. doi:10.1017/ehs.2020.26

Scheidecker, Gabriel. 2016. Kindheit, Kultur und moralische Emotionen. Zur Sozialisation von Furcht und Wut im ländlichen Madagaskar. *Childhood, Culture and Moral Emotions. About Socialization of Fear and Rage in Rural Madagascar*. Bielefeld, Germany: Transcript Verlag.

Scheidecker, Gabriel. 2023. "Parents, Caregivers, and Peers: Patterns of Complementarity in the Social World of Children in Rural Madagascar." *Current Anthropology* 64(3): 286–320.

Scheidecker, Gabriel, Nandita Chaudhary, Heidi Keller, Francesca Mezzenzana, and David F. Lancy. 2023. "Poor Brain Development in the Global South? Challenging the Science of Early Childhood Interventions." *Ethos*, January 31. https://doi.org/10.1111/etho.12379

Schieffelin, Bambi B. 1986. "Teasing and Shaming in Kaluli Children's Interactions." In *Language Socialization across Cultures*, edited by Bambi B. Schieffelin and Elinor Ochs, pp. 165–181. Cambridge: Cambridge University Press.

Schieffelin, Bambi B. 1990. *The Give and Take of Everyday Life: Language Socialization of Kaluli Children*. Cambridge: Cambridge University Press.

260 REFERENCES

Schieffelin, Bambi B., and Elinor Ochs. 1986. "Language Socialization." *Annual Review of Anthropology* 15: 163–191.

Schildkrout, Enid. 1981. "The Employment of Children in Kano (Nigeria)." In *Child Work, Poverty, and Underdevelopment*, edited by Gerry Rodgers and Guy Standing, pp. 81–112. Geneva, Switzerland: International Labour Office.

Schildkrout, Enid. 1990. "Children's Roles: The Young Traders of Northern Nigeria." In *Conformity and Conflict*, edited by James P. Spradley and Davie W. McCurdy, pp. 221–228. Glenview, IL: Scott Foresman.

Schlegel, Alice, and Herbert L. Barry, III. 1980. "The Evolutionary Significance of Adolescent Initiation Ceremonies." *American Ethnologist* 7(4): 696–715.

Schlegel, Alice, and Herbert L. Barry, III. 1991. *Adolescence: An Anthropological Inquiry*. New York: The Free Press.

Schmidt, Marco F. H., Hannes Rakoczy, and Michael Tomasello. 2011. "Young Children Attribute Normativity to Novel Actions without Pedagogy or Normative Language." *Developmental Science* 14: 530–539.

Schölmerich, Axel, Birgit Leyendecker, and Heidi Keller. 1995. "The Study of Early Interaction Contextual Perspective: Culture, Communication, and Eye Contact." In *Child Development within Culturally Structured Environments: Comparative-Cultural and Constructivist Perspectives*, edited by Jaan Valsiner, pp. 29–50. Norwood, NJ: Ablex.

Schulz, L. E., and Elizabeth B. Bonawitz. 2007. "Serious Fun: Preschoolers Engage in More Exploratory Play When Evidence Is Confounded." *Developmental Psychology* 43: 1045–1050.

Schütze, Yvonne, Kurt Kreppner, and Sibylle Paulsen. 1986. "The Social Construction of the Sibling Relationship." In *Children's Worlds and Children's Language*, edited by Jenny Cook-Gumperz, William A. Corsaro, and Jürgen Streek, pp. 128–145. Berlin, Germany: Mouton de Gruyter.

Scribner, Sylvia, and Michael Cole. 1973. "Cognitive Consequences of Formal and Informal Education." *Science* 182: 553–559.

Sefton-Green, Julian. 2015. "Negotiating the Pedagogicisation of Everyday Life: The Art of Learning." In *Cultural Pedagogies and Human Conduct*, edited by Megan Watkins, Greg Noble, and Catherine Driscoll, pp. 45–60. Abingdon, UK: Routledge.

Sefton-Green, Julian. 2019. "Outing the 'Out' in Out-of-School." In *Learning Beyond the School: International Perspectives on the Schooled Society*, edited by Julian Sefton-Green and Ola Erstad, pp. 193–208. Abingdon, UK: Routledge.

Serpell, Robert. 1993. *The Significance of Schooling: Life Journeys in an African Society*. Cambridge: Cambridge University Press.

Serpell, Robert, and Giyoo Hatano. 1997. "Education, Schooling, and Literacy." In *Handbook of Cross-Cultural Psychology, Vol. 2: Basic Processes and Human Development*, 2nd ed., edited by John W. Berry, Pierre R. Dasen, and T. S. Saraswathi, pp. 339–376. Needham Heights, MA: Allyn & Bacon.

Setalaphruk, Chantia, and Lisa L. Price. 2007. "Children's Traditional Ecological Knowledge of Wild Food Resources: A Case Study in a Rural Village in Northeast Thailand." *Journal of Ethnobiology and Ethnomedicine* 3: 33. doi:10.1186/1746-4269-3-33

Shea, John J. 2006. "Child's Play: Reflections on the Invisibility of Children in the Paleolithic Record." *Evolutionary Anthropology* 15: 212–216.

Shepler, Susan. 2014. *Childhood Deployed: Remaking Child Soldiers in Sierra Leone*. New York: NYU Press.

REFERENCES 261

Shneidman, Laura A., and Susan Goldin-Meadow. 2012. "Language Input and Acquisition in a Mayan Village: How Important Is Directed Speech? *Developmental Science* 15: 659–673.

Shneidman, Laura, and Amanda L. Woodward. 2016. "Are Child-Directed Interactions the Cradle of Social Learning?" *Psychological Bulletin* 147: 1–17.

Shore, Brad. 1996. *Culture in Mind: Cognition, Culture, and the Problem of Meaning.* Oxford: Oxford University Press.

Shostak, Marjorie. 1981. *Nisa: The Life and Words of a !Kung Woman.* New York: Vintage Books.

Silva, Katie G., Maricela Correa-Chavéz, and Barbara Rogoff. 2011. "Mexican-Heritage Children's Attention and Learning from Interactions Directed at Others." *Child Development* 81: 898–912.

Silva, Katie G., Priya M. Shimpi, and Barbara Rogoff. 2015. "Young Children's Attention to What's Going on: Cultural Differences." In *Children Learn by Observing and Contributing to Family and Community Endeavors: A Cultural Paradigm. Advances in Child Development and Behavior*, edited by Maricela Correa-Chávez, Rebeca Mejía-Arauz, and Barbara Rogoff, 49: 207–227. Cambridge, MA: Academic Press.

Simenel, Romain, Yildiz Aumeeruddy-Thomas, Morgane Salzard, and Lahoucine Amzil. 2017. "From the Solitary Bee to the Social Bee: The Inventiveness of Children in the Acquisition of Beekeeping Skills (Southwestern Morocco)." *Anthropochildren* 7: 1–29. https://popups.uliege.be/2034-8517/index.php?id=2772

Simmons, Leo W., ed. 1942. *Sun Chief: The Autobiography of a Hopi Indian.* New Haven, CT: Yale University Press.

Singleton, John. 1989. "Japanese Folkcraft Pottery Apprenticeship: Cultural Patterns of an Educational Institution." In *Apprenticeship: From Theory to Method and Back Again*, edited by Michael W. Coy, pp. 13–30. Albany: SUNY Press.

Smith-Hefner, Nancy J. 1988. "The Linguistic Socialization of Javanese Children in Two Communities." *Anthropological Linguistics* 30: 166–198.

Smith, Patricia E. 2008. "Children and Ceramic Innovation: A Study in the Archaeology of Children." *Archaeological Papers of the American Anthropological Association* 15: 65–76.

Sofue, Takao. 1965. "Childhood Ceremonies in Japan: Regional and Local Variations." *Ethnology* 4: 148–164.

Solomon, Olga. 2012. "Rethinking Baby Talk." In *The Handbook of Language Socialization*, edited by Alessandro Duranti, Elinor Ochs, and Bambi B. Schieffelin, pp. 121–149. West Sussex, UK: Wiley Blackwell.

Solway, Jacqueline. 2017. "The Predicament of Adulthood in Botswana." In *Elusive Adulthood: The Anthropology of New Maturities*, edited by Deborah Durham and Jacqueline Solway, pp. 39–60. Bloomington: Indiana University Press.

Sonoda, Koji. 2016. "'Give Me the Meat, the Child Said': Cultural Practice among the Children of the Baka Hunter-Gatherers." *Hunter Gatherer Research* 2(1): 39–62.

Sonoda, Koji, Daša Bombjaková, and Sandrine L. Gallois. 2018. "Cultural Transmission of Foundational Schemas among Congo Basin Hunter-Gatherers." *African Study Monographs*, Suppl. issue, 54: 155–169.

Sorenson, E. Richard. 1976. *The Edge of the Forest: Land, Childhood and Change in a New Guinea Protoagricultural Society.* Washington, DC: Smithsonian Institution Press.

Spencer, Mary L. 2015. *Children of Chuuk Lagoon.* Guam: University of Guam Micronesian Area Research Center.

262 REFERENCES

Spencer, Paul. 1970. "The Function of Ritual in the Socialization of the Samburu Moran." In *Socialization: The Approach from Social Anthropology*, edited by Philip Mayer, pp. 127–157. London: Tavistock Publications.

Sperber, Dan, Fabrice Clément, Christophe Heintz, Olivier Mascaro, Hugo Mercier, Gloria Origgi, and Deidre Wilson. 2010. "Epistemic Vigilance." *Mind & Language* 25(4): 359–393.

Sperry, Douglas E., Linda L. Sperry, and Peggy J. Miller. 2019. "Reexamining the Verbal Environment of Children from Different Socioeconomic Backgrounds." *Child Development* 90(4): 1303–1318.

Sperry, Douglas E., Peggy J. Miller, and Linda L. Sperry. 2020. "Hazardous Intersections: Crossing Disciplinary Lines in Developmental Psychology." *European Journal of Social Theory* 23(1): 93–112.

Spindel, Carol. 1989. "Kpeenbele Senufo Potters." *African Arts* 22(2): 66–73.

Spittler, Gerd. 1998. *Hirtenarbeit*. Köln: Rüdiger Köppe.

Sprott, Julie W. 2002. *Raising Young Children in an Alaskan Inupiaq Village: The Family, Cultural and Village Environment of Rearing*. Westport, CT: Bergin and Garvey.

Stafford, Charles. 1995. *The Roads of Chinese Childhood*. Cambridge: Cambridge University Press.

Stamm, Jill. 2008. *Bright from the Start: The Simple, Science-Backed Way to Nurture Your Child's Developing Mind from Birth to Age 3*. New York: Penguin.

Stapert, Dick. 2007. "Neanderthal Children and Their Flints." *Pal/Arch's Journal of Archaeology of Northwest Europe* 1(2): 16–38.

Stengelin, Roman, Robert Hepach, Daniel B. M. Haun. 2019. "Being Observed Increases Over-Imitation in Three Diverse Cultures." *Developmental Psychology* 55: 2630–2636.

Sterelny, Kim. 2021. "Veiled Agency? Children, Innovation, and the Archaeological Record." *Evolutionary Human Sciences* 3: e12. doi:10.1017/ehs.2021.9

Strauss, Sidney, and Margalit Ziv. 2012. "Teaching Is a Natural Cognitive Ability for Humans." *Mind, Brain and Education* 6(4): 186–196.

Strauss, Sidney, Margalit Ziv, and Adi Stein. 2002. "Teaching as a Natural Cognition and Its Relations to Pre-Schoolers' Developing Theory of Mind." *Cognitive Development* 17: 1473–1787.

Sugiyama, Michelle S. 2017. "Oral Storytelling as Evidence of Pedagogy in Forager Societies." *Frontiers in Psychology* 8 (March 29). doi:10.3389/fpsyg.2017.00471/full

Suina, Joseph H., and Laura B. Smolkin. 1994. "From Natal Culture to School Culture to Dominant Society Culture: Supporting Transitions for Pueblo Indian Students." In *Cross-Cultural Roots of Minority Child Development*, edited by Patricia M. Greenfield and Rodney R. Cocking, pp. 115–132. Hillsdale, NJ: Lawrence Erlbaum Associates.

Super, Charles M. 1976. "Environmental Effects on Motor Development: The Case of African Infant Precocity." *Developmental Medicine and Child Neurology* 19: 561–567.

Super, Charles M., and Sara Harkness. 1986. "The Developmental Niche: A Conceptualization at the Interface of Child and Culture." *International Journal of Behavioral Development* 9: 545–569.

Swadling, Pamela, and Ann Chowning. 1981. "Shellfish Gathering at Nukakau Island, West New Britain Province, Papua New Guinea." *Societe des Oceanistes* 37: 157–167.

Taggart, Jessica, Megan J. Heise, and Angeline S. Lillard. 2018. "The Real Thing: Preschoolers Prefer Actual Activities." *Developmental Science* 21(3): e12582. doi:10.1111/desc.12582

REFERENCES   263

Takada, Akira. 2005. "Mother-Infant Interactions among the !Xun: Analysis of Gymnastic and Breastfeeding Behaviors." In *Hunter Gatherer Childhoods: Evolutionary, Developmental, and Cultural Perspectives*, edited by Barry S. Hewlett and Michael E. Lamb, pp. 289–308. New Brunswick, NJ: Aldine Transaction.

Takada, Akira. 2020. *The Ecology of Playful Childhood: The Diversity and Resilience of Caregiver-Child Interactions among the San of Southern Africa.* New York: Palgrave-Macmillan.

Tanaka, Aya. 2022. "Attachment Behavior of a Baka Infant and His Participation in Song and Dance." Paper presented at 13th meeting of the Conference for Hunter-Gatherer Studies, Dublin, Ireland, June.

Tanner, Courtney, Alastair L. Bitson, and Sheila R. McCann. 2022. "Assimilated: How Utah Boarding Schools Stripped Native Students of Their Culture." *Salt Lake Tribune*, 1(75), A1–5. Accessed December 17, 2022. https://local.sltrib.com/utah-boarding-schools/utah-boarding-schools.html

Tanon, Fabienne. 1994. *A Cultural View on Planning: The Case of Weaving in Ivory Coast.* Tillburg, Netherlands: Tilburg University Press.

Tassinari, Antonella Imperatriz, and Clarice Cohn. 2009. "Opening to the Other": Schooling among the Karipuna and Mebengokré-Xikrin of Brazil." *Anthropology and Education Quarterly* 40(2): 150–169.

Tayanin, Damrong, and Kristina Lindell. 1991. *Hunting and Fishing in a Kammu Village: Revisiting a Classic Study in Southeast Asian Ethnography.* Copenhagen, Denmark: Curzon Press.

Tehrani, Jamshid J., and Mark Collard. 2009. "On the Relationship between Interindividual Cultural Transmission and Population-Level Cultural Diversity: A Case Study of Weaving in Iranian Tribal Populations." *Evolution and Human Behavior* 30: 286–300.

Thiessen, Erik D., Emily A. Hill, and Jenny R. Saffran. 2005. "Infant-Directed Speech Facilitates Word Segmentation." *Infancy* 7: 53–71. doi:10.1207/s15327078in0701_5

Thornton, Alex, and Nichola J. Raihani. 2008. "The Evolution of Teaching." *Animal Behaviour* 75: 1823–1836.

Tian, Xiaojie. 2021. "Un apprentissage 'par les pieds.' L'éducation des enfants de pasteurs Maasaï." *Techniques & Culture* 76: 70–83.

Tian, Xiaojie. 2017a. "Ethnobiological Knowledge Generation during 'Herding Games' in Pastoralist Maasai Society (Southern Kenya)." *Anthropochildren* 7: 1–22. doi:10.25518/2034-8517.2825

Tian, Xiaojie. 2017b. "Ethnobotanical Knowledge Acquisition during Daily Chores: The Firewood Collection of Pastoral Maasai Girls in Southern Kenya." *Journal of Ethnobiology and Ethnomedicine* 13(2): 1–14.

Tizard, Barbara, and Hughes, Martin. 1985. *Young Children Learning.* Cambridge, MA: Harvard University Press.

Tomasello, Michael. 1999. *The Cultural Origins of Human Cognition.* Cambridge, MA: Harvard University Press.

Tomasello, Michael. 2009. *Why We Cooperate.* Cambridge, MA: MIT Press.

Tomasello, Michael, and Amrisha Vaish. 2013. "Origins of Human Cooperation and Morality." *Annual Review of Psychology* 64: 231–255.

Tonkinson, Robert. 1991. *The Mardu Aborigines: Living the Dream in Australia's Desert.* San Francisco: Holt, Rinehart and Winston.

264 REFERENCES

Toren, Christina. 1988. "Children's Perceptions of Gender and Hierarchy in Fiji." In *Acquiring Culture: Cross-Cultural Studies in Child Development*, edited by Gustav Jahoda and Ioan M. Lewis, pp. 225–270. London: Croom Helm.

Toren, Christina. 1990. *Making Sense of Hierarchy: Cognition as Social Process in Fiji*. Houndsmills, UK: Palgrave-Macmillan.

Tovote, Katrine E., and Ashley E. Maynard. 2018. "Maya Children Working in the Streets: Value Mismatches from the Village to the Street Setting." *International Journal of Psychology* 53: 34–43.

Traig, Jennifer. 2019. *Act Natural: A Cultural History of Misadventures in Parenting*. New York: HarperCollins.

Trias, Manuel C., Jaume G. Rosselló, David J. Molina, and Daniel A. Santacreu. 2015. "Playing with Mud? An Ethnoarchaeological Approach to Children's Learning in Kusasi Ceramic Production." In *Children, Spaces and Identity*, edited by Margarita Sánchez-Romero, Eva A. García, and Gonzalo A. Jimenez, pp. 88–104. Oxford: Oxbow Books.

Trivers, Robert L. 1974. "Parent-Offspring Conflict." *American Zoologist* 14: 249–264.

Tronick, Edward Z., Gilda A. Morelli, and Steven Winn. 1987. "Multiple Caretaking of Efe (Pygmy) Infants." *American Anthropologist* 89: 96–106.

Tuck Po, Lye. 1997. "Knowledge, Forest, and Hunter-Gatherer Movement: The Batek of Pahang, Malaysia." Unpublished PhD diss., University of Hawai'i.

Tucker, Bram, and Alyson G. Young. 2005. "Growing up Mikea: Children's Time Allocation and Tuber Foraging in Southwestern Madagascar." In *Hunter-Gatherer Childhoods: Evolutionary, Developmental, and Cultural Perspectives*, edited by Barry S. Hewlett and Michael E. Lamb, pp. 147–171. New Brunswick, NJ: Aldine/Transaction Publishers.

Tulkin, Steven R. 1977. "Social Class Differences in Maternal and Infant Behavior." In *Culture and Infancy: Variations in the Human Experience*, edited by P. Herbert Leiderman, Steven R. Tulkin, and Anne Rosenfeld, pp. 495–537. New York: Academic Press.

Turnbull, Colin M. 1965. *The M'buti Pygmies: An Ethnographic Survey*. New York: American Museum of Natural History.

Tuzin, Donald. 1980. *The Voice of the Tambaran: Truth and Illusion in Ilahita Arapesh Religion*. Berkeley: University of California Press.

Turke, Paul W. 1988. "Helpers at the Nest: Childcare Networks on Ifaluk." In *Human Reproductive Behavior*, edited by Laura Betzig, Monique Borgerhoff Mulder, and Paul Turke, pp. 173–188. Cambridge: Cambridge University Press.

Turnbull, Colin M. 1961. *The Forest People*. New York: Simon and Schuster.

Turnbull, Colin M. 1965. *The Mbuti Pygmies: An Ethnographic Survey*. New York: American Museum of Natural History.

Turnbull, Colin M. 1978. "The Politics of Non-Aggression." In *Learning Non-Aggression: The Experience of Non-Literate Societies*, edited by Ashley Montague, pp. 161–221. Oxford: Oxford University Press.

Ullrich, Hellen E. 2017. *The Women of Totagadde: Broken Silence*. New York: Palgrave Macmillan.

UNICEF Data. 2022. "Education: Primary Education." Updated June 2022. https://data.unicef.org/topic/education/primary-education/

Uno, Kathleen S. 1991. "Japan." In *Children in Historical and Comparative Perspective*, edited by Joseph M. Hawes and N. Ray Hiner, pp. 389–419. Westport, CT: Greenwood Press.

REFERENCES 265

Uziel, Joe, and Rona S. Avissar Lewis. 2013. "The Tel Nagila Middle Bronze Age Homes—Studying Household Activities and Identifying Children in the Archaeological Record." *Palestine Exploration Quarterly* 145(4): 268. doi:10.1179/0031032813Z.00000000070

van Gennep, Arnold. 1908/1960. *The Rites of Passage*. Chicago: University of Chicago Press.

Van Groningen, Derk 2023. *Kilenge: A Pictorial Ethnography*. Wiesbaden, Germany: Harrosswitz Verlag.

Vandermaas-Peeler, Maureen, Jackie Nelson, Melissa von der Heide, and Erica Kelly. 2009. "Parental Guidance with Four-Year-Olds in Literacy and Play Activities at Home." In *From Children to Red Hatters*, edited by David Kuschner, pp. 93–112. Lanham, MD: University Press of America.

Veldhuis, Niek. 2011. "Levels of Literacy." In *The Oxford Handbook of Cuneiform Culture*, edited by Karen Radner and Eleanor Robson, pp. 68–89. Oxford: Oxford University Press.

Vermonden, Daniel. 2009. "Reproduction and Development of Expertise within Communities of Practice: A Case Study of Fishing Activities in South Buton." In *Landscape, Process, and Power: Re-Evaluating Traditional Environmental Knowledge*, Studies in Environmental Anthropology and Ethnobiology, edited by Serena Heckler, pp. 205–229. Oxford: Berghahn Books.

Vinden, Penelope G. 1999. "Children's Understanding of Mind and Emotion: A Multi-Culture Study." *Cognition and Emotion* 13(1): 19–48. https://psycnet.apa.org/record/1999-00731-002

Voeks, Robert A., and Angela Leony. 2004. "Forgetting the Forest: Assessing Medicinal Plant Erosion in Eastern Brazil." *Economic Botany* 58: 294–306. doi:10.1663/0013-0001(2004)58[S294:FTFAMP]2.0.CO;2

Vogt, Paul, J. Douglas Mastin, and Diede M. A. Schots. 2015. "Communicative Intentions of Child-Directed Speech in Three Different Learning Environments: Observations from the Netherlands, and Rural and Urban Mozambique." *First Language* 35(4–5): 341–358.

Vygotsky, Lev. (1930) 1978. *Mind in Society*. Cambridge, MA: Harvard University Press.

Wagley, Charles. 1977. *Welcome of Tears: The Tapirapé Indians of Central Brazil*. New York: Oxford University Press.

Waldfogel, Jane. 2006. *What Children Need*. Cambridge, MA: Harvard University Press.

Walker, Harry. 2013. *Under a Watchful Eye: Self, Power, and Intimacy in Amazonia*. Berkeley: University of California Press.

Wallaert, Hélène. 2001. "Learning How to Make the Right Pots: Apprenticeship Strategies and Material Culture, a Case Study in Handmade Pottery from Cameroon." *Journal of Anthropological Research* 57(4): 471–493.

Wallaert, Hélène. 2008. "The Way of the Potter's Mother: Apprenticeship Strategies among Dii Potters from Cameroon, West Africa." In *Cultural Transmission and Material Culture: Breaking Down Boundaries*, edited by Miriam T. Start, Brenda J. Bowser, and Lee Horne, pp. 178–198. Tucson: The University of Arizona Press.

Wallaert, Hélène. 2012. "Apprenticeship and the Confirmation of Social Boundaries." In *Archaeology and Apprenticeship: Body Knowledge, Identity, and Communities of Practice*, edited by Willeke Wendrich, pp. 20–42. Tucson: University of Arizona Press.

Warneken, Felix. 2015. "Precocious Prosociality: Why Do Young Children Help?" *Child Development Perspectives* 9(1): 1–6.

266 REFERENCES

Warrick, Gary. 1984. "Reconstructing Ontario Iroquois Village Organization." Mercury Series, Paper 124, National Museum of Man, Archaeological Survey of Canada, National Museum of Canada, Ottawa.

Watson-Gegeo, Karen Ann. 2001. "Fantasy and Reality: The Dialectic of Work and Play in Kwara'ae Children's Lives." *Ethos* 29(2): 138–158.

Watson-Gegeo, Karen A., and David W. Gegeo. 1989. "The Role of Sibling Interaction in Child Socialization." In *Sibling Interaction Across Cultures*, edited by Patricia G. Zukow, pp. 54–76. New York: Springer-Verlag.

Watson-Gegeo, Karen A., and David W. Gegeo. 1992. "Schooling, Knowledge, and Power: Social Transformation in the Solomon Islands." *Anthropology and Education Quarterly* 23: 10–29.

Wayne, Derrick. 2001. *Bushman of the Kalahari: A Bushman Story*. Princeton, NJ: Discovery Channel Video.

Weber, Ann, Anne Fernald, and Yatma Diop. 2017. "When Cultural Norms Discourage Talking to Babies: Effectiveness of a Parenting Program in Rural Senegal." *Child Development* 88: 1513–1526.

Weisfeld, Glenn E., and Harold E. Linkey. 1985. "Dominance Displays as Indicators of a Social Success Motive." In *Power, Dominance, and Nonverbal Behavior*, edited by Steve L. Ellyson and John F. Dovidio, pp. 109–128. New York: Springer-Verlag.

Weisner, Thomas S. 1996. "Why Ethnography Should Be the Most Important Method in the Study of Human Development." In *Ethnography and Human Development: Context and Meaning in Social Inquiry*, edited by Richard Jessor, Anne Colby, and Richard W. Shweder, pp. 305–324. Chicago: University of Chicago Press.

Weisner, Thomas S., and Ronald Gallimore. 1977. "My Brother's Keeper: Child and Sibling Caretaking." *Current Anthropology* 18: 169–190.

Wenger, Etienne. 1999. *Communities of Practice: Learning, Meaning, and Identity*. Cambridge: Cambridge University Press.

Wenger, Martha. 1989. "Work, Play and Social Relationships among Children in a Giriama Community." In *Children's Social Networks and Social Supports*, edited by Deborah Belle, pp. 91–115. New York: Wiley.

Werbner, Pnina. 2009. "The Hidden Lion: Tswapong Girls' Puberty Rituals and the Problem of History." *American Ethnologist* 36: 441–458.

West, Elliott, and Paula Petrik, eds. 1992. *Small Worlds: Children and Adolescents in America, 1850–1950*. Lawrence: University Press of Kansas.

White, Ben. 2012. "Changing Childhoods: Javanese Village Children in Three Generations." *Journal of Agrarian Change* 12: 81–97.

White, Merry I. 2002. *Perfectly Japanese: Making Families in an Era of Upheaval*. Berkeley: University of California Press.

White, Robert W. 1959. "Motivation Reconsidered: The Concept of Competence." *Psychological Review* 66: 297–333.

White, William A. 1946. *The Autobiography of William Allen White*. New York: Macmillan.

White, J. Peter, Nicholas Modjeska, and Irari Hipuya. 1977. "Group Definitions and Mental Templates." In *Stone Tools as Cultural Markers*, edited by R. V. S. Wright, pp. 380–390. Atlantic Highlands, NJ: Humanities Press.

Whiten, Andrew, and Penny Milner. 1984. "The Educational Experiences of Nigerian Infants." In *Nigerian Children: Developmental Perspectives*, edited by H. Valerie Curran, pp. 34–73. London: Routledge & Kegan Paul.

REFERENCES 267

Whiten, Andrew, Victoria Horner, and Sarah Marchall-Pescini. 2003. "Cultural Panthropology." *Evolutionary Anthropology* 12: 92–105.

Whiting, Beatrice B., and Carolyn P. Edwards. 1988. *Children of Different Worlds: The Formation of Social Behavior.* Cambridge, MA: Harvard University Press.

Whittemore, Robert D. 1989. "Child Caregiving and Socialization to the Mandinka Way: Toward an Ethnography of Childhood." Unpublished PhD diss., UCLA.

Weiss, Florence. 1993. "Von der Schwierigkeit, Über Kinder zu forshen. Die Iatmul in Papue Neuginea." In *Kinder: Ethnologische Forschungen in Fünf Kontinenten*, edited by Marie-Jose van de Loo and Margaret Reinhart, pp. 96–153. München, Germany: Trickster Verlag.

Wiessner, Polly W. 2014. "Embers of Society: Firelight Talk among the Ju/'hoansi Bushmen." *PNAS* 111: 14027–14035.

Wikipedia. 2023a. "Pedagogy." Updated January 9, 2023. Accessed January 14, 2023. https://en.wikipedia.org/wiki/Pedagogy

Wikipedia. 2023b. "Indigenous Peoples." Updated January 22, 2023. Accessed January 23, 2023. https://en.wikipedia.org/wiki/Indigenous_peoples

Wilbert, Johannes. 1976. "To Become a Maker of Canoes: An Essay in Warao Enculturation." In *Enculturation in Latin America*, edited by Johannes Wilbert, pp. 303–358. Los Angeles: UCLA Latin American Center Publications.

Willemsen, Annemarieke. 2008. *Back to the Schoolyard: The Daily Practice of Medieval and Renaissance Education.* Turnhout, Belgium: Brepols Publishers N.V.

Willerslev, Rane. 2007. *Soul Hunters: Hunting, Animism, and Personhood among the Siberian Yukaghirs.* Berkeley: University of California Press.

Williams, Ronald J. 1972. "Scribal Training in Ancient Egypt." *Journal of the American Oriental Society* 92(2): 214–221.

Williams, Thomas R. 1969. *A Borneo Childhood: Enculturation in Dusun Society.* New York: Holt, Rinehart, and Winston.

Wimsatt, William C., and James R. Griesemer. 2007. "Re-producing Entrenchments to Scaffold Culture: The Central Role of Development in Cultural Evolution." In *Integrating Evolution and Development: From Theory to Practice*, edited by Roger Sansome and Robert Brandon, pp. 228–323. Cambridge, MA: MIT Press.

Wober, Mallory M. 1972. "Culture and the Concept of Intelligence: A Case in Uganda." *Journal of Cross-Cultural Psychology* 3: 327–328.

Wolfenstein, Martha. 1955. "Fun Morality: An Analysis of Recent American Child-Training Literature." In *Childhood in Contemporary Cultures*, edited by Margaret Mead and Martha Wolfenstein, pp. 168–178. Chicago: University of Chicago Press.

Wright, David, and Hana Karar. 2010. "Prenatal Learning Products Draw Expert Skepticism." *ABC News: Nightline*, January 8, 2010. Accessed October 3, 2022. https://abcnews.go.com/Nightline/science-skeptical-prenatal-products/story?id=9513543

Wyndham, Felice S. 2010. "Environments of Learning: Rarámuri Children's Plant Knowledge and Experience of Schooling, Family, and Landscapes in the Sierra Tarahumara, Mexico." *Human Ecology* 38: 87–99.

Wynn, Thomas. 1993. "Layers of Thinking in Tool Behavior." In *Tools, Language and Cognition in Human Evolution*, edited by Kathleen R. Gibson and Tim Ingold, pp. 389–406. Cambridge: Cambridge University Press.

Yale University. N.d. "Human Relations Area Files: Cultural Information for Education and Research." Accessed December 27, 2022. https://hraf.yale.edu/

268 REFERENCES

Young-Bruehl, Elisabeth. 2012. *Childism: Confronting Prejudice against Children*. New Haven, CT: Yale University Press.

Young, Frank W. 1985. *Initiation Ceremonies: A Cross-Cultural Study of Status Dramatization*. New York: Macmillan.

Yousafzai, Malala. 2013. *I Am Malala*. New York: Little, Brown.

Yovsi, Relindis D. 2014. "Parenting among the Nso of the Northwest Province of Cameroon." In *Parenting Across Cultures: Childrearing, Motherhood and Fatherhood in Non-Western Cultures*, edited by Helaine Selin, pp. 253–266. Cham, Switzerland: Springer.

Zarger, Rebecca K. 2002a. "Acquisition and Transmission of Subsistence Knowledge by Q'eqchi' Maya in Belize." In *Ethnogioloby and Biocultural Diversity*, edited by John R. Stepp, Felice S. Wyndham, and Rebecca Zarger, pp. 592–603. Athens, CA: International Society of Ethnobiology.

Zarger, Rebecca K. 2002b. "Children's Ethnoecological Knowledge: Situated Learning and the Cultural Transmission of Subsistence Knowledge and Skills among Q'eqchi' Maya." Unpublished PhD diss., University of Georgia.

Zarger, Rebecca K. 2011. "Learning Ethnobiology: Creating Knowledge and Skills about the Living World." In *Ethnobiology*, edited by Eugene N. Anderson, Deborah M. Pearsall, Eugene S. Hunn, and Nancy J. Turner, pp. 371–387. New York: Wiley-Blackwell.

Zelazo, Phillip R., Nancy A. Zelazo, and Sarah Kolb. 1972. "'Walking' in the Newborn." *Science* 176: 314–315.

Zelizer, Viviana A. 1985. *Pricing the Priceless Child: The Changing Social Value of Children*. New York: Basic Books.

Zeller, Anne C. 1987. "A Role for Children in Hominid Evolution." *Man* 22: 528–557.

Zent, Stanford. 2001. "Acculturation and Ethnobiological Knowledge Loss among the Piaroa of Venezuela." In *Biocultural Diversity: Linking Language, Knowledge and the Environment*, edited by Luisa Maffi, pp. 190–211. Washington, DC: Smithsonian Institute Press.

Zernike, Kate. 2011. "Fast-Tracking to Kindergarten?" *New York Times*, May 13. Accessed September 25, 2002. http://www.nytimes.com/2011/05/15/fashion/with-kumon-fast-tracking-to-kindergarten.html?_r=1&emc=eta1

Zero to Three. 2022. "Early Learning." Accessed October 3, 2022. https://www.zerototh ree.org/issue-areas/early-learning/

Zukow, Patricia G. 1984. "Folk Theories of Comprehension and Caregiver Practices in a Rural-Born Population in Central Mexico." *The Quarterly Newsletter of the Laboratory of Comparative Human Cognition* 6: 62–67.

Index

For the benefit of digital users, indexed terms that span two pages (e.g., 52–53) may, on occasion, appear on only one of those pages.
Tables, Figures are indicated by an *t, f* following the page/paragraph number

Aari people, 61–62, 104–5
Abelam people, 147
academic intelligence, 198–202
Aché people, 76
Afikpo people, 151
after-school periods, 188
Agta people, 92, 107–8, 195, 197
Aka people, 11, 33*b*–34, 53*b*, 55, 90, 99n.3, 107, 130, 153, 157–58, 205
Akwete Ibo people, 126–27, 140–41
Alcalá, Lucia, 68
alloparenting, 43n.9
American Educational Research Association, 1–2
American Sign Language, 25, 182
Amhara people, 130
Amish, 167n.12
Apache people, 111
apprenticeships
    generally, 20–21, 59*b*, 175–76, 216
    autonomy and, 144
    crafts and, 140, 143
    defined, 139
    families and, 141–42
    gatekeeping mechanisms, 140–41
    "graduation" from, 145–46
    initiation rites compared, 150–51
    masters, 142
    observation and, 142–43
    paradox in, 139–40
    punishment in, 144
    secrecy in, 145
Arapesh people, 153, 154–55
Araucanian people, 202
Araweté people, 161
Argenti, Nicolas, 71–72

Aristotle, 20
artifacts, 61–65
asocial learning, 69
Assaf, Ella, 61–62, 99
"Assembly-Line Instruction," 205–6
Atran, Scott, 1
Attachment Reconsidered: Cultural Perspectives on a Western Theory (Quinn and Mageo), 208–9
attachment theory, 49
attention, management of, 202–6
Atzompa people, 103–4, 119
Australia, "chore curriculum" in, 193
autonomy
    generally, 5
    apprenticeships and, 144
    everyday classrooms, in, 105
    foraging, 73*b*–74*b*
    playgroups, 85

babies. *See* infant education
BabyPlus, 27–28
"Baby Signs", 25, 182
"baby talk," 26, 30–35, 212
Bacchiddu, Giovanna, 52–53
Bagwell, Elizabeth A., 103
Baining people, 118
Bakalanga people, 186
Baka people, 53–54, 69, 88n.1, 92, 150–51
Bakkarwal people, 129, 152
Baktaman people, 147–48, 149
Bamana people, 19, 58, 61–62, 67–68, 111, 120–21, 123, 171
Bamangwato people, 45*b*
Bangladesh, lesson creep in, 185
Bara people, 38, 70

270 INDEX

Barrett, Clark, 209
Barth, Fredrik, 149
basketmaking, 101n.5
Basotho people, 45*b*
Batek people, 55
Battiste, Marie, 53–54
Baulé people, 126–27
BaYaka people, 44*b*, 58, 95, 97, 122, 126, 128, 153–54, 157, 192, 195
bedtime stories, 79–80
Bengali people, 121, 130
Bentz, Bonnie, 153
Bequia Island, 196
Biersack, Aletta, 154–55
Bimin-Kuskusmin people, 148
Bird-David, Nurit, 8, 66, 109
Bjorklund, David, 30, 49–50, 64, 159
blacksmiths, 85–86
Bofi people, 90–91
Boko Haram, 174
Bolin, Inge, 122
Bonawitz, Elizabeth, 74
Bonerate people, 33*b*, 97, 152
Bourgeois, Kristine, 63
Boyd, Robert, 47
Bozo people, 140–41
Braff, Danielle, 183
Brahmin people, 178
Brandl, Eva, 209–10
Brazil
  "pitching in" in, 67–68
  traditional ecological knowledge (TEK) in, 195
Briggs, Jean L., 125, 127–28
Bright from the Start: The Simple, Science-Backed Way to Nurture Your Child's Developing Mind from Birth to Age 3 (Stamm), 28
Broch, Harald B., 97
Bronfenbrenner, Uri, 5n.3
Brooks, Douglas, 142
Brown, Penelope, 39
Bruner, Jerome S., 11, 54n.3
Buckingham, David, 184–85
"bush schools." *See* initiation rites
butchering, 109
Buton Island, 11, 123, 200

calming, 35–36

Cambodian people, 167–68
Cameroon, apprenticeships in, 140–41
Canela people, 150
canoes, 119–20
Cashdan, Elizabeth, 90
Casimir, Michael J., 36, 122
Castañeda, Nuria, 98
Center for Applied Anthropology, 210
Chabu people, 70–71, 114, 157
Chaga people, 79, 120–21
Chewa people, 116
Chiga people, 128, 171
child-as-agent perspective, 8
child circulation, 47n.11
child-directed speech, 38–40
"children's culture," 9, 84
Chiloé Island, 52–53
China
  Cultural Revolution, 167
  fetal instruction in, 27
  resistance to schooling in, 167
"chore curriculum"
  generally, 8, 17–19, 106–7, 217
  butchering example, 109
  canoe example, 119–20
  components of, 107–9
  crafts in, 19
  curriculum construed, 107–8
  decline of, 191–93
  errand running, 18, 113–16, 117
  failures of, 129–31
  gender differences in, 116–17, 126–27, 131–32, 217
  hunting example, 111
  identity, work and, 124–27
  informality of, 108–9
  "ladders," 107–8
  low threshold of, 113
  managing young workers, 130
  mandatory versus optional work, 106–7
  mentors and, 18–19
  middle childhood, in, 127–29
  milestones, 19, 126
  mortar and pestle example, 110
  "opting out," 129–31
  path to mastery, 110–12
  "pitching in" and, 109, 113
  planting example, 111–12
  play and, 17–18, 110, 112–13, 114

INDEX 271

reliable workers, children as, 129
role models and, 18–19, 120–22
self-esteem and, 125–26
shepherding example, 110
strategic intervention, 122–24
transition from play to work, 116–20
variability in, 131–32
"watch and learn," 108
Chutes and Ladders, 79
circumcision, 147–48
cognitive development, 30, 200–1
Cole, Michael, 198
collaboration, 66–67
collaborative learning, 206–8
collectivism, individualism versus, 8–9
communities of practice, 99
Conambo people, 75, 123
Cooper, Eugene, 140
core knowledge, 5
COVID-19 pandemic, 159n.9, 185
Coy, Michael W., 139
crafts
apprenticeships and, 140, 143
"chore curriculum," in, 19
innovation and, 72, 75
lost skills, 194, 196
Crago, Martha, 203–4
Cree people, 194
Csibra, György, 157–58
cultural anthropology, 6–7
culturally responsive schooling
(CRS), 197–98
cultural models, 8–9
cultural practices, 8
culture
distributed, as, 9
importance of, 4
Cunnar, Geoffrey E., 98
curiosity, 57

Davis, Helen, 201
Deák, Gedeon O., 63
declarative information, 199
de Haan, Mariëtte, 3, 183
Dennell, Robin, 100
Depaepe, Marc, 181
Deschooling Society (Illich), 187
developmental niches, 8, 16, 80–81
de Waal, Franz, 67

Dickens, Charles, 134–36
didactic method of teaching, 185–86
Dii people, 60, 104
Dilley, Roy M., 145
Dio Chrysostom, 138–39
Dioula people, 143
direct experience, 53–54, 213
Djenné people, 138–39, 145, 196
Dominica Island, 117
Donley-Reid, Linda W., 90
Dorland, Steven G., 102–3, 103n.6
Doumbia, Noumouké, 95
Dowayo people, 144, 145–46
Draper, Patricia, 90
Duffett, Ann, 190
Duha people, 200
Dunn, Judy, 157–58
Dusun people, 54–55

"Early Childhood Development Kits," 185
"Early Math Counts," 184
early schools, 135–39
eavesdropping, 56–57
Edel, May M., 128
educational play, 14
Efe people, 202
Egypt, early schools in, 135–36, 137
Einarsdóttir, Jónina, 124
Ellis, Elizabeth M., 86
Eluama people, 36
Ember, Carol, 131
emulation, 57–60, 95–96
Endicott, Karen L., 55
Endicott, Kirk M., 55
Erasmus, 22, 187
errand running, 18, 113–16, 117
Ese Eja people, 34b
ethnography, 6–7
ethnotheories, 8, 214
everyday classrooms
generally, 16–17, 82–83
autonomy in, 105
communities of practice, 99
developmental niches, 8, 16
family circle, 88–91 (See also family
circle)
forest, learning in, 92–93
make-believe, 17, 85
mother ground, 84, 85, 90

272 INDEX

everyday classrooms (*cont.*)
    natural classrooms, 216–17
    nonparticipants, learning as, 96
    observation and, 94–96
    playgroups, 83–88 (*See also*
        playgroups)
    rituals as, 94–96, 97
    social gatherings as, 94–96
    stone toolmaking sites as, 97–100, 217
    workshops, 100–5 (*See also*
        workshops)

Fais Island, 114
families
    apprenticeships and, 141–42
    pedagogization of, 183–85
family circle
    example, 88–89
    foraging and, 90–91
    kinship and, 89
    mother ground and, 90
    social learning in, 89
Fassoulas, Argyris, 52
Featherstone, Sally, 182
fetal instruction, 27–28
Fiji
    observation in, 58
    ritual in, 97
Fiske, Alan, 5, 154
Fiske, Alan P., 148
foraging
    autonomous foragers, 73b–74b
    family circle and, 90–91
    innovation and, 72, 73b–74b
forest, learning in, 92–93
formal education, 7
Friedl, Erika, 35–36
Frost, Ginger S., 134
future research, 23–24, 208–10

Ganda people, 58
Gapun people, 33b, 167, 190–91
Gardiner, Amy K., 64
Gaskins, Suzanne, 67, 96, 202
Gato, John, 203n.10
Gau Island, 42
Gbusi people, 147, 154
Geary, David C., 159

gender differences
    "chore curriculum," in, 116–17, 126–27,
        131–32, 217
    initiation rites, in, 153
    role models, in, 70
    structured learning, in, 173–75
    workshops, in, 100–1, 102
Gergely, György, 157–58
Germany
    collaborative learning in, 206–7
    school–village conflict in, 167–68
Ghana, collaborative learning in, 207
Giri, Birendra, 172
Giriama people, 125, 129–30
Gisu people, 149
Gladwin, Thomas, 157
global WEIRDing
    generally, 21–24, 179–81, 218
    lesson creep, 181–90 (*See also* lesson
        creep)
    lost skills, 190–98 (*See also* lost skills)
    schooled mind, 198–208 (*See also*
        schooled mind)
Goldschmidt, Walter, 151
Gonja people, 141–42
Goody, Esther N., 113, 141–42
Greece
    apprenticeships in, 143, 144
    early schools in, 137
Greenfield, Patricia M., 7, 71, 175, 200–1
Grendler, Paul R., 138
Griesemer, James, 82
Guara people, 115
Guatemala
    "chore curriculum" in, 111–12, 191
    errand running in, 115
    "pitching in" in, 65
guilds, 140n.2
Guinea, physical punishment in, 168
Gusii people, 35–36, 130
Gutiérrez, Kris, 189

Hadza people, 70, 87–88, 92, 114, 117, 118,
    122, 123, 126–27, 153, 158, 195
Hagstrum, Melissa B., 62
Hall, Granville, 208–9
Hampton, O.W. "Bud," 98
Hanawalt, Barbara A., 133

Hansen, Judith F., 168–69
Harkness, Sara, 84
Hatano, Giyoo, 159n.8
Hausa people, 33b, 139–40, 174
Hawcroft, Jennie, 100
Hays, Jennifer, 135, 163
Heckler, Serena L., 195
Heine, Stephen J., 4–5
Hemingway, Ernest, 155
Hendry, Jean C., 104, 119
Henrich, Joseph, 4–5, 208–9
Hewlett, Barry S., 153–54
Hewlett, Bonnie, 55, 90
*The Hidden Curriculum of Compulsory
    Schooling* (Gato), 203n.10
hierarchy
    avoiding, 53b
    initiation rites and, 178
    structured learning and, 169, 177–78
Highland Maya people, 71
Hilger, M. Inez, 202
Hobart, Angela, 94
Hogbin, H. Ian, 112–13
Holt, John, 187–88
homework, 80
Hopi people, 44b, 152
Huaorani people, 48, 66
Human Relations Area Files, 6–7, 210
hunting, 87–88, 88n.1, 111
Huron people, 75

identity, work and, 124–27
Ijo people, 154
Ikenwèn people, 52
Illich, Ivan, 187
Imbonggu people, 165–67
imitation, 57–60, 95–96, 215
India
    lesson creep in, 183n.4
    play in, 37–38
    structured learning in, 172–73
indigenous defined, 13
indigenous pedagogy. *See also specific
    people; specific topic*
    indigenes as poor research subjects, 211
    methodology of study, 6–7
    principles of, 59b
    terminology, 10–13

theory, 7–10
WEIRD education contrasted, 211–18
indirect chains of support, 120–21
individualism
    collectivism versus, 8–9
    WEIRD, in, 8–9, 26, 57
infant-directed speech (IDS), 14
infant education
    generally, 13–15, 25–27, 49–50
    "baby talk," 26, 30–35, 212
    calming versus stimulating, 35–36
    caretakers and, 28
    child-directed speech, 38–40
    cognitive development and, 30
    fetal instruction, 27–28
    infant-directed speech (IDS) and, 14
    kinship, 43–45, 44b
    "motherese," 26
    mother's education, relevance of, 32–35
    "Mozart effect," 27
    neuroscience and, 30
    overhearing, 40–41
    pattern detection training, 29f, 29–30
    "pitching in" and, 48–49
    play in, 14, 36–38, 213
    prosocial behavior and, 14
    sensitive responsiveness, 39–40
    sharing, 46
    social acceleration, 26–27, 41–43, 212
    social behavior, 45b–46b, 47
    social integration, 212
    speech development, 32
    swaddling and, 36
    untutored babies, 33b–35b
    walking, 42
    weaning, 42–43
    WEIRD, in, 25–26, 31–35
    womb education, 27–28
    work and, 48–49
informal education, 7
Ingold, Tim, 78, 82
initiation rites
    generally, 20, 147, 154, 176
    apprenticeships compared, 150–51
    gender differences in, 153
    "graduation," 150–51
    hierarchy and, 178
    purposes of, 151–55

274 INDEX

initiation rites (*cont.*)
  ritual in, 149–50
  secrecy in, 149–50
  setting apart, 147–49
innovation
  crafts and, 72, 75
  foraging and, 72, 73*b*–74*b*
  self-starting learners and, 71–75, 216
interdisciplinary approach, 6, 209
Inuit people, 44*b*, 58, 62n.4, 74*b*, 77,
  111, 114, 125, 127–28, 171, 185–86,
  193, 203–4
Iran
  calming in, 35–36
  crafts in, 75
Islam, 149n.6, 174–75
Izquierdo, Carolina, 66

Japan
  apprenticeships in, 59*b*, 142, 143
  collaborative learning in, 207
  fetal instruction in, 27
  initiation rites in, 150–51
  lesson creep in, 183–84
  social behavior in, 45*b*
Jarawa people, 93
Java
  calming in, 35–36
  "chore curriculum" in, 191
  fetal instruction in, 28
  social behavior in, 45*b*
  structured learning in, 173
Jenu Kuruba people, 195, 196
Jiménez-Balam, Deira, 66–67
Johnson, Jean, 190
Jordan, Fiona M., 89
journeymen, 145–46
Ju|'hoansi people, 35–36, 92, 164, 176–77

Kaland, Sigrid H., 48
Kaluli people, 34*b*
Kamea people, 154
Kammu people, 87, 100–1
Kamp, Katheryn A., 102–3, 104
Kaneko, Morie, 102, 104–5
Kanō people, 140–41
Kaoka people, 112–13, 126
Kaugel people, 152

Kayapó people, 161
Keil, Frank C., 157–58
Keller, Charles, 142–43
Keller, Heidi, 49, 206–7
Kenya, infant education in, 32–35
Kerkenneh Islands, 127
Khanty people, 114
kindergarten, 187
Kinkead, Joyce, 162n.10
kinship, 43–45, 44*b*, 89
Kipsigi people, 128
Knauft, Bruce, 147
Kogi people, 42, 156
Köhler, Iris, 103
Kokwet people, 84
Korea, fetal instruction in, 27
Kosrea Island, 192
Köster, Moritz, 91
Kpeenbele Senufo people, 141
Kpelle people, 84, 85–86, 94, 106–7, 110,
  116, 148–49, 150, 151, 160, 169–70
Kramer, Karen L., 117, 209–10
Kramer, Samuel N., 137
Kremer-Sadlik, Tamar, 189
Kumon North America, 186–87
!Kung people, 11, 42, 46, 53*b*, 90, 95, 108
Kusasi people, 114, 196
Kuttab schools, 149n.6
Kwara'ae people, 44*b*
Kyrgyz people, 40–41, 53*b*

lab science, 209n.13
"ladders," 107–8
The Ladybird Book of Handwriting
  (Gourdie), 162n.10
Lancy, David F., 77, 139, 160
Lapp people, 126
Lave, Jean, 7, 144, 175
learning cultures, 7
Lego, 185
Lese people, 156
lesson creep
  generally, 22, 180
  after-school periods and, 188
  COVID-19 pandemic, effect of, 185
  didactic method of teaching, 185–86
  "Early Childhood Development Kits," 185
  family, pedagogization of, 183–85

INDEX 275

kindergarten, in, 187
neuroscience and, 182
play and, 182–83
preschools, in, 186–87
reading, in, 190
recess and, 188
resistance to, 187
sports and, 188
"unschooling" and, 187–88
lessons defined, 10, 11–12
LeVine, Robert A., 173–74, 186
Lewis, Jerome, 156
Lew-Levy, Sheina, 72, 122
Liberia
  apprenticeships in, 144
  self-starting learners in, 76–77
  structured learning in, 169–70
  village schools in, 159–60
Lindell, Kristina, 87
listening, 56–57
livestock, 86
Locke, John, 49–50
Lofoten Islands, 74*b*
lost skills
  generally, 22–23, 180, 190–91
  "chore curriculum," decline of, 191–93
  crafts, 194, 196
  culturally responsive schooling (CRS)
    and, 197–98
  natural environment, withdrawal from,
    193–94, 195–96
  traditional ecological knowledge (TEK),
    11n.4, 11, 180, 194, 195, 197
  village schools and, 197–98
Lovevery, 29–30
Luo people, 131
Luria, Alexander, 199
Lurs people, 196

Maasai people, 55–56, 86, 93, 154, 195
Madagascar, "chore curriculum"
  in, 119–20
make-believe, 17, 85
Malaita Island, 164–65
Mande people, 143, 145
Mandinka people, 44*b*, 46, 83–84
Maninka people, 94–95, 96
Manu people, 157

Maori people, 58
Mapuche people, 33*b*
Marchand, Trevor, 138–39
Mardu people, 154
Maretzki, Hatsumi, 88–89
Maretzki, Thomas W., 88–89
Marlowe, Frank W., 153
Marquesas Islands, 121, 171
Martinez-Rodriguez, Maria R., 160–61
Martu people, 117
masters, 142
Matses people, 76, 161–62
Matsigena people, 108–9, 130
Mayangna people, 91
Maya people, 59*b*, 66–68, 120–21, 130,
  185–86, 196, 211
Maynard, Ashley E., 71
Mazahua people, 3, 33*b*, 40, 43, 59*b*, 78,
  116, 167–68, 171, 192n.8
Mbendjele people, 53*b*, 108–9, 170, 172
Mbuti people, 78, 93, 126
Mbya Guarani people, 73*b*
McNaughton, Peter R., 145
Mead, Margaret, 7, 113–14, 150, 157,
  205, 208–9
Medaets, Chantal V., 67–68, 89–90
Mehinacu people, 41–42, 97, 150
Mellor, Maureen, 102–3
Menander, 20
Menominee people, 194
mentors, 18–19
Meriam people, 78, 121
Mesopotamia, early schools in, 136
Mesoudi, Alex, 51
methodology of study, 6–7
Mexico
  "chore curriculum" in, 191–92
  collaborative learning in, 207
  infant education in, 32–35
  lesson creep in, 185–86
  origami study, 3–4, 8, 202–3, 205–6
  "pitching in" in, 65, 68
  puesto study, 2–3, 202
Mezzenzana, Francesca, 109
Mikea-Madagascar people, 73*b*
milestones, 19, 126
Minangkabau people, 40–41
Miskito people, 91

276 INDEX

Mitchell, Alice, 89
Modiano, Nancy, 168
Mongolia, play in, 46*b*
Montessori, Maria, 187
Moore, Richard, 10
Morelli, Camilla, 161–62
Morice, Alain, 144
Morocco, imitation in, 60
mortar and pestle, 110
"motherese," 26
mother ground, 84, 85, 90
Mozambique, child-directed speech in, 40
"Mozart effect," 27
Murphy, William P., 150
Musharbash, Yasmine, 65

Native Americans. *See also specific people*
    collaborative learning, 207
    physical punishment and, 168–69
    resistance to schooling, 167n.12
Nativo, Joseph, 186–87
natural classrooms, 216–17
natural environment, withdrawal from,
    193–94, 195–96
Navaho people, 53*b*
Naveh, Danny, 9, 77
Nayaka people, 34*b*, 59*b*, 66, 77, 78, 109,
    123, 161, 170
Nepal, lesson creep in, 186
Nerlove, Sarah B., 115
Netsilik people, 11, 19, 126
neuroscience, 30, 182
newborns. *See* infant education
Ngaanyatjarra people, 86
Ngandu people, 33*b*–34
Ngoni people, 45*b*
Nicolas Nickleby (Dickens), 135
Nielsen, Mark, 207
Norenzayan, Ara, 4–5
Norway, "chore curriculum" in, 193
Nso people, 39–40, 94
Nuer people, 124
Nukakau Island, 73*b*
Nukak people, 87
Nyae Nyae peple, 162–63, 164
Nyaka people, 8
Nyarafolo people, 141

observation
    apprenticeships and, 142–43

everyday classrooms and, 94–96
    participation versus, 169
    self-starting learners and, 56–57, 58
Ochs, Elinor, 22, 66
Odden, Harold L., 57
Ohmagari, Kayo, 194
Oku people, 71–72
Old Enough (television program), 116n.1
Omura, Keichi, 77, 111
Oneida people, 197
opacity problem, 155–59
opportunity, 135, 172–75
Our Mutual Friend (Dickens), 134–35
overhearing, 40–41
overimitation, 205, 209

Pagel, Mark, 74
Pakistan, structured learning in, 174–75
Pala'wan people, 85
Paliyar people, 129
Papel people, 46, 124
Paradise, Ruth, 3, 43, 202
parental engagement, 22
Pashtun people, 36, 70, 120–22
pattern detection training, 29–30, 29*f*
pedagogical tools, 147–51
pedagogy. *See also specific topic*
    defined, 10, 12–13
    pedagogy in culture, 1
peers as role models, 120–22
Penan people, 78, 200
Philippines
    Department of Education, 197
    Indigenous Peoples Education
        Initiative, 197
Philips, Susan U., 207
physical punishment, 168–69
Piaget, Jean, 128–29, 200–1
Piaroa people, 59*b*, 168, 195
Pigeot, Nicole, 96
pioneers, 53–76
"pitching in"
    "chore curriculum" and, 109, 113
    infant education and, 48–49
    self-starting learners and, 65–69,
        213, 215
planting, 111–12
play
    "chore curriculum" and, 17–18, 110,
        112–13, 114

educational play, 14
indigenous education, in, 37–38
infant education, in, 14, 36–38, 213
lesson creep and, 182–83
self-starting learners and, 79
tools and, 54n.3, 98–99
transition to work, 116–20
WEIRD, in, 36–37
playgroups
generally, 16–17
autonomy of, 85
blacksmith example, 85–86
"children's culture," 84
hunting example, 87–88, 88n.1
livestock example, 86
make-believe, 17, 85
mother ground and, 84, 85
tools in, 87
Po, Tuck, 82
Polak, Rainer, 68, 95, 111, 120–21
Politis, Gustavo G., 87
Pomponio, Ali, 163–64
Ponam Island, 164–65
pottery, 101–5, 103n.6
Powhatan people, 148
practical intelligence, 198–202
Prenatal Education System, 27–28
preschools, 186–87
procedural information, 199
prosocial behavior, 14
Puebloan people, 102
Pumé people, 61, 78, 87–88, 93, 117
Punan Bah people, 78–79
P'urhe'pecha people, 191–92

Q'eqchi' Maya people, 69, 93, 118, 121, 130
Quechua people, 59b, 197

Rabain-Jamin, Jacquelin, 42
Rai, Tage S., 148, 154
Raramuri people, 199
Raroia Island, 117
Raum, Otto F., 120–21
recess, 188
redundancy, 5–6
Reichard, Gladys, 65
resistance to schooling, 21, 164–65, 177
Revel, Nicole A., 85
Richerson, Peter J., 47
Riesman, Paul, 116

risk, 54–56
rituals, 94–96, 97
Rival, Laura M., 48, 66
Rochat, Philippe, 57
Röder, Brigitte, 85
Rogoff, Barbara, 23, 191, 206, 207
role models
adolescents, for, 70–71
"chore curriculum" and, 18–
19, 120–22
gender differences in, 70
middle childhood, in, 70
peers as, 120–22
self-starting learners and, 69–71, 214
toddlers, for, 70
Rome, early schools in, 137–38
Rotuman Island, 79, 164–65
Runa people, 49, 109
Russia, "chore curriculum" in, 125
Rutherford, Markella, 125–26

Saami people, 126
Samburu people, 92
Samoa
errand running in, 113–14
imitation in, 57, 60
infant education in, 33b
"pitching in" in, 65, 66
Sangopari people, 103
San people, 53–54, 69, 74b, 209
"scaffolding," 65, 80
Scanlon, Margaret, 184–85
Schildkrout, Enid, 174
schooled mind
generally, 23, 181, 198
"Assembly-Line Instruction," 205–6
attention, management of, 202–6
collaborative learning, 206–8
declarative versus procedural
information, 199
overimitation, 205, 209
practical versus academic intelligence,
198–202
self-regulation, 204–5
The Scientist in the Crib (Gropnik), 49–50
secrecy
apprenticeships, in, 145
initiation rites, in, 149–50
self-esteem, 125–26
self-regulation, 204–5

278 INDEX

self-starting learners
  generally, 15–16, 51–56
  artifacts and, 61–65
  collaboration and, 66–67
  core beliefs, 52–56
  crafts and, 72, 75
  curiosity and, 57
  developmental niches, 80–81
  direct experience and, 53–54, 213
  eavesdropping, 56–57
  emulation, 57–60
  foraging and, 72, 73*b*–74*b*
  hierarchy, avoiding, 53*b*
  imitation, 57–60, 215
  innovation and, 71–75, 216
  listening, 56–57
  observation, 56–57, 58
  pioneers, 53–76
  "pitching in" and, 65–69, 213, 215
  play and, 79
  risk and, 54–56
  role models and, 69–71, 214
  social capital and, 65–66, 215
  "strategic rejection" and, 67–69, 216
  teaching, avoiding, 75–81, 213, 216
  things, learning from, 61–65
  tools and, 54n.3, 61–65, 214–15
  WEIRD, in, 51–52, 54
  work and, 65–69
Senegal
  infant education in, 34*b*
  observation in, 59*b*
sensitive responsiveness, 39–40
Serpell, Robert, 159n.8
sharing, 46
sharing knowledge, 170
shepherding, 110
Shepler, Susan, 171–72
Shore, Brad, 149
Shostak, Marjorie, 25, 108
Siassi Islands, 164–67
silo effect, 4–5
Simenel Bonnie, 60
Smeyers, Paul, 181
social acceleration, 26–27, 41–43, 212
social behavior, 45*b*–46*b*, 47
social capital, 65–66, 215
social gatherings, 94–96
social integration, 212

social learning
  generally, 69
  family circle, in, 89
Solomon, Olga, 30–31
Solomon Islands, 190–91
Soninke people, 35*b*
Sonoda, Koji, 192
sources of data, 2
speech development, 32
Sperber, Dan, 1
Spindel, Carol, 141
Spittler, Gerd, 110
sports, 188
Sprott, Julie W., 106
Stamm, Jill, 28
stimulating, 35–36
Stone Age, stone toolmaking sites from, 97–100, 217
stone toolmaking sites, 97–100, 217
strategic intervention, 122–24
"strategic rejection," 67–69, 216
structured learning
  generally, 20–21, 133, 217–18
  apprenticeships, 138–46 (*See also* apprenticeships)
  "bush schools" (*See* initiation rites)
  conforming to expectations, 152
  early schools, 135–39
  gender differences in, 173–75
  hierarchy and, 169, 177–78
  historical background, 20–21
  impact of, 175–78
  initiation rites, 147–51, 154 (*See also* initiation rites)
  observation versus participation, 169
  opacity problem, 155–59
  opportunity and, 172–75
  pedagogical tools, 147–51
  physical punishment in, 168–69
  resistance to, 21, 164–65, 177
  sharing knowledge, 170
  verbal interaction, 171
  Victorian era, in, 133–35
  views on pedagogy, 167–72
  village schools, 159–63, 197–98
  work versus school, 163–67
Sudbury School, 187–88
Sumer, early schools in, 135–36
Super, Charles M., 84

INDEX 279

swaddling, 36
Swazi people, 128
Sweden, "scaffolding" in, 80

Tahiti, 53*b*
Tainae people, 211
Taira people, 88–89, 122
Takada, Akira, 95
Talensi people, 97
Taliban, 174–75
Tannese people, 185n.5
Tanzania, lesson creep in, 185
Tao people, 211
Tapirapé people, 101, 150
Tarong people, 126–27
Tayanin, Damrong, 87
Tchokwé people, 125
teaching. *See also specific topic*
    defined, 10–11
    self-starting learners, avoiding teaching,
        75–81, 213, 216
teaching cultures, 7
Telefol people, 76
Temne people, 148–49
terminology, 10–13
theory, 7–10
things, learning from, 61–65
Thomson, Christopher, 135
Tian, Xiaojie, 55–56, 86
Tibetan people, 129
Tiwi people, 44*b*
Tobian people, 5
Togo, apprenticeships in, 144
Tomasello, Michael, 11, 51, 66
tools
    everyday classrooms, stone toolmaking
        sites as, 97–100, 217
    play and, 54n.3, 98–99
    playgroups, in, 87
    self-starting learners and, 54n.3,
        61–65, 214–15
Tools for the Mind, 186–87
traditional ecological knowledge (TEK),
    11n.4, 11, 180, 194, 195, 197
Traig, Jennifer, 137
Trobriand people, 58
Truk Island, 65, 78
Tsimané people, 160, 161, 196, 201
Tswapong people, 152

Tuareg people, 110, 126–27
Tukolor people, 143, 145–46
Tzeltal Maya people, 35*b*, 39
Tzotzil Maya people, 168

Uganda
    lesson creep in, 185
    social acceleration in, 42
Ullrich, Hellen E., 173
Ulukhaktok people, 162
UNICEF, 185
United Kingdom, lesson creep in, 184–85
United Nations, 169–70
United States
    bedtime stories in, 79–80
    "chore curriculum" in, 193
    Indian Bureau, 168–69
    infant education in, 32–35, 80
    lesson creep in, 186–87, 189–90
    Million Book March, 190
    National Reading Month, 190
    Peace Corps, 169–70
    play in, 79
    preschools in, 186–87
    USAID, 169–70
"unschooling," 187–88
untutored babies, 33*b*–35*b*
Urarina people, 42
Ute people, 169
Uzbek people, 199

Vaish, Amrisha, 66
van Gennep, Arnold, 148–49
Vanuatu
    infant education in, 36
    play in, 37–38
Venda people, 59*b*
Venezuela, lesson creep in, 186
verbal interaction, 171, 213
Vermonden, Daniel, 11, 123, 200
Victorian era, pedagogy in, 133–35
Vietnam, play in, 45*b*–46
village schools, 159–63, 197–98
Vygotsky, Lev, 76

Wagenia people, 148n.5
Wagley, Charles, 101, 150
Walker, Harry, 42, 48–49
walking, 42

280 INDEX

Wallaert, Hélène, 60, 142
Walpiri people, 33*b*, 39–40, 44*b*, 65
Wanku people, 62
Warao people, 59*b*, 123
Warneken, Felix, 48
Warrick, Gary, 104
"watch and learn," 108
Wayne, Derrick, 176–77
weaning, 42–43
Weisner, Thomas S., 120–21
Wenger, Etienne, 99
Western educated industrialized rich
  democracies (WEIRD)
  generally, 2n.1
  adolescents in, 151
  agency in, 8
  bedtime stories in, 79–80
  child-directed speech in, 38–39
  children's culture in, 9
  core knowledge in, 5
  fetal instruction in, 27
  global WEIRDing (*See* global
    WEIRDing)
  homework in, 80
  imitation in, 57–58
  indigenous pedagogy
    contrasted, 211–18
  individualism in, 8–9, 26, 57
  infant education in, 25–26, 31–35
  innovation in, 72
  opportunity in, 172–73
  play in, 36–37
  preschools in, 186–87
  "scaffolding" in, 65, 80
  self-esteem in, 125–26
  self-starting learners in, 51–52, 54
  silo effect and, 4–5
  "strategic rejection" in, 68–69
  work in, 118–19, 163
White, Ben, 173
White, J. Peter, 200

White, William, 165
Whittemore, Robert D., 83–84
Why Youth Is Not Wasted on the Young
  (Bjorklund), 30
Williams, Ronald J., 137
Williams, Thomas Rhys, 54–55
Wimsatt, William C., 82
Wogoa Island, 113
Wolfenstein, Martha, 37
Wolof people, 200–1
womb education, 27–28
work. *See also* "chore curriculum"
  identity and, 124–27
  infant education and, 48–49
  school versus, 163–67
  self-starting learners and, 65–69
  transition from play, 116–20
  WEIRD, in, 118–19, 163
workhouse schools, 147n.4
workshops
  basketmaking, 101n.5
  gender differences in, 100–1, 102
  pottery, 101–5, 103n.6
Wunambal people, 154
Wyndham, Felice S., 199

Xikrin people, 60

Yanomami people, 117
Yemen, apprenticeships in, 139
Yoruba people, 143, 145–46, 156–57
Yousafzai, Malala, 174–75
Yucatec Maya people, 118, 170
Yukaghir people, 53–54, 202
Yupiaq people, 162

Zarger, Rebecca, 69
Zero to Three, 28, 49
Zinacantec Maya people, 55, 67, 123, 186
Zukow, Patricia G., 185–86
Zulu people, 42